"An astute, wide-ranging analysis of the directions British travel writing on Arabia have taken since Thesiger and the 1950s. Jenny Walker combines practical knowledge of the Arabian desert with sensitive readings of how writing about it has been formed by postmodern trends and twenty-first century contexts. This book is more than an update it is an invaluable aid to our understanding of the desert writing genre".

Geoffrey Nash, author of, *From Empire to Orient,*
Travellers to the Middle East

The Arabian Desert in English Travel Writing Since 1950

Broadly this book is about the Arabian desert as the locus of exploration by a long tradition of British travellers that includes T. E. Lawrence and Wilfred Thesiger; more specifically, it is about those who, since 1950, have followed in their literary footsteps. In analysing modern works covering a land greater than the sum of its geographical parts, the discussion identifies outmoded tropes that continue to impinge upon the perception of the Middle East today while recognising that the laboured binaries of "East and West", "desert and sown", "noble and savage" have outrun their course. Where, however, only a barren legacy of latent Orientalism may have been expected, the author finds instead a rich seam of writing that exhibits diversity of purpose and insight contributing to contemporary discussions on travel and tourism, intercultural representation, and environmental awareness. By addressing a lack of scholarly attention towards recent additions to the genre, this study illustrates for the benefit of students of travel literature, or indeed anyone interested in "Arabia", how desert writing, under the emerging configurations of globalisation, postcolonialism, and ecocriticism, acts as a microcosm of the kinds of ethical and emotional dilemmas confronting today's travel writers in the world's most extreme regions.

Jenny Walker is Consultant to the CEO of Oman's national accreditation agency. Fellow of the Royal Geographical Society and Member of the British Guild of Travel Writers, she has written for Lonely Planet for 20 years in 40 guidebooks, curated a book of Silk Road drawings, and co-authored, with husband Sam Owen, an off-road guide to Oman.

Routledge Research in Travel Writing
Edited by Peter Hulme, University of Essex
Tim Youngs, Nottingham Trent University

French Political Travel Writing in the Interwar Years
Radical Departures
Martyn Cornick, Martin Hurcombe, and Angela Kershaw

Travelling Servants
Mobility and Employment in British Fiction and Travel Writing
1750–1850
Kathryn Walchester

The Desertmakers
Travel, War and the State in Latin America
Javier Uriarte

Time and Temporalities in European Travel Writing
Paula Henrikson and Christina Kullberg

Revisiting Italy
British Women Travel Writers and the Risorgimento (1844–61)
Rebecca Butler

Travel, Travel Writing, and British Political Economy
"Instructions for Travellers," circa 1750–1850
Brian P. Cooper

The Arabian Desert in English Travel Writing Since 1950
A Barren Legacy?
Jenny Walker

For more information about this series, please visit:
https://www.routledge.com/Routledge-Research-in-Travel-Writing/
book-series/RRTW

The Arabian Desert in English Travel Writing Since 1950
A Barren Legacy?

Jenny Walker

NEW YORK AND LONDON

First published 2023
by Routledge
605 Third Avenue, New York, NY 10158

and by Routledge
4 Park Square, Milton Park, Abingdon, Oxon, OX14 4RN

*Routledge is an imprint of the Taylor & Francis Group, an
informa business*

© 2023 Jenny Walker

The right of Jenny Walker to be identified as author of this work
has been asserted in accordance with sections 77 and 78 of the
Copyright, Designs and Patents Act 1988.

All rights reserved. No part of this book may be reprinted or
reproduced or utilised in any form or by any electronic, mechanical, or other means, now known or hereafter invented, including
photocopying and recording, or in any information storage or
retrieval system, without permission in writing from the
publishers.

Trademark notice: Product or corporate names may be trademarks or registered trademarks, and are used only for identification and explanation without intent to infringe.

Library of Congress Cataloging-in-Publication Data
Names: Walker, Jenny (Jenny Fiona Hawkes), author.
Title: The Arabian desert in English travel writing since 1950 : a barren
legacy? / Jenny Walker.
Description: New York, NY : Routledge, 2022. | Series: Routledge research
in travel writing | Includes bibliographical references and index. |
Contents: Introduction : Arabia, the Land of Legend -- In Literary
Footsteps : The Prevalence of "Second Journeys" -- Desert and Sown : The
Narration of Progress and Modernity -- Gendering the Desert :
Women and Desert Narratives -- Wonderment and Wilderness :
Desert Science Writing -- Desert as Shared Space
Identifiers: LCCN 2022030247 (print) | LCCN 2022030248
(ebook) | ISBN 9781032053523 (hardback) | ISBN
9781032399263 (paperback) | ISBN 9781003197201 (ebook)
Subjects: LCSH: Travelers' writings, English--History and
criticism. | Travelers--Arabian Peninsula. | Deserts--Arabian
Peninsula. | Arabian Peninsula--Description and travel.
Classification: LCC PR808.T72 W35 2022 (print) | LCC PR808.
T72 (ebook) | DDC 820.9/3253--dc23/eng/20221027
LC record available at https://lccn.loc.gov/2022030247
LC ebook record available at https://lccn.loc.gov/2022030248

ISBN: 978-1-032-05352-3 (hbk)
ISBN: 978-1-032-39926-3 (pbk)
ISBN: 978-1-003-19720-1 (ebk)

DOI: 10.4324/9781003197201

Typeset in Sabon
by SPi Technologies India Pvt Ltd (Straive)

This book is dedicated to my beloved husband and fellow desert traveller, Sam Owen.

Contents

Acknowledgements	xi
Preface	xiii

Introduction: Arabia, the land of legend   1

The margins of Western desert travel in Arabia 3
Locating Arabia 5
Arabia as a country of the mind 11
The Lawrence and Thesiger legacy 14
Mapping the chapters 18
Notes 24

1 In literary footsteps: The prevalence of "second journeys"   30

A tradition of intertextuality 34
Learning from the past – Blackmore in the footsteps of
  Lawrence 38
Writing about the present – Kirkby and Hayes in the
  footsteps of Thesiger 45
Opportunities for the future – Evans in the
  footsteps of Thomas 53
Notes 61

2 Desert and sown: The narration of progress and modernity   67

Desert but not deserted – Asher's modern Bedu 68
The desert mechanised – Toy's travels by Land Rover 75
The desert politicised – Morris and a Sultan's pageant 80
The desert urbanised – Raban and a camel-free account 85
The desert historicised – Mackintosh-Smith's inverse
  archaeology 91
Notes 99

x *Contents*

3 **Gendering the desert: Women and desert narratives**   106

Where are the women? Western women's travels in Arabia 108
"Pay, pack and follow" – Women as desert writers 113
The siren trope 119
The "veiled best-seller" 121
Desert as an inconstant space 129
Notes 135

4 Wonderment and wilderness: Desert science writing   142

Delighting in sand grouse 144
George and the neo-sublime 151
Walker and Pittaway in amateur pursuits 156
Winser in search of solutions 160
Staging the desert for Western audiences 166
Notes 171

5 **Desert as shared space**   176

Post-tourism and the accelerated sublime 179
The modern secular pilgrimage 183
Democratisation of the desert experience 187
Notes 191

Conclusion: Barren legacy?   195

Notes 199

Bibliography   201
Index   218

Acknowledgements

There are many people I am glad to have the opportunity to thank in the development of this book. First and foremost, I am very grateful to Professor Tim Youngs, whose generous guidance, depth of knowledge, and critical insights have helped bring this work to fruition. The project originated from a doctoral thesis (completed at Nottingham Trent University under my married name Jenny Owen), and I continue to be indebted to my supervisory team, led by Professor Youngs and assisted by Dr. Anna Ball and Dr. Jenni Ramone, for their gentle and patient help in broadening my scholarly horizons. Working under their inspirational guidance has been a special privilege.

Writing this book has been rather like crossing a desert – an adventure in which I have had to confront apparently barren ground but in which seams of productive thought have bloomed unexpectedly in the wilderness. Provoking those thoughts have been the many friends, colleagues (especially Dr. Ahmed Al-Bulushi and Dr. Salim Radhawi), supporters (especially Dr. Geoffrey Nash to whom I am deeply grateful for his encouragement to publish), and fellow travellers I have met along the way – encountered while studying Lawrence and Doughty for a dissertation at the University of Stirling, while writing an MPhil thesis on the Romantic origins of Orientalism at the University of Oxford, and latterly during over two decades of living in Oman. Many desert-goers have generously allowed me to interview them in the context of my doctoral studies, professional work in higher education, and as a guidebook writer. Specifically, I would like to thank (in alphabetical order) His Excellency Jamie Bowden, Sir Simon Bryant, Mark Evans MBE (Member of the Order of the British Empire), General Charles Fattorini, Anthony Ham, Tim Mackintosh-Smith, General Rupert Smith, Tony Wheeler, Nigel Winser, Levison Wood, and Mohamed Al-Zadjali. The oral and written accounts of these distinguished Arabian desert travellers not only formed the primary inspiration in my wanting to consider the desert trope in modern travel literature but have also demonstrated that the genre is reinvigorated in each new generation.

xii *Acknowledgements*

I love the desert, and I owe my deep respect of this provoking landscape to my father, the late D. H. Walker, who took my beloved mother and me, nets waving in the wind, across the interior of Saudi Arabia in the hunt for bugs. He went on to write a book on insects, illustrated by one of my three brothers, Professor Allan Walker (a cherished mentor), and the memory of those field trips made an impression on me that has lasted a lifetime.

And so to beloved Sam Owen, my husband, fellow traveller, and joint author of an off-road guide to Oman. Quite simply, this project would not have been possible without his loving support and encouragement. I dedicate this book to him.

Preface

There is a point in Oman's Sharqiya Sands where the undulating rhythm of the dunes as they extend into the distance appears to be without human interruption. At a casual glance, it may appear as if nothing other than the name has altered in that landscape for centuries, or at least since geographer Nigel Winser and his team set up Taylorbase nearby from which to conduct a survey that still represents the most complete study of any desert anywhere in the world. But then on closer inspection, a series of tracks leading to the left and right of the ergs comes into focus, and along each of those tracks, some kind of despoliation has occurred – a snapped branch of acacia, a dung beetle that was too slow in the path of oncoming traffic, and sadly the trail of litter that is an inevitable part of the local picnic culture. On further inspection, it becomes clear that other factors have transformed this view – a telephone mast and the glint of water in a swimming pool at one of the tourist camps that now dot the landscape. It is to these camps, in motorised convoys of a hundred cars, that tourists head, seeking in the surrounding dunes the kind of sublime wilderness that Winser describes so affectingly in his expedition narrative, *Sea of Sands and Mists*.[1]

To be clear, this is not to suggest that Winser's 1980s project led directly to the incursion of roads and the setting up of camps; rather, it facilitated the sense that once the sands were known and mapped, they were less alien and less hostile. In the expedition's wake, emboldened amateur naturalists followed in the footsteps of the scientists, and they were followed in turn by visitors whose desire to frame the same view with less energy and less risk has generated an entire desert tourist industry. This industry, of which guidebooks form a part, somewhat disingenuously offers the semblance of a wilderness experience without the attendant dangers, instructing the visitor how to access the dunes while supplying checklists on how to minimise the risk. I know this because I am complicit in this activity. Indeed, I have spent the best part of two decades not just travelling through the deserts of the region but also promoting them as a tourist destination in my role as a professional guidebook writer and as a contributor to the higher education sector in Oman. It was through

xiv *Preface*

these activities that I recognised that I am part of a modern dilemma, wanting both to share and celebrate the desert wilderness while lamenting a despoliation for which I am partly responsible – in other words, romanticising the desert and those who occupy its settled fringe (some of whom stand to gain from increased tourism), while also contributing to the agencies of change therein. If this appears to be overstating the case, then it is worth considering that guidebooks are ubiquitous, cover every country in the world, purport to be authoritative in their unique combination of fact interlaced seamlessly with authorial voice and, in this way, shape the ways in which millions of people organise their routes and engage with their destinations. Of the relatively few scholars who have explored the influence of guidebooks in the context of travel literature, Scott Laderman recently contends that guidebooks may even be considered as the "most influential form of travel writing of the twentieth century".[2] It could be argued, therefore, that even at the point where guidebooks are being replaced by more representative forms of destination advice, or at least are metamorphosing into something new, it remains beholden on every guidebook writer to consider the responsibility entailed in their contributions to the genre.

This book, which examines mostly British travel writing connected with the deserts of Arabia since 1950, came about, then, through a desire to probe the ethical dimensions of my professional practice – as perhaps one of the "planes of activity and praxis" advocated by Edward Said – and I looked to travel literature as a point of departure.[3] When Wilfred Thesiger wrote of his 1945–1950 desert expeditions with the Bedu, "I went to Southern Arabia only just in time", he appeared to be signalling the end of an era, both in terms of exploration of the desert wilderness and of the long literary engagement with the region.[4] But the fascination with the arid lands of the Middle East has continued regardless, ironically intensified by the challenge for authenticity that Thesiger's epitaph to desert travel represents. The resulting expeditions, motivated by science, adventure, or by tourism, have left a new legacy of what is referred to here as "desert literature" and have contributed in their own way to the "common grounds of assembly" accruing to the subject of Middle Eastern travel narratives.[5]

Arabia, as the locus of exploration by a long tradition of British travellers that includes Richard Burton, Charles M. Doughty, and T. E. Lawrence, is "haunted, holy ground" – a land greater than the sum of its geographical parts.[6] My main objective in this book has been to use desert literature connected with Arabia as a lens through which to examine whether Orientalism continues to be relevant to the perception of the Middle East today or whether its laboured binaries have been superseded by the emerging configurations of globalisation. This subject is specifically approached by analysing how modern travellers have engaged nostalgically with the Oriental legacy connected with the region and the

Preface xv

extent to which their work either incidentally or consciously reinforces, contests or extends beyond Orientalism. While this discussion sets desert literature *within the scope of* Orientalism, however, it is not specifically a study *about* Orientalism, a subject which, as the focus of intense modern scholarship for over four decades, has left limited opportunity for new comment. Instead, by considering why the Arabian desert should continue to exert a strong fascination for Western writers and analysing the presentation of the desert and the human story therein, this book identifies desert literature as one strand of a dynamic and complex intercultural practice of representation and cultural self-reflection. The modern desert texts selected for discussion herein are released, in other words, from being read only as a continuum of the now-familiar project of othering; instead, they are interrogated to reveal more productive discourses, befitting of a postcolonial travel experience that – in anxieties about identity and representation, the effects of globalisation and the human impact on the environment – are essentially modern.

Notes

1 Nigel Winser, *The Sea of Sands and Mists – Desertification: Seeking Solutions in the Wahiba Sands* (London: RGS, 1989), p. 137.
2 Scott Laderman, "Guidebooks", in *The Routledge Companion to Travel Writing*, ed. by Carl Thompson [2016] (London and New York: Routledge, 2020), pp. 258–68 (p. 258).
3 Edward W. Said, "Orientalism Reconsidered", in *Literature, Politics and Theory: Papers from the Essex Conference, 1976–84* [1986], ed. by Francis Barker et al (Abingdon and New York: Routledge, 2003), pp. 210–29 (p. 228).
4 Wilfred Thesiger, *Arabian Sands* [1959] (Harmondsworth: Penguin, 1984), p. 11.
5 Said, "Orientalism Reconsidered", p. 228.
6 George Gordon Lord Byron, *Childe Harold's Pilgrimage* [1812], Canto II, LXXXVIII, line 1.

Introduction
Arabia, the land of legend

When Wilfred Thesiger left Arabia in 1950 and published *Arabian Sands* in 1959, stating that other travellers "will bring back results far more interesting than mine, but they will never know the spirit of the land nor the greatness of the Arabs", he was suggesting the end of an era both in terms of an Arab way of life and of the exploration of the desert region he described.[1] Despite Thesiger's foreboding, however, the past 70 years have been marked by a significant number of desert journeys undertaken by those who have found the experience sufficiently rewarding to publish an account; in so doing, these travellers participate in a tradition within anglophone literature, the origins of which stem back at least to the eighteenth century. Many of these travellers respond overtly to the writing of earlier explorers and especially to the key desert narratives of Charles M. Doughty, T. E. Lawrence, and Wilfred Thesiger. This rich intertextuality informs the way in which modern writers construct their own travelling persona, either through the lens of nostalgia for presumed heroic endeavour or in deliberate and ironic opposition to the same. These constructions of self differ from the narratives of their travelling forebears in the levels of self-doubt and anxiety of purpose that frequently foreground their accounts. The reasons for this apparent loss of confidence in the travelling project belongs to a larger discourse pertinent to travel as a whole; it registers a moment of crisis in a globalised age and suggests that something intangible may have been forfeited in the quest for ever greater mobility and exploitation of the world's diminishing wild places. The imaginative nature of that loss and whether it is indeed lamentable forms one major theme of this book.

Focusing specifically on the anglophone literature of those expeditioners, scientists, and travellers who have been inspired to write about their experience of the Arabian desert in the period since 1950, the following chapters consider the reasons why the region continues to provoke literary output despite being saturated by previous accounts. Whether consciously or not, modern writers connect with the region through this literary legacy finding in the desert an "imagined geography" as much as a physical space.[2] While some of these writers are unable to entirely

DOI: 10.4324/9781003197201-1

2 Introduction

eschew the inherited tropes of the Arab context with which they engage (described by Edward Said as "latent Orientalism"), most are at least in part able to step beyond the received "wisdom" of their predecessors to provide a more nuanced view of the modern Middle East appropriate to an era of postcolonial sensibility.[3] While presentations of the Other are an intrinsic feature of the travel writing genre as a whole, these texts reveal a particular awareness of the perplexities and politics involved in arriving at an equitable description of cultural encounter and provide rich commentary about the land left behind. While this form of cultural introspection and/or of comparison has been a consistent feature of the desert genre, writers since Thesiger include a greater sense of nostalgia in their work while also expressing troubling suspicions about the relative merits of their own culture in contrast. Indeed, fractures within the presumed cultural hierarchy form a prominent feature of modern desert writing, with many travel accounts striving at least partially towards the postcolonial; the way in which these texts offer opportunities for a more equitable assessment of "the Other" are highlighted throughout this book in a second broad theme.

In an era when it is predicted that 68 per cent of Earth's population will live in cities by 2050, there is arguably a human need for wild spaces.[4] This need can be read, in ecocritical terms, as a "deep nostalgia for a unity with the natural world that seems for ever lost".[5] The desert fulfils an imaginative function in providing a locus of that connection with nature and many of the writings examined herein revel in describing the desert in what appears to be unpoliticised, topographical detail. If, however, travel literature as a whole cannot be read naively as being, in Carl Thompson's words, "just a transparent window on the world", then neither can desert literature.[6] In a third broad theme, this book probes modern desert texts for a counter-narrative regarding national Arab modernities; in doing so, it contributes a contemporary perspective to discussions on the "desert and the sown" – and crucially the one bordered within the other.

In examining the three aforementioned broad themes (which can be summarised as studies in self, other, and the margins in between), this book considers whether writing focusing on the Arabian desert, which arguably reached its apotheosis in the work of Thesiger, offers only a barren legacy for belated Western writers, beguiled by the long history of imaginative and outmoded engagement in the region. This would be an obvious interpretation of many of the texts under scrutiny, but it is something of a reductive interpretation. Through detailed reading of new desert writing, opportunities present to observe, albeit in microcosm, many of today's critical issues relating to cultural interaction and appropriation, the re-evaluation of the contribution of women in the genre, responsible and sustainable travel, the protection of unique environments, and the nature of authentic travel in ever-more globalised and urbanised contexts.

Introduction 3

Primarily focusing on texts written in the first-person that give an account of non-fictional desert encounter, whether presented as works of science, cultural commentary or mainstream travel account, some of the texts chosen for discussion (for example, work by Charles Blackmore, Barbara Toy, Marguerite van Geldermalsen, and Nigel Winser) are relatively obscure. These hybrid "subspecies of memoir" have hitherto attracted little or no scholarly attention;[7] the intention of drawing them into this work, alongside more prominent modern desert texts (by Jan Morris, Geraldine Brooks, and Tim Mackintosh-Smith), is to establish the existence of a subgenre of modern Arabian desert literature that both engages with the canon of anglophone literature connected with the region while providing new ways of reflecting on cross-cultural representation.

The objective herein is not an exhaustive survey of modern desert literature in the anglophone tradition but rather a discussion on the ways in which the selected texts participate in key critical discourses surrounding the much broader themes of travel and wilderness encounter. There are some deliberate omissions: only passing reference is made, for example, to the works of Ranulph Fiennes and Nicholas Clapp, whose desert explorations in Oman in search of the lost city of Ubar mirror much that is already covered here under the analysis of footstep journeys. While not wishing to underestimate the contribution these travel writers make to the genre and whose work may warrant a separate study, their omission makes way for the productive inclusion of contemporary texts relating to other desert regions. These include Geoffrey Moorhouse's Saharan odyssey, *The Fearful Void* (1974); Robyn Davidson's Australian desert classic, *Tracks* (1996); Sara Wheeler's Antarctic desert descriptions in *Terra Incognita* (1996); Jay Giffiths, who writes a chapter on various deserts in *Wild* (2006); and, in passing, Lois Pryce, who describes a motorbike incursion into the Iranian desert in a chapter of *Revolutionary Ride* (2017). The work of all these travellers to "non-Arabian" deserts is referred to in this book either in contrast to the imaginative geography of the Arabian region or, conversely, to show that Arabian desert literature participates in broader, globalised discourses about the distinction between traveller and tourist, and gendered narrations of wild space.

The margins of Western desert travel in Arabia

Given the influence of Thesiger on almost all modern Arabian desert literature, the year 1950 makes an obvious opening parameter in this book, as it marks the point at which Thesiger withdrew from the field, leaving it open to a new generation of Western expeditioners.[8] While there has been a small but growing number of studies recently about the work particularly of male desert travellers who preceded Thesiger,[9] there has been very little systematic study of those who followed thereafter.[10] This book bridges that gap by considering the work of subsequent desert

4 Introduction

travellers up to 2016, the date of the last major crossing of an Arabian desert (by Mark Evans and his Omani co-expeditioners). There has been opportunity to give only passing reference to desert journeys since 2016, such as Levison Wood's circumambulation of Arabia from 2017 to 2018. An extended trek entitled "Her Faces of Change" across the Eastern rim of the Omani Empty Quarter by three women (Baida Al-Zadjali, Atheer Al-Sabri, and Janey McGill) in February 2019 is as yet undocumented in a full travel narrative; similarly, "YallaGo", a so-called bee-line trek in 2020, by women adventurers Anisa Al Raisi and, for part of the journey, Natalie Taylor, has been recorded only through commentary in social media. The Covid-19 pandemic, resulting in restricted travel into many of the countries of the Arabian Peninsula, has inhibited subsequent formal expeditions, including a much-publicised trek in Oman by British military veterans under royal patronage, while encouraging informal indigenous desert excursions; these are yet to be documented in the form of extended, published travel narratives in either Arabic or English. The pre-2016 texts discussed in this book are mostly considered chronologically within (but not across) chapters to show how each discourse develops from one generation of travellers to the next.

In a survey on British travel writing on Oman prior to 1970, the Omani scholar Hilal Al-Hajri writes as his reason for choosing 1970 as the farthest limit of his own study:

> The inaccessible Inner Oman is quite open to foreigners, the "unknown people" of the southern Oman have been "discovered", and the dangerous Empty quarter has been "penetrated". Thus, the curiosity of exploration, the allusion of untrodden paths, the lure of the unknown, and the risk of adventure that imbued travel writing in the past began gradually to vanish after 1970. In short, travel to Oman after 1970 became a kind of tourism.[11]

Al-Hajri's stated enterprise focuses on a historical account that is part of a wider project to document overlooked aspects of regional history. In a recent essay entitled "Arabic Travel Writing, to 1916", Nabil Matar corroborates the fact there have been relatively few travel accounts in Arabic after the Sykes-Picot partition of the Arabic-speaking world in 1916; this he attributes in part to the "artificial borders requiring passports and permits" which curtailed travel between Arab nations thereafter. Matar goes on to make the point that travel writing has "continued to be a popular genre in Arabic" but is now almost exclusively by "men who can get visas, have money, and who want to tell stories about themselves and their acquaintances in foreign lands"; this Matar notes is a far cry from traditional *rihla* – earlier journeys that produced travelogues associated with the "happy combination of piety and curiosity that marked the civilization of Islam".[12] Al-Hajri's own discussion ends with the succession

Introduction 5

of the former sultan, Qaboos bin Said, in 1970 – a point in Omani history generally referred to as the "renaissance". This term, akin to *al-nahda*, and sometimes translated as "enlightenment", has been used in Arab anglophone literature to refer to the concept of "Arab awakening" and, as Tarik Sabry and Joe Khalil show, spans a diverse lexicon of meanings from cultural productions originating in the nineteenth century and a growing consciousness of Arab modernity in the twentieth century.[13] More recently it has come to define the period of intense modernisation and infrastructure development since the discovery of oil in Arabia.

By broadening the scope beyond 1970, then, this book deliberately engages with Arab modernities, albeit through the lens of a Western perspective. It examines the extent to which recent desert literature challenges traditional tropes of the supposed immutability of the desert and those who live there and thereby explores the fault lines between exploration, travel, and tourism, as problematised by rapid globalisation. This in turn sets the texts under scrutiny within a broader range of concerns common to all modern travel literature. In adopting an interdisciplinary approach, the insights of various fields, including literary criticism, postcolonialism, anthropology, feminism, and ecocriticism, are applied to the analysis of modern desert literature to make sense of the modern discourses in which it participates.

If these opening paragraphs have hitherto sketched out the broad scope of this book in terms of genre, time, and approach, they have yet to address the "geography" of the enterprise. While it may be easy to define "desert" (generally regarded as an area receiving "less than ten inches of precipitation annually"),[14] attempting to define "*Arabian* desert" is made challenging by both the "imaginative geography and history" – in other words Orientalism – that impinges upon it.[15] Some tangible geographical and historical parameters are therefore needed to anchor the examination of texts in the chapters that follow in both a concrete and an abstract space; indeed, without the context of Orientalism, it is difficult to explain why modern travellers continue voluntarily to undertake journeys of deliberate hardship in the Arabian desert, spending time, money, and energy in the process and for uncertain reward.

Locating Arabia

As a result of Orientalism, the representation of Arabia may be somewhat fluid in terms of imagined and imaginative borders, but that does not mean the term lacks specificity entirely. According to Zara Freeth and Victor Winstone, the first Western geography of Arabia was produced in 1592 by the Medici Press in Italy, and it covered a much broader territory than currently embraced by today's Arabian Peninsula.[16] A German map published by Christoph Weigel in 1720 shows Arabia as covering three distinct zones: Arabia Felix occupying the southwestern diagonal of the

6   Introduction

Peninsula, Arabia Deserta occupying the north-eastern diagonal, and Arabia Petraea, covering the Sinai and parts of the Syrian Desert. A similar demarcation is shown in the J. Rapkin map, published in London and New York by J. and F. Tallis in 1851.[17] Today, however, the term "Arabia" is generally avoided locally in preference for "Arabian Peninsula", which covers the six members of the Gulf Cooperation Council (founded in 1981) and Yemen, unified since 1990.

The "Arabian desert", which according to McColl's *Encyclopaedia of World Geography* is the fifth largest in the world, extends beyond the Peninsula to encompass parts of Jordan and Iraq.[18] In this, it comes nearer to, in ecocritical terms, a "bioregion", a common ecosystem "that has its own distinctive natural economy".[19] It comprises many specific arid zones, including stony plains, volcanic *harrat*, and the largest sea of sand in the world; shared by Saudi Arabia, Oman, United Arab Emirates, and Qatar, these sands are known in the West as the Rub Al-Khali, or "Empty Quarter". Despite its Arabic translation, the name is a Eurocentric one, implying *terra nullius* – empty land. For Arab people, in contrast, the area is known simply as *al-ramlah* (the sands) and is recognised as the home of nomadic and semi-nomadic tribes, generally referred to as "the Bedu". While Thesiger used the term "Arab" interchangeably with "Bedu" to refer to the nomadic "camel-breeding tribes" of the Arabian desert, he was somewhat out of step with the evolution of the term; through the nationalistic movements of the early twentieth century, the term "Arab" came to encompass "anyone who speaks Arabic as [their] mother-tongue … regardless of origin".[20] In summary, this book uses the term "Arabian desert" in its physical geographical sense to allow discussion of desert travel that encompasses modern-day Jordan but excludes travels in Iraq and neighbouring Levantine countries, as made distinctive by an entirely different modern history. The term "Arab" is used in its modern sense as denoting someone from the Arabian Peninsula, but the diasporic dimensions, of "Arab modernity" for example, are beyond the scope of this study. Taking the lead from Alan Keohane, the term "Bedu" is used throughout as the term used by Arab nomads in their own language. It is used in its anglicised, plural form to avoid confusion. The term "Bedouin", a Westernised term, is only used in citation and occasionally adjectivally where the use of Bedu would appear otherwise forced.[21]

While geographical specificity is important in giving a physical context to modern works of desert travel literature, it is inadequate when trying to describe the psychological impact of the term "Arabia". For this, we have to turn to the "Orient" and to chart in its delineation some of the features that act as waypoints in the study of Europe's "cultural contestant, and one of its deepest and most recurring images of the Other".[22] It is useful, therefore, to consider the location of "Arabian desert" in its amplified sense as part of "a created body of theory and practice" and to set it in a brief epistemological history of Western travel to the region.[23]

Introduction 7

In a study entitled *Desert: Nature and Culture* which synthesises the responses of geographers, explorers, artists, and anthropologists to wild, desolate places, Roslynn Haynes singles out the deserts of Arabia as the locus of a particularly rich seam of intellectual and imaginative literary involvement for Western writers:

> Long before Lawrence of Arabia captivated the West with romantic images of desert Bedouin, the Arabian Desert and its traditional inhabitants held a fascination for the Western mind, woven from stories of the Crusades, nineteenth-century travellers' tales of danger and disguise, and associations with harems and the holy places of Islam forbidden to infidels.[24]

In the preceding passage, Haynes identifies some of the key tropes of this literary engagement. There is the "fascination for the Western mind" that translates into a quest for knowledge; there are the woven "stories of the Crusades" which inform Orientalism's blurring of fact and fiction; the "tales of danger and disguise" that signal a relationship between the self and the landscape, and the encoded encounter with "the other" (through the harem and "holy places of Islam"). This is the Orient that Said describes as being "almost a European invention", the place which "since antiquity" has been associated with "romance, exotic beings, haunting memories and landscapes, remarkable experiences".[25] Haynes, then, in highlighting these tropes is firmly positioning her own text within a tradition that spans more than three centuries.

It is hard to define the exact moment at which Arabia became embedded in the British imagination, but it certainly dates back at least to the work of Joseph Pitts.[26] Pitts is widely accredited with writing one of the earliest substantiated accounts by an English traveller to the Arabian Peninsula (in 1704) and "the first detailed account through Western eyes of the observances of Mecca".[27] Whether his narrative lives up to its title as *A True and Faithful Account of the Religion and Manners of the Mohammetans, with an Account of the Author's Being Taken Captive* has been the subject of enquiry by subsequent explorers and scholars of the region who have questioned his enforced conversion to Islam and some of his descriptions of captivity – but that is hardly the point.[28] Pitts's profession that "I cannot pretend to abilities that are required in a person who writes such a history", whether a cynical attempt to disguise his mendacity or not, show how Western travellers have for centuries felt at liberty to write just such a history.[29] Towards the end of the eighteenth century, under the purview of that exercise, there was little that fell beyond a traveller's attention, partly encouraged in their endeavours by the apparatus of colonial administration at home. The instructions that the Society of the Dilettante, for example, issued to their Eastbound travellers reflects the empiricism of the era:

8 *Introduction*

> You will be exact in making distances and the direction in which you travel, by frequently observing your watches and pocket compasses, ... and you will ... report to us for the information of the society whatever can fall within the notice of curious and observing travellers.[30]

In this exhortation to be observant, and to apply the instruments of Western measurement to the dimensions of the East (in a fashion that pre-empts the measuring of Bedouin heads by Bertram Thomas and his callipers in the twentieth century), it is clear that the mapping of the Orient had begun. Indeed, it was remarkable the kinds of things that fell within the notice of "curious and observing travellers". J. L. Burckhardt, one of the first Europeans to explore the Arabian desert in earnest at the beginning of the nineteenth century, records the 31 tobacco shops in Jeddah, the 18 dealers in fruit and vegetables, 2 men selling sour milk, and spice shops run by East Indians selling rosebuds from Taif (which scented the washing water of Jeddah wives) and he notes that men drank 3 to 30 cups of coffee per day.[31] The recording of such minutiae several decades later, in the voluminous footnoting of Richard Burton's travels and those of subsequent Victorian travellers to Arabia, becomes almost obsessive in nature – as parodied by Thackeray, in an article in *Punch* in February 1845, who allegedly "pasted up the Standard of our glorious leader ... at 19 minutes past 7, by the clock of the great minaret at Cairo, which is clearly visible through my refracting telescope".[32] If partly validating the observations of these travellers, the recording of customs and manners in Arabia also contributed to the validation of a received representation of the region; in this, it can be seen as part of the growing resource – the "considerable material investment" – that Said argues helped to prop up the imperial project in the region.[33]

While much information gathering took place in the cities, however, the deserts of the region remained largely unexplored. Helen Carr reminds us that the trains and steamships of the 1840s facilitated longer-distance travel for a wider franchise of travellers, helped upon their way by Karl Baedeker's guidebooks, and that Thomas Cook's first tour of the Continent took place in 1855, the same year that the first edition of Richard Burton's *Personal Narrative of a Pilgrimage to Al-Madinah and Meccah* appeared in print.[34] The desert heartland of Arabia, however, remained the locus of specialist travel reserved for diplomats and explorers for most of the nineteenth century.[35] Even later in the century, when, as Carl Thompson notes, "it was possible to travel by train all the way from Paris to Istanbul, in modern-day Turkey, on the famous *Orient Express*", few casual travellers ventured beyond the Ottoman Empire or strayed from the beaten track along the Nile.[36] Various modern anthologies and biographies, including Andrew Goudie's relatively recent Royal Geographical Society publication, *Great Desert Explorers*, chart the

Introduction 9

occasional intrepid exploration that probes the Arabian desert expanse at this time, but by and large Arabia proper, despite (or some suggest because of) being the home of the two holy cities of Islam, lay largely beyond the purview of Western travel interests.[37]

Towards the end of the nineteenth century, there begins to be more curiosity in exploring the region. Gifford Palgrave, Wilfrid Scawen Blunt, and Charles M. Doughty were all drawn to the Arabian desert, albeit for significantly different reasons. In a study that considers the contribution of these writers to Orientalism, Kathryn Tidrick identifies the desire of each to find in the East something that eludes them at home. Palgrave was highly religious and a Jesuit priest but plagued with doubts, Blunt a minor aristocrat early orphaned and left without estate, while Doughty might best be described as a misfit. Tidrick relates their white, male, upper-middle-class, public school experience to the desire to purge the "sins of their fathers" in a sacrificial, hard, loveless environment and the desert presented a good opportunity for this. All these travellers found Arabia fulfilling because of "the oddness of their own personalities; for various reasons, all of them were ill at ease in Victorian and post-Victorian England".[38] Ill at ease with the reality, perhaps, they remained consistent with the presentation of Englishness in their texts, a fixed identity that Robert Young argues was "doubtless a product of, and reaction to, the rapid change and transformation of both metropolitan and colonial societies".[39] Reading (through Young) fixity of identity as evidence of a culture in flux, these travellers become marginal or "hybrid" figures that occupy the space between two cultures while belonging fully in neither. While the reading public may have enjoyed tales of derring-do with the Bedu encountered by these travellers, and the exotic otherness of the Orient, few would have welcomed the reality. As Young writes, "Exotic romance is one thing. But its dusky human consequences are another" (p. xi). In the Victorian era, few believed that the Orient offered a workable alternative to Western culture, and the narratives of these *fin-de-siècle* travellers shows the extent to which all kinds of subversive fears and desires could be legitimised by externalising them to an alien landscape and thus rendering them harmless. In this, the desert texts of these writers conformed to the Orient's function to maintain the status quo – not to change it.

In the early twentieth century, desert travel in Arabia became more strategic, and mapping the space, both literally and politically, took on particular urgency during the First World War. Western travellers until at least the middle of the twentieth century continued to assume a superior moral and intellectual centre, peripheral to which were arrayed an assortment of inferior cultures. What changes, perhaps, is the degree to which their accounts interfere with the lives of those they observe. The information they place in the hands of politicians, diplomats, and generals in the first half of the twentieth century, for example, demonstrates the power of racial stereotyping in influencing the course of history in the region.[40] T. E. Lawrence and Gertrude Bell are not objective observers and explorers of Arab lands

10 Introduction

and their inhabitants: they are part of a general license to meddle, and their work marks a shift in the desert travel writing genre from picaresque to political that prevails throughout the early twentieth century.[41]

After the First World War, travel narratives become motivated less by politics than by geography; undertaken ostensibly in the interests of the emerging discipline of anthropology, journeys to the Arabian desert became an opportunity to test new theories regarding primitivism and racial stereotyping.[42] It was also an opportunity to engage in intense competitive endeavour, demonstrated in the rivalry between Bertram Thomas and St. John Philby to be the first to cross the Empty Quarter. The quest for "firsts" becomes the race for "lasts" in the travels of Freya Stark, and more especially Wilfred Thesiger who many regard as bringing the era of desert exploration to a close.

After this point, many dismiss subsequent desert journeys, where they receive critical attention at all, as the journeys of commercial expeditioners and tourists. "Some of the great desert explorers are now very little remembered or appreciated", writes Andrew Goudie, "in comparison, say, with those who ventured to the poles, climbed Everest, or sought the source of the Nile", despite the comparability of the challenge.[43] Searching for a reason for this, Billie Melman notes that Arabia's "geography and climate have made its hinterland almost inaccessible to non-mechanised travel" leaving Arabia "peripheral from both touristic and imperial viewpoints".[44] Between the mid to the end of the twentieth century, at the point when an increase in jet travel and oil production in the Gulf region (together with regional political determination to promote tourism as a means of diversifying local economies) may have encouraged more comprehensive travel across Arabia, interest was deflected from the desert at its core to the cities of the Peninsula's urban edge. As a result, the desert, or "the *locus idealis* of the Arabist utopia", has become peripheral in many recent travel narratives as writers such as Jonathan Raban and Tim Mackintosh-Smith moved their attention towards the new cityscapes.[45]

So why, it may be wondered, do modern travellers continue to organise expeditions into the Arabian desert; what is the continuing appeal? Mark Evans, who in 2016 completed the first crossing of the Empty Quarter since Bertram Thomas's landmark journey of 1930, recorded in *Arabia Felix* (1932), observed that the sands have never been more empty, never been more wild, as the Bedu by and large have migrated to towns and the hermetically sealed camps of oil companies move on when wells run dry:

> Some 85 years after Thomas's crossing, the Empty Quarter is today emptier than it has ever been. The tribes that once occupied the central sands have long since migrated to the periphery, where blacktop roads and electricity offered an easier life, with employment opportunities, the option of keeping a toehold on the edge of the sands, and a connection to their animals and their heritage.[46]

Introduction 11

This somewhat surprising observation by Evans reminds us that while all deserts are by their nature wild, some are more wild than others. Part of the Arabian desert's unique appeal has involved the sense of remoteness that the region's isolation has implied. Human incursion (through scientific study, resource exploitation, urbanisation, modern tourism, and travel) appears to dent that perception of wilderness to some extent, while in reality making relatively little mark on the expanding desertification – what geographer Uwe George terms the "apparently inevitable spread of deserts" – across the region.[47]

At the same time as the Arabian desert has attracted relatively few travellers, then, it has nonetheless been the site of disproportionately more imaginative speculation. If, as F. A. Patrick wrote in 1927 in an early appreciation of travel literature, travel writing "more than any other both expresses and influences national predilections and national characteristics", the Arabian desert has similarly proved sufficiently unknown and sufficiently unpopulated to work as a perfect *tabula rasa* upon which to play out three centuries-worth of primarily Western preoccupations.[48] These preoccupations may have evolved or dissipated over time, but some remain constant, including the quest for self-knowledge, pitting self against nature in an extreme landscape, the sense of encounter with "the other", the desire for escape (albeit briefly) from urban sophistications achieved vicariously through the supposedly authentic lives of the Bedu. The Arabian desert functions, in other words, as a "country of the mind more real than any place on a map" and continues to draw those whose journeys are "undertaken in search of themselves" – or indeed those who are trying to leave the self in its "normal life" behind.[49] Constructing that country, as Said famously pointed out, has been the project of Orientalism and the discussion pauses here to consider briefly the study of Orientalism – a subject that continues implicitly to motivate much desert travel, through both its latent and manifest tropes, and to play a significant role in shaping the contours of the resulting desert literature.

Arabia as a country of the mind

While not necessarily explicitly aware of Orientalism as a theoretical concept, most modern Arabian desert travellers deliberately reference the East and its attendant discourses, either overtly – as in treading the path of a former desert explorer and using a former text as a pretext for a modern journey – or in more subtle, self-authenticating ways that show the writer is part of a continuum of Arabian encounter. In this way, some (but not all and not all of the time) belong to the imaginative category of Orientalism postulated four decades ago by Said that is characterised by those who "have accepted the basic distinction between East and West as the starting point for elaborate theories, epics, novels, social descriptions,

12 *Introduction*

and political accounts concerning the Orient, its people, customs, 'mind,' destiny, and so on".[50] The familiar tropes arising out of the East-West binary are easy enough to detect in modern desert travel literature: there is the portrayal of the Bedu as offering glimpses of a prelapsarian past; the notion of the desert (and indeed Arabia as a whole) as being a feminine, gendered space upon which to launch penetrative, pioneering assaults; fascination with the exotic (generally sought in the *souqs* or bazaars along the desert's fringe), the sense of the sublime (with the desert representing ruins of empire on the one hand, and the location of British imperial quest on the other); all offer a contrast with the comforts and emasculations of life back home. But the identification of these tropes in modern desert literature is not necessarily to condemn the genre as a wholesale reproduction, or manifestation, of an outmoded discourse. In recognising that some modern writers – but not all and not all the time – continue to be seduced by Oriental stereotypes, it is possible to concur with modern critics who look to Edward Said for a useful vocabulary of East-West representation while remaining alert to many of the criticisms levelled at Said's project in *Orientalism*.

Influenced by Nietzsche, Foucault, and Derrida, and the Italian Marxist thinker Antonio Gramsci, Said's *Orientalism* was of course groundbreaking in the way in which it popularised theories of perception and representation, and the way in which it contributed to the emergence of the newly configured discipline of postcolonialism.[51] The central tenet of *Orientalism*, that the standard tropes concerning the depiction of the East and its inhabitants are a primarily Western construct, struck a chord with many of Said's advocates who attempted to further his work through practical application to literature. Rana Kabbani, for example, argued in *Imperial Fictions* that the Orient was constructed partly through Western fiction, and she convincingly traced tropes such as the "indolent, superstitious, sensually over-indulgent and religiously fanatical" Oriental in Edward Lane's nineteenth-century translation of the *Arabian Nights*.[52] This, Kabbani argues, is part of Orientalism's reproductive or (to use Said's term) "latent" energy – the stereotypes reappear consistently over time, apparently unchallenged by the observations of travellers and scholars.[53]

Over the four decades since *Orientalism* was published, Said's ideas have provoked a constant stream of debate. The main criticisms, articulated mostly at the end of the last century, centred on his ahistorical or polemical approach in which selective reading from related literature is made to fit an overall thesis. This, critics such as Bernard Lewis and Dennis Porter argued, conflated Classical scholarship with modern scholarship and illogically ignored the specificities of time and geography.[54] Then there is Said's "monolithic", or "homogenising" approach,[55] which suggests that "every European, in what he could say about the Orient, was consequently a racist, an imperialist, and almost totally ethnocentric",

Introduction 13

regardless of the evidence to the contrary – a problem that mischaracterises the work of those deeply immersed in their subject or instances where cultural self-criticism is apparent.[56] Furthermore Said's work was considered polarising in the way it relied on binaries that leave little room for those who are marginalised by the discourse.[57] Marxist scholars Aijaz Ahmed and Robert Young argued, for example, that there is a long history of political resistance that is overlooked by Said's project of othering while Sara Mills has shown how "colonial discourse theory and postcolonial theory have troubled Edward Said's homogenising views of colonial texts".[58] Those who advocated for a more heterogenous approach (such as Lisa Lowe and Mary Louise Pratt) noted that there may be multiple strands of argument even within a single text – some supporting the thesis of Orientalism and some that destabilise notional tropes.[59] Despite the criticisms, few deny that Said's work, together with that of Homi Bhabha and Gayatri Chakravorty Spivak (affectionately termed the "Holy Trinity" by Robert Young), has helped to establish a new and practical way of studying other cultures that extends, as Said acknowledges in the 1995 edition of *Orientalism*, well beyond the scope of his 1978 project. "Too often", wrote Said in the original publication, "literature and culture are presumed to be politically, even historically innocent", a criticism that could be levelled at the humanist approach to studying Orientalist texts in the 1970s and 1980s.[60] Now, it is arguably impossible to consider literature in relation to the East without reference to whether the representations being made are at least fair. This is surely to be welcomed, but it does not provide a neat platform for the making of cultural pronouncements. Since the turn of this century, as the proliferation of postcolonial studies has shown, it is important to keep exploring what "fair" might mean. Old tropes have a habit of being recycled, re-emerging, for example, in the figure of the "eccentric gentleman traveller", as categorised by Patrick Holland and Graham Huggan. This figure, as Claire Lindsay describes in a recent essay, continues to be fundamentally "elitist and exploitative".[61] While some critics (for example, Debbie Lisle) have hitherto insisted that conservatism is inherent to the genre of travel writing as a whole, many others (most recently, Corinne Fowler) make the case that it has always had an ethical dimension and that this has resulted in modern travel literature as "serious cultural critique".

Of importance to the current discussion from the preceding brief theoretical survey is the way in which the twin discourses of Orientalism and postcolonialism remain valuable in "decolonising the mind";[62] they provide, in other words, ways in which to be vigilant towards "latent Orientalism" in the texts under scrutiny while remaining open to moments of productive cultural insight.[63] British desert travel literature since 1950, however, is not a homogenising project in which all texts line up in defence of either logic: on the contrary, a whole range of motivations, backgrounds, genders, and other specificities based on time and encounter

14 *Introduction*

naturally impinge on the reading of these works. While the old Orient continues to exert an influence on the way in which the modern Middle East is perceived, modern desert writers often identify this within their own work and recognise that this is at odds with the pioneering and modernising projects of the specific cultures being encountered. It is this tension that creates the interesting dynamics of the modern form of the desert genre; however small and largely unobserved by current criticism, it plays its part not just in reflecting but in shaping the "nature of perception" that is central to Orientalism's highly charged aftermath.

If modern desert texts belong to, rather than are entirely defined by a heritage that is Oriental in nature, they owe an equal debt to the legacy of desert exploration with the work of T. E. Lawrence and Wilfred Thesiger casting the longest shadows over modern desert accounts. Lawrence's Arabian travels, between 1916 to 1918, were undertaken as part of the imperial administration of the region and British ambitions during the Great War, while Thesiger's Arabian desert journeys (from 1945 to 1950) were initially launched as part of a locust-eradication project and latterly motivated by a fascination with the lives of the Bedu.[64] It is possible to read the work of both Lawrence and Thesiger as entirely within the Oriental paradigm, but they both show many points of sympathy with their subject that unseat the homogenising assumptions of Orientalism. The cultural ambivalence within their work is one of the reasons, perhaps, they continue to exert an influence on today's desert travellers, striking a chord with the equivocation that underpins the modern quest for authenticity and the heroic endeavour, and the realisation that cultural appropriation is not the place to find it. The narratives of Lawrence and Thesiger are not the only texts to be referenced by modern travellers – Bertram Thomas's achievement is the motivation for Mark Evans's recent journey across the Empty Quarter, for example – but theirs are the most often quoted; indeed, they are often bracketed together (not altogether helpfully, given their radically different purpose and approach) as the last of a kind. Given their impact on successive generations of travellers, it is useful to reflect, albeit briefly, on their broad legacy as identified in the following section.

The Lawrence and Thesiger legacy

In glossing the life of Thesiger in *Atlantis of the Sands* (1992), former soldier and desert expeditioner Ranulph Fiennes writes, "[A]t Oxford [Thesiger] read *Arabia Felix* by Bertram Thomas and *Revolt in the Desert* by T.E. Lawrence. He began to dream of the Empty Quarter".[65] Within this biographical fragment, the entire imaginative geography of Arabia with its totemic deserts is telescoped, providing a lens within a lens for the way in which the reader should approach Fiennes's own work. Nearly all modern desert travel writers employ a similar device, or shorthand, for

Introduction 15

summoning up the old Orient. Indeed, nearly 30 years after Fiennes's search for the lost city of Ubar in the deserts of Oman, Levison Wood (another ex-military traveller) writes of his own desert journey in *Arabia* (2018): "I was cheered by the fact that plenty of explorers had been to the region and left a great raft of literature on the subject", and he goes on to refer to Ibn Battuta, Richard Burton, Gertrude Bell, T. E. Lawrence, Freya Stark, and Wilfred Thesiger, among others.[66] The problem with shorthand is it can be read differently from the way intended by the writer. If today's travellers see in Lawrence a soldier and a man of action, and in Thesiger a man heroically wandering in an immutable wilderness, others see men of breath-taking arrogance writing at the height of British imperialism.

In the epilogue to his opus magnus, *Seven Pillars of Wisdom*, Lawrence writes that he had dreamed "at the City School in Oxford, of hustling into form, while I lived, the new Asia", and throughout his account of the Arab Revolt he casts himself as a leader and a crusader: "I meant to make a new nation, to restore a lost influence, to give twenty millions of Semites the foundation on which to build an inspired dream-palace of their national thoughts".[67] Anthony Nutting appears to be the first to identify the Lawrence of *Seven Pillars* with a divinity complex and points out that war, sacrifice, and the spirit of crusade, all part of the Christian heritage, are similarly part of the book and the literal pilgrimage away from Islam's Mecca.[68] This reading is continued by Simpson and Knightley who comment that Lawrence "saw himself as one of England's crusaders, not only in the physical sense but in the metaphysical as well – strong, just, and chaste".[69] Certainly in *Seven Pillars* Lawrence presents himself as a preacher (p. 603), a prophet (p. 366), and ultimately a martyr (p. 452); the infamous Dera'a incident, in which an infidel soldier pulls up a fold of "the flesh" over Lawrence's ribs and punctures it with his bayonet – "the blood wavered down my side"– even has overtones of the crucifixion. Phrasing such as "offered up my own life", and, of the Arabs after the war, "I was glad they felt grown up enough to reject me" (p. 681), not only establish Lawrence as a messiah figure, who is both persecuted and rejected, but they suggest that without Lawrence the birth of the "New East" would not have been possible – a view so obviously Eurocentric in its perspective that it has been contested by many since.[70] In the foreword to *Seven Pillars*, Lawrence may write that it is his intention to show "how natural the success was and how inevitable, how little dependent ... on the outside assistance of the few British" (p. 21), but this intention contrasts with his heroic self-presentation throughout the text. As "imperial agent" of the West, the implications of a Christian Occidentalist bringing salvation to the Islamic Orient naturally help replay contentious representations of conquest and cultural interaction that Said suggests have characterised relations between West and East for centuries.[71]

While the aforementioned is one reading of Lawrence's *Seven Pillars*, it is not the only reading, however, and critics since Said have sought to

16   *Introduction*

salvage Lawrence's reputation (and with it redeem the heterogeneity of Western Oriental scholarship). Dennis Porter, for example, in a famous riposte to *Orientalism*, interrogates the moments in the text where Lawrence appears to be troubled by, or at least shows ambivalence towards, the imperial project of which he is part. To be clear, Porter of course accepts that *Seven Pillars* is likely to disgruntle "those whose sensibilities have been heightened to racial doctrines by twentieth-century history" and understands the offence caused by "the myth that a white European male in a position of leadership is an essential ingredient" to the success of nationalist ambitions. He also recognises that *Seven Pillars* is "apparently written from a position of privilege and authority – the privilege of race, class and gender – within the Western hegemonic world order". Porter goes on, however, to find moments within the text (such as the introduction) that unsettle the status quo and, together with the Orientalist discourse as a whole, allow "counter-hegemonic voices to be heard":[72]

> The complexity of the narrator's persona, his aspirations and self-doubt, his sense of estrangement from his own culture, the sympathy for and distance from the Arab culture he shared for roughly two years, are part of the story Lawrence tells.[73]

These ambivalences, Porter suggests, contribute to Lawrence's status as a legend, turned into such by the contemporary press, the American journalist Lydell Hart, and latterly by David Lean's Academy Award–winning film, *Lawrence of Arabia* (1962).[74] Lawrence himself, however, was uneasy about his status, admitting to a "craving to be famous; and a horror of being known to like being known";[75] perhaps more convincingly, as Geoffrey Nash writes, "he both enjoyed and affected to disdain the 'Lawrence myth'".[76] Either way, the comment demonstrates the difficulty in representing a consistent image of self within the text, let alone Orientalism or indeed the Orient itself.

Porter ends his evaluation of Lawrence by asserting that, in *Seven Pillars*, "the desert Arab becomes in part an expression of the age-old nostalgia for the supposed lost wholeness of the primitive world, a modern noble savage, who is different not only from the half-Europeanised and decadent Turk but also from city Arabs" (p. 159). Porter identifies now familiar binaries between primitive and civilised, desert and sown that create sympathy towards rather than division from the East. Despite Lawrence's ability to turn a self-critical eye on British culture and its essentialist notions of progress, his legacy is nonetheless a problematic one. Indeed, the Lawrence legend, together with the Orientalist frame-tale that it evokes, is recognised among more erudite modern desert travellers as something of a poison chalice. When asked, for example, whether he was an "Orientalist", Tim Mackintosh-Smith (in his travel narrative in

Introduction 17

the footsteps of Ibn Battuta) writes that he "winced inwardly", recognising through parody that the word had "undertones, dark ones; an Orientalist went around in native dress, carried a pocket theodolite and worked for the ultimate and total dominance of the West".[77] The imbrications of the Oriental legacy, overlapping the heroic with the self-deprecating, the scholarly with the experiential, are not lost on Mackintosh-Smith who manipulates the fractures within Orientalism throughout his *Travels with a Tangerine* with postmodern bravura.

Rightly or wrongly, modern desert travellers find in Thesiger a less contentious figure. Thesiger's project in *Arabian Sands*, the Arabian travelogue by which all modern travel narratives tend to be measured, appears anodyne enough. Unlike *Seven Pillars*, Thesiger's *Arabian Sands* does not set out to capture any great acts of heroism, other than the indomitability of the human spirit in lives lived at the edge of physical endurance. Instead, it entails a description of 10,000 miles of journeying by camel and on foot across the Peninsula, beginning with an explanation of how Thesiger came to love wild places from his early life in Abyssinia and Sudan. The book's greatest merit (Thesiger claimed to be an explorer first and a writer second) is in capturing a way of life through minutely detailed descriptions of Bedu tribes and their customs and manners that Thesiger believed would not long survive into the latter half of the twentieth century and the desert incursion of oil companies. His regret regarding this monumental change of a centuries-old culture is one of the key notes of the text and the original preface is one of the most famous and poignant pieces of nostalgia for a pre-automotive world in travel literature. Or at least, it is a reflection of Thesiger's own inability to be reconciled with modernity, which he later came to accept was no such impediment for the Bedu.

On closer scrutiny, embracing the Thesiger legend can be as problematic as referencing Lawrence. Like Bertram Thomas a decade or two earlier, "Umbarak" (Thesiger's Bedu name), had a mission – to chart for the Western world the unknown interior of the Arabian sands. More crucially, he also had a job, as part of the locust control mission, trying to identify outbreaks of locust infestation in what is now call Oman. The fact that he had a reason to be there, gives his writing an immediate authority. He applies this authority in *Arabian Sands*, continuing the Orientalist assessment of the desert and the sown by levelling sharp criticism at what he describes as the "gutter Arabs" of towns. In contrast, he is highly respectful of the Bedu, whom he describes as a people under terminal threat from modernity, and his account of their lives functions, in Thesiger's own estimation, as a "memorial to a vanished past, a tribute to a once magnificent people".[78] With a sense of the cultural superiority of the British, anticipated in someone writing before the end of empire, he describes the Bedu as childlike in their naivety and immutable in their collective character, a point that his own biographer, Michael Asher, sets

18   *Introduction*

out to dispute.[79] This concept, the "fallacy" in the words of Tim Youngs "that so-called traditional societies never change", is one of the most enduring myths associated with the Arabian desert.[80]

It is within this gloss that many travellers have tried to retrace Thesiger's footsteps and recreate his experience. In so doing, they are neither successful in being authentic to the journeys he engaged in (because times have changed and most importantly the purpose is gone), nor are they able to engage in an authentic "modern" experience with today's desert inhabitants, as they are consumed with tracing a lost past in the Bedu's modern practices. The embrace of the Thesiger perspective contributes to a sense of belatedness that even those who go in search of a vanished past recognise as being misplaced: "[I]t is irresponsible to suggest", writes Bruce Kirkby, a recent desert traveller, "that a remote culture should remain in the past, denied modern advances, only to present a sideshow for Western travellers", but at the same time, Kirkby finds he cannot help himself lamenting the "spread of a generic world culture, a shocking loss of diversity, a growing sameness".[81] The relationship between present and former travellers is problematised through passages such as this which bring to crisis, through the disconnect between expectation, experience, and expression, the inherited tropes of an Orientalist past and the postcolonial and global sensibilities of the present. Put more simply, Bruce Kirkby, in comparing himself with Thesiger "feels bad for feeling sad" but spreads the cloak of Orientalism over the deserts of the Middle East regardless and this, he recognises, has real-world implications. Those implications are revealed through closer reading of the relationship between one generation of desert texts and the next, and an examination of this "intertextuality" is the specific focus of the first chapter of this book, which considers presentations of self in modern desert texts. This and succeeding chapters (characterised, respectively, by presentations of the Other, gender, nature, and the travelling persona in Arabian desert literature since 1950) are mapped out in greater detail in the remaining part of this introduction.

Mapping the chapters

In tracing the concept of intertextuality through an anglophone history, Graham Allen writes that "contemporary literature seems concerned with echoing and playing with previous stories, classic texts and long-established genres such as the romance and the detective story".[82] One might add to these examples, the classic tales of exploration. Maria Leavenworth is one of several critics to identify that second journeys – that is those conducted in the footsteps of a distinguished earlier traveller – form a distinct genre in modern travel writing. These journeys tend to use a travel text as both a pretext for the current journey and as a source of inspiration informing the new journey, and strands of the former text are

Introduction 19

generally quoted at length in the modern text, thereby setting up interesting dynamics between the two.[83] This book identifies a similar phenomenon at work in modern desert literature and Chapter 1 of this study identifies those narratives, written since 1950, that follow a footstep path written overtly within the very specific tradition of desert exploration. The deserts of Arabia offer a particularly fertile landscape for this kind of invested travel because the space they occupy, as we have already seen, is more than just physical. Journeying into the deserts of Arabia, modern travellers engage with a past that is "encoded in narrative form".[84] In other words, the region far exceeds the sum of the individual journeys of exploration and adventure that helped map the region for Western interests. The intertextuality involved in these footstep endeavours, therefore, creates an interesting opportunity to consider the extent to which new generations of desert travellers continue to plod through the well-trodden territory of the Orient or whether they cut new imaginative ground in their presentation of Arab encounter. Significantly, the texts these footstep travellers write, in setting the past against the present, and expectation against experience, help delineate the country left behind. Often, this referentiality exposes a sense of regret, or to use Ali Behdad's phrase "belatedness", that is highly revealing of modern preoccupations with the loss of authenticity in the travel experience or a sense of foreboding about the encroachments of globalisation – strands that are explored with the aid of literary criticism throughout the chapter.

While Chapter 1 establishes that the work of footstep travellers is often illuminating about the nature of "self" in the modern narrative, particularly as defined in relation to the protagonists of prior desert texts, Chapter 2 turns, with the aid of postcolonial theory and anthropology, to those modern writers whose main aim is to reveal the "other" in their Arabian desert encounters and in an explicitly different way from their predecessors. Implicit in some criticism of the footstep narrative is a sense of redundancy of form (in that it attempts to replicate the route and manner of an earlier journey); this criticism in turn implies that there can be nothing interesting in a second account because everything of value has been already covered in the original and there is nothing further to learn of the destination despite the elapsed time; in other words, within the intervening years between first and second journey, the destination and those who live there have remained static and resistant to change. The supposed immutability of the desert and its inhabitants is a frequently recurring trope throughout the history of literary engagement in Middle East exploration. In this, it conforms to one of the two types of travel writing identified by Paul Fussell that centres on a nostalgic engagement with a vanishing way of life.[85] Western travellers purport to find characteristics and cultural practices that appear to stem from biblical times and describe the way in which both succumb to the impingement of the modern world as the particular calamity of the moment in which they travel.

20   *Introduction*

Thesiger famously charts the demise of the Bedu way of life in the Arabian desert, laying the curse of futility on all those endeavouring to repeat his journey: "If anyone goes there now looking for the life I led [among the Bedu] they will not find it".[86] He omits to say that the traveller will of course continue to find the desert and the Bedu, and the life the one lives within the other, evolving and adapting, as has ever been the case, to the circumstances and contexts of their contemporary lives.

If Chapter 2 looks at the way some modern travel writers have continued to treat the Bedu as a fossilised culture with, as Tim Youngs states, "the air of preserving for us in the text lifeways that are about to disappear", the chapter also looks beyond stereotypical accounts to find a more sympathetic approach to the Other.[87] By treating the desert in contrast with the sown – the desert's supposed age-old binary – the discussion shows that not all modern desert journeys conform to the need to find things as they were. Some travellers, including Thesiger's biographer, Michael Asher, are interested in the destination as a living entity and their motivation for travel is less about recapturing the past than exploring the present. This gives an opportunity, through texts that deliberately expose the mechanised nature of the modern desert journey, or which explore urban cities within the desert context, to engage with presentations of Arab modernities in contemporary, interdisciplinary studies by Arab scholars.[88] The most convincing recent accounts of travel in the Arabian desert, particularly the work of Tim Mackintosh-Smith, do not necessarily reject the past; they incorporate it into the present in much the same way as the Arab city selects elements of heritage to shape the character of the modern. This blurring of past and present aids in the shifting of unhelpful, outmoded binaries and – in the same spirit of engagement that marked earlier journeys to the region – opens up opportunities for dialogue and discourse in the space in between.

A whole critical discourse is devoted to in-betweenness, inspired by Said and elaborated upon by Bhabha and Spivak in the emergent field of subaltern studies. Chapter 3 of this book turns the attention to one strand of what amounts to a feminist and postcolonial discussion – namely, the way in which women are marginalised in desert travel literature, both as the subject of such travels and as the object of attention in male travels. Said recognised in Flaubert's Egyptian courtesan, a "widely influential model of the Oriental woman; she never spoke of herself, she never represented her emotions, presence, or history. *He* spoke for and represented her".[89] As Said goes on to note, this is a model of Orientalism itself, and indeed, Arabia has often been projected as a seductive, gendered space in relation to the Western, white, and most especially male gaze. Such, at least, is the dominant narrative of travel in the region, but again it is not the only narrative and the discussion herein, in common with a general modern critical tendency to redeem the voice of women in travel literature, seeks out examples of female travel in desert accounts. This is

Introduction 21

undertaken partly to contest Oriental stereotypes and partly to redress the omission of female-authored travel accounts that remain under-represented in critical surveys despite the distinguished accomplishments of women travellers such as Gertrude Bell and Freya Stark. The work of modern desert traveller Marguerite van Geldermalsen, among others, is also presented as an example of hitherto overlooked female desert writing, helping thereby to broaden the field. The point of the discussion in Chapter 3, however, is not simply to resurrect or promote the female voice in this area but to engage in contemporary discussion about the extent to which the desert travel writing of women can be seen as a liminal activity that offers a contrast to what Holland and Huggan call the "propensity for self-congratulation", particularly of the middle-class, white and primarily male traveller.[90]

For help in understanding the nature of the in-between role that women may play in this context (as privileged, for example, to step into realms that are not accessible to male travellers such as the harem, Bedu tent, or marriage celebration in today's urban cities), the discussion draws on postcolonial theory. Anne McClintock is one of a series of influential modern critics who took issue with Said's omission of women from the discussion in *Orientalism* and who emphasised that gender matters in postcolonial discourse.[91] As Sara Mills points out, men and women do not necessarily experience colonialism in the same way – some were empowered by their role in relation to the lands through which they travel, but most were also disempowered in relation to men.[92] Chapter 3 brings this discussion to bear on the work of recent female writers that can broadly be categorised as "desert context literature" and finds reasons why the modern political, social, and cultural context of Middle Eastern travel has continued to disadvantage (but not completely deter) female travel in the region. The purpose of this approach is to contribute to, in Reina Lewis's words, a "recognition that gender, race and subjectivity are complex, plural and contingent" and thereby unsettle the norms of the prevailing *his*torical discourse.[93] The chapter concludes with a discussion about the way in which the very taxonomy of desert encounter (the categories employed, the vocabulary used and labels imposed) reflects an inbuilt gender bias that reveals much about the continuing construction of East-West binaries and that these binaries prove stubbornly resistant to postcolonial attempts to champion the liminal and the in-between.

The theme of liminality is continued in Chapter 4 but within the context of nature rather than gender. In continuing to explore how modern desert writing reveals much about the land left behind, the work of desert scientists, captured in moments of sublime contemplation of the natural world, is examined for the commentary it offers about the human place bordered within nature. In identifying the artificial nature of boundaries between disciplines (for example, between scientific documentation and travel literature) that has become a feature of exploration narratives since

22   *Introduction*

the 1950s, this chapter employs ecocriticism to show how modern desert texts often reach towards a more equitable definition of the human relationship with the environment.

In common with Orientalist tropes, the deserts of Arabia have often been gendered as feminine – either as "pristine", "virgin" space, or as "seductive", "alluring", and "dangerous"; both entice the "penetration" of male exploration. The traditional representation of desert exploration assumes other familiar binaries, such as wild, negative, empty space, or *terra nullius* (albeit a term applied more usually to the Australian desert), that require the positive energy of science to define, map, and tame. A depopulated landscape that appears both ominous and anonymous but also siren-like in its seductiveness is obviously not a trope that is limited to the desert context; John McLeod, for example, elaborates Rudyard Kipling's jungle as emptied out of indigenous Indians and he makes the point that "this depiction of the landscape is clearly mediated by the limited perception of the British and shapes a particular and selective envisioning of space".[94] With the help of ecocritical theory, this chapter examines the envisioning of the desert space through science and probes the way in which a number of modern science writers cross the boundary of their traditional discipline to extemporise on the beauty or sublimity of the desert landscape.[95] This appears radical and almost transgressive but, as Mary Campbell writes of early travel literature, "the travel book is a kind of witness: it is generically aimed at the truth".[96] Science and ethnographic information, in other words, have always had a role in informing and giving pleasure to the reader, and the modern desert writers considered in Chapter 4 are shown to continue in this tradition.

Notions of the "truth" have troubled writers since the earliest travel narratives – even before Marco Polo earned his reputation for being economical with it. Seeing with one's own eyes has since Classical times been linked with acquiring knowledge, but it has also been linked with embellishment as successive generations of travellers have journeyed in search of the constructed realities of their travelling forebears. This was particularly the case with Eastern-bound travellers who carried with them an entire Oriental baggage. Disappointed by what they found, they often resorted to imagination to supply the missing dimensions, and exposing them in this practice became a pastime of successive travellers. The need to verify assumed a particular character in Arabian desert literature where the desert proper remained a place of conjecture. While a travel writer in the *Eclectic Review* of 1824 lamented that "no one can now pretend to have seen the world who has not made one of a party of pleasure up the Nile or taken a ride on camel-back across the Syrian desert", the reality was that desert exploration remained the experience of very few.[97] As such, desert travel narratives as we have seen became obsessively annotated in a bid to illustrate not just the authority of the author but also the authenticity of the experience. Some of this

Introduction 23

obsession with authenticity has become the legacy of modern desert writers who find authenticity invested in the tales of daring expedition and seek, by "getting off the beaten track", to share that authenticity by association.[98] Focusing on authenticity and what that might mean in an age when desert exploration is mostly confined to specialist oil prospecting and fully supported by modern technology (motorised transport, satellite communications, aerial search and rescue), Chapter 5 brings the discussion on authenticity in the work of desert travellers into a twenty-first-century context. It looks at the way selected recent writers continue to position themselves as travellers while their activities are becoming ever-more accessible and replicated by tourists. In finding that the space between traveller and tourist is, as they would describe it, disappointingly narrow, some desert travellers make ironic use of the term "tourist" and include it in their titles. Tom Chesshyre's *A Tourist in the Arab Spring*, Tony Wheeler's *Bad Lands: A Tourist on the Axis of Evil*, and *Misadventure in the Middle East* by Henry Hemming are all examples of the way in which some travellers look for ever-more extreme ways of distinguishing their journey – part of a phenomenon that Claudia Bell and John Lyall (and latterly Graham Huggan) refer to as the "accelerated sublime" – a concept examined in the context of desert literature within the chapter.[99] As some travellers grapple with the modern dilemma of how to find meaning in their journeys through exaggerating the differences between home and away, others seek out universal commonalities by turning inwards and emphasising the inner journey. Chapter 5 concludes by examining two recent travel accounts that chart the nature of personal transformation encouraged by desert encounter; in so doing, the discussion identifies the reinvention of the pilgrimage genre, albeit calibrated in secular terms, out of which desert travel writing originally grew.

With the perceived need of some travellers to find extremes of experience to make a desert journey special enough to write about, inevitably it is necessary to ask the question, posed in the title of this book, of whether the Arab desert has at length become a "barren legacy". In conclusion, this question is specifically addressed by reflecting to what extent today's travel writers have been able to take old themes and forge something new. Throughout this study, the discussion turns to critical discussions on modernity to understand this phenomenon in a broader context and finds in the work, for example, of Marc Augé, concepts of the "supermodern" that explain how the desert can appear to have contracted even at the moment at which it is technically expanding. The book concludes by considering how globalisation is contributing to this process, causing the imaginative geography of the Arabian desert, and the landscape of Orientalism contoured within it, to recede into the distance as Arjun Appadurai's new topography of "ethnoscapes, mediascapes, technoscapes, financescapes and ideoscapes" begin to form in their place.[100]

24 *Introduction*

Notes

1 Wilfred Thesiger, *Arabian Sands* [1959] (Harmondsworth: Penguin, 1984), p. 11.

2 Carl Thompson, "Introduction", in *The Routledge Companion to Travel Writing*, ed. by Carl Thompson, [2016] (Abingdon and New York: Routledge, 2020), p. xviii. Carl Thompson describes "imagined geographies" as the relationship between travel writing and the various constructs "which exist for us through a complex interaction of personal experience ... and a tangled web of culturally-mediated prior associations, expectations and images", all of which influence the way in which a geographical region is approached.

3 Edward W. Said, *Orientalism* (Harmondsworth: Penguin – Peregrine, 1978), p. 206.

4 United Nations, "68% of the World Population Projected to Live in Urban Areas by 2050, Says UN" [online], United Nations Department of Economic and Social Affairs (2018), available at https://www.un.org/development/desa/en/news/population/2018-revision-of-world-urbanization-prospects.html [accessed 12 July 2019].

5 Karla Armbruster, "Creating the World We Must Save: The Paradox of Television Nature Documentaries", in *Writing the Environment: Ecocriticism and Literature*, ed. by Richard Kerridge and Neil Sammells (London and New York: Zed Books, 1998), pp. 218–38 (p. 228).

6 Carl Thompson, *Travel Writing* (Abingdon and New York: Routledge, 2011), p. 30.

7 See relevant chapter for bibliographic details. The term "subspecies of memoir" is taken from Paul Fussell, *Abroad: British Literary Travelling between the Wars* (New York: Oxford University Press, 1980), p. 30, in relation to travel books in general.

8 Although his acclaimed desert text, *Arabian Sands*, was not published until 1959, Thesiger left Arabia in 1950. See Wilfred Thesiger, *The Life of My Choice* [1987] (New York and London: W. W. Norton, 1988) and Michael Asher, *Thesiger: A Biography* (Harmondsworth: Viking, 1994).

9 See, for example, Richard Trench, *Arabian Travellers* (London: Macmillan, 1986); Andrew Taylor, *Travelling the Sands: Sagas of Exploration in the Arabian Peninsula* (Dubai: Motivate Publishing, 1997); Geoffrey Nash, *From Empire to Orient: Travellers to the Middle East 1830-1926* (London: I. B. Tauris, 2005), and James Canton, *From Cairo to Baghdad: British Travellers in Arabia* (London: I B Tauris, 2014). Anthologies of women travellers are referenced in Chapter 3 of this book.

10 Only one such work is cited here: Hilal Al-Hajri, *British Travel-Writing on Oman: Orientalism Reappraised* (Bern: Peter Lang AG, 2006). This helpful study focuses, however, on texts written prior to 1970 and relating only to Oman.

11 Al-Hajri, *British Travel-Writing*, p. 23.

12 Nabil Matar, "Travel Writing and Visual Culture", in *The Routledge Companion to Travel Writing*, ed. by Carl Thompson (London and New York: Routledge, 2020), pp. 139–49 (pp. 148–49).

13 Tarik Sabry and Joe F. Khalil, *Culture, Time and Publics in the Arab World: Media, Public Space and Temporality* (London and New York: I. B. Tauris, 2019), p. 169.

14 An area is technically "classed as a desert if it receives less than ten inches of precipitation annually"; see Uwe George, *In the Deserts of this Earth* [1976], translated by R. and C. Winston (New York and London: First

Harvest/HBJ, 1977), p. 10. The international Aridity Index also measures the potential evapotranspiration (P/PET) in relation to precipitation by "rain or fog or dew"; see William Atkins, *The Immeasurable World: Journeys in Desert Places* (New York: Doubleday, 2018), p. 12.

15 Said, *Orientalism*, p. 55.

16 Freeth, Zara and Victor Winstone, *Explorers of Arabia: From the Renaissance to the Victorian Era* (London: George Allen and Unwin, 1978), p. 295.

17 I am indebted here to the Royal Geographical Society for access to rare maps of Arabia.

18 R. W. McColl, ed., *Encyclopaedia of World Geography* (New York: Facts on File, 2005, 3 Vols.).

19 Johnathan Bate, "Poetry and Biodiversity", in *Writing the Environment*, ed. by Kerridge and Sammells, pp. 53–70 (p. 54).

20 Thesiger, *Arabian Sands*, p. 12. The Bedu are not confined to the Empty Quarter but range across Arabia.

21 Alan Keohane, *Bedouin Nomads of the Desert* [1994] (London: Kyle Books, 2011).

22 Said, *Orientalism*, p. 1. Despite the inherent vagueness of the term, the Orient usually comprised "those countries, collectively, that begin with Islam on the Eastern Mediterranean and stretch through Asia". Martha Pike Conant, *The Oriental Tale in England in the Eighteenth Century* (New York: Columbia University Press, 1908), pp. xvi–xvii. Where Conant argues that the Orient generally excludes Palestine on the grounds that, as a zone of Christian pilgrimage, it registers less successfully as an imaginative "Other", this book adopts the more common approach to the term that is inclusive of Palestine.

23 Said, *Orientalism*, p. 6.

24 Roslynn D. Haynes, *Desert: Nature and Culture* (London: Reaktion Books, 2013), p. 13.

25 Said, *Orientalism*, p. 1.

26 Pitts did not date his travels, but Richard Burton postulated approximate dates. See Richard Burton, *Appendices to Pilgrimages to Al-Madinah and Meccah* [1855], ed. by Isabel Burton (London: Memorial Edition, 1893, 2 Vols.).

27 Freeth and Winstone, *Explorers*, p. 50.

28 See Claire Norton, "Lust, Greed, Torture and Identity: Narrations of Conversion and the Creation of the Early Modern 'Renegade'", *Comparative Studies of South Asia, Africa and the Middle East*, 29, no. 2 (2009), 259–68, and Douglas Pratt et al., eds., *The Character of Christian-Muslim Encounter: Essays in Honour of David Thomas* (Leiden: Brill, 2016), p. 248.

29 Freeth and Winstone, *Explorers*, p. 60.

30 Lionel Cust and Sidney Colvin, eds., *History of the Society of Dilettanti* (London: MacMillan, 1898), p. 85.

31 John Lewis Burckhardt, *Notes on the Bedouins and Wahabys, Collected During His Travels in the East* (London: Henry Colburn and Richard Bentley, 1831, 2 Vols.); quoted in Brent, *Far Arabia*, p. 75.

32 William Makepeace Thackeray, *Contributions to "Punch", Etc.* (New York and London: Harper and Brothers, 1903), p. 86.

33 Said, *Orientalism*, p. 6.

34 Helen Carr, "Modernism and Travel (1880–1940)", in *The Cambridge Companion to Travel Writing*, ed. by Peter Hulme and Tim Youngs [2002] (Cambridge: Cambridge University Press, 2010), pp. 70–86 (p. 70).

35 See historical timeline in Hulme and Youngs, *Cambridge Companion*, p. 292.

26   *Introduction*

36   Thompson, *Travel Writing*, p. 54.
37   Andrew Goudie, *Great Desert Explorers* (London: Royal Geographical Society with IGB, 2016).
38   Albert Hourani, "Preface", in Kathryn Tidrick, *Heart Beguiling Araby: The English Romance with Arabia* [1990] (London: Tauris Parke, 2010), p. xiv.
39   Robert J. C. Young, *Colonial Desire: Hybridity in Theory, Culture and Race* (Abingdon and New York: Routledge, 1995), pp. 3–4.
40   See Robert Irwin, *For Lust of Knowing: The Orientalists and Their Enemies* [2006] (London: Penguin, 2007), p. 217. Irwin's defence of Orientalist scholarship concedes a link between Oriental scholarship and politics and traces elements of racial stereotyping (p. 184), although he does not explicitly make the link between all three.
41   See Billie Melman, "The Middle East/Arabia: 'The Cradle of Islam'", in *Cambridge Companion*, ed. by Hulme and Youngs, pp. 112–19. Melman writes that engagement with Arabia at this time "took on institutional form; with the exception of the Blunts, all the major explorers of the peninsula were affiliated to British political and military agencies" (p. 113).
42   Peter Whitfield, "Post-War English Travel Writing", in *Travel: A Literary History* (Oxford: Bodleian Library, 2012), 263–270.
43   As Andrew Goudie points out in his preface, there are "many books on exploration but remarkably few" on desert exploration, *Great Desert Explorers*, p. xi.
44   Melman, "Middle East/Arabia", p. 112.
45   Melman, "Middle East/Arabia", p. 118.
46   Mark Evans, *Crossing the Empty Quarter in the Footsteps of Bertram Thomas* (UK: Gilgamesh Publishing, 2016), p. 31.
47   George, *Deserts of this Earth*, p. 285.
48   F. Patrick, *Cambridge History of English Literature* (New York: Cambridge University Press, 1927), pp. 2–3.
49   Tidrick, *Heart Beguiling Araby*, p. 37. See also Gillian Tindall, *Countries of the Mind: The Meaning of Place to Writers* (Boston, MA: Northeastern, 1991).
50   Said, *Orientalism*, pp. 2–3.
51   John McLeod notes that Said's *Orientalism* "is considered to be one of the most influential books of the late twentieth century": John McLeod, *Beginning Postcolonialism* [2000] (Manchester: Manchester University Press, 2010), p. 24. See also John MacKenzie, *Orientalism: History, Theory and the Arts* (Manchester: Manchester University Press, 1995).
52   Rana Kabbani, *Imperial Fictions: Europe's Myths of Orient* (London: Pandora, 1994), p. 39.
53   Edward William Lane, *An Account of the Manners and Customs of the Modern Egyptians* (London: C. Knight, 1836). As Kabbani points out, Lane's influential book, together with his translation of *The Thousand and One Nights* (London: Chatto and Windus, 1883), helped fuel general misconceptions about the East. See also Leila Ahmed, *Edward W. Lane: A Study of His Life and Works and of British Ideas of the Middle East in the Nineteenth Century* (London: Longman, 1978).
54   Bernard Lewis, *Islam and the West* (Oxford: Oxford University Press, 1993) and Dennis Porter, "Orientalism and Its Problems", in *Postcolonial Theory: A Reader*, ed. by Patrick Williams and Laura Chrisman (New York: Columbia University Press, 1994), pp. 150–61.
55   F. Barker, P. Hulme, M. Iverson, and D. Loxley, eds., *Literature, Politics and Theory* (London: Methuen, 1986), pp. 210–29.

Introduction 27

56 Said, *Orientalism*, p. 204.
57 Bill Ashcroft, Gareth Griffiths, and Helen Tiffin, *The Empire Writes Back: Theory and Practice in Post-colonial Literatures* (London: Routledge, 1989).
58 Sara Mills, *Discourse* (London and New York: Routledge, 1997), p. 129; see also Aijaz Ahmad, *In Theory: Classes, Nations, Literatures* (London: Verso, 1992), and Young, *Colonial Desire*.
59 Lisa Lowe, *Critical Terrains: French and British Orientalisms* (Ithaca, New York: Cornell University Press, 1991), p. 29; see also Mary Louise Pratt, *Imperial Eyes: Travel Writing and Transculturation* [1992] (London: Routledge, 2008).
60 Said, *Orientalism*, p. 27.
61 Claire Lindsay, "Travel Writing and Postcolonial Studies", in *The Routledge Companion to Travel Writing*, ed. by Carl Thompson (London and New York: Routledge, 2020), pp. 25–34 (p. 32).
62 Ngũgĩ wa Thiong'o, *Decolonising the Mind: The Politics of Language in African Literature* (Portsmouth, NH: Heinemann, 1986).
63 Said, *Orientalism*, p. 206.
64 Given the lives and work of both Lawrence and Thesiger have been extensively analysed elsewhere, the discussion herein focuses only on their broad legacy as drawn upon by subsequent desert travellers. See Lawrence's authorised biographer, Jeremy Wilson, *T.E. Lawrence Studies* [online], available at http://www.telstudies.org/ [accessed 12 July 2019] for an overview of studies on Lawrence; see also Asher, *Thesiger: A Biography*.
65 Ranulph Fiennes, *Atlantis of the Sands: The Search for the Lost City of Ubar* [1992] (London: Signet, 1993), p. 21. See also Graham Dawson, *Soldier Heroes: British Adventure, Empire and the Imagining of Masculinities* (Abingdon: Routledge, 1994).
66 See Levison Wood, *Arabia: A Journey Through the Heart of the Middle East* (London: Hodder and Stoughton, 2018), p. 35.
67 T. E. Lawrence, *Seven Pillars of Wisdom: A Triumph* [privately printed 1926, published 1935] (Harmondsworth: Penguin, 1986), pp. 412–13.
68 Anthony Nutting, *Lawrence of Arabia: The Man and the Motive* (London: Clarkson N Potter, 1961), p. 243.
69 P. Knightley and C. Simpson, "The Secret Lives of Lawrence of Arabia", *The Sunday Times* (9 June 1968, Col 1), p. 50.
70 Tidrick, *Heart Beguiling Araby*, pp. 172–74 cites Richard Aldington (1955) and Suleiman Mousa (1966) as attempting to establish the truth of Lawrence's contribution to the Arab Revolt (see Bibliography).
71 Said, *Orientalism*, pp. 241 and 58.
72 For the way in which Said's *Orientalism* gives "insufficient account of resistance or contradiction within imperial culture itself" see Bart Moore-Gilbert, *Postcolonial Theory* (London: Verso, 1997), p. 50.
73 Porter, "Orientalism and Its Problems", in *Postcolonial Theory*, p. 157.
74 Lydell Hart, quoted in Wilson Knight, *Neglected Powers* (London: Jonathan Cape, 1971), pp. 315 and 349. See also Steven C. Caton, *"Lawrence of Arabia": A Film's Anthropology* (Berkeley, Los Angeles, and London: University of California Press, 1999).
75 T. E. Lawrence, *Seven Pillars of Wisdom*, p. 580. For a reassessment of Lawrence's legacy, see Harold Orlans, *T.E. Lawrence: Biography of a Broken Hero* (London: McFarland, 2002).
76 Geoffrey Nash, ed., *Travellers to the Middle East from Burckhardt to Thesiger: An Anthology* (London and New York: Anthem Press, 2011), p. 199.

28   *Introduction*

77 Tim Mackintosh-Smith, *Travels with a Tangerine* [2001] (New York: Random House, 2004), p. 118.
78 Thesiger, *Arabian Sands*, p. 9.
79 Michael Asher, *The Last of the Bedu: In Search of the Myth* (Harmondsworth: Viking, 1996).
80 Tim Youngs, *The Cambridge Introduction to Travel Writing* (Cambridge: Cambridge University Press, 2013), pp. 127–28.
81 Bruce Kirkby, *Sand Dance: By Camel Across Arabia's Great Southern Desert* (Toronto: McClelland and Stewart, 2000), p. 219.
82 Graham Allen, *Intertextuality* (London and New York: Routledge, 2000), p. 5.
83 Maria Lindgren Leavenworth, *The Second Journey* [2009] (Umeå: Umeå Universitet, 2010).
84 Jacinta Matos, "Old Journeys Revisited: Aspects of Postwar English Travel Writing", in *Temperamental Journeys: Essays on the Modern Literature of Travel*, ed. by Michael Kowalewski (Athens: University of Georgia Press, 1992), pp. 215–29 (p. 215).
85 Thompson, *Travel Writing*, p. 17.
86 Thesiger, *Arabian Sands*, p. 11.
87 Youngs, *Cambridge Introduction*, p. 184. Said contended that "Orientalism assumed an unchanging Orient" (Said, *Orientalism*, p. 96) but detractors suggest in using the term "traditional – the very word has notions of inferiority" when applied to nomadic communities, he does the same. See Ziauddin Sardar, *Orientalism* (Buckingham: Open University Press, 1999), p. 74.
88 Full references are given within the chapter, but the work of Yasser Elsheshtawy, Jaafar Aksikas and Tarik Sabry, representing the academic fields of architecture, cultural studies, and media respectively, are highlighted in the discussion.
89 Said, *Orientalism*, p. 6.
90 Patrick Holland and Graham Huggan, *Tourists with Typewriters: Critical Reflections on Contemporary Travel Writing* [1998] (Ann Arbor: University of Michigan Press, 2000), p. 122.
91 McClintock, Anne, "The Angel of Progress: Pitfalls of the Term 'Post-Colonialism'", in *Colonial Discourse/Postcolonial Theory*, ed. by F. Barker, P. Hulme, and M. Iversen (Manchester: Manchester University Press, 1994), pp. 253–66.
92 Sara Mills, *Discourses of Difference: An Analysis of Women's Travel Writing and Colonialism* (London and New York: Routledge, 1992).
93 Lewis, *Gendering Orientalism*, p. 1.
94 John McLeod, *Beginning Postcolonialism* [2000] (Manchester: Manchester University Press, 2010), p. 72.
95 Bibliographical details are given in the chapter, but for an overview of ecocritical scholarship, see Kerridge and Sammells, *Writing the Environment* and Graham Huggan and Helen Tiffin, *Postcolonial Ecocriticism: Literature, Animals, Environment* [2010] (Abingdon and New York: Routledge, 2015).
96 Mary B. Campbell, *The Witness and the Other World: Exotic European Travel Writing, 400–1600* (Ithaca, New York: Cornell University Press, 1988), pp. 2–3.
97 R. Bakewell, "Travels in Switzerland", *Eclectic Review*, N.S.21 (1824), 306–27 (pp. 306–07).

Introduction 29

98 James Buzard, *The Beaten Track: European Tourism, Literature, and the Ways to "Culture" 1800–1918* (Oxford: Clarendon Press, 1993). Buzard states that tourism offers a homogenous, shared experience that is impersonal, fixed to specific itineraries and superficial (p. 91).

99 Graham Huggan, *Extreme Pursuits: Travel/Writing in an Age of Globalization* (Ann Arbor: University of Michigan Press, 2009), p. 6.

100 Arjun Appadurai, *Modernity at Large: Cultural Dimensions of Globalisation* (Minneapolis: University of Minnesota Press, 1996).

1 In literary footsteps
The prevalence of "second journeys"

While broadly diverse in their approach, almost all recent travel writers to the deserts of the Arabian Peninsula share one common characteristic: they refer in some measure, whether as a foreword to their travel account or through a more involved, intertextual referencing, to the canon of celebrated explorers – and particularly T. E. Lawrence and Wilfred Thesiger – who preceded them. In this, they share the company of many of their literary forebears who have made it a point to acknowledge the desert explorations of the previous generation before expounding on their own. Often, the referencing is intended as a genuine homage to the achievements of earlier desert travellers; at other times, it is intended to foreground the merits of the present journey. In the past half-century, an exaggerated form of this kind of referencing has emerged wherein an entire modern journey is built around the itinerary of a former traveller allowing for the original account to act as both a "pretext for and a pre-text of a second journey".[1] The motivations for undertaking one of these footstep journeys (the term "footstep" often occurs in the title of the expedition narrative) are various and worthy of study on account of what they reveal about the modern quest. It is no coincidence, for example, that the footstep phenomenon has proliferated at a time when some contend there is little or "no meaningful distinction between the tourist and the traveller".[2] As modern desert travellers, in common with travellers in many other contexts, struggle with issues of authenticity, the connection with a former journey helps give a rationale for undertaking the modern journey while also lending it the gloss of respectability that once used to attach to expeditions of an exploratory nature.

Of course, it could be argued that searching for authenticity through imitation is something of a self-defeating exercise, and some critics have indeed pointed this out. Described by Peter Hulme, for example, as forming an "ambulant gloss" of the original text, footstep accounts use the original journey not just for guidance and inspiration but to give form and structure to the modern endeavour and equally to the resulting account.[3] Inevitably, then, there is a sense of predictability inherent in the very nature of the subgenre that invites criticism of some of these second

DOI: 10.4324/9781003197201-2

texts as "thin and dreary offerings", at best trawling over stale content and at worst hagiographical in their treatment of the original author.[4]

While this may sometimes be justified criticism in terms of their literary merit, footstep accounts nonetheless offer many interesting insights into intertextuality; the close relationship between reader, writer, and traveller; and the expectations raised by the original journey in contrast to the experience of the second journey. The desire, furthermore, to "imagine a form of travel literature forever original in all essentials" is, as James Buzard suggests, a specious quest wherein an escape from the "prison of prior texts" is neither wholly sustainable nor wholly desirable.[5] Indeed, as Jay Clayton points out, intertextuality can be highly productive in that it allows the flow of ideas to be recognised not simply as a matter of influence exerted on the present by the past but, in the interpretation of the reader, an influence extending forward. The idea of a more "flexible relation among texts", is built upon by Maria Lindgren Leavenworth, who writes,[6]

> Instead of a steady line of descent through the history of travel writing, maintaining canons and reinforcing modern distinctions between high and low art, between past reality and contemporary experience, intertextuality stresses the mosaic quality of the narrative: parallel, overlapping, complementing or conflicting strands of inspiration or discussion.[7]

The "mosaic quality" referred to here allows for a fragmented approach to time in which ideas can be applied without the straitjacket of temporal logic. Read in this light, footstep accounts can be seen as fruitful ways of bringing fresh insights to bear on the elements of the original journey. In the context of the Middle East, with its richly invested landscapes of religious and Oriental connotations, they invite the reader to reconsider an inherited set of tropes traditionally associated with the location, while also probing the original motivations and claims of the first journey authors. While it may be stretching the point to suggest that any of the modern footstep writers considered in this chapter offer a specifically postcolonial counter-narrative, their observations on the impact of globalisation and modernisation on the lives of the Bedu, the inclusion in the narrative of Bedu companions as equal explorers rather than incidental facilitators, and the reflections on the nature of statehood and ownership of land where previously borders were defined along tribal lines, inevitably set up interesting points of contrast with the original texts and perspectives of the Arabian desert therein. As Adrian Hayes recognises in the epilogue to his own footstep journey, while Wilfred Thesiger "fondly remembers the good parts of the 'traditional lives' of the Bedu", there is of course a darker side "that is often forgotten …: that of brutal infighting, death and cruelty".[8] Observations such as these invite a critical rereading of the original text and thereby contribute in turn to the

32   *In literary footsteps*

"mosaic quality" of narrative represented by modern desert texts, and within the integral tessera, questions naturally arise as to whether journeys propelled by nostalgia alone are appropriate in a postcolonial age. At a time when, as Chris Rojek argues, "nostalgia industries continuously recycle products which signify simultaneity between the past and the present",[9] it takes courage on the part of the footstep traveller to spell out what ought to be obvious – that the people they encounter are not there simply for the benefit of "the tourist gaze".[10]

This chapter looks closely at footsteps accounts of present-day Western desert travellers to Arabia. It examines the various tropes that are common to this recently recognised subgenre of modern travel literature, as particularly identified by Jacinta Matos, Heather Henderson, Alison Russell, and Maria Lindgren Leavenworth,[11] and argues that despite the general critical pessimism about the value of these footstep journeys, they play a useful role in serving to rescue "from oblivion" the literary "monuments of the past", while also highlighting, through the lens of elapsed time, the way in which the original texts could or should be read.[12] The chapter goes further in suggesting that far from being a redundant or anachronistic form of travel writing (in that it is by its nature backward-looking), many footstep travels can be considered expressly modern, at least in the way in which they connect with a wider discourse on the difficulties of representing encountered others; the way in which opportunities are afforded for a fairer representation of the Arabian "Other", and the way in which they employ methods of self-irony to probe the value of their endeavour. Indeed, all of the desert footstep travellers highlighted in this chapter are acutely aware of their diminished status in relation to the supposed elite whom T. E. Lawrence termed the "real Arabian veterans",[13] and if not exactly representing themselves as "clowns and as cowards", they do at least acknowledge the limitations of their enactments in contrast to the explorers whom they seek to emulate.[14] Whether this amounts to acts of glorification of the past or simply an ironic undermining of the chosen pretext of the footstep journey is further problematised during the course of this chapter.

Part of the motivation of desert travel has traditionally been the desire to veer off the beaten track. A shared anxiety among modern desert travellers, in common with many modern travellers in general, is the realisation during their respective journeys that their quest is founded on the unlikelihood of finding an untrodden path in a world which has comprehensively been mapped and explored. This is an intensified concern for footstep travellers who generally undertake the journey to demonstrate that genuine exploration is still possible despite the fact that the text of the original traveller has already left waypoints along the route. Their quest for authenticity is therefore undercut by the awareness that they may be living out a self-deluding fantasy. Their postulation in this way as "post-tourist", in the sense in which Maxine Feifer defined the term, is also explored herein.[15]

In literary footsteps 33

The identification of footstep travel accounts as a distinct literary phenomenon is a relatively recent one, and Leavenworth – one of the few critics to identify the form and give it critical prominence – defines this type of travel thus: "second journeys are carried out with the express aim of duplicating an earlier traveller's itinerary and as far as possible re-live past experiences".[16] Leavenworth's emphasis on itinerary and re-enactment focuses attention on the traveller's relationship with the past, and she regards the phenomenon positively as one of the ways in which travel writing reinvents itself over time. She refines her definition of these journeys as ones in which an original travelogue provides the map for the second journey. Although she makes no explicit reference to Western desert travel accounts in Arabia, much of her theory of second journeys has many points of commonality in its application; this chapter builds upon Leavenworth's work, therefore, by identifying similar tropes in the context of Arabian travel while pausing to consider the uniquely location-specific features of this subgenre. One such unique specificity is that, due to the inaccessibility of Arabian desert locations and the restrictions of modern political realities (such as border crossings and visa restrictions), it is seldom feasible or desirable for modern travellers to follow identical itineraries to those of their chosen predecessor. In the course of the current discussion, therefore, the term "footstep travel" is used to denote the endeavour of following a primary text to give shape to a modern journey but takes a looser interpretation with regard to the retracing of an exact itinerary. For this reason, although it has inspired the discussion, Leavenworth's term "second journey" is mostly avoided, except occasionally as a way of distinguishing a modern journey from the original journey by which it was motivated.

For a footstep journey to work well, it has to be predicated on the right kind of *pre*text. Carl Thompson notes that travel writers are "keenly aware" that they follow in the footsteps of "true explorers, heroic figures who reported real discoveries and made genuine contributions to knowledge".[17] Footstep writers travelling in Arabia are not just "keenly aware": they have chosen their mark, very often, with an eye on the potential to be earned through association. It is perhaps no accident, for example, that as yet there are no footstep journeys that trace the paths of lesser-known writers in Arabia such as H. H. McWilliams, who travelled from Tel Duweir in the Levant to England in 1933 and recorded his journey in *The Diabolical* (1934), or of lesser-known journeys, such as Norman Lewis's travels by car captured in *Sand and Sea in Arabia* (1938). For a footstep journey to have maximum credibility, it usually has to follow the path of a "looming giant",[18] in literary as well as historical terms, or it has to re-establish the calibre of the forgotten. Above all, the journey has to be recorded in a text.[19]

The right kind of *pre*text is easily identified in what might be called (in a somewhat irreverent nod to Said, Bhabha, and Spivak)[20] an "*un*holy trinity" of desert narratives that have inspired a half-century of renewed

34 *In literary footsteps*

interest in Arabian desert encounter by Western travellers – namely, Bertram Thomas's *Arabia Felix* (1932), T. E. Lawrence's *Seven Pillars of Wisdom* (1935), and Wilfred Thesiger's *Arabian Sands* (1959). The emphasis of this chapter, however, is not on these texts themselves but on the travel accounts of four travellers – Charles Blackmore, Bruce Kirkby, Adrian Hayes, and Mark Evans – who deliberately set their journeys in the context of these twentieth-century explorers and whose narratives interact dynamically with the texts that gave rise to their modern journeys. Their work is selected to demonstrate that while aspects of footstep travel can seem predictable and tedious because of the imitative nature of form (in following the itinerary of the original journey), their content exemplifies a productive engagement with many of the concerns that inform modern desert travel literature as a whole. The explicit nature, furthermore, of this genre's "intertextuality" (to use the term in one of its original meanings as first articulated by Julia Kristeva in the late 1960s, and still useful in determining the kind of mediation of meaning involved in reading within a hyper-referential sequence of texts) is in itself of interest, helping the reader to "read back", or reinterpret white, male, Western texts in the light of new or modern postcolonial perspectives.[21]

While the discussion cuts new ground in determining the prevalence of the second journey concept among modern accounts of Arabian desert travel, it resists the impulse to treat those footstep accounts as a single, homogenous phenomenon. On the contrary, it identifies that the form evolves over time from a confident undertaking that shares some of the pioneering qualities of the original journey, through a period of self-doubt in the footstep project itself and the commercial gimmickry that it often entails, to emerge as an opportunity for a more inclusive enterprise through what might be called the "indigenisation" of the footstep journey. As such, the desert footstep accounts act as a parallel journey of a different kind, charting in microcosm many of the inherent complexities and anxieties traced by postcolonial travel literature as a whole. The chapter is shaped, therefore, in chronological terms, analysing the work of each of the modern footstep travellers in turn, in the order in which their work was published.

Before turning to these accounts in detail, it is helpful to consider the tradition of intertextuality, both of a religious and a secular nature, within which the modern footstep narratives have emerged. Within the circular referencing, there is a competitive kind of posturing that, while it may not be unique to Western accounts of Arabian desert travel, is at least highly pronounced and revealing about the modern literary quest for authenticity.

A tradition of intertextuality

By journeying into the Arabian desert, as we have seen in the previous chapter, modern travellers engage with a past that is "encoded in narrative form".[22] One form of encoding is specifically Christian in nature and involves using the Bible and other religious books as a way of mapping the geographies of the Middle East in terms of the histories represented therein. These can be traced to the very earliest tradition of Western travel writing when Englishman William Wey, "almost a medieval *Baedeker*" according to Peter Whitfield, made two trips to Jerusalem in 1458 and 1462.[23] Using the Bible as the pretext for his journey, the resulting narrative can be described as a practical guidebook for pilgrims.[24] This tradition of using a holy text to inspire and inform a journey into the desert continues to the present day – for example, in the work of James Cowan. Cowan's journey into the Egyptian wilderness in the footsteps of Saint Anthony is charted in *Desert Father* (2006), a narrative that translates the Middle East of the present into the land of the past for the purpose of theosophical introspection. Commenting on the "discipline of silence" and "doctrine of emptiness" he encounters in a monastery during his journey, Cowan projects these two qualities onto the landscape as he considers Anthony's withdrawal into the desert and the opportunity that the wilderness affords in terms of a recalibration of the "individual's relationship to secular society".[25] The dynamic established between the two texts – ancient scripture and modern travelogue – can be seen as a literary landscaping of the past within the present, allowing for channels of inspiration, in this case spiritual, to resonate through the centuries and enrich the sense of revelation. The resonance is reflected metaphorically in movement as Cowan follows along the "road to salvation" (p. 55), literally and literarily crossing the desert in Anthony's footsteps.

If biblical texts (and the diaries of former pilgrims) form a natural inspiration for religious footstep travel in the region, the texts of Western explorers provide the opportunity for a secular counterpart. The Arabian desert, with its topographical features of exposure and austerity, stripped back to geological essentials, provides a natural site of experiment wherein human endurance is tested under extreme conditions. As each desert explorer charts the limits of not just his (and occasionally her) endeavour but that of human endurance itself, it is inevitable that they should set their account of that enterprise within the context of past achievers. This habitual referencing in the search for superlatives – to be the longest-suffering (like Doughty), to be the most enduring (like Lawrence), to be the first (like Bertram Thomas), or, best of all, to be the last (like Thesiger) so that no desert traveller thereafter can upstage the achievement – leads to one of the defining characteristics of Arabian desert literature as a whole: namely its keenly competitive nature. While each eminent desert explorer adopts a gloss of modesty, this technique is usually unsuccessful in disguising the competitive edge. In the foreword, for example, to *Arabia Felix* (Bertram Thomas's largely forgotten *opus magnus* written after his momentous but equally largely forgotten

36   *In literary footsteps*

journey by camel across the Empty Quarter) T. E. Lawrence writes, "Thomas shocked me when he asked me for a foreword to his great journey-book ... because he had recourse to me".[26] Not only is "great journey-book" a somewhat belittling term that contrasts with more usual references to "exploration account", but there could also be little shock value in Thomas's "recourse to me", as Lawrence is quick to position himself within a long lineage of great Arabian travellers:

> You see, in my day there were real Arabian veterans. Upon each return from the East I would repair to Doughty, a looming giant, white with eighty years, headed and bearded like some renaissance Isaiah. Doughty seemed a past world, in himself: and after him I would visit Wilfrid Blunt.
>
> (p. xv)

Lawrence goes on to write of Gertrude Bell, who "by twenty years of patient study, had won some reputation, too". His choice of the words "some" and "too", suggestive of limitation and afterthought, respectively, helps diminish Lawrence's female rival, despite her legacy, at least in terms of British imperial administration, being perhaps the greater.[27] Lawrence makes the point that in the past "the seeing [of] Arabia was an end in itself. [Earlier explorers] just wrote a wander-book and the great peninsula made their prose significant". He contrasts this with his own day where travellers "must frame excuses for travelling. One will fix latitudes, the silly things, another collect plants or insects" (p. xvi). Lawrence deliberately elevates his own journey by placing himself in the company of the literary elite of desert literature and diminishes Bertram Thomas whose achievement in being the first European to cross the largest sand desert in the world is overlooked in favour of a possible jibe at Thomas's keen botanical and entomological interests.[28] Thomas may not have read it this way, but the competitiveness of desert endeavour at this time is evidenced by the fact that Thomas's "plans were conceived of in darkness" to avoid them being thwarted by the authorities, or worse eclipsed by his contemporary rival, Harry St. John Philby. In a telegraph dated 7 March 1931, Philby wrote on hearing the news of Thomas's success, "Heartiest congrats", two words that according to modern-day explorer, Mark Evans, who crossed the same desert in Thomas's footsteps, "must have been painful to write"; Evans goes on to note the "bitter disappointment" felt by Philby, who for years had been "hatching his own plans" to cross the Empty Quarter.[29]

"Bitter disappointment" is a useful term when considering any travel writing to the region as each explorer recognises his own deficiency in relation to the journeys of these illustrious forebears, or the lands they cross and the people they meet fail to measure up to expectation. For modern writers, this sense of belatedness is exaggerated because their

In literary footsteps   37

journeys are conducted post-Thesiger. In the introduction to *Arabian Sands*, Thesiger writes a eulogy for what he perceives as a dying way of life, and in so doing, he literarily inked a "full stop" on desert travel:

> I went to Southern Arabia only just in time. Others will go there to study geology and archaeology, the birds and plants and animals, even to study the Arabs themselves, but they will move about in cars and will keep in touch with the outside world by wireless. They will bring back results far more interesting than mine, but they will never know the spirit of the land nor the greatness of the Arabs. If anyone goes there now looking for the life I led they will not find it.[30]

Given the competitive nature of the genre, these statements act as something of a textual tease; indeed, an overwhelming sense of belatedness is visited upon all future travelogues by those words: "If anyone goes there now looking for the life I led they will not find it". This is a cruel legacy to leave to future travellers, but it is also an inspired insurance policy that locks the value of the original project in a period of time that no one left alive can vouch for. Thesiger's journeys, captured in *The Life of My Choice* and *My Life and Travels: An Anthology*, therefore mark a watershed in British exploration, as noted by many distinguished reviewers. Richard Holmes, for example, writes that Thesiger "belongs to an endangered species; he is one of the last, great gentlemen explorer-adventurers of our time" – a time before sponsorship and the needs of television and social media impinge upon the journey.[31]

Modern Arabian desert travellers have attempted to rise to Thesiger's challenge through deploying different strategies, one of which is to circumvent the issue of comparative merit through humour and self-irony. Jan Morris, in *Sultan in Oman* (1957), for example, appears to plant her journey (carried out in her former male identity) alongside "the greater explorations of the Burtons, the Doughtys, the Philbys and the Thesigers", but the pluralisation of these figures allows an element of bathos in the comparison that invites the reader not to take Morris, nor her final estimation of the value of the journey, too seriously: "[It opened] a corner of Arabia to the scrutiny of the world, it set a travellers' precedent, and it had its effect upon the course of Arabian history".[32] These claims would have been difficult to substantiate in terms of Sultan Taimur's accomplishment in initiating the journey: for Morris, a lowly expatriate reporter in his retinue, they are deliberately hyperbolic. Other modern writers take an opposite approach: by not just conceding to the fame of "the Burtons, the Doughtys, the Philbys and the Thesigers" but by prostrating in front of former achievements, the endeavours of some modern acolytes, as we shall see, are usefully benchmarked.

The competitive nature of the relationship between original explorer and those who follow thereafter informs not just the choice of hero

38   *In literary footsteps*

selected for emulation but also sets up a dynamic in the modern journey that belongs to the "cult of nostalgia".[33] Contained within the vague sense of longing for past heroism is a wistfulness regarding the hero figure himself (there is yet to be a footstep account focusing on a female desert explorer). As social theorists such as John MacInnes have identified, masculinity has been brought to crisis by modernity, and as such, it is unsurprising to find some male travellers looking back to a time when former characteristics such as "heroism, independence, courage, strength, rationality, will, backbone, virility" were manly virtues rather than potential vices.[34] By casting themselves in heroic roles, these modern travellers are in some senses cloaked in masculine robes or are "remasculated" at least for the short period of the journey. Within that notion, each of the four footstep travellers discussed in this chapter takes up their own competitive positions – to be the most faithful to the original (Charles Blackmore), to be the most honest in estimation of the outcome (Bruce Kirkby), to be the strongest leader (Adrian Hayes), and to be the one with the most enduring legacy (Mark Evans). By looking at each of their narratives in turn, the discussion adds to Leavensworth's category of second journeys by identifying a distinct subgenre of footstep texts within Arabian desert travel. Further, it attempts to go beyond their categorisation as itinerary-following re-enacters of the past, by treating their texts not as a homogeneous subset but as one that develops and matures over the course of the 30 years in which the four texts are written.

Learning from the past – Blackmore in the footsteps of Lawrence

In a book the title of which explicitly references the footstep nature of his journey, Charles Blackmore weaves a reverence for a hero of the past into the fabric of the current adventure as part of the texture of enrichment invested in the journey:

> My thoughts are of the 700 miles we have ridden in the steps of Lawrence of Arabia, and the reward of an adventure shared with the Bedouin, the profits of their company, the sharing of a simple and traditional life. These are the investments of memory for the future.[35]

Using words such as "reward", "profit" and "investment" in his estimation of the 700 miles he has made in tracing Lawrence's footsteps, the past for Blackmore is not just enveloped in the present through thought; the present is also combined with the future through anticipation. The encounter with the Bedu, and the value placed on their "simple and traditional life" weighed against unspoken comparisons of "life back home", is represented as integral to the footstep experience. This is not a journey, then, that is merely imitative of the past, in the tracing of former itineraries; it is one in which the present-day experience is allowed to resonate in

In literary footsteps 39

the future and provide sustenance after the return home. As such, it makes an interesting case study of the resulting text.

Blackmore's camel-back journey (in February 1985) involved leading a team of four soldiers in the company of their Bedu guides across the deserts of modern-day Jordan in T. E. Lawrence's footsteps. The resulting travelogue is not just a good example of a desert journey that is both inspired and informed by an original text, it also represents, in all probability, the first of the footstep subgenre in modern Arabian desert travel literature.[36] Throughout Blackmore's account, Lawrence's text intrudes upon his own, and Blackmore reminds the team of the purpose of their footstep journey in almost nightly readings of *Seven Pillars*. Preparatory and contextual readings, according to James Buzard, not only "help to establish future travellers' expectations" but also help to test and strengthen remembered expectations and experiences "recharging the reader's sense of having accomplished something meaningful by travelling".[37] In this sense, Blackmore's close reading of Lawrence's *Seven Pillars* is part of a long heritage of what Buzard has described as a "complementary connection between travelling and reading". The relationship between travelling and reading helps to establish an Arabian desert context for Blackmore's travels that taps into an entire literary tradition of expedition in the region; in so doing, it lends authority to Blackmore's travels in a way that would have been hard to achieve in a random and anachronistic journey by camel across late twentieth-century Jordan.

If reference to *Seven Pillars* adds literary authority to the footstep journey, the choice of Lawrence, as soldier and ascetic, capitalises on the hardships involved. Beginning and ending in Wadi Rum, the place most closely associated today with Lawrence, Blackmore's journey is conducted commemoratively (as is often the case with footstep journeys, whether as a marketing hook or as valid review associated with centenary, or other significant dates),[38] to mark the fiftieth anniversary of the *death* of Lawrence; as such, it resonates as much with the legend of Lawrence as with his "real-life" endeavours.[39] The Blackmore team members are encouraged by thoughts of their hero and find inspiration during the hardships of their own journey in frequent references to Lawrence's military exploits which give them a "new sense of purpose" (p. 59). These exploits famously included attacks on the Hijaz Railway; for Blackmore, reaching the location of an abandoned railway carriage supposedly targeted by Lawrence became the mission of their footstep journey. When they failed to find it, Blackmore turns to Lawrence's book to escape the disappointment:

> I study closely the picture of him in native dress, *thinking myself into him*, and wondering at the exact nature of the man: the complicated intellect, the charisma which attracted people, the romantic and the visionary, the chivalrous knight in the desert, and the extraordinary

40   *In literary footsteps*

vulnerability of the post-war Lawrence, the subsequent architect of his own enigma and the pursuing legend which inwardly destroyed him.

(p. 58, emphasis added)

The power of the legend and the magnetism of the charismatic figure at the heart of his own journey feature almost as an inverse haunting as Blackmore "thinks himself into" Lawrence, trying to inhabit "the exact nature of the man". In fact, a sense of haunting pervades his account. The first journey, its narrator, and the encoded past represented in the form of the original text of *Seven Pillars of Wisdom* (a copy of which is treated with talismanic reverence during the footstep journey) manifest in quotation, and there is a séance-like quality, furthermore, to the regular in-situ readings of the treasured volume. These readings around the campfire at night are used to conjure up benign encouragements from the past for the edification of the present company. When one of the party intuits Lawrence's ghost at Azraq Fort, in the room once occupied by Lawrence, the haunting is complete. Blackmore writes after that incident, "Our feelings and thoughts about Lawrence grow day by day" (p. 101), and if there is a sense of intimate engagement of one soldier with another in Blackmore's account, there is an equal sense of intimacy between Blackmore as reader and Lawrence as writer. The desert "harshness and, above all, the life we are sharing with the Bedu have enriched our understanding", writes Blackmore of his rereading of *Seven Pillars of Wisdom*, "and given colour, sight and sound to the faded black and white picture" of Arab life described therein (p. 101). Blackmore's enterprise, therefore, can be read less as passive re-enactment and more as active reinvigoration of the past, blowing breath – "colours, sight and sound" – into the act of imagining the resurrected hero.

The depth of connection sought by reader with writer is illustrated notably in Blackmore's account when he encounters the Bedu who give him the "unexpected opportunity to retrace the Lawrence legend" (p. 60), not through meeting anyone who physically met Lawrence but through a hoped-for meeting with the son of Auda, with whom Lawrence rode into battle.[40] The excitement generated by even such a tenuous link is interesting because it shows the extent to which Blackmore's journey is about more than the desire, to use Sara Wheeler's term, to "pay homage" to a fellow traveller: it is about identifying a history of the heroic endeavour itself.[41] In writing about Captain Scott (albeit in a polar desert context), Beau Riffenburgh delineates the characteristics of heroic endeavour that can usefully be applied to Lawrence.[42] There is the provocation for adventure supplied by a military subject plucked from obscurity (Lawrence is keen to emphasise his non-commissioned status, and in 1927, changed his name by Deed Poll to Shaw); there is the wilderness threshold (in Lawrence's case the Arabian desert) and the necessity of being a leader (a status repeatedly claimed in Lawrence's relationship with the Arabs);[43] there are the trials evidenced through years of often unsuccessful planning (Lawrence suspects he was not a natural choice for the Arab Campaign when the authorities were casting about for someone to represent British interests),[44] and there are challenges of adjustment on arrival (in Lawrence's case, he found it difficult to acclimatise).[45] Other defining features of the Riffenburgh hero identifiable in Lawrence include close-knit brotherhood, extreme journeying, doomed endeavour, inspiration sent home in the form of letters and travelogue, and the role played by the media in the creation of the Lawrence of Arabia myth. Blackmore's account casts his own team's enterprise in similar if coincidentally heroic terms. The team comprises obscure military figures in the British army; they travel across desert wilderness, the harshness of which becomes a defining part of their journey; they have many trials in launching their expedition, including the financial expectations of the Bedu, which remain unresolved at the start of the journey.[46] A sense of brotherhood extends between the members of the team and their guides, and the "icons of myth", garnered from Blackmore's expedition, are captured in the press in a post-journey debate regarding the expedition's credibility.[47] Only doomed endeavour is lacking from a tale of modern-day heroism – a factor that has not hindered the book's reception, at least according to the dust jacket, as a modern "classic travel book". The footstep construction, then, has allowed Blackmore to transpose the supposed heroism of the original into the subtext of his own journey, making more of the present endeavour than may have been possible without the Lawrence motif.

Blackmore's mission is underpinned by a desire to recapture not just the spirit of hero Lawrence but also something of the heroic context in which Lawrence operated. That context has a particular lineage in Arabian desert literature that can be observed in the retrospective gaze upon ruins of empire. Contemplation on the sites of former grand civilisations, such as those at Petra, Medain Salah, Yarub Dam, or Abu Simbel, and the way in which they evoked thoughts of human frailty ("Look on my works, ye mighty, and despair!") is a familiar trope of early desert writing, closely connected with the aesthetic of the Burkean sublime.[48] Early Romantic accounts deliberately dwell on ruins in set piece reflections on former empires to the extent that, as Romantic-era traveller John Galt observed, travellers began to "attach more value to the past than it deserves, and to regard the present with far less esteem than it merits".[49] The enjoyment of exquisite emotions occasioned by rambling around old ruins lay, as Jonathan Wordsworth identified, in contemplations of immortality and the paradoxical way in which art "defies the erosion of time".[50] The emphasis, however, is generally on the *fall* of empire and the way the present compares unfavourably with the greatness of the past. As John Smith notes in 1804, for example, "Greece, Egypt, Syria, Anatolia, Arabia, recall a thousand pleasing recollections, which can no longer be associated with

42   *In literary footsteps*

them in their present state of barbarism, slavery and degradation"; these kinds of obsessive comparisons continue to characterise Arabian desert literature throughout the nineteenth and early twentieth century.[51]

It is within this context that Blackmore and his team trudge across the deserts of Wadi Rum in today's Jordan, looking for old carriages and sons of Auda, not so much in a search for Lawrence but in a search, unconsciously or otherwise, for the ruins of empire – an empire in which Blackmore defines Lawrence as "the chivalrous knight in the desert" (p. 58), with all that implies of his contrast with the Bedouin other. Previous travellers, from Clarke to Doughty, wrote their travelogues from the perspective of imperial confidence with Britain at the height of her influence abroad. Wilfrid Scawen and Lady Anne Blunt, Freya Stark, St John Philby, and Bertram Thomas, were all part of the so-called imperial project in Arabia. Lawrence was not an explorer sponsored by the Royal Geographical Society – he was a soldier and a diplomat whose mission it was to nurture Arab allegiance in the fight against the old Ottoman Empire. His endeavours helped pave the way for the consolidation of British interests in the Sykes-Picot Agreement of 1918 which, with the establishment of Israel, signalled the beginning of the end, in many respects, of Britain's imperial influence in the region and the onset of many decades of unrest.[52] When Robin Maugham, a soldier of the Second World War, comes to write *Nomad* (1947) in which Lawrence and *Seven Pillars* are frequently referenced, the note of nostalgia for an empire slipping away is already present: "I had been thrilled by the *Seven Pillars*. But the peoples and events seemed of another world, heroic and refined, which had few points of contact with the bit of Levant we had known". Maugham goes on to write that "Lawrence seemed too god-like, too remote from those few things of the East an ordinary soldier could see, too unattainable".[53] Lawrence and his legend, for Maugham, have become wrapped in the nostalgia for a supposed golden age before the Suez crisis signalled the first cracks in the empire.[54]

For Charles Blackmore, riding a camel in Lawrence's footsteps with his team of fellow army officers, it is inevitable then that he should be tracing not just a biography of Lawrence the desert explorer, not just the history of a desert military campaign, but the imperial heritage of the nation to which they belong. Something of the arrogance of the imperial heritage is nuanced in Blackmore's conflicting interactions with the Bedu: he describes them as lazy (p. 36), yet is surprised and impressed by their grasp of history (p. 49); he states they look "noble" (p. 19), yet he doubts their motives and insists on his own compass bearings (p. 72); citing the virtues of "English mental strength, endurance and adaptability to change situations", he reflects that it is these qualities that made Lawrence "so respected" by the Bedu (p. 36). But if Blackmore's account amounted to a simple recycling of discredited imperial tropes, it would be easy to dismiss it as a nostalgic throwback to old colonial values that have been "wholeheartedly rejected".[55] Blackmore's account, however, is as full of fracture and uncertainty as the British imperial project in Arabia, post-Suez, that it mirrors, and one fault line occurs within the very choice of Lawrence as the inspiration of Blackmore's own journey.

The problem for footstep travellers when they tie their search for national glories to literary heroes is that they are vulnerable to the vicissitudes of those figures. "Lawrence had been here on this exact spot", Blackmore writes at Aba El Lassan, the site of an important battle against the Turks that Lawrence was involved in, "yet the bare rock carries no record, no epitaph and only those in search of the past would be aware of it". He adds wryly that with no evidence, "it may not have happened at all" (p. 147). A niggling doubt creeps into the text but rather than come to the obvious conclusion that the battle was a fabrication on Lawrence's part, Blackmore rationalises the doubts away: "[W]ho am I to sit there in 1985 casting opinion on an incident in 1917 … in any case my recollections of our journey in one year will be distorted by time" (p. 148). While Blackmore was willing to accept the distortions of time, his travelling companion, Jamie Bowden, was less sympathetic. Commenting on their return on an event in Tafila where Lawrence was awarded a Distinguished Service Order for his part in a battle, Bowden stated, "Having seen the terrain, and having lived and ridden in it just as he would have done, I am very dubious about some of Lawrence's claims. Some of his exploits were just impossible". Addressing the resulting furore surrounding this revelation, Bowden felt obliged to write an open letter to *The Times* that verges on apology, stating that it was not the team's intention to spoil the Lawrence legacy by "quibbles over historical accuracy", nor by "totally defaming a British hero".[56] Some modern historians, such as Scott Anderson, contend that Lawrence was just "mischievous" with the facts; others find a life's work in trying to disaggregate fact from fiction, using the contradictions of the Lawrence myth to spur "descents into minutiae" and leading to "arcane squabbles between those seeking to tarnish his reputation and those seeking to defend it".[57] It may not matter to Anderson whether Lawrence "truly made a particular desert crossing in forty-nine hours, as he claimed, or [it] might … have taken a day longer", but as the Bowden incident shows, doubts about credibility appear to hurt more than Lawrence's posthumous reputation: at some level, they touch on the uncomfortable possibility that the imperial presence in Arabia had been less significant too and similarly subject to myth-making through exaggeration and embellishment.

Accuracy is a significant theme in footstep narratives, although there is of course no accepted yardstick by which it can be measured or ascertained. Most footstep journeys are at pains to point out which aspects of the first journey can be substantiated through observation and which cannot, but this seldom results in discrediting the original because, at some level, to do so would similarly undermine the value of the second journey.

44 *In literary footsteps*

When confronted about the truth of his own adventures, Lawrence states in a letter sometime after the writing of *Seven Pillars* (the crucial first draft of which he allegedly lost on a train to Reading raising questions about the likely inaccuracies of the second draft, given the difficulty of re-remembering that level of detail) that "history isn't made up of the truth anyhow, so why worry".[58] In recognising "that history was malleable, that truth was what people were willing to believe",[59] Anderson argues that Lawrence was ahead of his time, and indeed, the literary traditions of life-writing studies and biographical studies are full of examples of the fictionalisation of the past.[60] When asked about the credibility of Lawrence nearly 30 years after the expedition, however, Bowden makes the important point that "it is important to be honest about [describing] what you see, as false accounts can have a negative impact on those that are being described" – a subject covered through a quarter-century of postcolonial criticism.[61] Unravelling fact from fiction, however, is complicated because at some level, heritage replaces history, and heritage is tied up with a communal sense of collective or national self-esteem.[62] Footstep travellers help create that heritage by selecting those travellers whose experience they believe is worth recreating and capturing for a new generation. Any criticism of the validity of the first journey undermines the authority of the second journey and to some extent the selection process upon which heritage accrues. Lawrence in particular, as a national treasure, belongs to something bigger than history: "even today", writes Oliver Smith in a relatively recent article, "the legend of a romantic figure – dressed in Arab robes, sweeping across hostile landscapes and capturing holy cities – has endured, thanks to David Lean's epic film, *Lawrence of Arabia*".[63] When Blackmore eventually comes across the Hijaz Railway, one of his party hums the theme tune, adding another accretion to the layers of the legend.

If footstep accounts were limited to the revival of a romanticised past, they would probably be of equally limited interest. As we have seen, however, the frisson of encounter is laced with doubt – about authenticity and credibility, about the value of the modern project in comparison with the original – and this doubt casts a productive pall over our reading of both the original and the second journey and the context in which the texts of both interact. Towards the end of his account, Blackmore reflects that it is only on encountering the desert and the Bedu that he has been able to gain an understanding of Lawrence's self-glorification and alternating modesty, of his masochism and "intellectual path of self-discovery" (p. 101). In this recognition is the understanding of a shared quest and ultimately *Seven Pillars* functions more usefully for the footstep travellers as a pretext for their own journey of discovery, rather than as a satisfactory *pre*text. For the reader, this layering of one history within another is potentially endlessly revived the further the reader is distanced from either journey by time, adding a third dimension to the narrative and deepening its interest.

In literary footsteps 45

An inevitable legacy of "re-creational" history that threatens the value of a footstep project is the sense of travelling in the region too late, and indeed, belatedness appears intrinsic to the form. The article in *The Times* that appeared on Blackmore's return describes the team arriving at Heathrow Airport "still attired in headdress and *galabeyas*, louse-ridden and unwashed for a month, having eked out sparse water supplies and chewed desert plants for salt".[64] In a first journey, this would have been the stuff of mythmaking, but in a second journey, it appears somewhat staged. Indeed, Blackmore's journey marks a watershed in desert travel. Subsequent expeditioners are less able to fashion a heroic persona for themselves, exhibiting instead what Leavenworth has described as "feelings of disorientation, anxiety and loneliness".[65] As later travellers begin to question the precepts of the original journey, inevitably the nascent anxieties begin to extend to their own journey, and this, as discussed in the following section, can lead to productive, post-imperial doubts.

Writing about the present – Kirkby and Hayes in the footsteps of Thesiger

When modern-day adventurers Michael Swan and Roger Mear retraced Scott's footsteps across Antarctica, they were partly drawn by the notion of unfinished business. Scott famously never accomplished his aim, and the sense in which Swan and Mear attempt to close the circle on that endeavour on his behalf has been analysed by a number of critics, including Jennifer Laing and Warwick Frost.[66] Claiming to be motivated by the "simple bravery of men against the elements", their real reasons for following Scott appear rather more complex.[67] In an age when "those who seek adventure can no longer set out under the banner of science", they were drawn to an earlier era when the value of exploration enjoyed unquestioned legitimacy.[68] Today's sophisticated navigational aids, easy access to wilderness through modern transportation, a school of ecology that promotes wilderness preservation as opposed to conservation, the branching of science into specialisms that generally require patient observation focused on a single location, a modern obsession with health and safety (and rescue at the cost of other people's lives) – all these technological, environmental, and sociological developments have circumscribed the modern journey in remote landscapes and cast doubt on its value and purpose.[69] By pegging an adventure to celebrated exploration, however, modern travellers endeavour to legitimise their modern journeys with borrowed authenticity.

It is possible to detect a shift in motive from Blackmore and his team (and for that matter, Mear and Swan) who exhibit a genuine and deep-rooted interest in the hero figure of their journey, and the motives of their footstep successors a generation later. While Blackmore, as we have seen, couches his experience in financial metaphor ("reward", "profit", and

46   In literary footsteps

"investment"), the earning of an income through either the journey or publication of the resulting travelogue does not appear to be a significant motivating factor in the journey. In contrast, both Bruce Kirkby, author of *Sand Dance* (2000), and Adrian Hayes, an ex-officer of the British Army who describes his journey in *Footsteps of Thesiger* (2012), both undertake their journeys as part of a career plan. While both ostensibly travel in homage to Wilfred Thesiger,[70] they are ultimately more interested in the quest for adventure itself and indeed the potential for financial gain that the journeys present. Hayes, for example, admits to being "addicted to a life of adventure, exploration and travel" and treats the destination as something of an afterthought.[71] Kirkby similarly measures up the desert wilderness as a commodity with a commercial value, expressed as literary output: "[W]e all liked the fact that deserts were not a popular destination in the world of adventuring … [but] remained foreign landscapes".[72] His choice of the word "foreign" sets up the psychological context in which his team will approach the desert as a contrast to the tamed landscapes of home and an otherwise random arena for human challenge. A sense of cashing in on the Thesiger legend is apparent throughout the resulting book, as Kirkby relies on the connection to foreground a "mythical age of exploration and romantic imperialism" (p. 36). The allusion by a Canadian to "romantic imperialism" is problematic, as Oman (the part of Arabia mostly crossed by Kirkby) had "in a past era" its own significant empire that stretched across the Gulf and along the shores of East Africa with only brief periods under Portuguese rule and latterly British protection.[73] The use of the term suggests a lack of interest in the historical specificity of the desert region Kirkby travels through and reveals a more commercially driven desire to reference, in B. J. Moore-Gilbert's words, "the myth of the gorgeous East".[74] Indeed Kirkby and his friends appear to know little about either "Arabia's Great Southern Desert" (the subtitle of his book) or Thesiger (despite meeting him for what amounts to a blessing before their journey begins). This site-specific ignorance is a fact that Kirkby acknowledges, or even celebrates, as he declares that he and his friends, the two Clarke brothers, are "grossly underqualified for the expedition" (p. 25); this strategic self-deprecation may be intended to deflate any exaggerated expectations on behalf of the reader that may lead to unfavourable comparisons with Thesiger, but it is also suggestive of a complacent lack of preparedness.

Adrian Hayes, in contrast, admits to researching Thesiger "much like actors or actresses who read up on their characters when representing real-life people in films" (p. 26); the preparation forms part of his identity as a "de facto professional adventurer", casting about the Middle East for the next paid assignment: "[L]iving in the region with a good knowledge of the area … it seemed a no-brainer to not consider something on my doorstep" (p. 31). Thesiger's travels, however, provide for Hayes no more than an excuse for the next professional exploit; the "concept"

In literary footsteps 47

involves "myself and one or two locals only, rather than ... fellow westerners" and without the support of GPS, guides, or mechanised transport and relying only on local knowledge, "just as Thesiger had experienced". The phrasing risks turning the relationship with Thesiger into a gimmick and objectifying the "one or two locals only". Despite stating that he wanted to avoid succumbing to the "prevalent game of firsts" (p. 11), Kirkby is similarly explicit in needing his journey to be noteworthy in order to capture sponsorship, identifying that from this perspective, living with the Bedu is "crucial" (p. 12). For Hayes and Kirkby, the appropriation of the Arabian desert and its inhabitants as "glibly homogenised" Orientalist tropes employed to lend credibility to their journeys does not, at least at the planning stage, appear to concern either traveller.[75]

As adventure texts, both Kirkby's account and Hayes's account function predictably enough. Both outline the challenges of trying to launch the journeys, with the obligatory complaint about the lack of interest and help by the authorities, the perfidiousness of the camel owners, the arduousness of the journey once underway, and the picaresque anecdotes about "the locals" encountered on route. These elements were present in Blackmore's account of his journey too, but now a new sense of anxiety about the purpose and merit of the endeavour can be detected. In 1985, while probing aspects of authenticity surrounding the original journey, Blackmore does not question the value of his own. A decade and a half later, in 1999, this question is repeatedly presenting itself. Kirkby, for example, writes of the lack of pride in their endeavour: "[D]espite the apparent success of the expedition ... I struggled with what our expedition had meant". Kirkby recognises that he and his team had been so "blinded by expectations" that they failed to "embrace the experience [they] actually found" (p. 218). In the expedition account, there is a poignant photograph of Kirkby and team standing in front of Abu Dhabi's skyline before meeting with Sheikh Zayed bin Sultan Al-Nahyan, president of United Arab Emirates. The travellers are mounted on camel back – conspicuously so, given this is the country's wealthy, sophisticated capital. It was here that the travellers found the presumed old world of Bedu hospitality and charismatic sheikhs that they had sought in vain in the desert, but as this experience ran counter to their expectations of either Arabian desert or Gulf city, they failed to see it. Not only has reading back through Thesiger's text proved an illusory way of capturing the past, then, but the endeavour itself has obscured the present, limiting the value of the modern journey. The "past site", in other words, has blinded the "present sight".[76]

Involved in the focus on the past is generally an expression of regret or disappointment that the best is over. If this "belatedness" was given nascent expression in Blackmore's text, it dominates Kirkby's account and indeed is a highly prevalent feature of Oriental travel texts in general. These often display, as Ali Behdad notes, an "obsessive urge to discover an 'authentic' Other".[77] In today's desert footstep accounts it suggests

48   *In literary footsteps*

retreat as if the authentic other resides in the past rather than, as Tim Youngs observes, in today's "less interesting period with [its] fewer and smaller accomplishments".[78] In a desert context, this is very often expressed inversely, and most desert footstep travellers lament at some point in their narrative that the Arabian Peninsula (with its roads, trucks, pylons, oil derricks, and urban sprawl) is not the "Orient" of received tropes. Before Kirkby even stepped foot in Arabia, he was launched on his way by Thesiger's own mournful disappointment: "As I packed my brief-case, [Thesiger] shook his head. 'You will be in Riyadh tomorrow ... the world has changed and it is dreadfully sad'" (p. 43). When Kirkby and his team finally reach Oman, they try to stick faithfully to the path that Thesiger took in the hope that it will hint at the lost world he described, but there is no way back, neither literally nor metaphorically, and it is significant that Kirkby is eventually talked out of the endeavour of his-torical re-enactment altogether. As his party approaches Liwa (in mod-ern-day United Arab Emirates), towards the more physically challenging end of the journey, he is persuaded by the Bedu guides, who do not share the commemorative value of his project, to take a shortcut. This is a defining moment for Kirkby who writes, "[O]ur vision had remained elu-sive. I realised it may have disappeared forever, passed to a bygone era", and he concedes that "perhaps the problem lay in our expectations" (p. 179). This is particularly the case in the team's expectations of the lives of the Bedu. To be fair, Kirkby notes the modernisation of desert dwelling as a positive development, nonetheless he calibrates those advancements as "not ... without a cost", and the cost is calculated in specifically Western terms as the "spread of a generic world culture, a shocking loss of diver-sity, a growing sameness" (p. 219). The "shocking loss of diversity" bor-ders on panic and makes it clear that the Arabian desert experience is more than just an ethnographic exercise; in such an exercise, the Bedu encounters of Kirkby's adventure could have, and perhaps should have, been rendered interesting by virtue of the ways in which they conflicted with received preconceptions (of the traditional characteristics of endur-ance, patience, hardiness), but this opportunity to reflect on specific dif-ference is lost in the emphasis on an elusive, generalised "bygone era".

Interestingly, the point at which Kirkby acknowledges that the "prob-lem" does not lie in a less traditional Bedu but in the eye that perceives them, is also the point at which the author becomes more interesting to the reader. The self-reflection opens up another channel of enquiry to the reader, namely that of the character of the writer, and this helps to remove Kirkby from the past of Thesiger and lifts him into the present, thereby making the account more modern.

For Kirkby, and indeed most desert travel writers, the desert mostly represents a zone of private challenge, an otherness to the tamed experi-ence of home; the resulting narrative holds the travelling individual to account, demonstrating how well he or she measured up in the quest. Any erosion in the severity of the challenge impacts on the measurement of the journey's worth and the author's achievement within it. Blackmore, Kirkby, and Hayes all rue the kind hospitality lavished on them during their journeys because, as Blackmore laments, "we treasure our insular, isolated life in the desert. Frequent contacts threaten to erode it to the point where James [one of the team] even objects if an old vehicle track is seen in the sand". There is no obligation upon these writers to acknowledge their disappointment in the intrusion of modern life and its comforts in their desert journeys, but they choose to draw attention to it. Charles Blackmore laments the Mars bar that James produces from a shop two-thirds of the way through their journey and writes, "[W]hat of the Toyota pick-ups? ... Should I turn a blind eye to them in order to maintain ... impressions of a desert unchanged by encroaching technology?"[79] Bruce Kirkby writes with similar anxiety of various people turning up uninvited in four-wheel drive vehicles to cook them an ad hoc supper and dispense soft drinks, stating that "the trucks we found following us at every turn diminished the sense of adventure that we had come seeking".[80] Adrian Hayes resents the presence of the media and asks the news crews to leave them alone, writing, "[D]espite appreciation for the media support, we were all becoming disillusioned at the intrusion and interference to the journey".[81] For footstep travellers, modern impingement on the journey is problematic on several levels. Firstly, it breaks in upon the sense of enactment, reminding the traveller that recapturing history is impossible; secondly, it spoils the illusion of adventure, inherent in the original journey, as extreme physical endeavour is tempered by the sense of help being near at hand; and thirdly, it challenges the notion of authentic experience, encapsulated in a journey that seeks to get off the beaten track. But the net result of all this lamentation about the intrusion of the present is that the reader is made to feel a new kind of authenticity being expressed – one in which only those who have been to the modern deserts of Arabia would know that Mars bars, fizzy drinks, and satellite media are as part of the reality of these destinations as they are "back home". This helps close the gap, then, not just between author and reader but also between the land of the travelled and the land left behind.

It may seem counterintuitive that second travellers use first journeys to create *authentic* experience, but, as Dean MacCannell suggests, this is closely connected with the ways in which modern travellers distinguish themselves from tourists. MacCannell identifies front regions that equate with "the production that is projected to tourists" and back regions which are accessed through interaction with native populations and through redundant forms of travel.[82] All these footstep travellers journey by camel, and they share a common surprise in the inability of the modern beast to cope with the extended journeys of a now mostly defunct nomadic lifestyle. Disappointment in the lethargy and lack of fitness of their camels exposes holes in the back region: "[T]o have done the

50   *In literary footsteps*

journey on a camel when I could have done it in a car", wrote Thesiger, "would have turned the venture into a stunt".[83] Thesiger rode on camels because there was no other way to get about. In contrast, Kirkby and company were deemed ridiculous by the Bedu for even attempting the journey on camel, and supply trucks kept turning up to their chagrin to ensure their safety and, perhaps as importantly, that of the camels. The journey thus becomes something of an extreme sport rather than a genuine wilderness expedition with the camel providing the means with which to "get off the beaten track". This is a common trope in modern travel literature and is suggestive of a need to reach, as James Buzard terms it, "the authentic 'cultures of place' – the genius loci ... lurking in secret precincts 'off the beaten track' where it could be discovered only by the sensitive 'traveller', not the vulgar tourist".[84] Thesiger lived and travelled with the Bedu with apparently little thought about authenticity because there was nothing to authenticate. In contrast, Kirkby and Hayes look to repeat the authentic Bedu experience because there is little that marks their endeavours from a desert adventure, except that their journeys involve more time, money, and effort than most tourist exploits.

One way in which Kirkby and Hayes attempt to distinguish their experiences as travellers rather than tourists is through the management of their expedition team. Earlier travellers, including Thomas and Thesiger, attempt no intervention in either the habits of their guides nor the specific direction of their journeys; they earn the respect of the Bedu precisely because of their willingness to undergo personal hardship in order to observe nomadic life and be counted, at least for the duration of the journey, as one of the tribe. In contrast, Kirkby and Hayes both assume, in something of a retrograde glance at an imperial past, that the interaction with Bedu works best through white Western male oversight of subservient local guides. In *Footsteps of Thesiger*, for example, Hayes imperiously cautions "the boys" (the Bedu guides), apparently in Arabic, about the hazards of fasting during the early part of the journey in case it impedes progress. For this, he rightly earns their rebuke: "Yes Adrian, we know, we not stupid. We be OK" (p. 93). The broken English is not "nation language", as defined by Edward Brathwaite, in which the language has been transformed productively by its users; this is bastardised language, selected to demonstrate cultural authority over the Bedu guides.[85] Whether accurately recalled or not, this piece of dialogue functions to reassert the author's dominance – at least over the text, if not over "his" team. If Hayes talked to the guides in Arabic, then why, it may be wondered, did he choose to report their answer in a substandard form of English. The translation helps to silence the Bedu and their challenge of his command. This signifies a much larger act of marginalisation, especially of people descended from a largely oral tradition, that Emma LaRocque argues (in relation to First Nations peoples of Canada) is institutionalised in English literature.[86] Ultimately, the passage reads as an

In literary footsteps 51

unresolved usurpation of authority from which Hayes, in the direction of his journey, never fully recovers. Kirkby is similarly given the illusion of leadership of his expedition by his Bedu guide, whereas in fact all the important decisions (about route, when to leave, and how far to go) are made on his behalf. Both Kirkby and Hayes describe various attempts to wrest control of their plans, but the reality of their journeys is of modern commercial enterprise: they finance their respective trips, and their guides take over the arrangements. As such, there is little to distinguish their expeditions from a tourist trek in Wadi Rum or a guided trip to Oman's Sharqiya Sands where the payment of money similarly gives the illusion of decision-making.[87]

But even if footstep travellers *are* engaged in glorified tourism, even if they find their own journeys unconvincingly authentic, this does not mean that the resulting accounts are without value. In a globalised context, where critics such as Jean Baudrillard and Marc Augé posit a world in which there is a crisis of meaning brought about by "more and more signs, but less and less meaning",[88] the reader can identify with the existential angst of Blackmore, for example, when he writes, "I am trying to find something in this desert ... only I am not sure what it is".[89] The search for "something in this desert" is calculated differently over time. For Thesiger, in *The Life of My Choice*, the inherent value of the desert journey is expressed primarily in terms of the individual human spirit:

> I was exhilarated by the sense of space, the silence, and the crisp cleanness of the sand. I felt in harmony with the past, travelling as men had travelled for untold generations across the deserts, dependent for their survival on the endurance of their camels and their own inherited skills.[90]

On reaching Abu Dhabi and being met by the late Sheikh Zayed, who questions why he took such a lengthy route to reach his destination, Thesiger reputedly replies, "I was not travelling to get here, Your Highness, I was just travelling".[91] Travel for its own sake is at the heart of footstep travel too. Destination and journey are bound up in the original itinerary.

While Leavenworth suggests that the second traveller "disappears from the text", appearing only as sighs of disappointment, I would contend that, on the contrary, nostalgia helps makes the footstep traveller more visible as they give expression to their feelings of belatedness.[92] This in turn highlights the moments in which, almost despite themselves, footstep travellers burst from the straightjacket of the past with interjections concerning the present. These crucial moments tend mostly to be in connection with the wilderness: Blackmore, for example, writes, "[W]e are silent, dwarfed by nature and, I feel, timeless amongst it all" (p. 32). Elsewhere, he reflects with similar awe on the virtues of his chief guide:

52   *In literary footsteps*

"He is a desert nomad … as I watch him it seems to me as though he has pushed everything I know far away" (p. 19). The desert and its inhabitants may not fully live up to expectations, and none of the footstep travellers are particularly triumphant on arrival at their destination, but like Thesiger, they come to celebrate that the journeying is all. As Hayes states in the epilogue to his travel account: "stripped of all luxury and material goods … one takes a very different perspective on the world", and he recognises during the stark desert journey the things that are "truly important in life … family, friends and health … relationships, communication and life" (p. 264). The appreciation of travelling for the sake of travelling, and the benefit of a renewed reappraisal of life's priorities finds resonance in the rhythm of crossing great tracts of either featureless plain or the incessant plodding through dunes. They may not enjoy the experience (Kirkby finds the desert "foreign" and cannot understand its reputed allure) but each of the footstep travellers find great personal reward in what Hayes describes as the "peace, tranquillity, serenity" of being alone with their thoughts (p. 159).

Thesiger famously wrote in the prologue to *Arabian Sands* that "no man can live this life and emerge unchanged", and the sense of this psychological metamorphosis finds an objective correlative in the wearing of Bedu clothing and the assuming of an Arabic name, which all the first and second travellers considered hitherto in this chapter willingly succumb to. As Kirkby writes,

> I thought about how I was Saleh now. The names Sheikh Salem had given us only three weeks earlier now seemed intrinsically tied to each of us, representing our existence here – a life so different from that we knew at home as to be almost irreconcilable.
>
> (p. 115)

The desert seems to offer a way for these travellers to let go of their modern realities and adopt alter egos; the monotony and hardship of the journey encourage internal reflection and heightens their sense of observation, both inwardly as well as outwardly. The desert journey remains, in other words, the ultimate ascetic experience where time is suspended and there is a paring back of the soul to necessities.[93] Blackmore reflects on how the desert satisfies his inner quest with two poignant rhetorical questions: "Why do I need to see this journey into the desert as an escape? Why am I incapable of facing up to the reality of my own time?" (p. 142). In its hardship, the journey legitimises escape from a worse predicament, namely, as James Duncan puts it, "the social and psychological pressures of modernity".[94] Far from being reduced to a postscript of the original journey, then, the second traveller, in sharing inner thoughts about the nature of the journey and the anxiety represented in a perceived lack of authority in the enterprise, is fully present and takes the reader along the

In literary footsteps 53

same journey of quest. Only the quest has changed: the goal is no longer epistemological in the way that former desert travellers recorded Bedouin customs and manners but is theoretical in the way it searches for clarity of purpose in an era when modernity threatens to fracture meaning, question identity, and contest notions of gender, and where globalisation makes travel itself the subject of critical dilemma. Out of this unsettled purpose, as the discussion next explores, new meaning is brought to the genre.

Opportunities for the future – Evans in the footsteps of Thomas

"The metal blade of the shovel", Mark Evans writes with mock gravity at the beginning of his journey's account, "hit what might have been a human bone, and I had an increasingly uneasy feeling that we shouldn't be doing this" (p. 9). In a refreshingly novel start to a footstep narrative, in which the author is to be found rooting around a graveyard in Bristol looking for the last resting place of Bertram Thomas, guided in his somewhat macabre endeavour by the proceedings of the local historical society, Evans simultaneously and perhaps unconsciously hits upon a seam of modern critical theory that considers the palimpsestic space and the "interplay between personal and communal narratives of identity and belonging".[95] The tombstone he eventually unearths appears out of the undergrowth almost as a parody of itself, "covered in lichens and moss," and divested of the lead that had once made the lettering legible. From its outset, then, this desert account appears to invite a different kind of reading of a second journey, one in which new inscriptions are being made, as we shall see, in the space of erasure brought about by time.

The interplay between personal and communal narratives is a good way to describe both Evans's journey and the text that follows. A former polar explorer, Evans is credited in Oman with making the desert accessible as an educational experience for young Arab students who have become dissociated from their desert roots, and his most recent journey, retracing the route of Bertram Thomas (the first, although little remembered, Western explorer to cross the Empty Quarter), stands out as a "first" in its own right for its inclusive nature.[96] Where other footstep travellers have emphasised their own heroic qualities, Evans's attention is on reviving an interest in heritage among the Omani companions that accompany him and among the extended Omani team whom he involves in all parts of the preparation, execution, and post-event evaluation of the journey. Evans's perspective is firmly on the present and the future, therefore, rather than on a nostalgic engagement with the past, and as such the footstep nature of the journey is reduced to form, rather than content – a way of giving shape and publicity to a modern endeavour that is more about education and outreach rather than personal glorification. The resulting accounts, which take several forms, including digital tweets

54 *In literary footsteps*

and public lectures, include the expedition narrative entitled *Crossing the Empty Quarter in the Footsteps of Bertram Thomas* (2016). Despite the somewhat unpromising title, this book takes the footstep genre into new territory. Where in earlier footstep tomes (such as that of Hayes) the sub-genre threatens to collapse under the weight of its own intertextuality, tedious in its "saturation of cultural stereotypes",[97] Evans's book manages to "Make It New" by deliberately unseating the author's own supremacy in the journey and highlighting instead the Arab and expatriate facilitators and companions who make the journey possible; in so doing, the book restores depth to a project that may appear to have only surface value.[98] By reviving, furthermore, the indigenous patterns of travel through the desert and focusing on the navigational and survival skills of Thomas's companions, he reminds the reader that Western white men were not the first and certainly not the only expeditioners (in the sense of journey as purpose) in this particular landscape.

Recognising that "this journey would be as much about people as about place" (p. 40), Evans's choice to follow Bertram Thomas is apposite because of all the desert explorers in Arabia, Thomas is the one who exhibits more interest in tribal rather than desert encounter; indeed, the landscape is largely ignored in his descriptions except in rare moments of wonderment that interrupt the catalogue of itemisation. Observational, erudite, anecdotal without being judgemental, and with a subdued sense of authorial voice, Thomas, at least according to Tiddrick, is "the least flamboyant of Arabian explorers".[99] There is nothing conveyed of the writer's excitement in approaching the challenge of his journey and even less of his eventual accomplishment. Instead, the account acts as a quasi-anthropological work on "scattered and semi-barbarous nomad societies", undertaken by an amateur scientist, albeit with an impressive knowledge of tribal dialects.[100] His approach to the Bedu is similar to his approach to the animals and plants of the desert, which he traps, measures, pickles, and labels – the Bedu are the subject of his scrutiny, not his empathy. He even travels with a pair of callipers to measure tribal heads – "it was no easy task to find willing subjects", he writes, "there is always in the minds of rude people the fear of magic or worse, while the religious among them hate to be pawed by infidel hands".[101] While clearly a man defined by the cultural limitations of his time, Thomas at least was actively involved with the Bedu (unlike many modern travellers whose interactions with the Bedu are perfunctory at best), and appreciative of their many skills in withstanding a hostile environment.

Mark Evans's desert journey is similarly delineated in terms of modern political realities: he does not cross a *terra nullius* – a "nobody's land" – he explicitly travels through the Dhofar region of southern Oman, the Eastern Province of Saudi Arabia, and the Khor Al-Adaid of southern Qatar. Furthermore, the journey is planned partially as a celebration of a modern political reality, coinciding with the 45th anniversary of Sultan

In literary footsteps 55

Qaboos Al-Said's reign – a reign widely credited with ushering in a renaissance of learning, enterprise, and development in Oman. Evans celebrates the modern realities, recognising that re-enactment is neither a feasible nor a desirable part of the footstep journey:

> [Y]ou can't replicate what Bertram Thomas did – the environment has changed. You can replicate the food, the camels, but you have to deal with the here and now – there's a huge border to cross that wasn't there before, for example.[102]

In *Crossing the Empty Quarter*, then, there is refreshingly no attempt to disguise the twenty-first-century attributes of the journey, creating a more useful archive for those reading the account in years to come.

At many levels, Evans's footstep journey deliberately steps beyond the present, and courts instead the legacy of the enterprise. Authenticity, Evans argues, is not that important, or at least only to a degree: "Twenty-five per cent is about learning lessons from the past, fifty per cent of the journey is about the present but twenty-five per cent of our journey is also about creating opportunities for the future".[103] He goes on to explain that His Excellency Sayyid Badr Bin Hamed Al-Busaidi, one of the journey's official Omani champions, endorsed the journey as an opportunity, through media outreach in schools, to use the Bertram Thomas journey as a way of reconnecting young Arab people with their heritage through education, hard work, and endeavour. In *Crossing the Empty Quarter*, Evans describes a life that has changed radically since Thomas's journey, and this is why the focus of this footstep account is not so much on two or three white expeditioners (Evans, his photographers, and fixers) as on camel handler Amur Al-Wahibi and Outward Bound colleague Mohamed Al-Zadjali, who are the "first Omanis for 85 years to cross the Empty Quarter" (p. 33). It is their journey that sends an inspirational message to Arab youth, and it is this story that is told in the local media in daily updates and on Twitter. Evans writes,

> It was important to me ... we harness the power of technology and social media ... to communicate values and create positive role models for young people in Oman, Saudi Arabia and Qatar, at the same time as reconnecting them to their culture and heritage.
>
> (p. 34)

As such, Evans taps into the memory streams not of his own culture, in which the desert functions as empty and hostile, but into that of the Omanis whom he travels with, noting that the wells such as Bir Faisal and Bir Hadi – just "dots on maps" (p. 48) to Evans – represented "life-saving locations" for the Bedu. He is reminded, thereby, that "a map of Oman will show ... main roads, but the real stories" together with

56   In literary footsteps

Bedouin history, are located where there are no roads (p. 39). This is the Arabian desert, then, being redrawn both for the Western reader and also for the young local Arab, following the journey on a mobile application. The aim to communicate and connect is achieved at some cost to Evans, who spends the time he would rather give to sitting around the campfire at night resting, blogging about his journey through the Thuraya IP satellite terminal. This piece of technology becomes a vital and acknowledged part of the journey's paraphernalia; it is not treated as hitherto in footstep accounts as a guilty secret, hidden away for emergency and a source of dilemma compromising the supposed authenticity of the journey; on the contrary, it is directly related to the journey's stated goals and as such facilitates its hoped-for legacy.

The focus on legacy redefines the role of the original traveller, Bertram Thomas, in Evans's journey. Thomas is neither extolled as a hero figure (such as Lawrence in Blackmore's journey) nor relegated to convenient pretext (as Thesiger in Hayes's journey); rather, Thomas becomes a role model, a lesson in humility, for the current team. Their own achievement is measured constantly with that of both Thomas and of Sheikh Saleh Bin Kalut Al-Rashidi Al-Kathiri, his guide. As with Blackmore's evocation of Lawrence, these figures haunt the modern journey, manifesting in talismanic objects such as the *khanjar* (ceremonial dagger) worn by Thomas's guide on the original journey; this object acquires totemic potency as it is worn by the guide's grandson who joins Evans for part of the modern journey.[104] If mostly benign, the presence of the original travellers is also partly spectral, threatening to foreground the journey's limitations through the belittlement of the current endeavour: "[W]ithout doubt", writes Evans, "we are truly humbled by what those remarkable people did, and a key aim of this journey is to celebrate what they achieved" (p. 137). It is fitting, however, that a narrative that begins, as we have seen, with the exhumation of Thomas's ghost at the graveyard where the explorer is buried, lays the ghost to rest again at the end of the journey, stepping beyond Thomas to embrace the significance of the present-day accomplishment:

> Whilst one of our aims was to put these two forgotten explorers and one historic journey back into the spotlight (by the time we returned to Muscat we had 5,000 followers on Facebook, and media coverage elsewhere reached out to an estimated 165 million people from than 170 nations), the most important aim of all was to reconnect local young people to their heritage.
>
> (p. 194)

Unlike Blackmore's conjuring up of the past, this passage shows that Evans manages to avoid Thomas casting a long shadow over the expedition by utilising strategies that focus on a territory, namely the present, that Thomas cannot cross.

In literary footsteps 57

The key to the passage above is that it is about not one but *two* forgotten explorers. Evans is determined to bring Thomas's fellow traveller out of the shadows, in the same way that he continually draws his own Omani companions into the narrative:

> Whilst Thomas was undoubtedly a forgotten explorer, Bin Kalut was even more so. No global lecture tours and medals for him, yet Thomas had depended on him totally for support, guidance and safe passage across the Empty Quarter. The teamwork and trust between Oman and United Kingdom was something we wanted to replicate on our journey.
>
> (p. 34)

By giving credit where due, Evans manages to indigenise both his own and Thomas's journey. In so doing, he finds a way not just of bridging the past, present, and future, but also in crossing the cultural divide in a journey that emphasises intercultural dialogue. If this claim seems rather far-fetched, it is worth noting that the sultan of Oman, the king of Saudi Arabia, the now King Charles III – who writes the book's foreword – and Sheikh Joann Al-Thani of Qatar are all cited in the book's acknowledgements for their personal endorsement of the journey. Even the briefest of scans through the photographs in Evans's book, furthermore, shows the extent to which tribal leaders, dressed in their ceremonial finery, found value in the journey, pouring out to greet the travellers and lavishing their hospitality upon them. At one such gathering, the elders spoke encouragingly of a journey that replicated their own nomadic range in the time before borders; they saw Evans's journey as a nostalgic one, not for the implied imperialism of insignificant head-measuring Westerners with their incomprehensible thirst for unforced journeys, but for the pan-Arabism lost in the political realities of nationhood arising out of twentieth-century circumstances.[105] In crossing physical borders, then, Evans's journey prompts a wistful recollection among the tribal elders of "a time when political borders in Arabia were much less sharply defined" (p. 168); the journey as such seems to exist in a state of suspended animation, caught between the realities of past and present and the vague possibilities of a utopian future. It is a fragile zone, however, and just one year after the journey's completion, a deterioration in relations between Gulf neighbours would have rendered the journey impossible. For the duration of Evans's journey, then, the sense of one imagined community, defined by a desert at its core, is a potent one that blows out to the edges and beyond:

> Over the past few weeks, people from more than 150 countries have logged onto the website, and more than 4,500 people have been following our progress across the Empty Quarter on Facebook each day – all thanks to us being able to access the internet from the centre of the largest sand desert on earth.
>
> (p. 171)

58   In literary footsteps

This represents an achievement unmatched by the original journey which was communicated by telegram and caused only momentary interest among a limited audience of the British educated elite.

In one of the biggest understatements in travel literature, Bertram Thomas ends the account of his epic journey thus: "Half an hour later we entered the walls of the fort. The Rub Al-Khali had been crossed".[106] For Thomas, the Empty Quarter, with its continually smoothed sands, provided a blank canvas upon which to project extreme human endeavour, mostly white and male in complexion. For Evans, the canvas is already much more diversely marked, not only with the exploits of Thomas and Bin Kalut but also by the recollections of Evans's own Arab companions and the memories of the elders they meet. Fittingly, the canvas is further textured by the graffiti of ancient peoples that predate even tribal memory. In a journey that is expressly not about "firsts" but about "communication, and connection" (p. 79), it is appropriate that one of the significant finds of Evans's journey is a rare piece of pre-Islamic script etched into the rocks in the roof of a cave in southern Oman; a photograph of the writing is released on social media, and before the team leaves the vicinity, the image of the inscription has found its way to the Académie des Inscriptions et Belles-Lettres in France where it is scrutinised by a French scholar. Evans informs local explorer, Musallam Jedad, who discovered the inscriptions six years earlier, about their provenance, and the latter poses for a photograph beside them. Interestingly, the inscriptions resist translation as "there's no vertical line between words".[107] It might also resist translation, in a less literal sense, because there is no horizontal line (of "deep, horizontal comradeship") between Jedad and the people of the alien script, as it predates the origins of the Arab nation to which this local explorer belongs.[108] The desert as such is an archive of mysteries that modern human beings are no longer privileged to read.

As Evans sits on the cold sand one morning, he observes the hieroglyphics of animal tracks that imprint the sand and speculates about the "intricate stories of desert creatures ... and their various states of mind" (p. 142) and he turns to Jay Giffiths's *Wild: An Elemental Journey* in order to try to make sense of their inscriptions:

> In the desert, you are in fact sitting in the middle of a text, with lines, history, reference and narratives that remain until the wind wipes the slate clean, erases the pencil marks on the page, and then the tribes of tiny scribes of beetle and bird begin to write again.[109]

The act of writing and erasing captured in this passage, is also recorded, as Evans informs us, in Thomas's text where he writes that "no wild beast or insect pass but needs must leave its history in the sands, and the record lasts until a rising wind bears a fine sand along to obliterate it" (p. 143).

In literary footsteps 59

In this sense nature participates not just in the writing, erasure and rewriting of natural history but also, as one footprint replaces another as acted upon by the wind, in the palimpsestic sense in which a desert footstep journey is foregrounded within intertextuality.

Evans's journey is not confined to the narrow confines of the footstep genre but participates in much larger critical discourses summoned up by that concept. As modern critics David Marshall et al. define in their exploration of intertextuality, inscriptions are made through a "collaborative, digital storytelling that combines images, narration, and sound [in order to] provide a method that emphasises the polyvocality and multi-temporality that the term palimpsest implies".[110] As we have seen, Evans's work is collaborative in that it acknowledges his fellow travellers as equal partners in the enterprise; it is digital in that the account of the journey is broadcast around the world in nightly tweets, and it acts as storytelling, appropriate to the oral tradition of the desert, in the way it tells nightly versions of the modern journey (through diary excerpts) while the team members participate in regular readings of Thomas's *Arabia Felix* (1930). This multi-temporality shifts the reader's focus from the 1930s context of Thomas to the context of the modern-day journey and is further underpinned in the book's many images, such as in the reproduction of Thomas's map, for example, where the copy of the original map is photographed pegged out on a mat on the sand by the team's modern Garmin GPS unit. The multi-visual nature of the project is further captured in its collage of reprographic historical documents that include old photographs of Thomas, newspaper clippings, invoices, and sextant records. These, together with information boxes, some of which are supplied by subject experts, the large chunks of Thomas's original text, and the dovetailing of these with Evans's own diary excerpts and digital tweets, all contribute to the polyvocal nature of the work and emphasise the way in which Thomas's legacy is being reinscribed by the modern venture, replacing the lead in the letters of his tomb's forgotten headrest.

It is in this sense that I would argue that Evans's work is expressly modern. His account is not the "value-free, decorative, de-historicised quotation of past forms" that may be levelled as a criticism of the work of Kirkby and Hayes wherein Thesiger's text is provided as something of a clichéd way of reading the modern journey.[111] *Crossing the Empty Quarter*, in contrast, makes something new through the novel arrangement of familiar parts, through a process of giving visibility and voice to the indigenous people with whom Evans shares a journey and who were part of the original journey he seeks to retrace. This gives his footstep account a modern value that takes it beyond mere narrative device, as it chimes with local and regional attempts to re-indigenise their culture after a prolonged period of Western cultural domination.

There is an interesting comparison between Evans's account and that of Jan Morris, whose work is considered more closely in the following

60 *In literary footsteps*

chapter. Morris (travelling at the time as James) also undertook a second journey, albeit running a few minutes behind the first journey, following in the retinue of cars that trailed Sultan Taimur's progress across Oman's desert interior in the 1950s. In one of the few soul-searching parts of the resulting travelogue, *Sultan in Oman*, Morris drops the usual entertaining and ironic flippancy to reflect on the role of the expatriate in the future of the country:

> Some deep rooted imperial instinct within me kept me rigidly apart and divided from [the Omanis]. ... I remained – what? The administrator? The educator? The policeman? The exploiter? There was a patronising element in this instinct ... a subtle, lingering conviction that we had some indefinite rights or privileges denied to others. ... I saw myself standing there, looking towards the Arabian shore, as a chip in the huge antique mosaic of imperialism.[112]

Half a century on from these insightful self-reflections, the kind of travel Morris describes has become problematised by postcolonial anxieties, and while this chapter has sought to defend specific footstep travels as one way in which the past can be productively revisited through the hindsight of modern sensibility, there remains the risk that this mode of expression in general helps to perpetuate the very things – "the patronising element", the essence of privilege – that critical theory and the projects of postcolonial writers have tried to eschew. Footstep travel, after all, is fundamentally about reconstructing and reviving white male travel from the past in which indigenous people have been led, as we have seen, without appetite into places they have no particular desire to be in order to fulfil the economic imperatives (including book sales) of their white patrons. As such, it could be argued that while the winds of change have long since passed through the region in political terms, imperialism still impacts at a cultural level, helping to reinvest old stereotypes and intercultural relationships with outmoded value.

Evans is not completely immune from some of the aforementioned observations, but his attempt to recast the footstep journey into something more democratic is highly encouraging for the future direction of the genre. Where Morris was a visitor to Oman, Evans is a long-term resident in the country and region at large. Morris tagged along to observe his hosts; Evans planned his journey with his Omani colleagues around the needs of his adoptive country as identified by local sheikhs. It is primarily for this reason that Evans's journey succeeds, backed by regional governments, where many similar proposals to cross the Empty Quarter have met with difficulties and continuous postponement and are yet to occur.[113] For the subgenre of footstep travel to remain modern and relevant, then, it has to become less about the white Westerner and more about engaging with the local population in narratives that are relevant

In literary footsteps   61

to an Arab heritage, or at least a shared heritage. Without adopting that polyphonic approach, the Arabian desert footstep genre is in danger of descending into meaningless pastiche – into the kind of journeying that you can buy in Wadi Rum, complete with a Lawrence headdress and a camel led by the nose.

Notes

1 Jacinta Matos, "Old Journeys Revisited: Aspects of Postwar English Travel Writing", in *Temperamental Journeys: Essays on the Modern Literature of Travel*, ed. by Michael Kowalewski (Athens: University of Georgia Press, 1992), pp. 215–29 (p. 215).

2 Graham Huggan, *Extreme Pursuits: Travel/Writing in an Age of Globalization* (Ann Arbor: University of Michigan, 2009), preface, p. 5.

3 Peter Hulme, "In the Wake of Columbus: Frederick Ober's Ambulant Gloss", *Literature & History*, 3rd Series 6, no. 2 (1997), 18–36.

4 Tim Youngs, *The Cambridge Introduction to Travel Writing* (Cambridge: Cambridge University Press, 2013), p. 185. Youngs does not dismiss all such second texts; indeed, he states that "there are some very honourable exceptions, including Jonathan Raban's *Old Glory*" (pp. 184–85).

5 James Buzard, *The Beaten Track: European Tourism, Literature, and the Ways to "Culture" 1800–1918* (Oxford: Clarendon Press, 1993), p. 170.

6 Jay Clayton and Eric Rothstein, eds. *Influence and Intertextuality in Literary History* (Madison: The University of Wisconsin Press, 1991), p. 50.

7 Maria Lindgren Leavenworth, *The Second Journey: Travelling in Literary Footsteps* [2009] (Umeå: Umeå Universitet, 2010), p. 50.

8 Adrian Hayes, *Footsteps of Thesiger* (Dubai: Motivate, 2012), p. 265.

9 Chris Rojek, *Ways of Escape: Modern Transformations in Leisure and Travel* (London: MacMillan, 1993), p. 4.

10 John Urry and Jonas Larsen, *The Tourist Gaze 3.0* [1990] (London: Sage Publications, 2011).

11 Matos, "Old Journeys Revisited"; Heather Henderson, "The Travel Writer and the Text: My Giant Goes with Me Wherever I Go", in *Temperamental Journeys: Essays on the Modern Literature of Travel*, ed. by Michael Kowalewski (Athens: University of Georgia Press, 1992), pp. 230-248; Alison Russell, *Crossing Boundaries: Postmodern Travel Literature* (New York: Palgrave, 2000) and Leavenworth, *Second Journey*.

12 Leavenworth, *Second Journey*, p. 189.

13 T. E. Lawrence, in Bertram Thomas, *Arabia Felix: Across the Empty Quarter of Arabia* (London: Jonathan Cape, 1932), p. xv.

14 Nicholas Robinette, *Realism, Form and the Postcolonial Novel* (New York: Palgrave and Macmillan, 2014), p. 48.

15 Maxine Feifer, *Going Places: Tourism in History from Imperial Rome to the Present* (New York: Stein and Day, 1986).

16 Leavenworth, *Second Journey*, pp. 11–12.

17 Carl Thompson, *Travel Writing* (Abingdon and New York: Routledge, 2011), p. 92.

18 T. E. Lawrence in the Foreword to Thomas, *Arabia Felix*, p. xv.

19 See Douglas Curruthers, "Captain Shakespear's Last Journey", *Geographical Journal*, 59, no. 5 (1922), 321–44. Captain Shakespear's monumental journey in 1914 from Kuwait to Riyadh, of which he left no written record, is all but forgotten, despite Shakespear's heroic death in battle. The account of his

62 *In literary footsteps*

journey by Douglas Curruthers is similarly overlooked, possibly for the same reason that it is not predicated on a firsthand narration.

20 The allusion here is to Robert J. C. Young's reference to these founding post-colonial critics as the "Holy Trinity" in *Colonial Desire* (Abingdon: Routledge, 1995), p. 163. The reference is irreverent in the sense that their work has long since been viewed for the individual merits of each. The collective works of Edward Said, Homi K. Bhabha, and Gayatri Chakravorty Spivak, however, have helped in encouraging antithetical readings of the kind of canonical texts represented by the work of Thomas, Lawrence and Thesiger.

21 Julia Kristeva, *Desire in Language: A Semiotic Approach to Literature and Art* (New York: Columbia University, 1980). See also Graham Allen, *Intertextuality* (London and New York: Routledge, 2000), p. 3.

22 Matos, "Old Journeys Revisited", p. 215.

23 Peter Whitfield, *Travel: A Literary History* (Oxford: Bodleian Library, 2012), p. 251.

24 William Wey, *The Itineraries of William Wey* [1857], translated by Francis Davey (Oxford: Bodleian Library, 2010), and see Francis Davey, *Richard of Lincoln: A Medieval Doctor Travels to Jerusalem* (UK: Azure Publications, 2013).

25 James Cowan, *Desert Father: A Journey in the Wilderness with Saint Anthony* (Boston, MA: New Seeds Books, 2006), p. 57.

26 T.E. Lawrence, in Thomas, *Arabia Felix*, Foreword. Bertram Thomas was the first Western explorer to cross the entirety of the Rub Al-Khali (from south to north) with Bedouin guide, Sheikh Saleh Bin Kalut Al-Rashidi Al-Kathiri (the first recorded occurrence of this feat by a non-Westerner). Omani traveller, Mohamed Zadjali, accomplished the same in 2016, as co-expeditioner with Mark Evans. Author's unpublished interview with Mohamed Al-Zadjali, 26 April 2016.

27 James Canton, *From Cairo to Baghdad: British Travellers in Arabia* (London: I B Tauris, 2014), p. 9.

28 Thomas's appendices record his collections of flora and fauna; he endearingly notes that the hyenas will be glad to see him leave.

29 Mark Evans, *Crossing the Empty Quarter in the Footsteps of Bertram Thomas* (UK: Gilgamesh Publishing, 2016), p. 193.

30 Wilfred Thesiger, *Arabian Sands* [1959] (Harmondsworth: Penguin, 1984), p. 11.

31 Richard Holmes, cited in Alexander Maitland, *Wilfred Thesiger: My Life and Travels, an Anthology* (New York: HarperCollins, 2003). See also Christopher Morton and Philip N. Grover (eds.) *Wilfred Thesiger in Africa: A Unique Collection of Essays & Personal Photographs* (New York: HarperCollins, 2010), and Wilfred Thesiger, *The Life of My Choice* [1987] (New York and London: W. W. Norton, 1988).

32 James (now Jan) Morris, *Sultan in Oman* [1957] (London: Eland, 2008), p. 1.

33 See Rojek, *Ways of Escape* and Huggan, *Extreme Pursuits*.

34 John MacInnes, *The End of Masculinity: The Confusion of Sexual Genesis and Sexual Difference in Modern Society* (Buckingham: Open University Press, 1998), p. 47.

35 Charles Blackmore, *In the Footsteps of Lawrence of Arabia* (London: Harrap Limited, 1986), p. 157.

36 "Modern" here means post-1950. Blackmore's journey is pre-dated by that of Douglas Glen, who attempted to trace Lawrence's footsteps by car in 1938. See Douglas Glen, *In the Steps of Lawrence of Arabia* (London: Rich and Cowan, 1941).

In literary footsteps 63

37 Buzard, *The Beaten Track*, pp. 160–61.
38 Mark Evans commenced his commemorative journey on 10 December, 85 years to the day after Bertram Thomas (Evans, *Crossing the Empty Quarter*), and Bruce Kirkby marked the 50th anniversary of Thesiger's travels in *Sand Dance: By Camel Across Arabia's Great Southern Desert* (Toronto: McClelland and Stewart, 2000).
39 See the introduction to this book for a brief charting of the Lawrence legend.
40 Modern Bedu in the region delight in creating mythical links to "El Aurens" for the gratification of gullible travellers, as noted in Jenny Walker, *Jordan* (Melbourne: Lonely Planet, 2012), p. 211.
41 Sara Wheeler, *Terra Incognita* [1996] (New York: Modern Library, 1996), p. 148.
42 Beau Riffenburgh, *The Myth of the Explorer* [1993] (Oxford: Oxford UP, 1994), p. 7.
43 Lawrence writes, "[M]y personal duty was command, and the commander, like the master architect, was responsible for all". Lawrence, *Seven Pillars*, p. 197.
44 On being placed under the command of Colonel Holdich, Lawrence writes, "[S]ince he clearly did not need me, I interpreted this ... as a method of keeping me away from the Arab affair". Lawrence, *Seven Pillars*, p. 63.
45 Shortly after arrival in Arabia, Lawrence writes that, in contrast to his desk job in Cairo, the desert experience was severe "since time had not been given me gradually to accustom myself to the pestilent beating of the Arabian sun, and the long monotony of camel pacing". Lawrence, *Seven Pillars*, p. 86.
46 The fixation on the trials of planning are a familiar trope of modern footstep journeys as if these trials are more of a test than the journey itself. Kirkby obsesses over the struggle to attain "exceedingly difficult diplomatic permissions" (Kirkby, *Sand Dance*, p. 218), and Hayes spends three whole chapters describing thwarted planning and preparations (Hayes, *Footsteps of Thesiger*).
47 "Britons Relive Desert Legend of Lawrence", *The Times*, Tuesday, March 19, 1985.
48 Percy Bysshe Shelley, *Ozymandias* [1817], *Shelley's Poetry and Prose*, ed. by Donald H. Reiman and Sharon B. Powers (New York and London: W. W. Norton, 1977), p. 103: "Round the decay/Of colossal wreck, boundless and bare/The lone and level sands stretch far away".
49 John Galt, *Letters from the Levant* (London: T. Cadell and W. Davies, 1813), p. 305.
50 Jonathan Wordsworth, Michael C. Jaye, and Robert Woof, *William Wordsworth and the Age of English Romanticism* (New Brunswick and London: Rutgers University Press, 1987), p. 131.
51 John Smith, *A System of Modern Geography* (London: Sherwood, Neely, and Jones, 1811, 2 Vols.), Vol. 2, pp. 738–39.
52 See James Barr, *A Line in the Sand: The Anglo-French Struggle for the Middle East, 1914–1948* (New York: W. W. Norton and Co, 2011) and *Setting the Desert on Fire: T.E. Lawrence and Britain's Secret War in Arabia, 1916–1918* (New York: W.W. Norton, 2008).
53 Robin Maugham, *Nomad* (London: Chapman and Hall, 1947), pp. 29–30.
54 As James Canton points out in his work on the twentieth-century travellers to Arabia, *From Cairo to Baghdad*, "[B]y the time that the dust of Suez had settled, Britain's position in Arabia had become irreparably fractured ... now it was down to a journalist to ... tell of the time when Britain started to lose its imperial footing in Arabia". Canton, *From Cairo to Baghdad*, p. 81.

64   *In literary footsteps*

55 John McLeod, *Beginning Postcolonialism* [2000] (Manchester: Manchester University Press, 2010), p. 30.

56 "Britons Relive Desert Legend of Lawrence", *The Times*, Tuesday, March 19, 1985.

57 Scott Anderson, *Lawrence in Arabia: War, Deceit, Imperial Folly and the Making of the Modern Middle East* [2013] (New York: Anchor Books, 2014), p. 3 [emphasis in the original].

58 T.E. Lawrence quoted in A.W. Lawrence ed., *T.E. Lawrence by his Friends* [1937] (New York: McGraw-Hill, 1963), p. 175.

59 Anderson, *Lawrence in Arabia*, p. 3.

60 Bart J. Moore-Gilbert, *Postcolonial Theory* (London: Verso, 1997).

61 Author's unpublished interview with Jamie Bowden, 18 March 2014.

62 James Clifford, *Routes: Travel and Translation in the Late Twentieth Century* (Cambridge, Massachusetts: Harvard UP, 1997), p. 216.

63 Oliver Smith, "In Search of Lawrence's Arabia", *Lonely Planet Magazine* (May 2010), 76–86 (p. 80); this article won Smith the AITO Young Travel Writer of the Year Award in 2011 and was reprinted in 2017, suggesting the Lawrence legend lives on.

64 "Britons Relive Desert Legend of Lawrence", *The Times*, Tuesday, 19 March 1985. Cross-dressing has a long history in Oriental travel; see John Rodenbeck, "Dressing Native", in *Unfolding the Orient*, ed. by Paul and Janet Starkey (Reading, MA: Ithaca Press, 2001), pp. 65–100. See also C.W. Thompson, *French Romantic Travel Writing: Chateaubriand to Nerval* (Oxford: Oxford University Press, 2012), pp. 166–67: while acknowledging that "exotic cross-dressing" implies a degree of imperial condescension, Thompson applauds the attempt "at least to get closer to alien worlds", p. 167.

65 Leavenworth, *Second Journey*, p. 71.

66 Jennifer Laing and Warwick Frost, *Books and Travel: Inspiration, Quests and Transformation* (Bristol: Channel View Publications, 2012), p. 142.

67 Roger Mear and Robert Swan, *A Walk to the Pole: To the Heart of Antarctica in the Footsteps of Scott* (New York: Random House, 1987), p. xii.

68 Mear and Swan, *Walk to the Pole*, p. 20.

69 See, for example, Paul Shepherd, *Man in the Landscape: A Historic View of the Esthetics of Nature* [1967, 1991] (London: University of Georgia Press, 2002). Shepherd discusses the tension between genuine wilderness and managed natural space focusing on human control of the environment.

70 See Introduction for an overview of Thesiger's legacy.

71 Hayes, *Footsteps of Thesiger*, p. 20.

72 Kirkby, *Sand Dance*, p. 11.

73 Richard Hall, *Empires of the Monsoon: A History of the Indian Ocean and Its Invaders* [1996] (London: Harper Collins, 1998).

74 B. J. Moore-Gilbert, "'Gorgeous East' Versus 'Land of Regrets'", in *Orientalism: A Reader*, ed. by A.L. Macfie (Edinburgh: Edinburgh University Press, 2000), pp. 273–76 (p. 276).

75 McLeod, *Beginning Postcolonialism*, p. 53.

76 Henderson, "The Travel Writer", p. 231.

77 Ali Behdad, *Belated Travelers: Orientalism in the Age of Colonial Dissolution* (Durham, NC: Duke University Press, 1994), p. 13.

78 Youngs, *The Cambridge Introduction*, p. 89.

79 Blackmore, *Footsteps of Lawrence*, p. 20.

80 Kirkby, *Sand Dance*, p. 120.

81 Hayes, *Footsteps of Thesiger*, p. 137. A similar dilemma is perhaps more famously expressed in Robyn Davidson's modern desert classic, *Tracks* [1980] (London: Picador, 1998).

In literary footsteps 65

82 Dean MacCannell, *The Tourist: A New Theory of the Leisure Class* (Berkeley: University of California Press, 1999), p. 105.

83 Thesiger, *Arabian Sands*, p. 278.

84 Buzard, *The Beaten Track*, p. 6.

85 Edward Kamau Brathwaite, *History of the Voice* (London: New Beacon Books, 1984).

86 Emma LaRocque, Jeanne Perrault and Sylvia Vance, eds., *Writing the Circle: Native Women of Western Canada* (Norman: University of Oklahoma Press, 1993), preface, p. xx.

87 See, for example, Jenny Walker and Paul Clammer, *Jordan* (Melbourne: Lonely Planet, 2015), p. 10.

88 Tarik Sabry, *Cultural Encounters in the Arab World: On Media, the Modern and the Everyday* (London: I. B. Taurus, 2010), p. 98.

89 Blackmore, *Footsteps of Lawrence*, p. 122.

90 Thesiger, *Life of My Choice*; quoted in Hayes, *Footsteps of Thesiger*, p. 24.

91 Recollected by Ian Fairservice, Chairman of the UAE publishing house, Motivate, who helped facilitate Thesiger's journeys, quoted in Hayes, *Footsteps of Thesiger*, p. 29.

92 Leavenworth, *Second Journey*, p. 45.

93 See Kathryn Tidrick, *Heart Beguiling Araby: The English Romance with Arabia* [1990] (London: Tauris Parke, 2010), pp. 210–11, for a discussion on the masochistic relish of hardship in desert travel.

94 James Duncan, "Sites of Representation: Place, Time and the Discourse of the Other", in James Duncan and Derek Gregory, *Writes of Passage: Reading Travel Writing* (London: Routledge, 1999), p. 46. Remote places offer, according to Duncan, a retreat "into a more 'natural' place and time".

95 Anna Ball, *Palestinian Literature and Film in Postcolonial Feminist Perspective* [2012] (Abingdon: Routledge, 2017), p. 149. Ball applies this term to the context of Palestinian poetry, writing of the "diasporic landscape as a palimpsest of spaces, times and experiences that come to be layered upon one another", but the concept remains broadly relevant here too. See also S. Dillon, *The Palimpsest: Literature, Criticism, Theory* (London: Bloomsbury, 2014).

96 Evans was made a Member of the British Empire (MBE) in 2015 and earned the Royal Geographical Society Geographical Award for encouraging young people from non-Arab cultures to explore the Middle East (2019).

97 Allen, *Intertextuality*, p. 183.

98 See Frederic Jameson, *Postmodernism, or the Cultural Logic of Late Capitalism* (London: Verso, 1991).

99 Tidrick, *Heart Beguiling Araby*, p. 197.

100 Thomas, *Arabia Felix*, p. xxiv.

101 Thomas, *Arabia Felix*, p. 25.

102 Author's unpublished interview with Mark Evans, 20 October 2014.

103 Author's unpublished interview with Mark Evans, 19 March 2016. Three of the subheadings in this chapter allude to the quotation referenced here.

104 This piece of memorabilia is illustrated in Evans, *Crossing the Empty Quarter*, p. 93.

105 I recorded the comments noted here during one such gathering in Shisr (Southern Oman), on meeting up with the expedition on Day 8 of Evans's journey towards the Saudi Arabian border on 17 December 2018.

106 Thomas, *Arabia Felix*, p. 299.

107 Professor Christian Robin, quoted in Evans, *Crossing the Empty Quarter*, p. 65.

108 Benedict Anderson, *Imagined Communities: Reflections on the Origin and Spread of Nationalism* [1983] (London: Verso, 1991).

66   *In literary footsteps*

109 Jay Griffiths, *Wild: An Elemental Journey* (London: Penguin, 2006), pp. 290–91.
110 David J. Marshall, Lynn A. Staeheli, Dima Smaira, and Konstantin Kastrissianakis, "Narrating Palimpsestic Spaces" in *Environment and Planning A: Economy and Space*, 49, no. 5 (2017), 1163–80.
111 Linda Hutcheon, *The Politics of Postmodernism* [1989, 2002] (London and New York: Routledge, 2004), p. 90; Hutcheon uses the quoted phrase to describe what she identifies as prevailing critical attitudes towards postmodern parody.
112 Morris, *Sultan in Oman*, p. 152.
113 The proposed journey of Harriet Griffey in the footsteps of James (now Jan) Morris, commemorating 60 years since Taimur's journey in 2014 to 2015 is one such example of a journey failing to materialise.

2 Desert and sown

The narration of progress and modernity

At the beginning of *The Last of the Bedu*, Michael Asher's extensive travel narrative published in 1996 in which he described thousands of miles of his own desert journeys, Asher quotes from the *Encyclopaedia Britannica*, hinting at the age-old tension, dating back to the story of Cain and Abel, between the desert and the sown:

> The Arabian Desert, until about 1940, had remained practically unaffected by other cultures, and particularly Western culture. In the future one may anticipate change. ... The desert, nevertheless, will remain the desert, although it will become less isolated, more comfortable, and possibly more productive. The question that remains to be answered, however, is whether or not the Arab individuality will become merged into an urban anonymity.[1]

Within this description, the familiar characteristic of the desert's supposed immutability is posited; the terrain can lose most of its defining characteristics as a zone of isolation, hardship, and apparent barrenness, and yet it is supposed, it "will remain the desert". The people who dwell within the desert, by contrast, are considered vulnerable to the vicissitudes of presumed human progress. The choice of quotation by Asher is an interesting one on several levels not least because, in referencing an encyclopaedia, the need to believe in the desert's immutability is underscored by its presentation in a book of apparent facts. Of relevance to the present discussion in a chapter that focuses on the human story within the desert wilderness, however, is the implied lament of "Arab individuality" being subsumed by the altogether more pejorative concept of "urban anonymity" as the supposed result of "Western culture". This hints at familiar binaries of nature and nurtured, savage and civilised, rural and urban, and suggests that there is something to regret about the one becoming globalised or "merged" into the other.

As demonstrated in the previous chapter, which analysed presentations of self, modern desert literature that focuses on presentations of the Arabian Other includes a set-piece on the disappointment that is

DOI: 10.4324/9781003197201-3

68 *Desert and sown*

occasioned by the eliding of supposed opposites. This is expressed either as a eulogy for traditional modes of being within the desert or as a complete expurgation of the modern within the account. But, as we have also already seen, not *all* desert literature is unremittingly anti-modern, and some recent travellers in particular make a point of deliberately contesting the familiar tropes of the Oriental literary inheritance by drawing attention to the modern Middle East; their work, as the subject of this chapter, challenges over-simplified, relativistic binaries that obscure more than they reveal and reaches towards a more nuanced understanding of the region today. The discussion covers a range of desert accounts published since 1950, with a particular focus on those by James (now Jan) Morris, Barbara Toy, Jonathan Raban, Michael Asher, and Tim Mackintosh-Smith, each of whom emphasises the contemporary nature of their enterprise. Their work, discussed herein in thematic sequence rather than chronologically, challenges established tropes by showing that the Arabia they journey within may be desert, but it is peopled, mapped, mechanised, and the context of some of the world's great modern cities. While each of the texts discussed has some limitations in terms of the extent to which they are able to eschew the tropes of the old Orient, they nonetheless contribute to a counter-discourse that explores various Arab modernities, whether found in the desert, in the city or in the "imaginative geography" in between. In order to give some sense of how much of a *counter*-discourse these narratives provide, the discussion first addresses more common representations of the human story within modern desert travel narratives, paying specific attention to the Bedu as a group of people whose lives have traditionally provided a "happy hunting ground" for Western speculation. If, as Mark Cocker writes, "abroad is always a metaphysical blank sheet on which the traveller could write or rewrite the story, as he or she would wish it to be", this chapter contends that the Arabian desert and those who dwell in it continue to act as similarly invested entities.[2] But while disentangling established binaries is often a self-deluding exercise, it is one which at least deserves credit for the attempt.

Desert but not deserted – Asher's modern Bedu

In Arabian desert literature, the phrase "desert and the sown" inevitably calls to mind the work of the pioneering travel writer, Gertrude Bell, who, in a title of the same name, described desert travels that focus on people rather than place.[3] The phrase predates Bell, however, and indeed, at least according to archaeologist Cherie J. Lenzen, it is now so widely assumed to be true it is as good as "a concept".[4] In Lenzen's definition, the desert is "the place of the nomad, who lives outside the city and is not limited by its constructs. The area of the sown is that of the city-dweller". According to this definition, the notion of "inside" and "outside" is

Desert and sown 69

established in almost Venn diagram terms, indicating the set of all things civilised represented by the city, and all things other, represented by the desert. The Bedu are not placed inside the desert but "outside the city", suggestive of the liminality of their role in the literary imagination – free, unanchored but also excluded, occupying only the interstices of Arab modernity and heritage. Despite the term's ability to conjure more than just the two opposite notions of wild and tame but also the border zone in between, the distinction is not universally embraced. Ethnographers such as Donald Powell Cole and Soraya Altorki, for example, seek to draw the two parts of the term into a dynamic that is continually evolving: "Ours is an anti-essentialist view of ... deserts and desert development. Where many see a vast divide between desert and sown, we see a long history of interaction that has recently accelerated rapidly in magnitude".[5] Theirs is not a view often shared in desert travel literature, however, where the distinction is kept artificially alive in order to preserve the imaginative possibilities invested therein. Furthermore, the distinction is often extrapolated to encompass a wider contingent, carrying with it the danger, in Anshuman Mondal's words, of conflating "the Bedouins with Arabs as a whole" and, in turn, keeping alive outmoded hierarchies of townspeople and their nomadic neighbours.[6]

If the established hierarchy is generally stacked in favour of the settled within the social and political realities of the Middle East, within Arab desert literature, the balance is tipped in the other direction. Traditionally, desert travel writers have made a point of avoiding all mention of the *fellaheen* [farmers, the urbanised] and, in as much as they refer to an urban experience at all, these references are generally couched in laments about the corrupting nature of the desert's industrial fringe upon the life of supposed freedom enjoyed by the Bedu. Charles Blackmore, for example, observes what he describes as the tainting effect of the urban on the Bedu way of life:

> Mohammed gracefully declines [a Miranda, popular fizzy drink] – it is as though he feels as I do, and will not indulge in anything which he considers "un-Bedouin". For this I admire him though I am saddened by the changes which will inevitably be forced upon him. ... He squats by his camel with the dignity and humility of the desert nomad – facing him are the town Arabs of a new era who are fascinated to see camels in the dirty streets of El Mureigha.[7]

Not only are the "Arabs of a new era" (whatever that era may be) edited out of, or apologised for, in accounts such as this, but so too are the urban and industrial realities of desert travel and the mechanisms that make modern travel possible within the desert. This leads to the somewhat bizarre spectacle in the previous passage of modern Western travellers leading reluctant camels across sands that are traversed more naturally

70 *Desert and sown*

these days by Bedu in pickup trucks and shrinking from the sight of a Mars bar and a fizzy drink offered by local sheikhs bemused by the unnecessary austerity of their endeavours.[8] In such avoidance of the modern in desert narratives, there is an inevitable reference, either conscious or unconscious, to Wilfred Thesiger, the literary behemoth looming over all desert quests of the second half of the twentieth century. Although he reconciled himself to urbanisation and modernisation in the 1991 preface to *Arabian Sands*, and even praised Abu Dhabi as an "impressive city", Thesiger is largely remembered by later travellers as the one who "craved for the past, resented the present and dreaded the future", and his work, as we have seen, sets the tone of nostalgia and belatedness for the next half-century.[9]

Historians and commentators of modern travel literature, such as Peter Whitfield and Carl Thompson, note a similarly elegiac tone in modern travel writing as a whole and identify a number of texts that cast a backward glance at the late eighteenth and nineteenth centuries and the literary preoccupations of the day.[10] In particular, they point to a revival of the Romantic celebration of primitivism or, to use Thompson's definition of the term, the "valorisation of the primitive".[11] As a notion partly popularised in *Totem and Taboo*, and in a statement that was controversial even in its own day, Sigmund Freud wrote that primitivism, as evidenced in totemism, is a "necessary phase of human development through which every race has passed".[12] Despite being widely discredited by anthropologists throughout the twentieth century, from Albert L. Kroeber writing in the 1920s to Richard Schechner in the 1990s, the idea of cultural evolution in which the apparently "primitive" are seen as static repositories of human ideals has proved an enduringly persistent one and it is an idea that finds its desert apotheosis in the work of Thesiger.[13] As Whitfield observes, "Thesiger carried the primitivist spirit to new heights. He seems a twentieth-century throwback to the explorer adventurers of a century before like Burton, eager to ... dissolve their identities, in the encounter with desert and mountain and savage people".[14] The anthropologist Marianna Torgovnick helpfully explains how the study of the primitive accomplishes this dissolution of identity by offering access to "an exotic world which is also a familiar world" and she shows how this results in misleading perceptions or tropes: "Primitives are like children, the tropes say. Primitives are our untamed selves, our id forces – libidinous, irrational, violent, dangerous. Primitives are mystics, in tune with nature, part of its harmonies. Primitives are free". They are also, according to these tropes, inferior, and it is this sense of hierarchy that, according to Torgovnick, informs the primitivist discourse that is "fundamental to the Western sense of self and Other".[15]

The work of Burton, Thesiger, and many of those who have travelled along similar desert paths, demonstrates that a principal result of the neo-primitivist account, whether the intended objective or not, is to anchor

Desert and sown 71

Arabia in a time warp. Within what McClintock describes as this "anachronistic space", the stereotypical image of the Orient is consolidated and repeated, spilling over into much of today's desert literature too.[16] But it would be unfair to ascribe the essentialist notion of the Bedu to *all* modern desert travellers. The work of Michael Asher is a case in point. Asher is perhaps best known not for his seminal work on nomads but for his biography of Thesiger. The concept was received with ill grace by the older traveller who declared the project to be a "complete waste of time", believing he had already written the definitive account of the Bedu in *Arabian Sands.*[17] Despite an eventual mutual respect between the two travellers, discrepancies in perspective remained, with Asher expressing concern about Thesiger's romantic tendency to portray the Bedu "in a purely aesthetic light – as one not trapped within their life forever".[18] The indulgence of glamorising lives of hardship for the sake of an aesthetic ideal has been well documented by both critics and admirers of Thesiger alike; Peter Brent in *Far Arabia*, for example, questions whether "poverty and hardship, danger and the constant possibility of sudden death is a price people should pay for the code of honour, the freedom, the peculiar courage they give rise to", and he goes on to ask whether "it is a price any of us would pay?"[19] The Omani scholar Hilal Al-Hajri thinks not, and reminds the non-resident reader of a point many commentators often overlook, that travellers, including Thesiger, pick and choose the best time to play at being Bedu – because they can:

> Thesiger and other romantic travellers to Arabia, unlike the natives, stayed there temporarily and had a choice of leaving. They chose, deliberately, to travel in the region in the winter, avoiding the unbearable heat and difficult conditions of the summer, which the natives had to live under.[20]

There is a perversity, as suggested in Al-Hajri's comments, in feeling fondly towards a life of hardship, with its "unbearable heat", that a traveller can choose to adopt for as long or as little as he or she has appetite for, while the Bedu, at least until the benefits of oil brought release, remained virtual prisoners of their environment.[21] As anthropologists such as Dawn Chatty show, "freedom", the defining feature of the Bedu way of life in travel literature, is largely an illusion, as necessity (to find water, to find grazing for camels, to escape the ferocity of summer temperatures, to avoid raiding tribes) usually dictates its own imperatives that are rarely perceived by travellers who undertake their journeys at more benign times of the year and during less socially turbulent times.[22]

Describing the Bedu as "pragmatists rather than romantics", Asher reminds the reader that the Bedu themselves are bemused by Western fascination with a way of life they mostly have no desire to perpetuate.[23] Observations on their ready embrace of government-sponsored settlement,

72   *Desert and sown*

for example, abound in his own desert text, *The Last of the Bedu*, and are further confirmed by Chatty, in her anthropological study of Bedouin mobility.[24] In fact, the only anachronistic part of the modern Bedouin experience is the Western perception of it: the expeditioner Charles Blackmore records his Arab fixer telling him, "You know … the Bedouin do not do these journeys [by camel] any more. Our country is changed and only a few remain in the desert". The guide adds, in a satisfying reversal of gaze not without hint of rebuke, "I think perhaps you have come fifty years too late".[25] Asher's work shows how, exhorted by their own governments to catch up culturally with the rest of the region, the Bedu have become acculturated to the urban experience (albeit with different degrees of assimilation depending on their location within the region), surrounded by schools, hospitals, and government housing, enjoying a varied diet and talking about the inanity of blood feud.[26] Instead of a "once proud people now condemned to the humdrum of modern life", he finds instead less of an "acquiescence of the Bedu in their own modernisation and settlement" and more of a culture in a healthy state of transformation. Where Thesiger "and the Orientalists" had regarded nomadic settlement as a betrayal of cultural ideals, Asher is left wondering "who or what had been betrayed".[27] Similarly, where Thesiger described the Bedu as living a "doomed" existence, Asher identifies the opposite – a vital, adaptive culture, flexible enough to survive and thrive in new circumstances.[28] Far from being immutable, then, he shows the Bedu to be masters of their own reinvention: "In shifting to cultivation and motor-cars they were merely doing what they had always done, using the same penchant for adaptation they had employed for 4,000 years" (p. 283). As such, Asher makes the point that the elusive Bedu of traditional Western literature, "clinging to the remote desert, shunning all contact with the outside world", has probably never existed, and the corrosive influence of Western civilisation similarly is nothing more than an illusion brought about by the projection of the desire of travellers to see in the nomadic lifestyle a freedom from their own sense of restriction and containment back home.[29]

At the same time as Asher writes applaudingly of the Bedu's ability to adapt, he cannot resist expressing an entirely contradictory disappointment that the quest for the Bedu of Western imagination has proved elusive. Indeed, the full title of arguably his most important book – *Last of the Bedu: In Search of the Myth* – foregrounds the tension between modern reality and Western construct that permeates his account.[30] But if Bedu culture is not in itself stranded in the desert fastness, then it may be wondered why Western writers cling to what Homi Bhabha in his work on hybrid identities calls "the concept of 'fixity' in the ideological construction of otherness".[31] The answer probably lies less in the specificities of Bedu life and more in the life left behind. In writing about the revival of romanticism in English travel literature between the two world wars, critics such as Paul Fussell and latterly Helen Carr identify a literature

Desert and sown 73

that "often appeared to be more about escaping from England than anything else"; this is exactly the tendency that Asher's contemporary, Jonathan Raban, notes in Doughty, Lawrence, and Thesiger:[32]

> [In the Bedu] they professed to find all the simplicity, the powers of personal endurance, the stoic independence, which they feared the Englishman was losing. They loved him for his poverty, his spiritual leanness, his ignorance of the "soft" life from which they themselves were on the run.[33]

In this respect, the appropriation of Bedu culture is offering, as James Buzard comments on travel writing in general, "an imaginative freedom not as a rule available in modern social life".[34] This is of course the subject of Said's *Orientalism*, but while one might excuse an earlier generation of travellers for being complicit in the imagining of the Arab Orient as one of the West's "deepest and most recurring images of the Other", it is somewhat dispiriting to see the old familiar binaries reappear even in an era of postcolonial sensibility.[35] Writing at the end of the twentieth century, Asher still feels the need to state that the Bedu are not some "rare and exotic species which should be preserved in its natural habitat" (p. 43) for the benefit of the Western imagination – a fact so obvious that it should not need repeating. Social theorists, furthermore, detect that the neo-primitive urge to conceive of an exotic other continues to motivate travel well into the twenty-first century. The psychologist Jessica Jacobs, for example, charts a new wave of interest in the valorisation of the primitive in a Middle East context (in her study on sex tourism in the Sinai) – if not in travel literature, at least in the behaviour of tourists – and she attributes this, through citing T. Oakes and Griselda Pollock, to a desire for belonging in an ever-more urbanised, globalised, and anonymised world.[36] In this condition, Pollock contends, only "a migration in time and space backwards to the premodern pasts" can deliver a sense of social fulfilment.[37] If this is a credible theory, then it is a perpetually self-defeating one: with their gaze turned towards the past, many modern travellers and tourists miss the experience of the present and the opportunity that brings to make meaningful cross-cultural connections that may help humanise the globalised, anonymous space.

Some Arab commentators are understandably wearied by the role the Middle East continues to play in the imaginative geography of the West. Hilal Al-Hajri, for example, claims that the obsession with "absolute binaries such as 'West' and 'East', 'European' and 'Other', 'coloniser' and 'colonised', 'us' and 'them'" (and we might add "desert and sown"), has obscured the specificities of individual contexts.[38] This has overshadowed the tangible gains in political, economic, and social development made in the last half-century of *nahda*, or Arab renaissance. Indeed, the daily English-language newspapers of the Gulf States portray a life widely at

74 *Desert and sown*

odds with the popular Western delineation.[39] As Tarik El Aris shows, Omanis, Emiratis, Saudis, and Kuwaitis across the region are immensely proud of the radical changes that have occurred since the 1970s and the economic and social revolutions brought about through the extraction of oil that commenced in the 1950s.[40] One might therefore question the integrity, even as it is possible to understand the purpose, of foreign writers harking back to a pre-oil era that nationals in the region are often trying hard to forget. Alan Keohane, in his sensitive study of the Bedu today, warns where this can lead:

> improved communications … are creating a global stereotype, where the richness of diverse cultures is simplified into catchphrases and soundbites. Today most of us know Arabs only as the villains in movies and novels, or the hooded faces on news bulletins. We know nothing of the vast majority of Arabs and Muslims who enrich the world through their creative talents [… or] we assume that their achievements are the result of their having adopted our own culture.[41]

The "vast majority of Arabs and Muslims who enrich the world through their creative talents" are, in other words, left disenfranchised, and this has real-world implications.

It is heartening, then, to find that not all writers are complicit in contributing to the "global stereotype" and the discussion now turns to those desert travellers since 1950 whose work goes against the grain. Their accounts (albeit still largely Western, white, relatively wealthy, and mostly male) contribute to a counter-discourse that runs contrary to the familiar tropes of the genre and occupies a critical space that contests established binaries by focusing on what, in the *Location of Culture*, Homi Bhabha called "border lives". While not a self-consciously coherent set of travellers, the writers providing this alternative narrative share a similar vocabulary but for the sake of this discussion, they are identified through four distinct themes – the "desert mechanised", wherein the desert is consciously described as accessible by motorised transportation; the "desert politicised", wherein the desert is presented as a context for emergent Arab nationalism and modern industry; "desert urbanised", where the focus is specifically on city encounter; and "desert historicised" that recalibrates the region's geography within a distinctly Arab rather than Western frame of reference. Instead of analysing the "desert *and* sown" in these texts, the discussion takes a more "post-Orientalist" approach by gauging to what extent the selected writers present the "desert *as* sown". At its most productive, in the work for example of Tim Mackintosh-Smith, this desert travel literature can destabilise the idea of the urban partitioned off from "Nature capital N", redeeming the space as part of a free-flow connection between the two – the "minds of nations", perhaps, kept human by the rural heart.[42]

The desert mechanised – Toy's travels by Land Rover

On getting stuck in the sands in Oman, Michael Asher and Gerry, his Indian driver, are rescued by a local Bedu man who, in common with many of his tribesmen, proves to be an expert sand driver. He is quick to extol the virtue of the car, in a time-honoured tradition that used to be reserved for camels: "Cars are wonderful. There is nothing like a car!" (1996, p. 173). This should come as no surprise to those familiar with Bedouin history, and, as anthropologist Dawn Chatty observes in *Camel to Truck*, her 1986 study of nomadic pastoralism in Arabia, motorised travel has been fully embraced by the Bedu as they "continue to adapt and change to make the best of the opportunities that surround them".[43] Chatty explains that the ships of the desert are now "a Toyota, Datsun, Nissan or General Motors pick-up", and modern Bedu herd their livestock with the assistance of these vehicles while also engaging in new economic activities (such as truck driving) connecting the desert with settled areas.[44] The prevalence of new forms of transportation has thereby been both the cause of dependency on greater connection with settled areas – for example, through the need to refuel – and the facilitator of a different kind of travel across the region that represents a broader access to the space that was once exclusively reserved for those hardy enough to endure desert conditions on foot.

If the Bedu have embraced mechanised travel, so too have modern desert travellers – if only out of necessity. All expeditions today rely upon mechanised transport to deliver the travellers, and indeed their camels, to the edge of the desert, and then to support them with water, supplies, medical assistance, and communications in the journey thereafter. As recent explorers of the region such as Mark Evans and Mohamed Al-Zadjali have noted, it is currently impossible to travel across vast portions of the Arabian Peninsula without such support, as many of the wells that formed the traditional network of oases that sustained long-distance desert travel have long since silted up or knowledge of their whereabouts has been lost.[45]

With the motor vehicle playing a pivotal role within the realities of contemporary Bedu life, then, as well as in the character and successful completion of modern desert journeys, it may be expected that it would feature more prominently in modern travel writing too, but this has not been the case. In trying to understand why the car is airbrushed out of modern desert accounts, it is helpful to cast a glance at scholarship regarding the reception and perception of the motor car in another context – namely within British travel literature – as it offers some interesting parallels. Tim Youngs identifies mechanised transport as one of three factors that have been "especially dominant in the shaping of travel writing since 1900". He goes on to state that "the Petrol Age" (Wyndham Lewis's term from his North African travel accounts), has "changed people's

76 Desert and sown

sense of speed, their engagement with the landscape and their relationship with one another", and shows how automobile narratives, which appeared from the beginning of the twentieth century, originally featured cars in a favourable light as bringing greater access to nature than journeys by train.[46] This general sense of optimism, however, is soon overshadowed by an ambivalence towards modes of transport that threaten the very environment that they are employed to explore. In her study of the history of motorised travel in Britain, Esme Coulbert charts this change of perspective and shows how the automobile comes to be seen as impinging on the wilderness experience – a concern foregrounded in automobile enthusiast J. J. Hissey's early description of the motor car as an "intruder upon the harmony of unspoilt Nature".[47] By 1935, as Youngs explains, the nascent anxiety about the impact of mechanised travel develops into a full recognition that the privilege of travelling into uncharted territory is not without consequence. He cites twentieth-century aviator, Anne Morrow Lindbergh, as an example of this growing unease: "A few years earlier, from the point of view of aircraft alone, it would have been impossible to reach these places; a few years later, and there will be no such isolation".[48] By the mid-twentieth century, the British romance with the car in travel literature appears to be largely over.

The growing dependence upon but mistrust of mechanised transport in travel literature is perhaps unsurprisingly paralleled closely by British travellers in a desert travel context. In 1935, pioneering mechanical engineer and travel writer R. A. Bagnold was able to extol the virtues of the motorcar in *Libyan Sands* in a highly acclaimed account. By 1950, in contrast, Thesiger, who famously abhorred all machinery, set the tone of mournful regret that characterises most desert travel accounts thereafter:

> All my life I had hated machines. I could remember how bitterly at school I had resented reading the news that someone had flown across the Atlantic or travelled through the Sahara in a car. I had realized even then that the speed and ease of mechanical transport must rob the world of all diversity.[49]

Although he came to revise his views of the changing Arab world, Thesiger's dislike of technology persisted, despite his embrace of it through necessity. Indeed, so strong is his rejection of all things mechanical in his writing that it is easy to overlook the fact that he began his encounter with the Arabian desert on aerial reconnaissance as part of a locust control project and that his travels to and within the region were entirely facilitated by air and by automobile. Mirroring Thesiger's general tone of regret, however, most subsequent Western travel writers lament the presence of cars in the sands or try to banish them from their narratives.[50] In so doing, they are exhibiting the kind of "belatedness" that Ali Behdad describes – a symptom of the postcolonial era that, as we have seen, can be detected running through much of Arabian desert travel literature in general and which manifests in a "nostalgia for a time when 'real' adventures in unknown lands were possible".[51] Cars clearly compromise the notion of wilderness experience and undermine the heroic quest, but they also impinge upon the special nature of limitless space, interrupting the phenomenon described by John Urry and Jonas Larsen as the "romantic gaze".[52] Under this gaze, "unspoilt Nature" invites a reverential approach by a pilgrim explorer entering on foot, preferably unshod, and with head covered; support vehicles intruding within this sacred space are described, therefore, as transgressive or guilty secrets of the modern journey that are by and large kept hidden from the reader. In most desert accounts, the mapping of the sacred space is seldom made clear, but at some point, roughly after arrival in-country is over, when the trips to and from the various ministries for permits are transacted, and where the assembly of supplies is complete, the secular world is left behind: beyond that point, the car is no longer welcome as a reference point in the narrative, leaving the author alone to commune with nature.

Thankfully (at least when calculated in terms of the integrity of an account) not all modern travellers in Arabia share this general squeamishness of the genre towards mechanised travel. Australian-born fellow of the Royal Geographical Society Barbara Toy, for one, builds on the legacy left by Bagnold.[53] If the Bedu have a love affair with their vehicles, then this is an affection shared by Toy who invests emotionally in the Land Rovers that perform centre stage in her travels of the 1950s. "Pollyanna" was the name she gave to one such vehicle – a car of which the author was sufficiently fond to buy it back from its retirement at several times the cost of the original purchase.[54] In one of the accounts featuring her car travels across Yemen and Saudi Arabia, *Travelling the Incense Route* (published posthumously in 2009), the reader gains a strong sense of the vehicle's sentimental value beyond its sum of mechanical parts, and it is introduced in the prologue as a protagonist in the drama described thereafter: "my Land-Rover midships below, stood on bags of rice and around it other passengers, Arabs and Indians, leant against its sides with a proprietary air which was endearing".[55] The vehicle is anthropomorphised throughout the book to the point where car and traveller become "a composite object of person-cum-Land-Rover" (p. 32), and the author's inner journey is projected onto its frame:

The retreat continued and by the time we finally limped into Mukalla the vehicle was in need of extensive and expensive repairs: which proves that damage and accidents to vehicles occur when their drivers are either tired, in pain, depressed – or all three.

(p. 33)

78 *Desert and sown*

Towards the end of her journey, Toy sees herself reflected in the mirror of the car

> with all the travel-stained mementoes around me, a pair of tiny Greek slippers hanging from the mirror, the policeman's truncheon, St. Christopher and the printed 23rd Psalm pasted on the dashboard; the things that make up so much of my life.
>
> (p. 135)

In this sense, she comes nearer to the Bedu experience of the age in which she writes, where, according to Chatty, Asher, and other travellers, cars are a valued part, not just of the modern journey, but of the family wealth and enhanced sense of mobility; their decoration, bedecked in sheepskins and often decorated with dangling objects to deflect the envious evil eye, is totemic of a tribal life on the move.

Tribal life on the move is as good a description as any of Toy's journeys which are distinguished from earlier desert accounts by a celebration not of the earnest plod into isolation but of the communal nature of crossing the desert that is as old as the trade routes she follows. Where Coulbert describes motoring in post-war England as something private and bespoke, Toy resists the individualistic experience of travel and celebrates being part of something bigger as she drives alongside the pilgrim convoys bound for Mecca.[56] Travel in Arabia for centuries has been associated with spiritual journey, and travel by convoy, albeit in trucks rather than on foot or by camel, is common to this day with the journey to the holy cities remaining as one of the world's largest examples of mass travel. In this sense, the desert journey in Arabia as experienced by Arabs is, and generally always has been, a shared human experience, not a lonely encounter with wilderness. Toy's description of the carnival of travel – not all of it flattering – reflects this and, in contrast to the privations described by Doughty, Thomas, and Thesiger, comes closer to embracing the traditional Arab essence of travel in all its colourful, vibrant complexity. As for the spiritual nature of the journey, this is made clear in the full title of Toy's work, *Travelling the Incense Route: From Arabia to the Levant in the Footsteps of the Magi.* "Religion isn't being in a church or a mosque, nor is God – you carry them around with you" (p. 181), says Toy in conversation with a Syrian Christian who replies, "You talk like a b... [sic] Moslem. ... But I am glad that I met you" (p. 181). This is a religious text, then, but not one of dogma; the quest cuts across cultures, allowing for a more sympathetic understanding of the Arab context of Toy's travels.

Many elements of Toy's motorised expedition reflect the sense of journeying across cultures, not just across landscapes. The journey may have been carried out on four wheels rather than on muleback, but in following the old incense trail – which once rivalled the Silk Trail in importance – Toy recognises that many of the age-old customs that once marked the

Desert and sown 79

route are still in practice, including the need to give bribes for accurate information about her route ahead. This unpleasant necessity is partially reconciled by the satisfaction of becoming part of a continuity of caravan dating back centuries: "And didn't the precious incense cost six hundred percent its original price by the time it arrived in Damascus because of the bribes and dues taken all along the line? I was no precious cargo, but customs die hard" (p. 48). It is significant here that Toy resists the temptation to brandish misconceived racial stereotypes inherited from Orientalism, choosing to conceptualise the experience in terms of economic exchange instead. But she also goes further than this. In casting herself as cargo, precious or no, she becomes an object within an alien transaction, rather than a subject with a specific cultural perspective. In so doing, she avoids the necessity of making a judgement or apologising for the practice she encounters. Rather, she recognises she is carried along by a different value structure.

In another example of cultural relativism, Toy tries to fathom the amount of petrol she needs and concludes,

> Finding the exact mileage of a journey is almost impossible. No Arab knows distances, other than by the time it takes to go from one place to another, and this applies to lorry drivers as well. "It is so many hours from here to there. But there are dunes – you might have to go a whole day out of your way to miss them. But kilometres?" They will put their right hand under their left elbow. "It is surely that far!"
> (p. 54)

The complaint about locals and timekeeping is a common one in travel narratives as Western travellers attempt to apply their own notions of time to systems that are foreign to them. Al-Hajri reminds us that while the Western concept of time and punctuality "were probably absent" in Arabia in the 1950s and 1960s, this does not mean that Arabs lacked *any* sense of time.[57] He states that Moslems are in fact fastidious timekeepers in their observance of prayer at five specific times each day and in the annual *eids*, including *hajj*, or the pilgrimage to Mecca.[58] Despite the intrinsic value of established norms that have arisen from local needs, the pressure to adopt Western forms of calendar, clock, and land measurement are self-evident in travelling in the region today but Toy, in being quick to redefine mileage in local terms, helps the reader to question which is a better way of mapping the space. In observing that people "will tell you what they think you wish to hear" (p. 54), lending an elasticity to concepts that are much more rigid in a Western tradition, Toy invites the reader to reflect on the applicability of supposed discrete values (cost, distance, time) to contexts beyond the ones in which they evolved.

While there is no attempt to find common ground in these fragments or to act as an apologist for practices she finds disconcerting, Toy's ability

80 *Desert and sown*

to reimagine supposed universal norms contributes to an exchange that lies "beyond Orientalism", or of "letting be". This approaches the kind of cultural solidarity envisaged by Hans-Georg Gadamer and famously expressed in the phrase "unity in diversity".[59] In this way, Toy proves that not all desert travel writers of the era are irredeemably bound up in the business of othering but can and do reflect other cultures from a "nonrepressive and nonmanipulative perspective", albeit at a microcosmic level.[60] Her participation in travel patterns that are nearer to those of her destination than that of the literary heritage in which she writes has a contemporary relevance, despite the pre-postcolonial nature of parts of her account. As such, her work prefigures a recent resurgence of automobile narratives about the region, such as Henry Hemming's *Misadventure in the Middle East* in a truck called Yasmine, and Lois Pryce's ride through "the Real Iran" on the back of a motorbike in *Revolutionary Ride*, both of which explore at some level the nature of shared travel.[61]

The desert politicised – Morris and a sultan's pageant

If Toy's account of her travels in Arabia captured the sense of tribal life on the move, this is also a feature of James (now Jan) Morris's *Sultan in Oman*, written similarly in the 1950s and equally enthusiastic about the mechanised nature of the journey. The subject of the resulting narrative is a journey by motorcade with Sultan bin Taimur and his huge entourage across the newly reconquered territories of Oman: "This journey had never been made before, least of all by motor vehicle. No such crossing had been made of the Jaddat Al-Harasis; nobody had driven from Dhufar to Muscat; [and] the mountains of Oman were almost unexplored".[62] Morris makes a case for the competitive positioning of this journey precisely because it is uncharted territory – "no motor vehicle had ever travelled across" the region (p. 44) – and the sense of excitement in the motorised nature of the journey is palpable throughout:

> The trucks leapt away like dogs from the leash, manoeuvring for position. Exhaust smoke billowed about the palace. We were off! At breakneck speed our convoy drove out of the yard. The slaves struck up a loud unison *fatha*, invoking blessings on our mission. The household retainers lining the several courtyards bowed low and very humbly, and some of the men prostrated themselves.
>
> (p. 36)

Morris's description of the journey, which is conducted at a fast pace over rough tracks, captures more than just a sense of the mechanical wizardry involved in the enterprise: it also captures the "loud unison *fatha*", the invocation of blessing on this pageant, typical of the descriptions of mediaeval pilgrimages. But where Toy's travels were of a broadly religious

Desert and sown 81

nature, Morris's mission is expressly political, dressing the text with the trappings of pilgrimage but making it strictly secular. The Chaucerian details of "two splendid desert sheikhs, crowded together over the gear-box, with their rifles protruding from the window" (p. 37), for example, serve as comic riffs that undercut Orientalist stereotypes and invite a political reading. Indeed, throughout the book, humour is used to encourage a re-evaluation of accepted tropes; rather than the setting up of opposites, the description of the journey splices together not just disparate regions of Oman (the sultan's aim in conducting the journey with his entourage) but also the old with the new, the traditional with the economically developed, the nomadic as represented by the journey with the settled as represented by the destination. The form is chosen with care to match the modern conspicuousness of a journey through a country that is described throughout the narrative as "among the most backward places on earth – a truck had never yet been seen, nor had a telephone rung, nor even had a machine gun chattered" (p. 12). Within this antiquated landscape, the "neat, plump, autocratic little Sultan, compass open on his lap, led the royal convoy up the wadi" (p. 158) as if driving a path towards the future.

The compass is an interesting detail, as it symbolises a modern journey (the Bedu often tease travellers about their reliance on new-fangled technology in orienteering) towards not just a particular geographical direction but also a distinction in political orientation: this is not a democratic convoy, heading out in a multitude of independent directions, but a single-line of road-making subjects that have fallen in behind the map-maker. The drivers are frequently blinded by the plumes of dust ahead, kicked up by the car in front, and when asked if they knew where the convoy was headed, the drivers responded in the negative, apparently happy to trust in Allah and in the wisdom of the man at the helm. In one sense akin to a Bedu caravan, with its distinctive tribal allegiance and absolute faith in the sheikh, this convoy in contrast has a homogenising perspective: this is a unification drive, both literally and metaphorically, across tribal territory with nation-building its aim. While urban Arab commentators, in common with many Western travel writers, often sentimentalise the life of the Bedu, there remains a common consensus (as anthropologist Mohamed Awad points out) that Bedu communities are non-commensurate with Western notions of progress; their semi-nomadic lifestyle is interpreted as interrupting practical policies, relating to education, medical facilities and land reform, that are an accepted part of modern infrastructure.[63] Furthermore, it is a common belief among Arab governments, as argued by Dawn Chatty, that "nationhood in the Arab world cannot be achieved on a stable and permanent basis unless the tribal segment becomes fully integrated with the rest of the nation".[64] This political orientation is reflected in Morris's account where the tribal entities must either fall in line with the convoy whose

82   *Desert and sown*

destination is the capital city, Muscat, or be left behind. In postcolonial terms, the dissenting tribes are therefore marginalised twice – once as being onlookers of a journey of which they are not part and once again in the metaphorical journey towards notional progress. As such, they are both "of, and not of" in the way that migrants have come to be viewed in postcolonial theory, occupying a border zone of the nation's modernising imperative, hovering between desert and city. This calls to mind Cherie Lenzen's definition (referred to in the introduction to this chapter) of the Bedu being "outside the city", occupying the in-between space that is yet to become. Morris's travel text articulates the Bedu's relegation, awaiting in a figurative sense the positive interventions of another generation of travel criticism and the place of creative reimagining suggested by Homi Bhabha's "locations of culture". For now, the Bedu are "in the moment of transit where space and time cross to produce complex figures of difference and identity, past and present, inside and outside, inclusion and exclusion", and as such are part of a political as well as an aesthetic contradiction.[65]

There is another political dimension to *Sultan in Oman*. Morris spends a considerable portion of her account describing the mechanisation of the desert for the purpose of oil production. Where Toy presented the elasticity of certain Arab concepts such as direction and distance, Morris is precise in their delineation and particularly in terms of the oil industry and where it is located within the country's goals for the future. As Edward Said's *Orientalism* made clear, precision of detail in accounts of the region is important for potential profit and gain. Asset-listing information in oil-rich territory clearly has material outcomes of a socio-economic nature, leading to the commercialisation of the desert and impacting on those who live there. Al-Hajri makes the point that there was some political merit in being suspicious of the motives of Western desert travellers, as acknowledged by some of the writers themselves;[66] Thesiger writes, for example, on being refused permission to explore the interior of Oman in 1955 that "if they allowed me to travel there at will I should be followed by other Christians in cars, looking for oil and intending to seize their land".[67] If, as Said suggests, and other travel historians such as Carl Thompson endorse, travel literature "at one level works simply to whet the appetites of traders and investors in Europe, suggesting numerous possibilities for profit and self-advancement in distant territories", this is an equation that both Morris recognises a decade or more before Said's *Orientalism* was published.[68] The commercial potential of the new route the sultan cuts across the desert, for example, and which Morris communicates to a wider audience as chief reporter of the journey, is described in detail in *Sultan in Oman*. The visit to the nascent oil industry in Fahud forms a major highlight of the convoy's journey and acts in itself as a catalyst for future access to a remote and formerly disputed territory:

Desert and sown 83

Our journey opened some windows into this remote and arcane place, but at the same time it admitted some momentous draughts: it was concerned essentially with oil, that irresistible agency of change, and its very accomplishment meant that the territory we were crossing for the first time was changed for ever.

(p. 1)

It is not just oil, therefore, but the journey, and the report of the journey, that acts as "irresistible agency of change", and Morris is explicitly aware of her role within that political dynamic – well ahead of her time.

Morris's description of the oil plant at Fahud is covered in interestingly sterile terms; it is portrayed as a clean industry where crude oil "passes silently along a myriad pipes, cocks and mechanisms, aboard ships and through refineries, into tanks and out of them" (p. 58) until it reaches the petrol station. The only dirt attaching to the process, Morris states, is the part connected with its sale. But while the process of extraction may be clean, it is also deeply disconcerting. This is the desert emptied out of people, replaced by an alien landscape that fascinates in its "hygienic mystique" (p. 58) while being repellently dead. Toy is similarly alienated by the sight of oil production, although she emphasises the dirty amalgam that accrues to the industry, its products, and its users, with highways "strewn with Coca-Cola bottles and caps, burst tyres, broken plastic bottles and discarded sandals". Discarded oil stains the ground and "broken axles told of gross over-loading" (p. 112). A generation later, Asher also remarks on a landscape "vacant, naked, meaningless, bereft of the people who had survived upon its scant resources for generations"; the desert's human inhabitation has been replaced with a dystopian landscape of unsightly machinery:

At Marmul, I saw half a hundred steel pumps, like horse-flies, bleeding crude oil from the desert, acrid gas-flares trailing smoke from their chimneys like flags. Once, where these oil-rigs now stood, the Bedu had stayed alive by squeezing the dew out of rags left on bushes overnight. But that was in another country, long ago.[69]

The "another country, long ago" raises the question, however, of "which country, when?" Perhaps predictably (given the author's dilemma as we have seen about whether to be nostalgic for a way of life lost or encouraged by the Bedu's ability to adapt and change), the Bedouin use of the desert appears in Asher's description of Marmul as the antithesis to modern oil production. But if the Bedu are no longer present within the landscape, it is largely because the revenue from this industry has given opportunities (for example through free schooling) to migrate towards a different kind of life, as anthropologists such as Neil Richardson and Marcia Dorr, in their comprehensive work on Omani craft heritage, have shown.[70] Morris, Toy, and Asher, then, may perhaps be charged with

84 *Desert and sown*

projecting onto the desert the cultural norms of their own culture rather than recognising in the outcome of oil production the chance of a life no longer lived in rags and watered by dew.

All three writers considered hitherto in this chapter appear conflicted by the role of industry in shaping desert lives and impacting the desert environment. This is the case even as they celebrate the mechanised outcomes – namely, the petrol-engine vehicles they use – of that industry and contribute to the desert's despoilation through the indelible tracks their vehicles leave and the discarded detritus of long-haul travel. This conflict is expressed by many other desert goers too, even if they arrived in Arabia as part of the oil industry. Edward Henderson, for example, writes encouragingly of "the fruits of oil", even while recognising it comes at a social and environmental cost: "I suppose just by working for an oil company I have in any case done my little bit to 'spoil' acres of beautiful desert and the old life [but] I am not one to put the brakes on".[71] Parallels to this sentiment can be found in other English-language motoring literature where "ideals concerning the countryside are predictably constructed against impressions of the metropolis which alienated contemporary industry in favour of a pre-industrialised rural idyll". These laments all overlook the fact that the wealth from the one fuels the motion of the other and as such ultimately reflects the values of the writer rather than of the destinations with which they engage.[72]

Not all Western writers in a desert context eschew the positive value of modernisation to change lives for the better, however, and it is to two writers who embrace the urban experience resulting from industrialisation that this discussion now turns. Jonathan Raban's *Arabia Through the Looking Glass* (1979) and a much later work, Tim Mackintosh-Smith's *Travels with a Tangerine* (2004), appear to be solely focused on the urban experience at the expense of virtually any reference to the desert context. It may be wondered why, therefore, they appear at all in a book that is about desert literature; my contention here is that both texts, which focus on travels that necessarily cross deserts to reach cities, arrive at definitions of modernity that are bound up with the surrounding "negative space", albeit for different ends (as explored under the headings of "desert urbanised" and "desert historicised" in the following sections). The desert is in this way defined, in Saidian terms, by its urban otherness, and the two texts have a role to play in understanding the totality of the desert experience. The dates of the texts are significant. Raban's work was published a year after Said's *Orientalism*; as such, it captures the sense of bipolarisation (East versus West, past versus present) that was prevalent in cultural theory at that time. In the account of his Arabian travels, Raban's deliberate omission of the desert context, being all things other than urban, contributes to the delineation of the cities he visits. Given that Arab commentators criticise this binary approach as "bypass[ing] *other* possible modernities, which arise from a series of events, movements, and performances in between the city and the village, the street and the text, and the literary and the political", one can argue that, far from the radically new vision of Arabia he set out to produce, Raban's perspective remains rigidly Western – a railing against Western stereotypes but using the same tropes to do so.[73] Mackintosh-Smith's *Travels*, by contrast, is influenced by two decades of postcolonial theory. As we shall see, in work that seeks to dissolve some of the binaries, particularly of past and present, he is able to present a more holistic view of urban life in desert lands and in turn a more nuanced notion of contemporary Arab culture.

The desert urbanised – Raban and a camel-free account

In writing *Arabia Through the Looking Glass* as a primarily urban account, Jonathan Raban was provoked by the misrepresentation he perceived in backward-glancing literature. Raban describes this conscious rejection of what he called the "whole desert experience of Arabia" and goes in search instead of the progressively urban, the multi-national investment corporations, the dynamic infrastructure growth of a truer "second world":

> The way in which the British have been inclined to think of Arabia as an unpopulated land of sand dunes, camels and people living in tents is so far from the actual history of Arabia which is a place of spectacular cities. I wanted to get into that second world, to a large extent the truer one.[74]

In challenging the prolongation of old stereotypes in modern depictions of the people of the region, Raban suggests that the focus on the old Orient is not only anachronistic and dishonest, discrediting the collective endeavours of the modern nations of the Middle East, but it is also deeply unimaginative. Raban thereby attempts to distinguish himself from other traveller writers by offering what he suggests is a more authentic experience.

Interestingly, if his account is to be believed, it is a stereotype of a different kind that apparently inspired Raban's own travels. He slips behind the gaze of a prostitute to observe a potential Arab client in Earls Court, London, in the early 1970s and perceives a whole new injustice of perception about to unfold. Raban imagines that the girl sees not a man of humble origins but instead an Arab of supposed great wealth:

> Looking at him, all she saw was a figure of contemporary legend, a creature of rumour and newspaper headlines. Her head must have been awash with them. Arabs had bought the Dorchester; Arabs owned half of Holborn; Arabs tipped business girls with Cadillacs and solid gold watches.

(p. 10)

86 *Desert and sown*

In some senses, Raban is projecting onto the prostitute his own process of dehumanising the people who have become his neighbours, aware of a sense of alienation occasioned by their distinct cultural difference – by the "strange, beak-shaped foil masks of Gulf women and the improbably white dishdashas of husbands who walked exactly four paces ahead of their wives". He finds their culture threatening and "uniquely inaccessible" (p. 12) and wonders how it happened that in a summer (the summer of the oil price hikes of 1973), "one day Arabs were a remote people who were either camping out in tents with camels and providing fodder for adventurous photographers, or a brutish horde threatening the sovereignty of the state of Israel; the next, they were neighbours" (p. 11). Acting to avoid what Reina Lewis in a later decade called "simple binary analyses of culpability and innocence", Raban puts aside his misgivings in an attempt to unravel the semiotics of a foil mask and a gold watch. Put simply he journeys to Arabia. There he searches in the big cities for a modern Arab identity – or at least a male Arab identity. While he may come no closer to an "understanding of how we are variously interpellated into the types of complex positionings that can lead to racism in the name of feminism" (and indeed women barely feature in his account other than as the objects of male gaze), he does at least engage in conversations with real people whose voices he endeavours to include in his account.[75]

Like many great quests, Raban's endeavour is a specious one. The image of Arabia as dystopian metropolis is no more real than the Arabia of Doughty, Lawrence, and Thesiger, but Raban's 1979 account in *Arabia Through the Looking Glass* at least provides the region with a literary alter ego. His early travels in the region are almost perverse in their choice of exclusions, taking the bid for originality to extremes: he visits Jordan and avoids Petra; he visits Egypt but avoids the Valley of the Kings; most interestingly for the purpose of this discussion, he visits Arabia and avoids the desert. Unlike his predecessors, Raban is not interested in the desert as an existential canvas upon which to project human endeavour; for him, it is much more prosaic – an inconvenience to be crossed before the real focus of travel as a locus for human activity begins again: "There must, I suppose, be some stretches of desert which really do correspond to that romantic image. ... Most desert, though, ... is simply boring – hundreds and hundreds of miles of it, stretching away like a flat Sunday afternoon" (p. 160). Raban's conceptualisation of the desert as a "flat Sunday afternoon" in a region where the weekend is arranged around Friday is significant. It imprints upon the supposed empty space notions of English leisure: it is empty, perhaps, because it has yet to be tackled on the Monday morning of Western enterprise. But the concept of a boring space is not the same as an empty space, and by negating the desert in his work, he leaves it free, somewhat perilously so, to become part of what Said termed an "imaginative geography".[76] In *Culture and Imperialism,*

Said comments on how "the earth is in effect one world, in which empty, uninhabited spaces virtually do not exist. Just as none of us is outside or beyond geography, none of us is completely free from the struggle over geography".[77] In glossing over the landscape, Raban contributes to the notion of *terra nullius*, empty land that seems suggestive of struggle-free geography and where the thinking of it as empty is tantamount to an invitation to exploit. If this seems farfetched in a postcolonial era, then it is interesting to turn to the example of Desertec, a largely European project that envisions creating electricity by "exploiting vast energy resources in the Sahara". While able to overcome technical hurdles and signing various memoranda of understanding with North African nations, the political and social problems prove hard to overcome: after all, who owns "the sun, wind, and land in a desert that is not, in fact, empty"?[78] Geographers such as Sharlissa Moore and J. Scheele show that the Sahara is far from empty and in human terms "is perhaps the fastest changing, most dynamic, and wealthiest region of the African continent".[79] Despite its growing population, rapid urbanisation, and development of resources, however, it is still perceived as empty by Western imaginations. If, as Said went on to state, the "struggle is complex and interesting because it is not only about soldiers and cannons but also about ideas, about forms, about images and imaginings", then Raban's decision to leave out the desert in what has become a well-read work of travel literature can be read as propping up, rather than resisting old modes of representation.

Raban spends his time in the great desert cities of Doha, Bahrain, Abu Dhabi, Dubai, Sana'a, Cairo, and Amman, and although the resultant travelogue is, as Peter Whitfield describes it, "a very incomplete survey of its subject", it does at least capture "a new awareness" of an urban landscape arising out of oil production and the politics of black gold.[80] Through a collection of encounters with the people he meets and the stories they have to tell, from taxi drivers to eccentric expatriates, Raban redefines the region as a place not that dissimilar to the country he left behind with the same preoccupations revolving around property ownership, trade deals, concerns over education and legacy, changing family values and stress-related health concerns that occupy people in any fast-growing, urban environment. At face value, the material seems subversive; this after all is no monologism purporting to give an authoritative perspective on Arabia but a polyphonic collection of perspectives drawn from those who live there. On closer inspection, however, Raban's selection of material is globalising in nature and is underpinned by his own distinctively Western agenda. This agenda is led not by the urban experience of the modern Middle East but by the literary legacy from which he is trying to escape.[81] He has read the regional classics by Doughty, Lawrence, and Thesiger and recognises the supposed "vivid, affectionate special relationship between the English and the Arabs" (p. 15) that springs out of their descriptions of alterity: in the desert of the nomad,

88   Desert and sown

Raban writes, previous writers found "a perfect theatre for the enactment of a heroic drama of their own – a drama whose secret subject was not really the desert at all but the decadent life of the London drawing room" (p. 15). Raban's avoidance of desert description can be read, then, as a writing back to the trinity of desert literati. In an interview with Canton, Raban writes, "I'm going to write a kind of 'anti-you' book. No camels; no little brown boys"; this kind of binary bias where the focus of his Arabian travels is artificially stripped of its desert hinterland, therefore, seems less of a "headlong plunge into [Arab] modernity" (p. 35) and more of a gallop away from the London drawing room.[82]

It is easy to be critical of Raban in hindsight, but it is obviously important to remember that he was writing in a specific historical moment; indeed, reading *Arabia Through the Looking Glass* before the popularisation of Said's *Orientalism* (I speak from first-hand experience here) offered a new perspective on the Middle East in travel writing that appeared at the time as fresh and exciting. Raban admires the audacity of the Gulf project, in the building of cities such as Abu Dhabi on a desert sand bar, steel and concrete taking the place of the poverty that belonged to the region's pre-oil history when people in inadequate housing scraped a living from pearling. In this regard, in the lack of nostalgia for an Arabia of unremitting hardship, the text continues to resonate today. "Europeans have idealised the Middle East as an almost timeless place", writes Sandy Isendstadt and Kishwar Rizvi in *Modernism and the Middle East*, "a region that stands in distinct and didactic contrast with the disruptive displacement and disillusionment that has resulted from its own industrialisation", so it is refreshing at one level to read a text that dared to celebrate the process of modernisation through "industrialised building processes and urban infrastructure" that is such an abiding feature of the modern Middle East.[83]

Much has been written on the subject of Arab modernities over the past few decades by Arab social theorists, with Aijaz Ahmad's critique of Said's *Orientalism* laying the foundations for Arab anglophone commentary.[84] As Yasser Elsheshtawy points out in *The Evolving Arab City*, the very words "Arab city" evoke "a multitude of images, preconceptions and stereotypes", and he defines it as "a setting where one can observe the tensions of modernity and tradition; religiosity and secularism; exhibitions and veiling; in short a place of contradictions and paradoxes". He goes on, however, to recognise that these perceived anomalies are largely Western preoccupations that play "into clichés about what constitutes an Arab or Middle Eastern city".[85] While the Arab city is caught between various struggles for modernity, Elsheshtawy states that in essence, it is an expression of the attempt "to ascertain one's place in the twenty-first century".[86] This touches on an entire discourse revolving around globalisation that lies somewhat beyond the scope of this chapter, but if we take Manfred Steger's "*very short* definition of globalisation" as being about "growing worldwide interconnectivity" and reduce it to its most simplistic terms, it is possible to detect in the West a concern regarding cultural homogenisation that is not shared to the same extent in the Middle East.[87] Indeed, the dynamic that involves a combining of the global with the local, or what Roland Robertson terms "glocalisation", has had an arguably invigorating effect on the individual cultures of the region.[88] Jaafar Aksikas offers an accessible way into the subject by describing the growing sense of urgency for modernisation in the region that grew out of the relationship with the West and the challenges of colonialism:

> Arabs developed a certain kind of consciousness of the necessity of modernization and national *nahda* [renaissance][sic]. As time went on, ideologies of national modernisation and renaissance became more and more powerful and more anti-colonial in nature ... these ideologies shared common concerns, which centred on the following issues: anti-imperialism and the search for political independence; the search for unity of all Arabs and/or Muslims; modernity and social development; and cultural authenticity.[89]

Modernisation does not necessarily signify Westernisation, and the key word here is "*nahda*" because it resists the Western binary of traditional and modern in the perception of the Arab Orient by capturing both in the same concept. The sense of rebirth arises out of a strong sense of Arab identity that draws for its inspiration on former periods of enlightenment and strength. The need to invest in cultural authenticity takes inspiration from this past, albeit underpinned by the continuity of Islam, while simultaneously reinventing some of the ways in which this is expressed through a modern, globally accessible cultural iconography. An Arabesque window in a new government building, *mashrabiy'yas* [lattice screens] appearing as motifs on tower blocks, bus stops with crenulations, the locally popular "McArabia" *hilal* burgers, jeans worn under *abeyas* [Gulf women's outer attire], these can all be read as symbols of an assimilation of the past within the present. As Jane Jacobs writes, "Rather than doing away with tradition, globalisation has delivered new conditions for its emergence; installed new mechanisms for its transference; and brought into being new political imperatives for its performance".[90] This is an encouraging thought and can be seen powering the 2040 visions of the Gulf countries in their drive to focus on a new kind of globalised nationhood. There is no locally perceived discrepancy or contradiction, then, in building modernity that both embraces what Gwendolyn Wright refers to as an urban "desert vernacular" inspired by Western preconceptions of an Arab city, while simultaneously promoting processes of indigenisation (replacement of reliance on an expatriate workforce with local Arab human resources).[91] No contradiction, in other words, between the global and the local – except in the texts of Western travel writers who attempt to make sense of it.

90 Desert and sown

Raban is a case in point. Naturally, not all people in the Middle East have embraced the new modernity, and this is something that Raban reflects upon during his journey through Arabia. One of his acquaintances, a playwright in Qatar, laments the loss of the old days when people were more sociable and intimate. An easier life – an urban life – he felt, had arrived at the expense of close community. Raban is surprised to encounter this kind of nostalgia for an austere past, a mythology he thought "peculiarly Western" (p. 117), and comments that it is "one of the privileges of the rich to idolize poverty from a safe distance" (p. 117), and it is significant that the wealthy young Qatari he chats with is too young to have known the hardship involved in a pre-oil Gulf existence. Oil has undisputedly transformed the lives of Arabs – but not of all Arabs equally. Not only are there vast differences in wealth and opportunity for the citizens of an oil-rich nation such as Qatar compared to a country such as Oman, which is of modest income, but there are also differences in the way the wealth is distributed among city and desert dwellers.

Raban's work reflects on the adaptability of the region's inhabitants, and in particular the Bedu, to the rapid change brought about by oil production. Billie Melman argues that the Bedu, such as described by Raban, have become part of an archive in an "urban mock-utopia built with oil money", written out of the landscape through the redundancy of their traditional way of life.[92] This is certainly one reading of the fate of the Bedu in Raban's work, but it is not the only reading. In fact, Raban is at pains to emphasise the modern mobility (social and physical) enjoyed by the Bedu: ostensibly their lives have changed, but fundamentally, the internal structure of their families, their tribal allegiance, their practised nomadism have contributed to settlement but not to their eradication or marginalisation. Describing the Emiratis of Al-Ain, a desert oasis town on the edge of the Empty Quarter, for example, Raban observes the shift in expectation of a Bedu family that has swapped the *bait ish shar* [goat-hair tent] of old for a house of breezeblocks, concrete, and air conditioning:

> Six years away from being desert nomads, they were talking confidently about careers in engineering and medicine; ... they gave every sign of having adapted gracefully to a life in which Modern Tissues, the Range Rover, the twin-tub washing machine, two televisions, floral Thermos flasks, air travel and the local Hilton were taken perfectly for granted.
>
> (p. 141)

This description of the Bedu is unrecognisable as the "lumpenproleteriat" that Thesiger had in mind when he predicted their demise through settlement in shanty towns.[93] State-funded education and inclusion in state-building through representational institutions such as *majlis a'shura*

Desert and sown 91

(lower house of the Omani State Council, or parliament) have helped the Bedu avoid marginalisation and irrelevance in the modern world. This is in encouraging comparison to their marginalisation as described, as we have seen, by earlier writers just half a century earlier. In this sense, Raban writes that the Bedu have "been better prepared for a world of cars and skyscrapers and jet travel than anyone in Europe or the United States", and he goes on to recognise that a city such as modern Abu Dhabi, "with its migrant tribes of exiles, had not made the skills of the desert nomad redundant; rather it was testing and straining them in a way that they had never needed to be so fully exercised before" (p. 146). This "development" is something that Raban attributes to the highly evolved internal social structures of the Bedu, enabling them to be flexible to change, comfortable with strangers, mobile in adverse environments, and ready settlers in favourable environments.

In his estimation of the Bedu's ability to adapt, Raban shows an insight that precedes the more self-reflective studies of later travellers. Indeed, his observations on the Bedu are very similar to those we have already encountered in Michael Asher's work at the end of the century. Nonetheless, *Arabia Through the Looking Glass* is primarily a text designed for Western readers, to challenge Western prejudices. The discussion now turns to a text the appeal of which is deliberately broader and addresses the Middle Eastern context that the author, Tim Mackintosh-Smith, has wholeheartedly embraced as resident Arabist, rather than in which he merely travels.

The desert historicised – Mackintosh-Smith's inverse archaeology

In an email exchange with James Canton, Mackintosh-Smith memorably wrote that travel writers belong to a "sort of Fibonacci sequence" where each influences the other: "I see us all as a series, in which travel becomes Travels and reading the Travels generates more travel, and so on *ad infinitum*. It probably goes all the way back to Gilgamesh".[94] While this, as we have seen, is not exactly an innovative approach in desert literature per se, it is made so in this case as the sequence for this particular author is predicated on a non-Western source. The use of the Old Testament as an inspiration for European travel in the Levant is well documented in pilgrimage literature, including in relatively modern books such as *The Way of a Pilgrim*, but other than this, Western travel writers tend to reference each other rather than focusing on regional or local texts.[95] In *Travels with a Tangerine* (2001), however, Mackintosh-Smith writes a celebrated account of going in search of the fourteenth-century traveller from Tangiers, "Ibn Battutah", whom he affectionately refers to as "IB".[96] While ostensibly writing a footstep account (a term referenced in the extended title: *From Morocco to Turkey in the Footsteps of Islam's Greatest Traveller*), Mackintosh-Smith's choice of a North African,

92 *Desert and sown*

mediaeval, Arabic-speaking Muslim as the inspiration of his journey sets up an immediate and interesting contrast with his footstep contemporaries. In an unpublished email interview, he writes,

> Maybe when you look at the Arab/Arabian/Islamic present through the eyes of someone born 700 years ago who, even if he wasn't Arabian, was culturally Arab and a Muslim, you're getting an unusual and useful perspective. Obviously Arabs/Muslims have changed in many, many ways over that time, but in some ways they haven't changed much; at least, I think it's true to say that they've changed far less than people in say Western Europe.[97]

Generally, footstep travellers in the region lament the changes wrought on the land and culture in the time between the two journeys. Mackintosh-Smith, in contrast, celebrates his experiences in the modern Middle East as proof of the "cultural eternal present" (interview) or as a continuity with the past, thereby shedding the nostalgic or elegiac framework that, as has been demonstrated, is a marked feature of the genre. This is not to level at the text the censure of what Johannes Fabian calls the "denial of coevalness" – the tendency of anthropologists to observe their interlocutors as if they are "Others" that are impervious to change, or which belong to static time rather than existing in the same timeframe.[98] Rather, it is to see in his work the ability to make two timeframes simultaneously relevant – one past, one present.

And then of course there is the 600-year time gap between the first and second journey. Mackintosh-Smith's relationship with Ibn Battuta is not one of competitive positioning but of touching moments of shared experience, established largely through the author's brand of self-deprecating humour.[99] This is particularly significant as Mackintosh-Smith is walking in the footsteps not of a fellow foreigner, but of someone whose religion and culture he does not share. His impressive knowledge of Arab history and the Arabic language helps ameliorate this fact, allowing for a much deeper reflection on the culture of the region than might be afforded otherwise, and indeed, the people the author meets become protagonists in the story, not just decorations of a narrative focusing only on Western preoccupations. This leads to an additional point of contrast between Mackintosh-Smith and other footstep travellers, which justifies his consideration in the present discussion – namely, the focus of his journey, like that of Raban, spans the desert heart of the Middle East but is nonetheless not intrinsically about the desert but upon those who dwell there. Where it is mentioned at all, the desert is incidental. Unlike Raban, however, Mackintosh-Smith's avoidance of the landscape is not a deliberate challenge of Western presentations of Arabia, but more empathetic with local travel patterns where the desert is an inconvenience to be tolerated en route between communities.

Desert and sown 93

The search for signs of Ibn Battuta within these communities functions as a device with which to string together diverse experiences across a number of countries with mediaeval history as the unifying theme; the result, in contrast with most footstep travel, is a focus on tracing continuity in a living past rather than nostalgia for a culture that has been lost. This fascination with the present is demonstrated through Mackintosh-Smith's work, despite the diversions into arcane reference and what he refers to as the "ghostly tread" of his predecessors.[100] The highlights of his journey are those moments when the past is tangibly present, as when he runs into the villager at the tomb of Al-Murshidi, in Upper Egypt, who quotes Ibn Battuta at him:

> As he read, or recited, it seemed that the years which had elapsed since the original visit were insignificant beside the constants of place and memory. I had chanced, I felt, on one of those fragments of existence withdrawn from time.
>
> (p. 68)

As we have seen, travel writing connected with the Arabian desert has a strongly elegiac quality, as epitomised by Thesiger's famous curse on his followers: "If anyone goes there now looking for the life I led they will not find it". Of course, he was referring to a very specific Bedu context, but nonetheless, this is a prevalent and enduring theme. Mackintosh-Smith's work, by contrast, insists on conjunction with rather than disjunction from the age of Ibn Battuta as he traces its continuity with the modern Arab world. In the email exchange with James Canton, the author is explicit about the features that distinguish his work from Thesiger and other writers on the region:

> The place we've written about has changed, since the thirties and forties, in social, political and other ways: but much has stayed the same, and it's that continuity that fascinates me. It's more the case that where I come from has changed – that I bring with me a different cultural kit-bag to the ones my predecessors brought, that I see through a different lens.[101]

Far from eyeing his subjects up in a quasi-anthropological way that is loaded with judgement (as revealed in Raban's surprise that Arabs express nostalgia for a past of hardship), Mackintosh-Smith reverses the gaze and recognises that he is the Other in this spatial and temporal dialogue. By decentring the location of his perspective, he sidesteps the need to compare his observations against those of his own literary forebears, allowing the narrative to become more of, and in, the moment.

The idea of using an aged text to reveal something about modern realities, of finding traces of the past in the customs and manners of the living,

94 *Desert and sown*

is a process that the author refers to as "inverse archaeology" (pp. 252–53). He uses this refractive device to make the point that while Arab culture has a deep conservatism that at times verges on superstition, the frequent referencing of the past in the present is indicative of a deep and satisfying cultural continuity. This sense of continuity is something the author prefigures in his own text:

> At the high noon on the Gulf of Oman, there was almost no shade; just a few crew-cut trees quivering in the heat haze. I turned off the track, made for one of them and lunched on Bombay mix in a meagre fretwork of shadow. Then I opened the *Travels*: "I turned off the road", wrote IB of this same track, "and made for a tree of *umm ghaylan*".
>
> (p. 197)

The apparent simplicity of the incident is nonetheless complex to unpack. On one level, it illustrates Ibn Battuta's text being used as a roadmap through the modern country, in this case of Oman, wherein the author coincidentally makes the same choices after 700 years. The description moves from the sublime to the ridiculous with the throwing in of the Bombay mix, a deliberate leveller that reminds the reader not to take the coincidence too seriously, deflates any sense of pomposity arising from kindred decision-making with the great IB, and emphasises the modern context of the author's own journey (assuming, that is, there was no Bombay mix in Ibn Battuta's time). The impingement of twentieth-century realities on the narrative, the embracing of details that foreground the journey in the present, is in marked contrast with accounts of other footstep travellers who are cautious of mentioning anything modern in case they undermine the authenticity of the footstep enterprise. Such incidents in *Travels with a Tangerine* have a contradictory quality: they telescope the time between the centuries while at the same time emphasise the unreachability of the past. Ibn Battuta is caught in glimpses but, like a mirage, the nearer the author approaches him, the farther away he appears until he dissolves into history. While there are echoes here of the ever-unattainable quest for knowledge that dangles ahead of any journey and that cuts across borders in both Western and Arab cultures, there is also an element of destabilisation of what Roxanne Euben calls "neat oppositions between, for example, the literary and the historical, political theory and *rihla*, Islamic and Western travel".[102] Fragments such as these, together with descriptions of local people rooting out unfamiliar shrines, help combat distorted Western perspectives of contemporary Arab travel as being solely associated with acts of sabotage and terrorism and replace them more positively in the Western imagination with *rihla*, or the travelling in search of knowledge for its own sake rather than as a means to an end.

Desert and sown 95

In common with Ibn Battuta, Mackintosh-Smith keeps his focus firmly on people rather than place throughout *Travels with a Tangerine*. Where he mentions the desert at all, it is a landscape stripped of physical or topographical features. It is true that he describes feeling "suddenly and utterly contented" on finding (near Edfu) all the necessities of desert life – "shade, tobacco and cool water stored in sweating earthenware jars" (p. 121) – but the desert itself is described in negative terms:

> Next morning a lorry of excruciating slowness took me across a minimal, almost a nihilistic landscape – a mere joint between earth and sky, both the colour of plaster. The rare verticals, a milepost or the odd lone bush, assumed enormous significance. At Thumrayt [in Oman] I boarded the minibus.
>
> (p. 220)

Here the desert is not just a contrast to the sown, it is something to be avoided on the ground and in the text; it has an existential quality that inspires and repels, hovering in the background as a psychological space that gives a context to human encounter. It is fitting, then, that in the author's childhood dream, which can be seen as a modern equivalent of William Wordsworth's "Dream of the Arab" in Book V of *The Prelude*, he describes flying over the desert in a telephone box, quintessential emblem of modern communication and time travel that any admirer of modern cult hero, Dr. Who, will recognise. In this dream, Mackintosh-Smith's desert is not one of intrinsic wilderness, but of nomad encampments.[103] His is a social history – a journey about people, not about "empty" landscapes. Hajj, as the biggest example of shared travel on Earth, is the context in which Ibn Battuta's journey is made, and it sets out a very different tradition to the Christian crusade that informs much Western desert literature. Mackintosh-Smith does see some parallels, however, with Western patterns of travel: "For the Maghribis, the whole experience was a sort of Grand Tour: travellers like IB were treading a similar road to the one which eighteenth-century Englishmen, nineteenth-century Americans and the Australasians of today would follow around Europe" (p. 28). He goes on to quote Ibn Jubayr and surmises that Ibn Battuta must have read this Maghribi author before venturing out (p. 30). What is striking here is that the opposition between East and West (*maghrib* in Arabic) is similar to that found in Western literature, but it is an Islamic West, not a Christian West that provides the point of reference. This comparison casts a shadow over the familiar contrast between East and West, suggesting that it is an artificial construct arising out of cultural ignorance and a lack of knowledge of the Arabic language. The author is able to redefine the relationship because, as he is at pains to point out (in the email exchange with Canton), he is fluent in the Arabic language and resident in the region, something he sees as distinguishing him from his predecessors:

96 *Desert and sown*

> [For Thesiger] Arabia was a place where he collected beautiful memories to take away and sigh over. Freya delighted in the strangeness of it all – and I think in her own strangeness in Hadhrami eyes. In contrast to them both, I'm at home here, not a transient, and the "strange" is familiar.[104]

Mackintosh-Smith's ability to feel at home with his subject gives him the confidence to take liberties with the literal truth – something that many modern travel writers to the region are in fear of doing in case it undermines the credibility of the narrative. When questioned about an inventive passage in *Travels with a Tangerine* where Mackintosh-Smith purportedly bumps into someone wearing his old school blazer in the souq in Sana'a, the author comments that the description may have been "very slightly naughty",[105] – "but not a lie".[106] The use of "comic riff", to use Carl Thompson's term, contributes to the general meaning of the moment, even if it may not be literally true.[107] The emblematic wearing of an English blazer by a Yemeni is less about the cloaking of the local in Western preconceptions and more about global commonality, highlighting shared experience. It is the blazer that is described (jackets are a common item of clothing in Yemen), not the *dishdasha* or *wizar* worn underneath, and the focus of the humour is presented at the expense of the author, not at the wearer of the jacket. The jacket becomes, as such, a symbol of the more encouraging face of globalisation, the one that celebrates interdependence and "enhances people's chances to acknowledge their common humanity across arbitrarily drawn political borders and cultural divides".[108] The idea that an English blazer, with its connotation of wealthy public-school ownership, has become available to someone from the "impoverished South" is a welcome reversal of the usual lament regarding the inequalities of globalisation. Furthermore, it reverses the general direction of cultural commodification, albeit in the category of "shirts and shoes" that David Harvey suggests are distinct from other "cultural products and events"; the blazer, with its totemic potential, becomes part of the "highly porous boundary" between the two and in this case takes on the "special character" of the Other.[109] It contributes, in other words, to breaking down reductive binaries.

The playfulness of Mackintosh-Smith's work not only makes it eminently readable in the tradition of modern picaresque adventure, but it also helps to parody the traditionally austere and sonorous literary treatment of the region, in accounts, for example, by Doughty, Thomas, and Palgrave. In so doing, the people and the places he describes take on a more familiar complexion where cultural difference is appreciated and shared humanity emphasised. This makes his writing partially postmodern, at least in the sense identified by Linda Hutcheon who argues that postmodernist parody is a "value-problematizing, de-naturalizing form of acknowledging the history (and through irony, the politics) of

Desert and sown   97

representations".[110] Through parody, Mackintosh-Smith destabilises the status quo of Orientalism by casting doubt on the authority of the authorial "I/eye". In the preface to *Yemen: Travels in Dictionary Land*, Mackintosh-Smith admits that he treads the "thin line between seriousness and frivolity" and that the repeating of "questionable anecdotes" is part of that equation.[111] In this sense, the thin line can be seen not just as the tension between travel literature and fiction but also between Western subject and Oriental object, and Mackintosh-Smith is keen to note throughout *Travels with a Tangerine* that he is no Mandeville or Marco Polo and that the time is long past when travellers "according to the old proverb, might lie by authority" as if they have some command over the truth of cultural representations (p. 215). Naturally, all such refutations help to establish the authority of the text, and ultimately, the reader is left guessing whether the wonders he describes, particularly of coincidence, could in fact be true. On bumping into Moroccans in the *jebel* at Wadi Darbat in Dhofar, Oman, for example, Mackintosh-Smith writes, "I stared at him. In Wadi Darbat, a migrant Tangerine was almost as improbable as a passing penguin" (p. 241). Even more improbably the visitor turns out to have written two papers on Ibn Battuta. In blurring the line between fact and fiction, Mackintosh-Smith finds a fitting objective correlative for Ibn Battuta's world of 1325, "a world of miracles and mundanities, of sultans, scholars, saints and slave-girls, in which outrageous fortune and dubious dragomen … steered a course that lurched between luxury and poverty, asceticism and hedonism" (p. 9). Like T. E. Lawrence, Mackintosh-Smith understands the malleability of history and, in the same way as Anderson recognised Lawrence to be ahead of his time in his manipulation of historical conceit, it is possible to suggest that Mackintosh-Smith is similarly ahead of his time in weaving a history that is multi-perspective in source and yet somehow avoids pastiche.[112] Through similarly avoiding the reproduction of "the past as nostalgia",[113] Mackintosh-Smith shows that history can be used in an interrogative way to arrive at something more prescient and instructive.[114] Creating a sense of Ibn Battuta's world of wonders, then, Mackintosh-Smith consciously problematises the relationship between history and fiction to reveal the inner world of travel, or at least capture insights revealed through the travelling experience that the reader can recognise as fundamentally truthful, even while remaining sceptical of passing penguins.

By way of an example of this kind of productive blurring of history and fiction, it is worth touching on an incident in the Arabian part of *Travels with a Tangerine* that occurs on the Hallaniyat Islands, off the coast of Oman. The author makes the (not altogether unwitting) mistake of calling them the Kuria Muria Islands, and the local sheikh takes him to task over it, entering into a discourse on nomenclature in which he is keen to emphasise the purpose behind the change of name. For the reader, the incident is less interesting for the politics of the name change than for

98   *Desert and sown*

what the incident represents. Indeed, it is impossible not to sympathise with the sheikh who laments the imposition of outmoded labels to describe modern realities merely to suit the sensibilities of the traveller – bringing us back to the Arabia that Raban describes and the pride with which local inhabitants express their new modernity. Mackintosh-Smith is a resident in one of the poorest parts of the Arabian Peninsula as well as a traveller who delights in writing about life in the region's urban metropolises, so he will of course be aware of the semiotics involved in delineating the region with outmoded vocabulary. Significantly, however, he chooses to report on the incident, apocryphal or otherwise, instead of simply correcting the mistake. This allows the reader to choose to extend empathy towards the sheikh of the Hallaniyat Islands, labouring under what he feels is the injustice of misrepresentation, or accept that there could be an alternative configuring of the reality. In other words, the reader is given the opportunity to embrace or reject the portrait of a people that the author describes. In this sense, Mackintosh-Smith moves beyond Orientalism, avoiding what Dallmayr refers to as the "bland assimilationism of a melting-pot cosmopolitanism" where everyone is obliged to use the same definitions in a neatly homogenised cultural production. If, as Dallmayr suggests, "global development can avoid turning into a global nightmare only if it is accompanied by a cultivation of deeper human potentials and aspirations, aspirations foreshadowed in different ways in the plurality of cultural traditions", Mackintosh-Smith's work, that allows for multiple readings of the same subject as seen through the perspective of a Yemeni or an Englishman, a Thesiger or an Ibn Battuta, is surely a cause for optimism.[115]

The work of all five travellers discussed in this chapter has attempted, in Colin Thubron's words, to "humanise the map" of Arabia.[116] Indeed, in their work, it is impossible to separate the desert from those who dwell in it, and it is notable that in a place largely devoid of people, the focus of their work is intensively on the few who do live there, rather than on the landscape itself. It might be thought that the erasure of the desert from their discourse is a belittling device in which the human story colonises the space and allows no room for the landscape to "speak", but this is not the only reading. In some senses, the desert looms all the larger for being just beyond the described – it leaves an intuited impression of, in Raban's term, its "heroic emptiness" (p. 160) or is chased through metaphor in the labyrinths (an Arabic synonym for desert) of town (p. 29). In this sense, the absent landscape foregrounds a kind of Via Negativa, a deconstructive theology that attempts to describe the divine by negation or, to quote Tim Woods, "to speak of God only in terms of what cannot be said about God: both conceive of saying as an *avoidance* of saying something".[117] This returns us to the immutability of the desert space posited by the *Encyclopaedia Britannica* in the opening citation of this discussion, wherein the distinction between desert and sown reinforces old tropes of the Orient that carry with them overtones of discredited ethnography. While bland pseudo-equivalents (for example of desert dweller equating with "noble savage"),[118] have been largely avoided by the writers analysed herein, it is clear that racial stereotyping continues to attach to modern representations of the region, making the "undoing [of] named binaries" all the more important as a task. In the work of Mackintosh-Smith, there are encouraging signs of the productive part of globalisation (or perhaps what Chakravorty Spivak might call "planetarity") that allows for a multiplicity of perspectives which in turn destabilises the authority of one culture as it seeks to know or represent another,[119] but if not all of the five writers considered herein have found a way to challenge all of the stereotypes all of the time, then they are at least to be credited with unpicking some of the binaries – at least some of the time.

Notes

1 *Encyclopaedia Britannica*, cited in Michael Asher, *The Last of the Bedu: In Search of the Myth* (Harmondsworth: Viking, 1996), foreword.

2 Mark Cocker, *Loneliness and Time: The Story of British Travel Writing* (New York: Pantheon, 1993), p. 18.

3 Gertrude Bell, *The Desert and the Sown: Travels in Palestine and Syria* (New York: E.P. Dutton and Co., 1907) and see Rosemary O'Brian, *The Desert and the Sown: The Syrian Adventures of the Female Lawrence of Arabia* (New York: Cooper Square Press, 2001).

4 Cherie J. Lenzen, "The Desert and the Sown: An Introduction to the Archaeological and Historiographic Challenge", *Mediterranean Archaeology*, 16 (2003), 5–12.

5 Donald Powell Cole and Soraya Altorki, *Bedouin, Settlers, and Holiday-Makers: Egypt's Changing Northwest Coast* (Cairo: American University in Cairo Press, 1998), p. 39.

6 Anshuman A. Mondal, *Nationalism and Post-Colonial Identity: Culture and Ideology in India and Egypt* (London: Routledge Curzon, 2003), p. 171.

7 Charles Blackmore, *In the Footsteps of Lawrence of Arabia* (London: Harrap Limited, 1986), p. 142. Two-and-a-half decades later Adrian Hayes similarly writes of disappointment in encountering a gas plant after crossing the Liwa dunes. When his companions suggest the plant represents jobs, Hayes replies, "They didn't see a wilderness spoilt like me; they saw progress and development". Adrian Hayes, *Footsteps of Thesiger* (Dubai: Motivate, 2012), p. 209.

8 Blackmore, *Footsteps of Lawrence*, p. 20.

9 Wilfred Thesiger, *Arabian Sands* [1959] (Harmondsworth: Penguin, 1984), p. 34.

10 See Carl Thompson, "Travel Writing from 1914 to the Present", in *Travel Writing* (Abingdon and New York: Routledge, 2011), pp. 56–61; see also Peter Whitfield, "Post-war English Travel Writing", in *Travel: A Literary History* (Oxford: Bodleian Library, 2012), pp. 263–70.

11 Thompson, *Travel Writing*, p. 57.

12 Sigmund Freud, *Totem and Taboo: Resemblances between the Mental Lives of Savages and Neurotics* [1913] (London: W.W. Norton, 1989), Chapter 1, footnote 2.

100   *Desert and sown*

13 See, for example, Richard Schechner, "Ritual and Performance", in *Companion Encyclopaedia of Anthropology: Humanity, Culture, and Social Life*, ed. by Tim Ingold (London: Routledge, 1994), pp. 613–47 (pp. 635–36).

14 Whitfield, *Travel: A Literary History*, p. 269.

15 Marianna Torgovnick, *Gone Primitive: Savage Intellects, Modern Lives* [1990] (Chicago, IL and London: University of Chicago Press, 1991), p. 8.

16 Anne McClintock, *Imperial Leather: Race, Gender and Sexuality in the Colonial Contest* (New York: Routledge, 1995), p. 30.

17 In preference, Thesiger supported the biography written by life-time companion, Alexander Maitland, *Wilfred Thesiger: The Life of the Great Explorer* (London: Harper Press, 2006).

18 Michael Asher, *Thesiger* (New York: Viking, 1994), pp. 376–87.

19 Peter Brent, *Far Arabia: Explorers of the Myth* (London: Weidenfeld and Nicolson, 1977), p. 228.

20 Hilal Al-Hajri, *British Travel-writing on Oman: Orientalism Reappraised* (Bern: Peter Lang AG, 2006), p. 239. Thesiger noted the contrast between desert travel and life in Britain: "I like keeping the two worlds utterly distinct": Alexander Maitland, "Wilfred Thesiger: Traveller from an Antique Land", *Blackwood's Magazine*, 328 (1980), p. 256.

21 "The Omani national oil company started drilling … in 1958. The first [Bedu] family acquired a truck in 1974 and within five years nearly every family owned at least one vehicle", Alan Keohane, *Bedouin Nomads of the Desert* [1994] (London: Kyle Books, 2011), p. 171.

22 See Robin Bidwell, *Travellers in Arabia* (London: Hamlyn, 1976), p. 93. In contrast, Doughty "never tried … to see the Bedouins … as leading an ideal life of freedom" but "showed the harshness of their lot … [and] their occasional respites".

23 Asher, *Last of the Bedu*, p. 22.

24 Dawn Chatty, *From Camel to Truck: The Bedouin in the Modern World* [1986] (Oxford: White Horse Press, 2013), p. 8.

25 Blackmore, *Footsteps of Lawrence*, p. 16.

26 Asher remarks that Arabs consider the Bedu as "stranded in a 'backward' state, from which the rest of mankind had long since progressed"; he argues this leads governments to condemn the nomadic life as an anachronism from which its victims must be "rescued, and made to settle as farmers". Asher, *Last of the Bedu*, p. 143 and pp. 18–19. See also SueEllen Campbell who writes similarly that, with no respect for borders or visas, nomads are "hard to govern" (p. 234). SueEllen Campbell et al., ed. *The Face of the Earth: Natural Landscapes, Science, and Culture* (Berkeley and Los Angeles, University of California Press, 2011), pp. 233–40.

27 Asher, *Last of the Bedu*, p. 21.

28 Thesiger, *Arabian Sands*, p. 329. While Thesiger equates modern with Western here, he resists the hierarchy of the Orientalist discourse in expressing: "Among no other people have I ever felt the same sense of cultural inferiority".

29 See Jörg Janzen, *Nomads in the Sultanate of Oman: Tradition and Development in Dhofar* (Boulder, Colorado: Westeview, 1986), and Donald Cole, *Nomads of the Nomads: The Al-Murrah of the Empty Quarter* (Chicago: Aldine, 1975). As an example of their adaptability, Asher notes that the Bedu traditionally always travelled with a planting stick in case growing conditions proved favourable. Asher, *Last of the Bedu*, p. 45.

30 Asher regrets, in one of several expressions of belatedness, his abiding memory of the "last of the Nabataeans" will be of watching the Petra Bedu

Desert and sown 101

"sitting glued to a TV set watching a soap opera that presented a pale imitation of a life they had left only a decade before, but to which they would never return" (Asher, *Last of the Bedu*, p. 73).

31 Homi K. Bhabha, *The Location of Culture* (Abingdon and New York: Routledge, 1994), p. 66.

32 Helen Carr, "Modernism and travel (1880–1940)", in *The Cambridge Companion to Travel Writing* [2002], ed. by Peter Hulme and Tim Youngs (Cambridge: Cambridge University Press, 2010), pp. 70–86 (p. 83).

33 Jonathan Raban, *Arabia Through the Looking Glass* [1979] (Glasgow: Fontana, 1980), p. 15.

34 James Buzard, *The Beaten Track: European Tourism, Literature, and the Ways to "Culture" 1800–1918* (Oxford: Clarendon Press, 1993), p. 81.

35 Edward W. Said, *Orientalism* (Harmondsworth: Penguin – Peregrine, 1978), p. 1.

36 Jessica Jacobs, *Sex, Tourism and the Postcolonial Encounter: Landscape of Longing in Egypt* (Farnham: Ashgate Publishing, 2010). Jacobs refers to T. Oakes, "Tourism and the Modern Subject: Placing the Encounter between Tourist and Other", in *Seductions of Place*, ed. by C. Cartier and A. Lew (London and New York: Routledge, 2005), pp. 36–55 and Griselda Pollock who writes that modernity appears to "uproot, deracinate [and] detraditionalise" society.

37 Griselda Pollock, "Territories of Desire: Reconsiderations of an African Childhood Dedicated to a Woman Whose Name Was Not Really 'Julia'", in *Travellers' Tales: Narratives of Home and Displacement*, ed. by G. Robertson et al (London and New York: Routledge, 1994), pp. 61–88 (p. 66).

38 Al-Hajri, *British Travel-Writing*, p. 18. "Renaissance" is a term used in Oman to express the rapid development since 1970 facilitated through oil revenue and sound leadership.

39 Widely read English-language newspapers in the region include *The National, Gulf News, Gulf Today, Khaleej Times* (United Arab Emirates), *Muscat Daily* and *Oman Observer* (Oman), *Arab News* and *Saudi Gazette* (Saudi Arabia), *Gulf Daily News* and *Bahrain Tribune* (Bahrain).

40 See Tarek El-Aris, *Trials of Arab Modernity: Literary Affects and the New Political* (New York: Fordham University Press, 2013).

41 Keohane, *Bedouin Nomads*, preface, p. 7.

42 *Gayatri* Chakravorty Spivak, *Death of a Discipline* (New York: Columbia University Press, 2003), pp. 94–95: Spivak traces a similar "parallel structural contrast – between nature and trade, universality and the nation" in José Martí's work.

43 Chatty, *From Camel to Truck*, p. 8.

44 See geographer Jörg Janzen, *Nomads in the Sultanate of Oman: Tradition and Development in Dhofar* (Boulder, Colorado: Westview Press, 1986), who offers a holistic view of the Bedu (and Jabalis) and settled communities.

45 Author's unpublished interview with Mark Evans, 19 March 2016 and author's unpublished interview with Mohamed Al-Zadjali, 26 April 2016. Al-Zadjali notes that at the time of their expedition "most of the wells are dry, deep or salty".

46 Tim Youngs, *The Cambridge Introduction to Travel Writing* (Cambridge: Cambridge University Press, 2013), p. 68.

47 J. J. Hissey, *Untravelled England* (London: Macmillan, 1906). p. 32. See Esme A. Coulbert, *Perspectives on the Road: Narratives of Motoring in Britain* (unpublished doctoral thesis, Nottingham Trent University, 2013).

48 Cited in Youngs, *The Cambridge Introduction*, p. 70.

102 *Desert and sown*

49 Thesiger, *Arabian Sands*, p. 278.
50 See, for example, "I would not myself have wished to cross the Empty Quarter in a car. Luckily this was impossible when I did my journeys". Thesiger, *Arabian Sands*, pp. 278–79.
51 Ali Behdad, *Belated Travelers: Orientalism in the Age of Colonial Dissolution* (Durham: Duke UP, 1994), p. 35.
52 John Urry and Jonas Larsen, *The Tourist Gaze 3.0* [1990] (London: Sage Publications, 2011). Blackmore writes, for example, "I stand holding the rein of Hashan [his camel] and take in the scene. A bright red and yellow juggernaut passes over a fly-over above the old railway half a mile away that I had not seen. The illusion dissolves". Blackmore, *Footsteps of Lawrence*, p. 50.
53 Barbara Toy, *Travelling the Incense Route: From Arabia to the Levant in the Footsteps of the Magi* [1968] (London: Tauris Parke, 2009) and Ralph A. Bagnold, *Libyan Sands: Travels in a Dead World* [1935] (London: Eland Publishing, 2010).
54 Fiona Tarrant, "Queen of the Desert" [online], *Oxford Mail* (1998), available at: https://web.archive.org/web/20140201102033/http://www.oxford mail.co.uk/archive/1998/09/29/6638325.Queen_of_the_desert/?ref=arc [accessed 13 July 2019].
55 Toy, *Travelling the Incense Route*, p. 1. The tendency to anthropomorphise the car in desert literature is a common trope; Bagnold writes, for example, "[E]ach driver should be his own vet to diagnose and cure any car ailment", Bagnold, *Libyan Sands*, p. 29.
56 Coulbert, *Perspectives on the Road*, p. 57.
57 Al-Hajri, *British Travel-Writing*, p. 266.
58 Arabic time (in which the new day begins at sunset) is still in use in mosques and remote parts of the Peninsula; for a description of this form of time-keeping, see James Budd, *Half Past Ten in the Afternoon: An Englishman's Journey from Aneiza to Makkah* (London: Arabian Publishing, 2014), pp. 9–10.
59 Hans-Georg Gadamer, quoted in Fred Dallmyr, *Beyond Orientalism: Essays in Cross-Cultural Encounter* (Albany: State University of New York Press, 1996), p. xv.
60 Edward Said, cited by Dallmyr, *Beyond Orientalism*, p. xvii.
61 Henry Hemming, *Misadventure in the Middle East: Travels as Tramp, Artist and Spy* (London: Nicholas Brealey Publishing, 2007) and Lois Pryce, *Revolutionary Ride: On the Road in Search of the Real Iran* (London: Nicholas Brealey Publishing, 2017).
62 James (now Jan) Morris, *Sultan in Oman* [1957] (London: Eland, 2008), p. 13; the valorisation of off-road adventure is another common trope; Edward Henderson, for example, writes, "The journey in those days was of considerable interest as there were then very few vehicles ... [and] there were no roads". Edward Henderson, *Arabian Destiny: The Complete Autobiography* (Dubai: Motivate, 1999), p. 46.
63 M. Awad, "Settlement of Nomads and Semi-Nomadic Groups in the Middle East", *Ekistics*, 7, no. 42 (1959), 338–43.
64 Chatty, *From Camel to Truck*, p. 20.
65 Homi K. Bhabha, *The Location of Culture* (Abingdon and New York: Routledge, 1994), p. 1.
66 Al-Hajri, *British Travel-Writing*, p. 251.
67 Thesiger, *Arabian Sands*, p. 279.
68 Thompson, *Travel Writing*, p. 138.

Desert and sown 103

69 Asher, *Last of the Bedu*, p. 174.
70 Neil Richardson and Marcia Dorr, *The Craft Heritage of Oman* (Dubai: Motivate Publishing, 2003), Vol II, p. 518.
71 Henderson, *Arabian Destiny*, p. 115 and p. 262.
72 Coulbert, *Perspectives on the Road*, p. 80.
73 El-Aris, *Trials of Arab Modernity*, p. 81.
74 Interview (12 June 2007), in Canton, *From Cairo to Baghdad*, p. 246.
75 Reina Lewis, *Gendering Orientalism: Race, Femininity and Representation* (Abingdon: Routledge, 1996), p. 240.
76 Said, *Orientalism*, p. 55.
77 Edward W. Said, *Culture and Imperialism* [1993] (New York: First Vintage Books, 1994), p. 7.
78 Sharlissa Moore, *Sustainable Energy Transformations, Power and Politics: Morocco and the Mediterranean* (Abingdon: Routledge, 2019), Chapter 4.
79 J. Scheele, *Smugglers and Saints of the Sahara* (Cambridge: Cambridge University Press, 2012), p. 7.
80 Whitfield, *Travel: A Literary History*, p. 273.
81 Raban, in interview with James Canton, *From Cairo to Baghdad*, pp. 245–53. Raban describes Lawrence, Doughty, and Thesiger, all of whom appear in *Arabia Through the Looking Glass*, as "figures to rebel against", p. 246.
82 Canton, *From Cairo to Baghdad*, p. 246.
83 Sandy Isendstadt and Kishwar Rizvi, eds., *Modernism and the Middle East: Architecture and Politics in the Twentieth Century* (Seattle: University of Washington Press, 2008), p. 3.
84 Aijaz Ahmad, "Orientalism and After: Ambivalence and Metropolitan Location in the Work of Edward Said", in *In Theory: Classes, Nations, Literatures* (London: Verso, 1992).
85 Yasser Elsheshtawy, ed. *The Evolving Arab City: Tradition, Modernity and Urban Development* [2008] (Abingdon: Routledge, 2011).
86 Elsheshtawy, *The Evolving Arab City*, p. 4.
87 Manfred B. Steger, *Globalization: A Very Short Introduction* [2003] (Oxford: Oxford University Press, 2017), p. 17.
88 See Roland Robertson, *Globalization: Social Theory and Global Culture* (London: Sage, 1992).
89 Jaafar Aksikas, *Arab Modernities: Islamism, Nationalism, and Liberalism in the Post-Colonial Arab World* (New York: Peter Lang, 2009), p. 5.
90 Jane Jacobs, "Tradition is (Not) Modern", *The End of Tradition?*, ed. by Nezar AlSayyad (London and New York: Routledge, 2004), pp. 29–44 (p. 32).
91 Gwendolyn Wright, "Global Ambition and Local Knowledge", in *Modernism and the Middle East*, ed. by Isendstadt and Rizvi, pp. 221–54 (p. 236).
92 Billie Melman, "The Middle East/Arabia: 'the cradle of Islam'", in *The Cambridge Companion to Travel Writing*, ed. by Peter Hulme and Tim Youngs (Cambridge: Cambridge University Press, 2002), pp. 112–19 (p. 119).
93 Melman, "Middle East/Arabia", p. 118. Thesiger wrote that urbanised Bedu lost their values and became "a parasitic proletariat squatting around oil-fields in the fly-blown squalor of shanty towns", Thesiger, *Arabian Sands*, p. 87.
94 Canton, *From Cairo to Baghdad*, p. 238.
95 Anonymous, *The Way of a Pilgrim and The Pilgrim Continues his Way* [1930] translated by R. M. French (San Francisco: Harper and Row, 1952).
96 Ibn Battuta is referred to in this book using the more common transliteration of the traveller's name – namely, without the concluding "h".

104   *Desert and sown*

97 Author's unpublished email interview with Tim Mackintosh-Smith, 22 March 2016.

98 Johannes Fabian, *Time and the Other: How Anthropology Makes Its Object* (New York: Columbia University Press, 1983), p. 31.

99 Mackintosh-Smith writes, "I love bathos, and IB is bathos personified, with a measure of pathos here and there too". Author's unpublished email interview with Tim Mackintosh-Smith, 22 March 2016. A master of bathos himself, Mackintosh-Smith writes, for example, on encountering a moray eel: "'It bites really hard,' they told me, 'specially when it sees something red.' I looked at its nutcracker jaws and made a mental note never to swim in Omani waters wearing red bathing trunks". Tim Mackintosh-Smith, *Travels with a Tangerine* [2001] (New York: Random House, 2004), p. 199.

100 Canton, *From Cairo to Baghdad*, pp. 242–43.

101 Canton, *From Cairo to Baghdad*, p. 238.

102 Roxanne L. Euben, *Journeys to the Other Shore: Muslim and Western Travelers in Search of Knowledge* (Princeton, NU: Princeton University Press, 2006), p. 15.

103 By way of explanation as to why so few references to the landscape occur in either Ibn Battuta's or his own work, Mackintosh-Smith suggests, "To write about deserts in Arabic you have to be a poet, which [IB] wasn't (and neither am I)". Author's unpublished email interview with Tim Mackintosh-Smith, 22 March 2016.

104 Canton, *From Cairo to Baghdad*, p. 239.

105 Canton, *From Cairo to Baghdad*, p. 241.

106 Author's unpublished email interview with Tim Mackintosh-Smith, 22 March 2016.

107 Thompson, *Travel Writing*, p. 89. Some modern travel writers, Thompson asserts, "claim … the authority of fiction, and by so doing side-step the requirement that they be strictly truthful in their reporting".

108 Steger, *Globalization*, p. xvii.

109 David Harvey, "The Art of Rent: Globalization, Monopoly and the Commodification of Culture", *Socialist Register 2002: A World of Contradictions*, 38 (2002), 93–110 (p. 93).

110 Linda Hutcheon, *The Politics of Postmodernism* (London: Routledge, 1989), p. 94.

111 Tim Mackintosh-Smith, *Yemen: Travels in Dictionary Land* [1997] (London: John Murray, 2007), Prefatory Note.

112 Scott Anderson, *Lawrence in Arabia: War, Deceit, Imperial Folly and the Making of the Modern Middle East* [2013] (New York: Anchor Books, 2014), p. 3.

113 Tim Woods, *Beginning Postmodernism* [1999] (Manchester: Manchester University Press, 2009), p. 69. Mackintosh-Smith's work displays features of postmodernism, including the presentation of "negatives and absences" (Ibn Battuta is not of course real as a companion); its aesthetic presentations of commodities (the Bombay mix), and the subversion of elitist culture (he makes an ancient travel tome written by a Islamic scholar accessible). See William Burroughs, *The Naked Lunch* [1959], ed. by James Grauerholz and Barry Miles, New York: Grove Press, 2001) for more on postmodern "negatives and absences" in general.

114 See Wood, *Beginning Postmodernism*, pp. 69–70 and his reference to Frederic Jameson, and to Linda Hutcheon's *The Politics of Postmodernism* (London: Routledge, 1989).

115 Fred Dallmayr, *Beyond Orientalism: Essays in Cross-Cultural Encounter* (New York: State University Press, 1996), p. xxii.
116 Colin Thubron, "Don't forget your toothbrush" [online], *The Guardian* (2000), available at: https://www.theguardian.com/books/2000/sep/23/travel.travelbooks [accessed 15 July 2019].
117 Woods, *Beginning Postmodernism*, p. 57.
118 The noble savage trope arose out of a concept popularised since the earliest European contact with indigenous Americans but has been adopted to characterise all those from a perceived "primitive" society in contrast with the city dweller who is equated with "the civilised".
119 Spivak, *Death of a Discipline*, p. 92 and p. 72.

3 Gendering the desert
Women and desert narratives

In the first chapter of *The Road to Ubar: Finding the Atlantis of the Sands* (1998), Nicholas Clapp places his wife, Kay, right beside him – not just on the plane to Muscat "her face pressed to the window", looking out on a destination in which they are both about to invest equal time and energies but also in his narrative of the expedition to find the lost city of Ubar.[1] This is in contrast to Clapp's fellow expeditioner, Ranulph Fiennes, whose own wife Ginnie is given the proverbial back seat. In *Atlantis of the Sands*, the minimisation of Ginnie Fiennes's role in her husband's account reflects no lack of interest, involvement in the expedition, or aptitude – she is after all involved in the original idea (p. 91), early planning (p. 94), and on-site logistics (p. 215), and she at length emerges from obscurity in an understated paragraph where Fiennes notes that she was the first woman to receive the Polar Medal. The same paragraph reveals that Ginnie Fiennes was also the first woman permitted into "the hallowed male portals of the Antarctic Club".[2] This information comes as a surprise to the reader, as she is barely acknowledged in the rest of the account of their travels, despite the attested closeness of their relationship.[3] If there are reasons why Ginnie is not brought to the fore in Fiennes's text, these are not given, and her own successes as an explorer receive only one other mention: the reader learns that she was to be honoured for her achievements as an explorer at the Antarctic Club's annual dinner, but Fiennes admits, "I managed to make a dreadful mix up in my diary and we failed to attend" (p. 135).

This dispiriting passage in *Atlantis of the Sands* begins to suggest the extent to which women are often erased from the text in the male-dominated accounts of wilderness exploration in general and in the genre of Arabian desert travel in particular. As shown by the accounts of modern footstep travellers in the region, such as those of Charles Blackmore, Bruce Kirkby, and Adrian Hayes, while they may make a mention in passing of women travellers among the distinguished sequence of explorers in which their own travels are contextualised, they do not dwell on the exploits of women travellers as if to do so may undermine the inherent authenticity of the endeavour and blunt its competitive, masculine edge. The historical

DOI: 10.4324/9781003197201-4

Gendering the desert   107

reasons for this are somewhat predictable; as Carl Thompson points out, "[A] common yardstick for demonstrating and asserting masculinity in travel has been the degree of danger and discomfort involved in the journey. The greater the risk and the difficulty, obviously, the more manly and heroic a traveller seems".[4] By extension, place a woman in the arena of extreme experience, and all the attendant challenges become lesser benchmarks of endurance. This is no newly observed phenomenon in desert literature: Colin Thubron in reviewing Michael Asher's biography of Wilfred Thesiger, spells it out: "This is a warrior's arena. Women are absent from it",[5] while Roslynn Haynes, in her cultural study on deserts, similarly determines it to be "a highly gendered space" where women "are absent, or hardly even referred to".[6] Where women do appear in male desert texts, they are generally present not as Western co-expeditioners but as Arab objects of male fantasy, consistent with old Orientalist tropes, or simply glossed over as a subject beyond the scope of the writer's gaze. This chapter seeks to contribute to the redressing of this imbalance by probing several strands of the "highly gendered space" within the genre of desert writing in order not just to pay tribute to women's travels in the region but also to amplify the wider cultural significance of their contribution.

The first part of this chapter begins by considering, in general terms, how and why women feature so minimally in the subgenre of Arabian desert travel literature and looks at whether the literature that they do write shares the same "position of enunciation" as that written by men.[7] While the discussion examines contemporary attempts at reappraisal of a female literary legacy in travel writing as a whole, it does so through the examination of women's travels in Arabia in particular and considers whether any change of register occurring in women's texts arises as a result of differences in experience rather than of gender. The chapter goes on to suggest some of the ways in which modern women travellers present a broader narrative of the region by virtue of their access to the domestic part of Arab culture normally hidden from men, but while their field of vision is guided by the type of experience they encounter, this does not necessarily mean that they speak a different language, have a lesser or greater insight, or are any the less impacted by the Oriental inheritance articulated by their male travelling counterparts.

The second part of the chapter traces the way Arab women have typically been presented in both male and female travel literature in the region. This precedes an examination of modern travel accounts by women writers who each embrace a distinctly feminocentric project in their writing by virtue of their chosen subject matter. For reasons that will be made clear, there are few works to choose from, but each of the women commentators selected for discussion (Adrienne Brady, Jean Sasson, Geraldine Brooks, Marguerite van Geldermalsen, and the photographer Helen Couchman) formulate an agenda with which they challenge, document, or collude in the traditional perception of the Arabian desert as

108   *Gendering the desert*

delineated by their male counterparts. These modern texts, all written in the past two decades, bear little in common with one another, and some stretch the definition of travelogue, but their inclusion in this discussion reveals whether the articulation of a counter-discourse based on gender represents a meaningful distinction within desert literature.

Running through many women's texts that focus on the region is a tension between the heroic and the domestic, the wild and the tame – themes traditionally of masculinity and femininity. In this context, the landscape provides not just a backdrop to the gendered space of desert travel literature but is also included in the act of linguistically gendering that space. To examine to what extent and purpose the desert is anthropomorphised, the discussion concludes by seeking parallels of the wilderness trope among three women's desert texts from beyond the immediate region (Robyn Davidson's *Tracks* (1980), Sara Wheeler's *Terra Incognita: Travels in Antarctica* (1996), Jay Griffiths's *Wild: An Elemental Journey* (2006), and, albeit tangentially, Jo Tatchell's *Diamond in the Desert* (2009)).

If, as June Hannam suggests, feminism can be taken to mean "a set of ideas that recognise in an explicit way that women are subordinate to men and seek to address imbalances of power between the sexes", then this chapter takes a feminist approach in concurring with much modern criticism that "women's voices should be heard"; in texts where they are not heard, then it is reasonable to ask the question as to what this implies of the desert literature under scrutiny.[8] In finding answers to that question, feminism and postcolonialism are seen to resonate or share common ground as notions of patriarchy (defined by John McLeod as "those systems – political, material, and imaginative – which invest power in men and marginalise women") are problematised by the relationship between first and so-called third world contexts.[9]

Where are the women? Western women's travels in Arabia

Even a brief survey of desert literature prompts the question: "Where are the women?" Although, as Nabil Matar reminds us, Muslim women have travelled from West Africa, Turkey, and India to Mecca and Medina for centuries, none appear in the Arabic language travel accounts of their husbands let alone in published written records of their own.[10] There are scarcely more accounts of the region by or featuring women in the English language. According to Edward Said, an estimated 60,000 books were written in English about the near East between 1800 and 1950, many of which, including the classics by J. L. Burckhardt, Richard Burton, Wilfrid Scawen Blunt, Charles M. Doughty, T. E. Lawrence, and Wilfred Thesiger, focused specifically on the Arabian Peninsula.[11] Many of these authors became household names to the reading public of the nineteenth and early twentieth centuries but, with the notable exception of Gertrude Bell and Freya Stark, few Western women appear in these accounts, and fewer

Gendering the desert   109

authored accounts of their own. Indeed, the absence of women in the body of desert literature associated with the region is so pronounced that it has become, according to Haynes, part of "desert mythology".[12] But to recognise there have been few visible women desert travellers is not to say there have been none. As Carl Thompson notes of travel literature as a whole, "women have in fact been prolific producers of travelogues, especially in the nineteenth and twentieth centuries".[13] In desert literature, their texts were overshadowed by the dominant male discourse until projects like Lesley Blanch's *The Wilder Shores of Love* brought a new critical interest to women's travel writing on the region. First published in 1954, this work established a fashion for group biographies of Eastern-bound women and prefigured the current appetite for a rehabilitation of this group of travellers reflected across the field of global travel literature as a whole. Anthologies such as Mary Morris's *Maiden Voyages* (1993), Jane Robinson's *Unsuitable for Ladies* (1994), and Dea Birkett's *Off the Beaten Track: Three Centuries of Women Travellers* (2004), which accompanied an exhibition of the same name at the National Portrait Gallery in London in 2004, all include accounts by women of travels through the deserts of the Middle East and, together with Virago's reprinting of women's travel literature, have helped champion a greater visibility of women's contributions to the genre.

As these anthologies show, Western women have been travelling and writing on the region since the fourth century when the Galician pilgrim Egeria, who numbers among the earliest Westerners to write of travels in the Middle East, recorded her journey to the region's Christian sites in letters home to the nuns of her sisterhood.[14] Although it was commonly assumed in subsequent centuries that women could not physically endure the privation of extreme wilderness travel and "must be protected from nature and bandits alike",[15] the travails of Lady Mary Wortley Montagu in the early eighteenth century and Lady Hester Stanhope in the early nineteenth demonstrated that women were more than equal to the task, and the difficulty shifted from "cannot" to "should not" as the century progressed. Nonetheless, there was never a point at which women "did not" travel to the region, and the list of Victorian female endeavour in desert lands during the nineteenth century was impressive, resulting in works on archaeology in the Holy Land published in 1846 (Lady Hester Stanhope), convalescence and letter-writing in Egypt in the 1860s (Lady Lucie Duff-Gordon), horse-breeding in the Nejd in the 1880s (Lady Anne Noel Blunt), administration as wives to noted Arabists and specialists in their own right (Isabel Burton and Mabel Bent in the last two decades of the nineteenth century, and Violet Dickson and Doreen Ingrams in the first half of the twentieth century), and even butterfly-collection and lovemaking in the Lebanon at the end of the Victorian era (Margaret Fountaine).[16]

The achievements of these women can be reckoned not just in terms of their endeavours but in the fact that they made their journeys at all.

110   *Gendering the desert*

Travelling beyond Europe, especially "without escort, chaperon, or husband", was perceived, according to Mary Morris, as a dubious activity that put women physically and morally at risk.[17] Constrained by the presumed perils of travel and by norms that, as Tim Youngs identifies, associated "travel with masculinity", and "stasis and domesticity with the feminine", women travellers to Arab lands were in some senses performing an act of trespass into distinctly male territory.[18] The few who, like Fountaine, strayed across the threshold of exploration, situated as it is at the far end of the travel continuum, either attracted social opprobrium or feared for their reputations on returning to polite society, sensing that they were engaging in activities that were not wholly "proper or befitting to [their] station in life".[19] A ditty in *Punch* addressed to the Royal Geographical Society (RGS) at the end of the nineteenth century shows their concerns were well-founded:

> A Lady an explorer? A traveller in skirts?
> The notion's just a trifle too seraphic:
> Let them stay and mind the babies, or hem our ragged shirts;
> But they mustn't, can't and shan't be geographic.[20]

Written in 1893 at around the time the RGS was debating the inclusion of women among its membership (and about the time Fountaine was beginning her considerations on free love as a precursor to the chosen context of her entomological expeditions in Syria a decade later), the verse has a menacing undertone that makes it clear that women are welcome neither in the field as expeditioners nor in the journals and proceedings as authors. The *Times Literary Supplement* of 1907 lamented that "delicately-nurtured women" have ceased to be a "*rara avis*", in traversing "sandy deserts"; the same paper later asserted in 1912 that no "piece of actual exploration of the first importance has yet been accomplished by a woman".[21] This rejection of female endeavour in a hitherto male enterprise is in contrast to the evidence supplied by the women themselves; Fountaine alone contributed one of the best records of *diurnal lepidoptera* of the period.[22] Rejection of women in the field is also mirrored in the history of the RGS itself which only finally admitted women in 1913, despite their initially being proposed for membership in 1887, and only after four failed attempts and one reversal of decision, 83 years after the society was founded.[23]

Margaret Fountaine's *Love among the Butterflies* makes a significant contribution not only to the field of Lepidoptera but also to the genre of desert travel writing as her book is suggestive of a new kind of female travel in the region. In common with the writing by her contemporaries, Isabella Bird and Mary Kingsley, in other parts of the world, Fountaine's journeys are propelled by the hitherto largely masculine goal of science, and it is significant that she describes her scientific inclination arising

Gendering the desert   111

directly from her nature: "I was a born naturalist, though all these years for want of anything to excite it, it had lain dormant within me".[24] Fountaine's various romantic encounters represent an act of editorial selection by her male editor, W. F. Cater, from a diary of "well over a million words". By focusing on these intimacies at the expense of her intellectual output, Cater repositions Fountaine in the more familiar female camp of romance rather than risking her representation in the male camp of geography. Fountaine remained unpublished, in accordance with her wishes, for exactly 100 years from the date of the diary's commencement. As one of only a handful of scholarly commentators on Fountaine's work, James Canton posits that the notion of unmarried intimacy between an English woman and an Arab man meant that her travelogue was destined to be only ever a "distinctly ... personal confession, not written for an audience".[25] While it is possible that the 100-year embargo may have been put in place to protect family members, this interpretation is hard to reconcile with a narrative that is celebratory and in Fountaine's own words, "far from feeling ashamed";[26] whatever the intention, the theatricality of the hundred-year embargo functions both as an act of "heroic self-fashioning" as good as any male attempt at the same, and an acknowledgement of Fountaine's own modernity as she waits for social norms to catch up.[27] Fountaine could have simply burnt the diaries, or given instructions for their destruction, but this would also have meant destroying the methodically curated knowledge of insect habitat that the diaries also contain and the destruction of knowledge is too high a price to pay, one suspects, for the sake of protecting a reputation Fountaine is only partly interested in maintaining.

Fountaine's concern for knowledge, hitherto perceived as the preserve of men, hints at the professionalism of later generations of women travellers, as they find reasons to travel in the region – engaged, for example, in the assumed masculine pursuits of political administration and nation-building as undertaken by Gertrude Bell in Iraq, religious exploration and conversion to Islam as illustrated by Isabelle Eberhardt in the Magreb, cartography that Freya Stark carried out in Yemen, and exploration by Rosita Forbes in North Africa. While women travellers in the region gradually became better accepted and some even admired in the early twentieth century, difficulties in access replace social opprobrium as the major impediment to travel, with the conservatism of many of the countries in the Middle East creating the perception of an unfavourable climate for Western women travellers, particularly those travelling alone.[28] Institutional hurdles, put in place by regional governments in their attempt partly to guard against a perceived dilution of culture through gender interaction, have until relatively recently further limited the access of Western women to the region; strict visa regulations forbidding the entry of women to much of Arabia, for example, except in specific circumstances related to employment or the accompanying of an

112 *Gendering the desert*

employed husband, remained in place in parts of the Peninsula until the 2020s. In addition, widespread war and conflict have largely sealed off much of Southern Arabia to all travellers regardless of gender, except those who are employed in a military or humanitarian capacity. It is largely for these practical reasons that so few desert travel accounts by women have emerged from the region in recent decades. There are a few notable early exceptions, including Jan Morris (although this is complicated by the fact that she travelled at the time as James), Barbara Toy, and Ethel Mannin (whose "Arabian" work is confined to Palestine).[29] Among the few more recent women writers to the region, most have tended to engage with desert travel as a context for socio-ethnographic accounts, journalism, and expatriate tourism.

While they may be few in number, then, women have nonetheless contributed richly to the diversity of travel literature pertaining to the region, and while it is tempting to categorise their output as a form of hybrid or alternative voice that lies outside the established and essentially male tradition of desert literature, this also does them a disservice, ensuring their work remains forever a postscript to the perceived main event. As Susan Bassnett points out, this often unwitting marginalisation has nonetheless been a common approach by many reviewers.[30] The titles of early anthologies of women's travel texts alone – including *Unsuitable for Ladies*, *Maiden Voyages*, and *Off the Beaten Track* – show the extent to which the focus is on the exceptional among women travellers, foregrounding only the more unusual, eccentric, or adventurous accounts and omitting those texts which may seem more mainstream or mundane. Dea Birkett, for example, states that women are "rarely as we expect them to be. They surprise us still", and even in the twenty-first century, a former BBC journalist is able to describe Lady Hester Stanhope as brave but mad in a piece entitled "Great British Nutters":[31]

> In an age when most upper-crust women couldn't fart without a chaperone, Lady Hester was charging around the Middle East on an Arab stallion, dressed as a bloke. She went where she wanted and did as she pleased. Her ladyship was a law unto herself.[32]

"A law unto herself" is the dominant discourse within which women travellers to the region have been considered, their journeys and their writing described as eccentric, breaking the mould, not entirely female, and certainly not feminine.[33] Women, it has been argued by some critics, including Debbie Lisle, must adopt the register of men in order to be heard and therefore cease to become typical of their gender. Lisle detects "a masculine, rational and aggressive organising scheme" in their work that "writes over feminine characteristics in the self and in others".[34] It could be argued, however, that at the heart of the project to evaluate women's travel writing as a species of transgendered discourse (in that

Gendering the desert 113

women are presented as assuming the characteristics of male discourse) is the suggestion that women have been obliged to borrow from a male register and that this voice is not their own. This in turn suggests that there is an unborrowed reality lurking under the surface of their travelling and writing that is intrinsically different from that of their male counterparts. A reassessment of women's travel writing, however, has been underway in some quarters since Shirley Foster and Sara Mills attempted to edit a different kind of anthology, entitled in an appropriately anodyne manner as *An Anthology of Women's Travel Writing* (2002). In this volume, Foster and Mills challenge the implicit notion that women's travel writing is eccentric by arguing that it is only made to seem so through the kinds of writing selected to illustrate the point. They show convincingly that the eccentric female traveller must be seen "as only one of a range of different roles which women travellers could and did adopt".[35] Despite this pioneering work, the notion of essential difference is a recalcitrant one that carries with it an inherent hierarchy affecting women not just as travellers but as writers too.

"Pay, pack and follow" – Women as desert writers

Robin Bidwell's comprehensive account, *Travellers in Arabia* (1976), refers to a few key female figures (such as Mary Wortley Montagu, Isabel Burton, Gertrude Bell, and Freya Stark) among the several hundred male travellers covered in his chronology but none earn a whole chapter, despite their contribution to the literature of Middle Eastern exploration. Similarly, in their list of major explorations in Arabia published in 1978, Zara Freeth and Victor Winstone note 56 distinct journeys, only four of which were undertaken by a total of three women – again none of whom earns a whole chapter. Two of the most famous Arabists, Richard Burton and Wilfrid Scawen Blunt, travelled frequently with their wives, and these women in turn played a significant role in their husbands' literary output: despite this, they are generally not accorded the title "Arabist" in their own right by biographers. Indeed, even in 1990, Kathryn Tidrick is able to dismiss Anne Isabella Noel Blunt as a "reliable but unimaginative companion" on her husband's journeys; Tidrick goes on to condemn Lady Anne's published accounts as "rather pedestrian narratives", mere preludes to the important work found in Wilfrid Scawen Blunt's own diaries, which form the main focus of Tidrick's discussion.[36] This is a harsh criticism of work that is fresh with lived experience, full of carefully observed detail, and infused with a genuine delight in the desert.[37] Tellingly, Blunt's style, as Freeth and Winstone point out, is "admirably clear and easy for the modern reader" – a comment not entirely intended, it seems, as a compliment.[38]

Ali Behdad identifies the way in which the "project of exotic adventure, as Victor Segalen has remarked, can only be singular and individualistic – and ... masculine". The female companion plays the role of "the observer,

114　*Gendering the desert*

the sketcher, and the recorder", the "deheroicised female witness".[39] Similarly, Lady Anne's contemporary, Isabel Burton, struggles to be known as anyone other than the woman who wrote a biography of her husband, Sir Richard Burton, and who horrified generations of subsequent Arabists by "sorrowfully, reverently, and in fear and trembling" consigning his journals to the fire.[40] The sense of "irreparable loss" threads through the description of the event by the biographer, Lesley Blanch, who surmises in *Wilder Shores of Love* (1954) that Isabel Burton has acted not in accordance with her husband's wishes as his executor but out of implied insignificant concerns for his reputation and through marital jealousy provoked by the time he spent away from her:

> It was these hidden, mysterious aspects of his life in the East of which she was jealous. She had always stood beside him, her presence belying the insinuations; now in death, she saw her chance. His name should live on, untarnished. She would protect the legend from the man.[41]

Isabel Burton is reduced in Blanch's assumption of her motives to a malignant or at best misguided caretaker of knowledge – of the "fruits of a lifetime's adventure and study" – whose only role is to execute decisions already taken and to "pay, pack and follow" her husband.[42] Burton's judicious destruction of a man's texts is portrayed by Blanch as a form of suffocating and posthumous mothering that tames the masculine endeavour of scientific understanding and makes it impotent and ungodlike – a cross-gendered fall from a garden of Eden perhaps:

> Isabel acted towards Burton very much as England was then acting towards the East. She colonized him. To Burton's East, she became the managing West, civilizing, refining, elevating, protecting, suppressing ... and her burning of his journal was the ultimate gesture of conquest.
>
> (p. 11)

Blanch states that with that deed, the "great and baffling character of Richard Burton vanished for ever" (p. 124), whereas, in fact, the deed helped fashion that character, allowing for the immodesties of speculation to replace circumscribing fact. Contrary to Blanch's assessment, then, the legacy of the "great and baffling character of Richard Burton" profited handsomely from the intimation of knowledge lost.

In focusing on the impact of the wife upon the hero husband's legacy, Isabel Burton's role as generator of knowledge in her own right (as writer of *The Inner Life of Syria, Palestine and the Holy Land* (1875) and in the studies she makes in *A.E.I. (Arabia, Egypt, India,* 1879)) is overshadowed. Indeed, Blanch and Tiddrick both treat their accomplished female subjects as a sideline to the main male project: in this, they conform to the pattern that Behdad identifies, where the man is presumed to fulfil the authorative role of Orientalist, while the woman is marginalised as incidental or a mere adjunct in the dominant business of Othering.[43] Said set the tone for this critical oversight in *Orientalism* – a work that many critics have, according to Geoffrey Nash, "found lacking from a gender point of view".[44] Said notes that in male writing associated with the East, "women are usually the creatures of a male power-fantasy. They express unlimited sensuality, they are more or less stupid, and above all they are willing", but Said does not interrogate women's writing to establish whether women resort to the same stereotypes and, through this omission, he contributes to their continued erasure from the Orientalist discourse.[45]

More recent feminist theorists such as Lisa Lowe, Sara Mills, and Billie Melman – whose book, *Women's Orients*, rescues many women writers from obscurity – have addressed the gaps left in Said's work.[46] In analysing how colonial discourses are "multiple, precarious, contested and more ambivalent than Said conveys in *Orientalism*",[47] Mills in particular argues that as women have occupied a subordinate position to men throughout much of the previous two centuries, they may share a certain kinship with the subordinate subject of colonialism too, even as the privileged nature of their status as Western, white, and educated holds them within the prism of colonialism.[48] Similarly, in the influential *Imperial Eyes*, Mary Louise Pratt attempts to show how female colonial writers attempt to distance themselves from the dominant male narrative, while Reina Lewis takes this work further by considering the "extent and manner of women's engagement with the discourse of Othering, and the possibility of their speaking with an alternative voice free from or subversive of the dominant (male) discourse".[49] This begs the question, as Nash poses, as to "what differences then, if any, we might expect to encounter in women travel writers as distinct from males?"[50] Or, as Susan Bassnett puts it, "Do women's travel accounts differ from those written by men in any fundamental way, and is there a way in which travel writing is inherently gendered?"[51] One might query, in contrast, whether any such differences imply a lesser contribution of East-bound Western women to either an understanding of the region they describe or, in the context of the current discussion, to the genre of desert travel writing to which their writing contributes.

Mills, one of many who have attempted answers to these questions, identified early women travellers as "proto-feminist" (although she reassesses this in later work), at least in their leaving of the domestic realm, and found in women's texts a strong storytelling tendency wherein "narrative incident … [forms] the focus of attention"; this is in contrast with men's accounts that often focus on the collection of facts and data with narration assuming only secondary, and often merely picaresque, importance.[52] Mills identifies further their focus on the "personal and on

116 *Gendering the desert*

relationship in general"[53] – an observation shared by Mary Morris who contends that in the writing of Freya Stark or Isabella Eberhardt, "the inner landscape is as important as the outer, the beholder as significant as the beheld", overlooking perhaps that an entire generation of Romantic writers shared the same focus, regardless of gender.[54] Jane Morrison belongs to the same generation of critics after Said who take it for granted that a gender distinction exists. She dedicates a chapter of her book to women travellers in Arabia, and finds that women's travels are "different, certainly, but not, as generations of critics might have us believe, less valid". While she contends they share the same urge to find freedom from the constraints of society, and are just as capable of adventure despite "being assumed the gentler, fairer, weaker sex, burdened by sexual harassment, menstruation and childbirth", she characterises their differences largely as a result of external factors, noting for example that women have often had an inferior education; they have needed to be mindful of reputation but have not generally needed to satisfy a patron. This, Morrison argues, means they can afford to be "more discursive, more impressionable, more ordinary"– better able to map the inner space while their male counterparts focus on mapping in a more literal sense.[55] Wendy Mercer, a champion of what Hélèn Cixous termed "écriture féminine", has sought to identify not so much a feminine content as a distinctively feminine register: one that replaces the conquering of the "them" by the "us" with a more fluid sense of boundary, one that replaces objective observation and judgement with something more spiritual, intuitive, and sympathetic.[56]

All these commentators, while disagreeing on *how*, take it for granted that women *do* write and travel differently from men simply because they *are* different from men. Later critics, however, including Foster and Mills – the latter in something of a revision of her earlier perspective – raise concerns about this kind of essentialist position. They address the problems of this assumption by applying the work of gender theorist Judith Butler and feminist theorists Anne McClintock and Beverley Skeggs, showing that while gender is one lens of a female traveller's perspective, it may not necessarily be the predominant lens and that ultimately one looks in vain for a style of women's writing that is clearly distinct from that of men.[57] This is a conclusion that can be readily applied to Arabian desert literature too where it is hard to discern anything appreciably different about women's travel writing other than their access to and descriptions of the domestic, and this is largely a difference of content rather than of form or voice. The writing style of Gertrude Bell, a distinguished agent of the government in Iraq in the early part of the twentieth century, for example, resonated with her mentee, T. E. Lawrence, by whom she was much admired, even if he was not always generous in stating as much.[58] She participated in the collection of intelligence useful to the imperial project of her age and as such can be seen as contributing to the mainstream in her literary output. By the same token, Freya Stark, to use James Canton's

Gendering the desert 117

phrase, "began in contradiction to a colonial perspective but [was] eventually co-opted by it", providing insights and assumptions that shared much with the prevailing discourse. As such, both women can be seen as part of the wider "problem" of Orientalism as much as their male counterparts.[59] This is not to say, however, that their perspective is male, just shared. Rather than define two fixed perspectives with transgendered narratives gliding between the two, it seems more useful in Arabian desert literature to avoid ascribing fixed attributes to male or female narratives altogether, accepting with Youngs and Thompson that there is no consensus on how to read women's travel literature and no value in generalising about the characteristics of their writing.[60]

It is not the purpose of this discussion, then, to probe modern women's desert writing to discover a quintessential feminine voice, nor to treat women desert-goers as either freaks or eccentrics who transgress gender expectations; rather, the intention is to consider their work as revealing of subjects that often lie beyond the opportunity of male experience. Barbara Toy, who as we have seen published an account in 1968 of crossing the deserts of Arabia in a Land Rover, affords one such opportunity, in writing of an encounter with a Bedouin harem:

> Five women sat on the floor with their backs to the light ... I sat opposite the women, our knees almost touching. They were animated and excited, fluttering their headscarves, whilst the bangles on their pretty wrists made a tinkling sound. They could have been a row of brightly coloured birds on a bough.[61]

In gaining access to an area forbidden to men, Toy has an opportunity to make women the rare focus of her account. In an account that is otherwise rewardingly innovative, however, that opportunity is missed: this passage treats the women of the haram as aesthetic objects in a manner familiar to the Orientalist male fantasy trope. Remove the exposure to the harem in this passage, and Toy is indistinguishable from a male desert traveller, something Toy herself points up with irony, noting that her "lack of husband, children, or even jewellery made me only half a woman". She watches the women of the harem disappear through "a minute door in the back wall, whispering again and departing in excited secrecy" and then gets back to matters of more importance to her: "The Sheikh and I returned to the sterner problems of inquisitive Bedu and the radio".[62] Some might read the explicit positioning of self among raiding parties and technology as Toy acting out the role of token male; more convincingly, however, this is Toy playing the part of resourceful female desert traveller with other things on her mind at that moment than family. One could argue about whether the imagery she uses ("fluttering", "tinkling", "brightly coloured birds", "whispering ... in excited secrecy") belongs to a male or a female vocabulary, but the more important point

118   *Gendering the desert*

is that Toy shares with her male counterparts an inability to reflect more deeply on Arab women's lives, dehumanising them as a collective piece of colourful landscape in which women are both voiceless and nameless.

The "anonymisation" of Arab women in this way is an enduring trait of both male and female desert literature. Adrienne Brady's work, *Way South of Wahiba Sands*, is a case in point. One of the few women to attempt a travel account of a journey across Arabia in recent decades, she describes a four-wheel drive trip across the United Arab Emirates and Oman. Offering at times a touching portrait of her relationship with her late partner, Richard, the narrative is less successful in its treatment of other women, objectifying rather than individualising the women she meets:

> Was it possible ... that the women disappearing between the trees were descendants from Persians, living in their mountain stronghold as their ancestors had done? ... Their slim build and colourful stylish clothes set them apart from black-cloaked village females. ... We decided that an attempt to follow the women to see where they were heading would be impossible without being intrusive. Contenting ourselves with silent speculation, we watched their retreat until, unable to resist a shot of their receding back views, I reached for my camera.[63]

These are not Arab women, or Omanis, let alone named individuals with jobs, husbands, families, and histories (or "herstories" to use Hazel Carby's term); these beings belong to a checklist of types (Persian descendants, villagers, the black-cloaked) observed at the end of the camera lens, and shot from behind as trophies of Brady's speculative gaze. Brady's lost opportunity to become acquainted with Arab women is slimly justified by a concern for their privacy, but this is immediately contradicted by the act of capture and subsequent exposure in print. The "black-cloaked" objectification of "village females" implies criticism that these women are "not like Us", that they are backward in their remoteness. Similarly the mountain women, with their "receding back views", are "in retreat" in the direction of Brady's imagined past, inviting rescue "by their modern, Western sisters".[64] Set in a broader context, this is the kind of writing that attracted the censure of early feminist critics such as Carby who see in feminist writing a similar "Orientalist" presentation of the social practices of other nations which posits that women require the intervention of Western, educated, elite intellectuals in order to lead satisfactory lives.

Whatever the other merits of the book, Brady is disappointingly unable to determine a counter-narrative for these village women. In this she is not alone; as Tim Youngs and latterly Dúnlaith Bird point out, women are not *de facto* any more empathetic towards women of other cultures than their male counterparts as they "seek out narrative strategies that allow them to negotiate the pitfalls of reader expectations and contemporary

Gendering the desert 119

gender norms, often at the expense of cultural sensitivity or solidarity".[65] The opportunity for a more productive kind of "international cross-cultural sisterhood", one that gives voice to the women encountered and articulates their needs from their own perspectives, such as one would hope to be the result of a generation of postcolonial studies, remains elusive in Brady's work.[66] This dehumanisation of Arab women, the failure to give them substance in literature, and the presumption of speaking on their behalf belong to a larger act of erasure and selective exposure that is explored in the next section.

The siren trope

Thus far, this chapter has explored the absence of women in desert literature as female travel companions and as female travel writers. It now turns to the even greater absence, at least until recently, of Arab women as subjects within desert travel accounts. Where Arab women are mentioned at all, they make an appearance largely as figures in an exotic tableau, without voice and conforming to the familiar representational binary in Western male literature of women "veiled or splayed naked" – either languishing in their irrelevance or corrupting with their availability.[67] Foster and Mills identify this binary as arising out of the cult of the harem (a subject also notably explored by Inderpal Grewal), which they describe as being "central to the fantasies which structure Orientalist discourse: in male-generated myth it is forbidden territory … charged with erotic significance about which knowledge can only be voyeuristically obtained".[68] In this way, the siren trope acts as a metaphor for the old Orient itself – a self-mythologising locus of desire and unattainability, wherein women are portrayed as objects "both desired and feared by men" and without the agency of self-representation.[69]

The siren trope can be traced back to late eighteenth and early nineteenth-century Europe and the Romantic movement in which poetry, fiction, and painting gave cultural capital to the scant knowledge and febrile imaginings about Arab women in the experience of desert travellers. Works such as Delacroix's celebrated "The Death of Sardanapalus" and Byron's Eastern tales, which sold in record numbers, helped create the defining image of the Oriental female that persisted throughout the century in English art and literature.[70] Presented as submissive, seduced by superior physical strength, and silent except in speech engendered by men, these notional Arab women are analogous to the Western colonial enterprise. This amounts, as Kirsten Holst Petersen and Anna Rutherford have suggested, to a "double colonisation", celebratory of patriarchal values and achievements, and indeed male dominance.[71] That Arab women are shown to approve this submissive, slavish role of theirs, as Rana Kabbani points out in her analysis of sexuality in Orientalist literature, is a convenient fulfilment of male and, by extension, colonial fantasy.[72]

120   *Gendering the desert*

Some travellers challenged this fictional presentation of Oriental women, including Lady Wortley Montagu who, in describing the activities of Turkish women, emerges as an early apologist for presumed local customs in an implied criticism of life back home. In explaining, for example, that although the law permits a Muslim man four wives, no "man of quality" would make use of this liberty, and no "woman of rank" would suffer it.[73] A century later, Karsten Niebuhr similarly condemns "ridiculous stories" about women's roles, noting that "Arabian women enjoy a great deal of liberty, and often a great deal of power, in their families".[74] Despite occasional attempts at demythologising the role of Arab women, nineteenth-century desert literature, including Richard Burton's exhaustive accounts of Arab sexual practices, served only to reinforce stereotypes of sensuality and sexual license. This contrasts sharply with the representation of Arab women in the twentieth century. Given their traditional eroticisation in Western literature, it is unsurprising perhaps that the ascetic desert travellers of the late nineteenth and twentieth centuries, Charles Doughty and T. E. Lawrence, avoid any engagement (physical or literary) with women; indeed, women are erased almost entirely from their texts. In Lawrence's work, their absence is replaced by discussions on chastity and the asexual, or homoerotic and male, camaraderie of the desert experience, establishing, as we have seen, the desert as a locus of uncompromising masculine endeavour. In a letter to Doughty, Lawrence described *Seven Pillars of Wisdom* as an adventure that he hoped would "appeal to Boy Scouts",[75] and misogynistic references (such as the "raddled meat" of prostitutes and the lack of anything "female in the Arab movement, but the camels") further establish Lawrence's account as unapologetically male in perspective.[76]

The proto-anthropological works of Bertram Thomas and Wilfred Thesiger in the mid-twentieth century are often singled out as providing detailed pictures of desert societies in Arabia, and yet they reflect only half of the story.[77] Given that family is at the heart of Bedu society and their endeavours largely revolve around marrying, having children and providing for that family, accounts that omit all mention of women and domestic arrangements can at best be considered partial, but Thesiger in particular appears dismissive of this aspect of Bedu life.[78] Where they gain any mention at all, Arab women are objectified in *Arabian Sands* as the abstracted fulfilment of physical need: "[W]e seldom spoke of sex", Thesiger writes, "for starving men dream of food, not of women, and our bodies were generally too tired to lust".[79] According to Thesiger, women are considered by the Bedu as the bearers of sons and as "provided by God for the satisfaction of men". Thesiger goes on to write of women, in reference to chastity, that "deliberately to refrain from using them would be not only unnatural but also ridiculous".[80] The term "using them" is highly problematic for a modern reader and yet is seldom commented upon in modern literary criticism of Thesiger's work; one explanation of

Gendering the desert 121

this may be because Thesiger presents his observations as quasi-anthropological fact rather than as his own perspective of an ultimately private intercourse that would have remained hidden from his view.

Women occur in successive desert narratives as incorporeal objects of desire that help distract from the tribulations involved in crossing wilderness zones. As Bruce Kirkby writes (perhaps with ironic self-consciousness), travelling through the Omani desert by camel towards the end of the twentieth century, women, then food ("crisp baby carrots" to be precise), and then water present to the mind of the weary, camel-sore traveller, as fantasised therapies.[81] Towards the later part of the twentieth century, for reasons that are explored in the next section, women in male desert literature assume an altogether more sinister place in the male narrative, while in female narratives, they become figures eliciting sympathy.

The "veiled best-seller"

The post-Orientalist transition in the perception of Arab women in modern feminist literature "from figure of sexual allure to object of sexual abuse" is charted by Graham Huggan, and he alights specifically on the veil as being "a symbol of oppression" in that discourse.[82] Huggan notes Gillian Whitlock's work on the "veiled best-seller" and shows how this genre commercialises "humanitarian imperialism" through sensationalised biographies of Arab women that offer "the pleasures of empathic identification".[83] Huggan concurs with Whitlock that these narratives give satisfaction to the self-congratulatory illusion offered to privileged Western readers of participating in the agencies of social change. This veiled best-seller genre in modern female Arabian desert literature is analysed in this section, but first, the discussion turns to modern male Arabian desert accounts where women are presented less as passive victims and as something more sinister – as inverse agencies of change.

In *Sultan of Oman*, an account of crossing the deserts of Oman in the 1950s, James (now Jan) Morris writes not just of the menace engendered by "women, severely held in check, veiled with a hideous and alarming black beaklike mask, stiff and stifling", but also begins to register the suspected tyranny of their attire, noting that "[the masks] gave them an air at once theatrical and pathetic".[84] There is an illogical loathing expressed in the "swarms of women in bright orange dresses like a shifting sea of orange peel, twittering together in the background" (p. 84) as if Arab women, in their veiled anonymity, represent a spreading malignancy:

> The cumulative effect of sixty or seventy women disfigured by these things [peaked masks] was horrifying; with their black hanging robes, their dirty hands, their screeching voices and their beaked concealed faces, they were like huge hungry birds of carrion.
>
> (p. 105)

122 *Gendering the desert*

Verging on the misogynistic, the description foreshadows a similarly menacing presentation of veiled women in Jonathan Raban's work. Writing after the oil boom of 1973, it is the anonymous encounters with Arab women in London that provoke the travels throughout the Gulf that he documents in *Arabia Through the Looking Glass*:

> It was the masks I noticed first. They made the women look like hooded falcons, and they struck me not as symbols of Islamic female modesty so much as objects of downright menace. It happened in a summer; one day Arabs were a remote people ... the next, they were neighbours.[85]

The sense of cultural anxiety towards the spread of an alien culture is concentrated in the depiction of women as predatory and malign ("hooded falcons"). The passage hints at an inversion of the desert trope that is normally associated with benign escape: here the desert is alluded to in terms of encroachment and desertification – always a negative concept in literature – as presumed desert dwellers are transformed from consumables (fodder for tourists) to consumers (rich urban neighbours).

Something of the hysteria provoked by Morris's "hungry birds of carrion" and Raban's "hooded falcons" is noted similarly in Tony Wheeler's *Bad Lands* (2007), where the author recoils at the "sinister forms" of women who, invisible for the rest of the day, reappear at sunset "like black-cloaked vampires" (p. 296).[86] Mostly in Wheeler's work, however, the shock of difference is dealt with through disconcerting travesty: "[W] earing your glasses outside the slit can look quite comical", Wheeler writes, "really serious Saudi women even wear black gloves so if they have to hand money out, or take something in, not a square centimetre of flesh will show" (p. 270). Later, he speculates on the difficulty of eating "when you've got a bag over your head" (p. 277). The descriptions are not intended to explore the custom of body concealment, to consider how Arab women may feel about the practice, nor to reveal anything about the specificity of the context in which this practice is adopted, such as Gayatri Chakravorty Spivak advocates in "Can the Subaltern Speak?"[87] The ironic tone is used only to discredit a practice that Wheeler finds distasteful from an aesthetic perspective as he asks, "[W]hy do Saudi men treat their women so abjectly and why do they brand them with this absurdly uncomfortable and impractical outfit?" His concern is that men oblige women to look unlovely, "something to be hidden away" as opposed to the acts of beautification he associates with other cultural practices such as ritual tattooing (p. 296). As such, Wheeler risks the kind of double colonisation that we met with earlier, once as a male imposing a male aesthetic on the women he observes and once as a Western traveller who assumes that women would be better served by the kind of costume with which he is familiar.

Gendering the desert 123

While perhaps intended as well-meaning on Wheeler's part, his defence of women whom he perceives to be under the tyranny of the veil is problematic for reasons that have been widely explored by modern postcolonial feminists. Chandra Talpade Mohanty in "Under Western Eyes: Feminist Scholarship and Colonial Discourses" takes issue with an approach, for example, that presumes a "discursive homogenisation and systematisation of the oppression of women in the third world"[88] and contests the very notion of "universal womanhood" on a number of grounds, one of which (as McLeod illustrates) rests on the "arithmetic method", which presumes that "certain forms of oppression are universal if they circumscribe large numbers of women".[89] For Mohanty, the fact that a large number of Muslim women wear a veil does not necessarily mean they all suffer from oppression and she posits that some may choose to use a veil as a way of expressing political empowerment. There is a danger, then, that without careful consideration of the context, without listening for example to the women who wear veils in parts of Arabia, the cultural practice of veiling can be (mis)appropriated to a Western feminist agenda that does not advantage the presumed subjects of the argument. Norma Khouri's *Forbidden Love* (2003), a controversial book about honour killing in Jordan that was subsequently exposed by the 2008 documentary *Forbidden Lies* as a fraud, is a case in point. Whitlock identifies that Khouri uses the book as a "vehicle of activism", speaking for the Arab culture "in terms of a binary logic that privileges the West as the representative of universal values of human rights, democracy and free speech".[90] In what has been described as "armchair travel disguised as humanitarian treatise", Khouri uses the Arab country placement with its "touristic snippets of cultural information" to transfer authenticity to a text, the main purpose of which is to reinforce relative notions of cultural hierarchy.[91]

Several other Western women writers who have travelled in Arabia have taken the same approach, taking the opportunity similarly to exploit their insider status, as women writing about women, to peer behind the veil and make value judgements about Arab culture. The term "lifting the veil", commonly used in paternalistic contexts implying liberation through disrobing, has become such a commonplace one that it is hard to trace its origin. It has even earnt a visual correlative as becomes obvious when placing Geraldine Brooks's *Nine Parts of Desire* (1995), Donya Al-Hani's *Heroine of the Desert* (2006), and Jean Sasson's *Princess: More Tears to Cry* (2014) side by side: the covers of each of these books feature a pair of kohl-rimmed eyes framed by a *hijab* intended to work as an abstract for the narrative inside.[92] The visual short-hand sometimes places these veiled faces in full frontal appeal to the reader or, in a reference to Oriental tropes, modestly deflects their gaze amid a border of head jewels and lace, with the cloth veil suggesting both a framing device and a restraining order on the wearer. Of course, the implication is that

124   *Gendering the desert*

the unsmiling subject of the outward gaze is imprisoned by her culture and, with mouth covered over, a silent victim of male patrimony, trapped in an unyielding and unforgiving environment. Of interest to the present discussion is the way that each book is set within a tangential desert context which acts as a symbol of that unyielding and unforgiving environment despite the predominantly urban landscape of the stories within. The images of sand dunes on the book covers, the selection of the word "desert" in book titles, and the many oblique references to desert in all three books shore up notions of isolation and alienation conjured by the desert trope which in turn carries with it, as we have seen, many of the old stereotypes of the Orient.

These books are undeniably popular: Sasson, for example, claims that her books have been "a huge success all over the world. Published in over 40 countries, they have been bestsellers in many lands", and this boast appears to be evidenced by at least ten similar titles of supposed non-fictional stories to Sasson's name, each charting the lives of Arab women, in an output spanning 20 years and copyright held by her own Sasson corporation.[93] With subtitles such as "The World's Most Beloved Saudi Princess Speaks Out about the Struggle for Women's Rights in the Kingdom", or "The Hidden World of Islamic Women", or "The True Story of a Woman Who Risked Everything to Reunite Kidnapped Children with Their Mothers", these kinds of books prey on sentimental impulses (snatched children, violent husbands, unfair imprisonment); in doing so, they help project onto the *abaya*-wearing women beyond the bookstands a prescribed view of Arab women as speechless victims. A useful description of all three "veiled best-seller" books,[94] by Brooks, Al-Nahi, or Sasson, can be taken from Huggan who builds on the work of Elisabeth Bronfen in defining an "Orientalist trauma fantasy that 'speaks through' the subaltern woman in the name of a liberated West".[95] This particularly fits the Princess series of victim tales written by Sasson over the past two decades as she purports to give voice to Princess Sultana who, for reasons ascribed to the "most rigid, male-dominated system, where … [the] appointed male guardian has complete control over the female, from her first moment of birth to the last second of her death" (p. 27), is presumed to have no opportunity to speak for herself. Sasson, who has travelled widely across Iraq, Kurdistan, Afghanistan, and Kuwait (p. 4) finding material for her monographs on Arab women's lives, becomes their supposed champion, giving voice where she claims they have none. The books use the desert as a framing device for a land of male dominance, unpunished honour killing, and restrictions of freedom within which her heroines are apparently imprisoned. Where there might have been some satisfaction to be had in, as Spivak suggests, "the subaltern giving witness to oppression" for the benefit of the "less oppressed other", there is little comfort in the suspicion of a hoax, and some of these kinds of works stretch credibility on many levels not least because of the

Gendering the desert 125

unlikelihood of a genuine victim being able or willing to allow her personal narrative to be exposed in a bestseller.

Huggan tries to rescue Khouri's *Forbidden Love* from just such a betrayal of trust represented in her travel memoir by arguing that time and space give distance to the tale and lightens the load on authenticity.[96] While it is hard to classify either the Sultana tales or *Forbidden Love* as travel texts, other than that they involve the authors drawing on their own knowledge of Arabia, they are deliberately presented as such, and this contributes to the attempted legitimisation of the content. There is a map at the beginning of Sasson's *Princess: More Tears to Cry*, for example, and an appendix for the culturally illiterate which includes guidebook-style information about Saudi Arabian history, geography, economy, and a glossary of terms – all details that are designed to emphasise the authenticity of the text for the incurious reader.

An altogether more considered contribution to the genre of women's travel writing in Arab lands, Geraldine Brooks's travel journalism *Nine Parts of Desire* communicates an underlying agenda of cultural relativism. Building her narrative on genuine encounter, she states, "I did something so obvious I couldn't believe it had taken me a year to get around to it. I started talking to women" (p. 11). It is not clear, however, whether she starts listening in the way that Hazel Carby urged in her seminal essay, "White Woman Listen!"[97] Indeed, Brook's presentation of apparent facts – about Islam, about Arab women, about domestic life in desert lands – is likely to satisfy the prejudices of the intended Western readership:

> Like most Westerners, I always imagined the future as an inevitably brighter place, where a kind of moral geology will have eroded the cruel edges of past and present wrongs. But in Gaza and Saudi Arabia, what I saw gave me a different view. From there, the future is a place that looks darker every day.
>
> (p. 166)

Brooks admits that it is hard to dissociate Arabia from what she calls the "background noise" (p. 226) of prejudice and "dire social practice" attributed to the cultural baggage surrounding Islam. This noise crescendos into what she describes as a "roar" after the events of 9/11, which she attributes to the "hate-mongering Islam" of Saudi Arabia and the betrayal of its own fundamental ideals. "I thought", she writes, "of the other weeping faces we were never allowed to see: the bruised and battered Saudi women, hidden by the veil and imprisoned behind the high walls of their houses" (p. 241). An exploration of Islam is the focus of *Nine Parts of Desire* where Brooks attempts to find links between the experience of twentieth-century Arab women, and indeed her own, in the imperatives given in the Quran:

126   *Gendering the desert*

> Getting to the truth about hijab was a bit like wearing it: a matter of layers to be stripped away, a piece at a time. In the end, under all the concealing devices ... under all the talk about *hijab* freeing women from commercial or sexual exploitation, ... was the body: the dangerous female body that somehow, in Muslim society, had been made to carry the heavy burden of male honour.
>
> (p. 32)

In this context, Brooks finds a way of recognising in the veil both emblems of the traditional representation of Arab women as desired and feared: in either case, she recognises their objectification from the perspective of the Western observer as body, not as soul, personality, opinion, or even as sentient partner in a relationship. While Brooks does not make the connection with the landscape explicit, the desert – which hovers at the edge of the narrative throughout – with its pared-down features, lack of vegetation, and the frequency of its nomination as an empty space, makes the ideal context for this stripping back to body and becomes in some senses as the locus of male competitive endeavour, a similarly encumbered space that has "been made to carry the heavy burden of male honour". The description of Brook's travels with King Hussein of Jordan captures the way in which the environment is transformative for those who surrender to it, turning the effete, "smooth-talking, Harrow- and Sandhurst-educated diplomat" into something "much more potent: the avatar of his ancestor the prophet Muhammad, prayer leader, warlord and father of the tribes" (p. 122) – in other words, something much more male. The camel's blood spilt in the king's honour outside the Bedu tent they visit becomes more than just a set piece from the "tableaux from the Arabian Nights"; it symbolises the male brutality traditionally associated with an environment in which Bedu women "swathed in black veils and marked on the face with blue tattoos" press petitions into the king's palms (p. 124). Brook's Arabia, then, despite the witness of the women she interviews, is a zone of continuing patriarchy in which women continue to be represented as silent supplicants.

There is one account, rare among modern Arabian desert texts by Western writers, male or female, that manages to get beyond the "concealing devices" of Muslim society to reveal a richer complexity of encounters with Arab women. Marguerite van Geldermalsen's *Married to a Bedouin* (2006) describes the author's initiation into the lives of the Bdoul Bedu in Petra in Jordan.[98] Given that she settles in Jordan midway through her travels, instead of continuing to move, it is perhaps fairer to term this book a memoir, although it shares many of the same characteristics of a travel text as defined by Jonathan Raban, the "essential condition" of which "is the experience of living among strangers, away from home".[99] Geldermalsen refreshingly dismisses the pretensions surrounding casual discourse on the subject of veiling early in the narrative by

Gendering the desert   127

noting that her travelling companion, Elizabeth, "felt it was polite to cover up because we were in a Muslim world, but I didn't care. If they wanted to cover themselves, fine. I didn't usually and I didn't see why I should change for anyone" (p. 5). Effortlessly, over the course of the remaining 260 pages, however, Geldermalsen moves literally and metaphorically under cover as she becomes a lover, then a wife, and, ultimately, Umm Raami, the mother of Bedu sons, dressing to fit in or to be practical as her adopted life among the Bedu required. Her change of costume (and she is pictured on the front cover with headscarf, local dress, and Western shirt) is the unconscious product of her assimilation into a life she grows to respect and value deeply for its sense of societal and familial loyalties. As she writes,

> I was welcomed and accepted by everyone, but it took me a long time to realise that by marrying Mohammad I had really become a part of something larger, and that it was never going to be just him and me.
>
> (p. 53)

Eventually, the Bdoul are moved out of the ruins of Petra, and Geldermalsen's home is relocated from ancient cave to modern concrete block and "so a way of life disappeared" (p. 271). There is a hint of elegy about the transition into a more modern way of life, but in interview, Geldermalsen is sanguine about the move, recognising that the value of Bedu society is traditionally associated not with place but with connection, family, and Islamic values.[100] Her account is an example of non-judgemental, non-comparative desert travel literature that reveals the life of Bedu women in the complexity of their relationships with each other and the outside world in a way that challenges assumed stereotypes:

> I have not told of the girl who crept from her husband's bed ... to meet her lover in the mountains, nor of how caring friends convinced her husband to overlook her behaviour and not commit a crime of honour but an act of *sutra* and forgiveness by treating her child as his own.
>
> (p. 271)

She does tell of plenty of other stories, however, that illustrate how veil or no veil, women's lives are just as nuanced, as Lady Montagu contended several centuries earlier, as those of her own New Zealand heritage, despite the differences in opportunity.

Married to a Bedouin is similar in the inclusiveness of its gaze to a travel account by Helen Couchman entitled *Omani Women* (2012). Couchman's commentary takes the form of a series of confrontational photographs rather than words, supported by a catalogue essay by the Iranian critic Sussan Babaie. The book arose from an exhibition of the works in Muscat whose subtitle, *About a Journey*, deliberately positions the work within

128 *Gendering the desert*

the Arabian desert travel writing tradition; it is also cast, however, within a growing number of works that experiment with what Margaret Topping has recently called "postcolonialist, post-Orientalist ... post-ocularcentric ... intermedial forms" that explore the ethical dimensions of travel through the destabilising possibilities of juxtaposing text and image.[101] The cover of the book features a vast, flat, almost monochrome desert plain uninterrupted by any animate image; this frames, or at least hints at, the backstory as we learn from the interpretative gloss that the work was inspired by Couchman's encounter with two Bedu women on the edge of the Empty Quarter, and this apparently led to the recognition that, in the catalogue of female representations, there were only ethnographic photos of indigenous women and only from nomadic tribes. Couchman sets out to redress this omission, featuring mostly urban, working women in an attempt to present, in the words of Babaie, "people with lives as complex individuals" not just women behind "veils, looms and cooking pots" (p. 82). The images contest the familiar presentation of Arab women in Western male depictions as vulnerable, available, or seductive: these are not women dressed to satisfy the male gaze; in fact, men are simply irrelevant in these portraits where women are posing for women.

Babaie's accompanying text provides a frame tale for the pictorial commentary; she paints the picture of Couchman travelling in Oman, encountering a man who claims that the last British person he met was Thesiger in the 1950s. Babaie's embrace of this detail is significant as she describes Couchman as bridging "a gap as far as local memory allows" and shows willingness to hand the baton of Western male travellers' narrative over to a woman. While Babaie claims that a woman is able to bring more to the project of capturing other women "in the way they wish to be photographed" by virtue of culturally privileged access (p. 79), there remains a tension in the work that shows that the issues of difference are not about gender alone. The portraits form, as Babaie acknowledges, an ethno-anthropographic project in which Arabs are delineated by a European, and as such, they are as telling about Couchman's own journey of discovery and her attempt to find something in common with her subjects as they reveal of each of the women portrayed. Interestingly, over half the hundred or more women, going against the common practice in Oman at that time, chose to be photographed wearing a veil or covering part or all of their face in some way, adding to the conflict of Couchman's attempt to see beyond the surface of each portrait. While Babaie claims that the "portraits make observations that remain neutral, thus running contrary to the tacitly censorious shadow cast on the practice of veiling by Muslim women" (p. 80), this is not wholly convincing as there is an irreconcilability about Couchman's perspective on each of her subjects compared with the chosen representation of self, betrayed by the sitter and further problematised by Babaie's textual gloss.

Given this interplay between observer and observed, European and Arab, desert and domestic, Couchman's images remain outside feminine stereotypes or feminist agendas. According to Babaie, "[W]hile this is a journey for the artist, we – the viewer – are also implicated in an exercise in disrupting the old Orientalist tropes" (p. 80) as we are involved in deciphering unexpected nuances surrounding the coded context of each woman. Mouza (p. 43), for example, is fully veiled with just her extravagantly beaded wealth on display, but before assumptions can be made about a traditional life of rural labour, emblems of a different reality resolve on the eye – the watch she is wearing, the stylish sandals, the sealed roadside venue she chooses to stand by, running across the unpeopled desert. Similarly, Zainab (p. 17), in her magnificent pink veil and hennaed feet appears to be deliberately evoking the siren trope, her black, menacing shadow stretching into the past while her eyes are directed towards the sunshine ahead. Ultimately, the self-fashioning portraits are not about ethnography, journalism, or psychology – they are about people and a curiosity about each of the sitter's lives that is not "detached from the loaded baggage" (p. 85) of Orientalism as Babaie suggests but is deliberately provoking of commentary on that discourse. For the genre of travel writing (and I still contend this work can be considered as such, augmented as it is with a map of the author's routes through Oman), this is relevant because it suggests a less divisive and less reductive account of Arab women's lives.[102] "The more I look at these images", Babaie writes, "the more it feels as though we are being viewed" (p. 85). The key, given Babaie's gender and ethnicity, is in the satisfyingly inclusive "we". This is travel beyond the "contact zone" that Mary Louise Pratt memorably identified as "social spaces where disparate cultures meet, clash, and grapple with each other, often in highly asymmetrical relations of domination and subordination ... as they are lived out across the globe today",[103] and into "planetarity" – the place where, as Dúnlaith Bird identifies in reading Pratt's work, there is a "willingness to enter into stuttering dialogues where the participants do not necessarily speak the same language" and where the emphasis lies in "performativity", "improvisation", and "imperfection".[104] This kind of travel and its reproduction in print disrupts the dominant discourse and allows the reader or observer productively to interpret and intuit the gaps in between.

Desert as an inconstant space

In *The Road to Ubar* (1998), Nicholas Clapp's account of a desert expedition to uncover the hidden city of the title, the author reflects on the race to be first across the Empty Quarter in deliberately eroticised if bathetic terms:

130   *Gendering the desert*

> Both Thomas and Philby saw the Rub Al-Khali as a beckoning yet veiled virgin. Thomas called the Rub Al-Khali "the sands of my desire". Philby called the same sands "the bride of my constant desire". But, though there were two suitors, there could be only one husband.[105]

Only one husband? Not so in Arab culture, of course, but Clapp's observation is not of Arab presence in the desert space but of Western penetration. Throughout the history of desert literature, the landscape has been anthropomorphised in this way and generally in the female form. If in male desert literature, as we have seen, women are often represented as paradoxically siren-like and chaste, similarly the desert in its feminine incarnation is projected as magnetically dangerous and virginal.[106] The word "pristine" occurs frequently in desert texts, and there is a strong coincidence between concepts of the pristine with the lack of women in that space. Similarly, masculine boasts – about penetrating the land, being the first to conquer the virgin territory of the sands, to map and chart in straight lines – abound in male desert literature, as the previous excerpt from Nicholas Clapp illustrates.[107] Clapp goes on to state that Thomas embraced the Empty Quarter less as an "enchanting bride" and more "a hungry void and an abode of death".[108] Death and cleanliness are intimately connected in desert literature; Lawrence, for example, in describing the desert as an arena of death was attracted to it, at least according to Tidrick, "because it was sterile and therefore 'clean'",[109] a word he uses repeatedly (58 times by my count) throughout *Seven Pillars of Wisdom*.[110]

The desert as emblematic of something pristine yet perilous continues in modern representations of the desert and is not confined to male travel writing. In *Tracks* (1980), the work of the celebrated Australian desert-traveller Robyn Davidson, for example, the elemental nature of the space, stripped to the minimal rhythms of life and death in their unencumbered simplicity, is described in similar terms. Indulging uncharacteristically in the kind of competitiveness more usually exhibited by men, Davidson takes a moment of pride in being the first to step into untrodden space:

> There was nothing but sandhills and spinifex and interminable space. I was perhaps treading now on country where no one had ever walked before, there was so much room – pure, virgin desert, not even cattle to mar it and nowhere in that vastness even an atom of anything human.[111]

This is familiar territory – the pioneering trek, the nostalgic association with the past symbolised through the use of camels (connected thereby with Oriental tradition by virtue of their Middle East origins and handlers), the anthropomorphised landscape, the sublime dimensions, the virginity, the first to encounter – but it is not necessarily feminine territory.

Gendering the desert 131

In the writing of Davidson, the space becomes gender-neutral, its virginity conceptualised as a tension between the human and "the rest".

In a later work similarly from beyond the Arab region, Sara Wheeler attempts with what she considers less success to wrest the desert (in this case a cold desert) from specific gender connotation.[112] In *Terra Incognita* (1996), a book that famously probes the maleness of the space, Wheeler quotes Admiral Byrd, the first to fly over the South Pole but one of many to couch the ice in feminine terms, describing it as "pale like a sleeping princess. Sinister and beautiful, she lies in frozen slumber" (p. xviii); similarly, Scott notes that the continent "possessed a virginity, in his mind, that provided an alternative to the spoiled and messy world" (p. 49). Within this environment Wheeler, as a woman, is made to feel especially alien by some of the men she encounters – particularly those on the British base: "[S]hort of erecting a sign outside the base saying GO AWAY, they couldn't have made me feel less welcome" (p. 212). She traces their hostility directly to a sense of contamination that a woman represents in the male locale, as explained by one of the male scientists: "They don't want the complication of women in such a pristine place" (p. 219).

Looking for reasons why the desert is so often projected as a feminine space that is therefore jealously guarded for male encounter, Jay Griffiths notes in *Wild: An Elemental Journey* (2006), "The Arabic word for desert, *badieh*, is feminine, as is the word for desert waste, *barrieh*".[113] This raises the question as to what makes this type of landscape feminine in character across cultures. In her analysis of Karen R. Lawrence's *Penelope Voyages* (1994), Sidonie Smith comments on the traditional idea of women as "earth, shelter, enclosure". She suggests that the idea of woman "as home" persists in modern literature, "anchoring femininity, weighing it down, fixing it as a compass point".[114] Land, in reverse, is often similarly gendered. Its association with earth, hence fertility and propagation, tend to construct the land as lover and mother to an assumed male inhabitant; it may be questioned, then, as to how it is possible that an arid desert, "which cuts against motifs of fertility", is able to satisfy these gendered parameters.[115] Griffiths helps provide an answer in *Wild's* section on "Fire", where she traces the essential character of the desert to an inconstancy that matches the supposed nature of women. Her highly referenced account is in itself innovatively wild in design (in that its chapters are not sequenced by time nor in countries visited but around the five elements) as well as wild in content (in the eclectic way, for example, in which references to Thesiger and the Bedu, the French Foreign Legion and the Turkana people, the author's own experiences and those of the aboriginal writer, Ruby Langford, are spliced seemingly chaotically, or as a stream of consciousness, into the text). Griffiths's polyphonic description destabilises the image of the landscape, making it vulnerable to the dynamics of the author's recollection and the connections she makes between those she references. This is exemplified in a passage about the

132 *Gendering the desert*

mathematics, or what the author terms "sand algebra" (p. 287) of desert dunes, where the words used to describe the landscape dissolve into different meanings through translation:

> The wind draws dented diamonds in the sand, patterns subetched by gravity. Maths has long been important to Middle Eastern cultures. ... Omar Khayyam, poet of deserts, wrote a treatise on algebra and used the Arabic term *shay* to mean the "unknown" in an equation. Translated into Spanish, the term was spelled *xay*, then abbreviated to *x*. The unknown, like *terra incognita*, this is *numerus incognitus*, desert space of mathematics.
>
> (p. 288)

In the "maths of sand", Griffiths is drawn to the "absolute in number", which hints at the paradox of infinite stabilities, limitless in concept but fixed by numerical expression. This contrasts with the more feminine principles represented by the erratic rainfall and *wadis* that flood and cease; the desert, with its shifting form in which sand dunes move and change shape, twisters which rearrange the desert furniture, and mirages that tremble with visual misinformation becomes subject to ebb and flow, and this, in turn, contributes to its binary representation as sinister and chaste, repellent and alluring.

The desert need not be defined, however, in terms of a simple binary of male fixture and female flux: in its constant transition between the two, it also operates within the imagination as a liminal space, a borderland of potential. In her work on Palestinian literature and film, Anna Ball discusses the liminality, or in-betweeness, of Palestinians as inhabitants of a stateless nation "lacking self-determination over its own boundaries".[116] In this state, Palestinians are subject to the "shifting regulations, boundaries and territorial claims cast upon them". Ball goes on to explore how those within this unstable state are constantly, in reference to Deleuzian theory, in a "state of 'becoming' rather than 'being'", and there are obvious parallels here with the Bedu whose tribal range in Arabia has been circumscribed by the imposition of borders that fail to take into account the logic of their community. Their condition finds its physical equivalent in the Empty Quarter, the dunes of which are equally liminal in that they are never resolved, never wholly on one side of a border or another but in a constant state of influx and exodus under the influence of the shaping wind; within this terrain, the sand forms a complex "assemblage" of minute and multiple parts that cannot easily be disaggregated. As postcolonial feminist theorists point out, this state of becoming smooths the differences between genders (and sexualities): the liminal space offers opportunities for radical transmigration and redefinition of those, including women in traditionally male territory, who are marginalised.[117] This is helpful in confirming why women are frequently erased from desert

Gendering the desert 133

texts as their "transgressive" presence is potentially destabilising of masculine certainties traditionally defined by Western desert travel.

If this is true in a metaphysical sense, there is a political dimension to the gendering of the desert too, and there are further obvious parallels in the way in which the land as a whole – particularly in the oil-bearing regions of the Middle East – has been characterised as an opportunity for penetration and domination by Western explorers. As Susan Bassnett recognises, "the early history of colonialism is one in which new territories were metaphorised as female, as virgin lands waiting to be penetrated, ploughed, and husbanded by male explorers".[118] In an era of postcolonial sensitivity, however, it may be expected that this characterisation of the desert as available for exploitation would give way to something more nuanced – a respect for the land in its own right, perhaps. And indeed this is the case in some narratives, at least for some of the time (as exemplified in some of the science and wilderness texts discussed in the next chapter). Traditional presentations, however, remain the norm. In Jo Tatchell's *A Diamond in the Desert*, for example, which is primarily about the oil-rich Emirati capital of Abu Dhabi in the twenty-first century, there is a passage that describes the author's visit to the Rub Al-Khali, or the Empty Quarter, "almost a million square miles of sand, billowing like a great golden blanket as far as the eye can see, the largest expanse of dunes on earth".[119] Tatchell reflects on the Bedu who "lived side by side with their expansive, omnipresent God, privileged enough simply to be" and in contrast thinks of her own life and its insignificance. The desert is the empty space that offers this opportunity for communion between creator and created and within which the author is able to reverse her gaze, tying human consciousness into the fabric of the desert landscape:

> Outside the cold leather interior of the car, there is nothing but the purest, most unselfconscious part of ourselves. The desert eases time and geography into one, and who does not dream of sailing along the sharp edge of the natural world, leaving buildings and ambition behind? It deserves to stay as it is, one of the last great uninhabited spaces in the world.
>
> (p. 60)

It is notable that Tatchell does not feel that the desert should stay the same because of its own intrinsic value – as a landscape of note, as a habitat for uniquely adaptive wildlife, as an ecosystem with its own dimensions and rhythms – but only as a refuge for those weary of the "buildings and ambition" that have complicated modern life. As such, the desert remains a locus of potential exploitation and as an arena for escape, recreation, and contrast from the tamed life of a globalised, urban experience. Into that opportunity steps all the modern infrastructure that helps facilitate wilderness encounter – the tour groups, the camps, the

134 *Gendering the desert*

roads – bringing with it a new wave of explorers and exploiters who in their wake destroy the wilderness element, the very character of the landscape that made it attractive in the first place. Given that a wilderness cannot be both virgin and explored, it remains to be seen how, in turn, the desert as trope can survive its collapse into an adventure playground – as part of the so-called accelerated sublime (and the topic of a later chapter).[120]

Throughout this book, the work of women travellers has been selected for analysis, and so it could be questioned why there was a need for a dedicated chapter on gender issues in desert literature; indeed, it could be argued that the very act of parcelling women into their own chapter somehow contributes to the act of marginalisation. In reply, I would contend that the erasure of women from the desert landscape has been so wholesale in the past, it takes more than just their routine coverage to understand why and how this has been the case and to help in the project of representation. This chapter has tried, therefore, to show that although few in number, women writers have throughout Western history contributed diversely to the genre of Arabian desert travel writing; despite the relative lack of opportunity in recent years to engage in extended desert travel, their contribution continues into the present day in texts that allude to the desert, if only (in some texts) for the apparent sake of marketability. That these texts, by women about women, appeal to the travelling public is illustrated in the sales and in the fact that a book such as *Married to a Bedouin* is still being reprinted over a decade after publication. However disappointing some of these books may be in terms of the failed opportunity to present any more complex a depiction of Arab women than their male counterparts, they nonetheless illustrate a new desire to write and read about this hitherto textually marginalised part of society that is in step with wider movements to "give voice to the subaltern". Dealing with their own marginalisation, as women writers in a highly gendered space, however, is perhaps more problematic. The nominal desert best-sellers are a case in point. They may represent dubious writing (as a result perhaps of a lack of critical mass), but it could be argued that these texts are held to a higher account than male accounts. There may not be much difference, in fact, in a woman crossing desert lands in search of veiled women (Geraldine Brooks) to men's travels in search of lost heroes (Adrian Hayes), but the former subject matter is considered domestic and outside the parameters of "real" desert travel writing. Within this book, there was a strong temptation to leave these examples out of the survey of modern Arabian desert literature but I chose to include them to avoid continuing the erasure of women within the history of the genre. The late twentieth and early twenty-first centuries may not be characterised by many desert texts authored by women, but the reasons for this, as discussed earlier in this chapter, are interesting in their own right. To ignore the few texts that do present as relevant to the topic on the grounds that they

Gendering the desert 135

represent clichéd writing is to hold women's writing to higher account than men's, and this in turn is ultimately as problematic as excluding them from the discussion. It appears, at one level, that Lisle is right when she states,

> [W]omen must overcome their "natural" limitations as women and become "extraordinary" in order to be manly enough to travel and write books about it. In this way, the discourse of masculinity in travel writing continue to install an attending message of "even women can travel – imagine that!"[121]

Not only do women writers have to prove they can travel in Muslim countries, and that they are able to write about their desert experiences, but they are also expected to be standard bearers for the postcolonial feminist project, bringing voice to the marginalised. This brings their endeavours to crisis, as it is difficult to be accepted as a *bona fide* desert writer when the subject of the text is a topic beyond the traditional boundaries of the genre. Where they succeed, such as in Couchman's and Babaie's eclectic exploration of Omani women's identity, their achievement can be celebrated as a double intervention not only in bringing visibility to Arab women in "desert texts" but also in recalibrating, in form and content, the delineation of that genre.

Notes

1 Nicholas Clapp, *The Road to Ubar: Finding the Atlantis of the Sands* [1998] (London: Souvenir Press, 1999), p. 10.
2 Ranulph Fiennes, *Atlantis of the Sands: The Search for the Lost City of Ubar* [1992] (London: Signet, 1993), p. 135.
3 Author's unpublished interview with Nigel Winser, 2 June 2016. Winser is well acquainted with Ranulph and knew the late Ginnie Fiennes.
4 Carl Thompson, *Travel Writing* (Abingdon and New York: Routledge, 2011), p. 176.
5 Colin Thubron, "A Lifelong Search for Just Deserts: Thesiger – Michael Asher: Viking, Pounds 20" [online], *The Independent* (1994), available at: https://www.independent.co.uk/arts-entertainment/book-review-a-lifelong-search-for-just-deserts-thesiger-michael-asher-viking-pounds-20-1451083.html [accessed 13 July 2019].
6 Roslynn D. Haynes, *Desert: Nature and Culture* (London: Reaktion Books, 2013), p. 165.
7 Shirley Foster and Sara Mills, eds., *An Anthology of Women's Travel Writing* (Manchester: Manchester University Press, 2002), p. 7. "Position of enunciation" is a term used by Foster and Mills in their evaluation of Edward W. Said's neglect of women's travel writing in *Orientalism*. See also Georgine Clarsen, *Eat My Dust: Early Women Motorists* (Baltimore, MD: John Hopkins University Press, 2008).
8 June Hannam, *Feminism* [2007] (Abingdon: Routledge, 2013), pp. 2–3.
9 John McLeod, *Beginning Postcolonialism* [2000] (Manchester and New York: Manchester University Press, 2010), p. 99.

136   *Gendering the desert*

10 See Nabil Matar, "Travel Writing and Visual Culture", in *The Routledge Companion to Travel Writing*, ed. by Carl Thompson (London and New York: Routledge, 2020), pp. 139–49, and Emily Ruete, *Memoirs of an Arabian Princess from Zanzibar* [1888] (Mineola, New York: Dover Publications, 2009). This nineteenth-century account is by an Omani woman writing under her adoptive German nationality and name (Emily Ruete) and writing of her experiences of elopement *from* the Arab culture of her childhood in Zanzibar. Matar suggests a 2007 travel account in Arabic by Halima Bankaer 'Ayy breaks the silence.

11 Edward W. Said, *Orientalism* (Harmondsworth: Penguin-Peregrine, 1978), p. 204. Said does not cite a reference for these figures, but he does quote a source for the greater numbers of travellers visiting the Islamic East from Europe in comparison with those travelling in the opposite direction: Ibrahim Abu-Lughod, *Arab Rediscovery of Europe: A Study in Cultural Encounters* (Princeton, NJ: Princeton University Press, 1963), pp. 75–76.

12 Haynes, *Desert*, p. 165.

13 Thompson, *Travel Writing*, p. 3.

14 *Peregrinatio ad terram sanctam*, or *Pilgrimage to the Holy Land*, written somewhere between the fourth and sixth century, was written by a nun, Egeria [Etheria], in a series of letters to the sisters of her religious order. See M. L. McClure and C. L. Feltoe, eds., *The Pilgrimage of Etheria* (London: Society for Promoting Christian Knowledge; New York: Macmillan, 1919).

15 Haynes, *Desert*, p. 165.

16 See "Primary Sources" in the bibliography for the published texts arising from these travels.

17 Mary Morris, ed., *Maiden Voyages: Writings of Women Travellers* (New York: Vintage, 1993), p. xv.

18 Tim Youngs, *The Cambridge Introduction to Travel Writing* (Cambridge: Cambridge University Press, 2013), p. 135.

19 Margaret Fountaine, *Love among the Butterflies: Travels and Adventures of a Victorian Lady*, ed. by W. F. Cater (Boston, MA: Little, Brown and Company, 1980), p. 155.

20 "To the Royal Geographical Society", *Punch*, 104 (10 June 1893), p. 269.

21 Dea Birkett, ed., *Off the Beaten Track: Three Centuries of Women Travellers* [accompanying 2004 Exhibition] (London: National Portrait Gallery, 2006), p. 120.

22 Sophie Waring notes that Fountaine collected 22,000 butterflies and published her findings extensively: "Fountaine herself is under-researched", according to Waring, whose own article contains a useful account of her entomological career: Sophie Waring, "Margaret Fountaine: A Lepidopterist Remembered", *Notes and Records: The Royal Society Journal of the History of Science*, 69, no.1 (2015), 53–68 (p. 53).

23 The first and only female president of the RGS was elected in 2012.

24 Fountaine, *Love among the Butterflies*, p. 55.

25 James Canton, *From Cairo to Baghdad: British Travellers in Arabia* [2011] (London: IB Tauris, 2014), p. 181.

26 Fountaine, *Love among the Butterflies*, p. 150.

27 Thompson, *Travel Writing*, p. 174.

28 See, for example, the advice given to female travellers in Anthony Ham et al., "Women Travellers", in *Middle East* (Melbourne: Lonely Planet, 2012), pp. 618–19.

29 Mannin was a socialist-leaning traveller and popular travel writer of the second half of the twentieth century who spoke out against the creation of Israel and the "monstrous injustice" perpetrated on the Palestine Arabs.

Ethel Mannin, *A Lance for the Arabs: A Middle East Journey* (London: Hutchinson, 1963), p. 43.

30 Susan Bassnett, "Travel Writing and Gender", in *The Cambridge Companion to Travel Writing*, ed. by Peter Hulme and Tim Youngs (Cambridge: Cambridge University Press, 2002), pp. 225–41.

31 Birkett, *Off the Beaten Track*, p. 13.

32 Simon Bendle, "Lady Hester Stanhope: Kooky Desert Queen" [online], *Great British Nutters: A Celebration of the UK's Pluckiest Adventurers* (2008), available at: http://greatbritishnutters.blogspot.com/2008/07/lady-hester-stanhope-kooky-desert-queen.html [accessed 13 July 2019].

33 See, for example, Sara Wheeler, *Terra Incognita* [1996] (New York: Modern Library, 1996): Wheeler writes that her lack of fear in Antarctica made her be regarded either as a token male ("Everyone's a guy here!" (p. 74)) or seen as "a benign, barking-mad free spirit, like the tweed-skirted Victorian 'lady' travellers" (p. 97).

34 Debbie Lisle, *The Global Politics of Contemporary Travel Writing* (Cambridge: Cambridge University Press, 2006), p. 95.

35 Foster and Mills, *An Anthology*, p. 2.

36 Kathryn Tidrick, *Heart Beguiling Araby: The English Romance with Arabia* [1990] (London: Tauris Parke, 2010), p. 112.

37 Desert descriptions abound in Blunt's diaries: "The view in front of us was beautiful beyond description, a perfectly even plain, sloping gradually upwards, out of which these rocks and tells cropped up like islands", Lady Anne Blunt, *A Pilgrimage to Nejd: The Cradle of the Arab Race* (London: John Murray, 1881, 2 Vols.), January 23, Vol. I, Chap. IX, p. 209.

38 Zara Freeth and Victor Winstone, *Explorers of Arabia: From the Renaissance to the Victorian Era* (London: George Allen and Unwin, 1978), p. 272.

39 Ali Behdad, *Belated Travelers: Orientalism in the Age of Colonial Dissolution* (Durham, NC: Duke University Press, 1994), p. 97.

40 Isabel Burton, cited in Lesley Blanch, *The Wilder Shores of Love* [1954] (London: Phoenix, 1993), p. 124.

41 Blanch, *Wilder Shores of Love*, p. 124.

42 The phrase "pay, pack and follow" refers to a famous note written by Richard Burton to Isabel Burton, his wife, on being recalled from Damascus, as cited in Blanch, *Wilder Shores of Love*, p. 82.

43 Behdad, *Belated Travelers*.

44 Geoffrey Nash, ed., *Travellers to the Middle East* (London: Anthem Press, 2011), p. xv.

45 Said, *Orientalism*, p. 107.

46 Lisa Lowe, *Critical Terrains: French and British Orientalisms* (Ithaca, New York: Cornell University Press, 1991); Sara Mills, *Discourses of Difference: An Analysis of Women's Travel Writing and Colonialism* (London and New York: Routledge, 1992), and Billie Melman, *Women's Orients: English Women and the Middle East, 1718–1918: Sexuality, Religion and Work* [1992] (London: Macmillan, 1995).

47 McLeod, *Beginning Postcolonialism*, p. 60.

48 Mills, *Discourses of Difference*, p. 29.

49 Foster and Mills, *An Anthology*, p. 8.

50 See also Nash, *Travellers to the Middle East*, p. xv.

51 Peter Hulme and Tim Youngs, eds., *The Cambridge Companion to Travel Writing* (Cambridge: Cambridge University Press, 2002), p. 227.

52 Sara Mills, *Discourses of Difference: An Analysis of Women's Travel Writing and Colonialism* (London: Routledge, 1991), p. 29.

53 Bassnett, "Travel Writing and Gender", p. 227 (in writing about Sara Mills).

138 Gendering the desert

54 Morris, *Maiden Voyages*, p. xvii.
55 Morris, *Maiden Voyages*, p. xii.
56 Wendy Mercer, "Gender and Genre in Nineteenth-Century Travel Writing", in *Travel Writing and Empire: Postcolonial Theory in Transit*, ed. by Steve Clark (London: Zed, 1999), pp. 147–63. Cited in Nash, *Travellers to the Middle East*, p. xv.
57 Foster and Mills, *An Anthology*, p. 3. See also Judith Butler, *Gender Trouble: Feminism and the Subversion of Identity* [1990] (New York and Abingdon: Routledge, 2006); Anne McClintock, *Imperial Leather: Race, Gender and Sexuality in the Colonial Contest* (New York: Routledge, 1995), and Beverley Skeggs, *Formations of Class and Gender* (London: Sage, 1997).
58 Lawrence mentions in the context of "Master Arabians" that "Gertrude Bell, by twenty years of patient study, had won some reputation, too", Bertram Thomas, *Arabia Felix: Across the Empty Quarter of Arabia* (London: Jonathan Cape, 1932), p. xv. The belittling phrase "some" and "too" aside, Bell is treated as a token male achiever in the field.
59 Canton, *From Cairo to Baghdad*, p. 121.
60 See Youngs, *The Cambridge Introduction*, p. 132 and Thompson, *Travel Writing*, pp. 185–86.
61 Barbara Toy, *Travelling the Incense Route: From Arabia to the Levant in the Footsteps of the Magi* [1968] (London: Tauris Parke, 2009), p. 22.
62 Toy, *Travelling the Incense Route*, p. 23.
63 Adrienne Brady, *Way South of Wahiba Sands: Travels with Wadiman* (London: Austin Macauley Publishers, 2013), p. 27.
64 McLeod, *Beginning Postcolonialism*, p. 207 in reference to Hazel V. Carby, "White Woman Listen! Black Feminism and the Boundaries of Sisterhood", in *The Empire Strikes Back: Race and Racism in 70s Britain*, Centre for Contemporary Cultural Studies (London: Hutchinson, 1982), pp. 212–35.
65 Dúnlaith Bird, "Travel Writing and Gender", in *The Routledge Companion to Travel Writing*, ed. by Carl Thompson (London and New York: Routledge, 2020), pp. 35–45 (p. 37). See also Tim Youngs, *The Cambridge Introduction to Travel Writing* (Cambridge: Cambridge University Press, 2013).
66 McLeod, *Beginning Postcolonialism*, p. 197.
67 Sussan Babaie in *Omani Women*, by Helen Couchman (Muscat: Soloshow Publishing, 2015), pp. 79–87.
68 Foster and Mills, *An Anthology*, p. 15. See also Inderpal Grewal, *Home and Harem: Nation, Gender, Empire and the Culture of Travel* (Durham, NC: Duke University Press, 1997).
69 Foster and Mills, *An Anthology*, p. 7.
70 The first two cantos of *Childe Harold*, for example, were published in March 1812 and all 500 copies were sold within three days; by the middle of the month, the author "awoke to find himself famous".
71 Kirsten Holst Petersen and Anna Rutherford, *A Double Colonisation: Colonial and Post-Colonial Women's Writing* (Sydney: Dangaroo Press, 1986).
72 See Rana Kabbani, *Imperial Fictions: Europe's Myths of Orient* (London: Pandora, 1994), Chapters 1 and 2.
73 Lady Mary Wortley Montagu, *The Letters of Lady M.W. Montagu during the Embassy to Constantinople, 1716–18* (London: John Sharpe, 1825), Vol. I, p. 114.
74 Carsten Niebuhr, *Travels through Arabia, and Other Countries in the East*, translated by Robert Heron (Perth, Edinburgh, and London: Morison et al, 1792, 2 Vols.), Vol.2, p. 214.

75 T. E. Lawrence, "Letter to Charles Doughty" (7 August 1920) in T. E. Lawrence, David Garnett ed., *The Letters of T. E. Lawrence* (London: Jonathan Cape, 1938), p. 310.

76 T. E. Lawrence, *Seven Pillars of Wisdom: A Triumph* [1935] (Harmondsworth: Penguin, 1986), pp. 28 and 221.

77 Thesiger did not claim to be an anthropologist: "Although I have no anthropological training it seemed to me worth recording what I saw and what I was told"; cited in Alexander Maitland, *Wilfred Thesiger: The Life of the Great Explorer* [2006] (New York: The Overlook Press, Peter Mayer Publishers, 2011), p. 121.

78 See Alan Keohane, *Bedouin Nomads of the Desert* [1994] (London: Kyle Books, 2011): "Children are a vital part of Bedu life", the result of intercourse that is considered "a great pleasure for both men and women" (p. 106); women, according to Keohane, carry the tribe's sense of honour (p. 117).

79 Wilfred Thesiger, *Arabian Sands* [1959] (Harmondsworth: Penguin, 1984), p. 125.

80 Thesiger, *Arabian Sands*, p. 168. Maitland comments that Thesiger "never talked about physical sex as an expression of love, or even of affection. His attitude to sex was perfunctory, immature and selfish"; Maitland further suggests he diverted his sexual energy into "physically demanding pleasures", such as crossing the desert (Maitland, *Thesiger*, Chapter 11).

81 Bruce Kirkby, *Sand Dance: By Camel across Arabia's Great Southern Desert* (Toronto: McClelland and Stewart, 2000), p. 166.

82 Huggan, *Extreme Pursuits*, p. 166, in relation to American feminist literature.

83 Gillian Whitlock, "Tainted Testimony: The Khouri Affair", in *Australian Literary Studies*, 21, no. 4 (2004), pp. 165–77 (p. 170), cited in Huggan, *Extreme Pursuits*, pp. 166–67.

84 James (now Jan) Morris, *Sultan in Oman* [1957] (London: Eland, 2008), p. 17.

85 Jonathan Raban, *Arabia through the Looking Glass* [1979] (Glasgow: Fontana, 1980), p. 11.

86 Tony Wheeler, *Bad Lands* [2007] (Melbourne: Lonely Planet Publications, 2010).

87 Spivak, Gayatri Chakravorty, "Can the Subaltern Speak?" [1988], in *Colonial Discourse and Post-Colonial Theory* ed. by Patrick Williams and Laura Chrisman (Hemel Hempstead: Harvester Wheatsheaf, 1993), pp. 66–111.

88 Chandra Talpade Mohanty, "Under Western Eyes: Feminist Scholarship and Colonial Discourses", in *Colonial Discourse and Post-Colonial Theory*, ed. by Patrick Williams and Laura Chrisman (Hemel Hempstead: Harvester Wheatsheaf, 1993), pp. 196–220 (p. 198).

89 McLeod, *Beginning Postcolonialism*, p. 214.

90 Whitlock, "Tainted Testimony", pp. 175–76.

91 Huggan, *Extreme Pursuits*, p. 164. For Arab scholarship on veiling, see Fatima Mernissi, *The Veil and the Male Elite: A Feminist Interpretation of Women's Rights in Islam* (Mary Jo Lakeland, trans., Reading, MA: Perseus Books, 1991) and Leila Ahmed, *Gender in Islam* (New Haven, CT: Yale University Press, 1992). According to postcolonial feminist scholar, Anna Ball, "scholars such as these present vital alternatives to Western feminist interpretations of gender discourses in the Middle East and in Arab culture"; Anna Ball, *Palestinian Literature and Film in Postcolonial Feminist Perspective* [2012] (Abingdon: Routledge, 2017), p. 11.

140 *Gendering the desert*

92 Geraldine Brooks, *Nine Parts of Desire* (London: Penguin Books, 1995), Donya Al-Nahi, *Heroine of the Desert* (Bhopal, Manjul Books, 2006), and Jean Sasson, *Princess: More Tears to Cry* (London: Transworld, 2014).

93 Sasson, *Princess*, p. 5.

94 Whitlock, "Tainted Testimony", p. 169.

95 Huggan, *Extreme Pursuits*, p. 166. See Elisabeth Bronfen, *Over Her Dead Body: Death, Femininity, and the Aesthetic* (Manchester: Manchester University Press, 1992).

96 See Huggan, *Extreme Pursuits*, pp. 167–69.

97 Carby, "White Woman Listen!", pp. 212–235.

98 Marguerite van Geldermalsen, *Married to a Bedouin* (London: Virago, 2006).

99 Jonathan Raban, "The Journey and the Book" [1982], in *For Love and Money: Writing, Reading, Travelling, 1969–1987* (London: Collins Harvill, 1987), pp. 253–60, cited in Youngs, *Travel Writing*, p. 12.

100 Jenny Walker, "Married to a Bedouin", *Jordan* (Melbourne: Lonely Planet, 2009), p. 221.

101 Margaret Topping, "Travel Writing and Visual Culture", in *The Routledge Companion to Travel Writing*, ed. by Carl Thompson (London and New York: Routledge, 2020), pp. 78–88 (p. 87).

102 I am using Tim Youngs's definition (or parameters of selection) for travel writing, here, which references "predominantly factual, first-person prose accounts of travels that have been undertaken by the author-narrator" in Youngs, *The Cambridge Introduction*, p. 3; the portraits are not prose accounts, but they conform to every other criteria of the definition.

103 Mary Louise Pratt, *Imperial Eyes: Travel Writing and Transculturation* [1992] (London and New York: Routledge, 2008), p. 7.

104 Bird, "Travel Writing and Gender", p. 42.

105 Nicholas Clapp, *The Road to Ubar: Finding the Atlantis of the Sands* [1998] (London: Souvenir Press, 1999), p. 21.

106 Thomas writes, for example, "Dunes of all sizes, unsymmetrical in relation to one another, but with the exquisite rounds of a girl's breasts, rise tier upon tier like a mighty mountain system". Thomas, *Arabia Felix*, p. 170.

107 This fanaticism for the straight line is discussed by surveyor Len Beadell as he worked on the planning for the Gunbarrel Highway across central Australia. Len Beadell, *Too Long in the Bush* (Adelaide: Rigby, 1965).

108 Clapp, *The Road to Ubar*, p. 23.

109 Tidrick, *Heart Beguiling Araby*, p. 178.

110 As counted in a digital form of Lawrence's *Seven Pillars*. Colin Choat, ed., *Seven Pillars* [online], Project Gutenberg Australia (2001), available at http://gutenberg.net.au/ebooks01/0100111.txt [accessed 12 July 2019].

111 Robyn Davidson, *Tracks* [1980] (London: Picador, 1998), p. 190.

112 References to the maleness of the Antarctic desert abound in Wheeler's polar account, including among the men who work there and "pine for the old days when boys could be boys and girls weren't there" (p. 247).

113 Jay Griffiths, *Wild: An Elemental Journey* (London: Penguin, 2006), p. 295.

114 Sidonie Smith, *Moving Lives: Twentieth-Century Women's Travel Writing* (Minneapolis and London: University of Minnesota, 2001), p. x.

115 Citing Anna Ball from unpublished interaction with the author.

116 Ball, *Palestinian Literature and Film*, p. 116. Ball makes reference to "smooth space"; see Gilles Deleuze and Félix Guattari, *A Thousand Plateaus: Capitalism and Schizophrenia* [1987] (London: Continuum, 2004), pp. 256–341.

Gendering the desert   141

117 See explanation of the "Third Space" in Homi K. Bhabha, *The Location of Culture* (Abingdon and New York: Routledge, 1994), pp. 53–6.
118 Bassnett, "Travel Writing and Gender", p. 231.
119 Jo Tatchell, *A Diamond in the Desert: Behind the Scenes in the World's Richest City* [2009] (London: Hodder and Stoughton, 2010), p. 60.
120 See Huggan, *Extreme Pursuits*, Chapter 3.
121 Lisle, *Global Politics*, p. 97.

4 Wonderment and wilderness
Desert science writing

In *The Desert and the Sown* (1907), in a passage that runs against the grain of the familiar trope of empty desert, Gertrude Bell refreshingly slips behind the gaze of those she travels with to identify a different desert narrative to the one normally associated with Western travel in Arabia. Identifying that "Arabs do not speak of desert or wilderness as we do", she writes,

> Why should they? To them it is neither desert nor wilderness, but a land of which they know every feature, a mother country whose smallest product has a use sufficient for their needs. They know ... how to rejoice in the great spaces and how to honour the rush of the storm.[1]

Bell's association of the desert inhabitant with a deep understanding of nature is in itself a familiar trope suggestive of an Eden lost to urban societies, but it also hints at a moment of empathy within her own experience. The rejoicing in "great spaces" the honouring of the "rush of the storm" suggests that Bell is able to perceive the connection between Arab and desert because she shares a similar respect towards the "mother country". This connection could be read in two ways. If read through the familiar Western travel perspective of the desert as a zone of masculine posturing through quest, exploration, and exploitation (often conflated as science), Bell's landscape, as the provider of the "smallest product" for human sustenance, may appear feminised, domesticated, or tamed for human need. A different reading, however, is the one that Bell posits as an Arab perspective: "to them" this desert is composed of a more harmonious balance between the human being and his or her place within the environment. Nature in this passage, then, is not mere scenery staged for a human story, it is represented as architect of its own space, and prompter of its own rhythms. With the human story reduced to only one small constituent part amid the "great spaces", this passage can be read as sharing less of the colonising preoccupations of Bell's own era while anticipating more of the postcolonial sensibilities of the end of the twentieth

DOI: 10.4324/9781003197201-5

Wonderment and wilderness   143

century. In other words, within a passage that appears to move desert as mother country into centre stage, there is a response to nature that not only runs contrary to the dominant discourse of Bell's day but also prefigures the ecocritical concerns of our own.

This chapter probes the familiar tropes of Arabian desert representation and considers to what extent they collapse into more nuanced constructions of the desert space under an ecocritical reading. Thus far, in chapters that argue that the desert is often used in travel literature as a *tabla rasa* upon which to project fundamentally Western preoccupations, the landscape has formed only the backdrop for human endeavour. To recap, the desert featured as the stage set for historical re-enactment in footstep travel in Chapter 1, providing the context of extreme otherness for heroic quest and endeavour. In Chapter 2, the desert formed, on the one hand, the locus of human nostalgia as observed vicariously through the lives of the Bedu; on the other, it functioned as a periphery that hovered beyond the urban, helping to define the metropolitan or as an inconvenience to be crossed en route between human settlements. In Chapter 3, the desert was explored more positively as an opportunity to redeem marginalised voices, in particular of women, hitherto written out of the dominant discourse; by extension, and less positively, it was projected as a gendered space awaiting human penetration to become fully real or present. In each case, the desert retreats into the background as the focus falls on narratives that concentrate on various human interests – on presentations of self, other, and gender. This chapter, in contrast, attempts to move the desert into the foreground and seeks to do so with the help of an ecocritical reading and through the study of three broadly scientific texts.

Scientific texts (given their vintage qualities of mapping and naming) may seem like an unlikely choice to demonstrate the foregrounding of nature or to advocate for nature and the wild from a non-human perspective. If, however, as Robert Kern suggests, ecocriticism "becomes most interesting and useful ... when it aims to recover the environmental character or orientation of works whose conscious or foregrounded interests lie elsewhere", the choice of scientific texts in this chapter may find some justification.[2] In recent decades, "scientific writing" has become increasingly focused on the published communication of objectively observed facts for a community of peers; "science writing", meanwhile, targets a broader readership and has allowed for a less technical approach. Both definitions assume a human centre, however, imposing order on a random otherness; neither generally admits to passages of lyrical prose.[3] In science writing connected with the Arabian desert, it is nevertheless possible to see moments when the author's observations are unable to be contained within their formal discipline, when the writer bursts out of the text to express a delight in the land and its occupants almost in spite of the field of study. At these moments, the scientist cross-dresses as travel

144 *Wonderment and wilderness*

writer, recording the experience, the strongly felt emotions, of encounter with nature. In resisting categorisation according to established taxonomies, for example of physics, of entomology, or of geography, the work of these scientists resists homogenisation and migrates across boundaries – in other words, it becomes "hybrid", both in a taxonomical sense as being heterogenous and in a postcolonial sense, as work that inhabits and reveals border zones. Such work mirrors the "magpie" approach of ecocriticism, which applies an "attitude of inquiry … that neither foregrounds nor ignores [human] involvements, [but] draws equally on knowledge from the sciences, the humanities, and the arts".[4] By applying an eclectic ecocritical perspective to these moments of transgression in late twentieth-century science writing, it is possible to identify a step towards the kind of Earth-centred writing that Lawrence Buell, one of the founders of ecocriticism, recognised as expressing a "more even relationship of nature with culture, society, and the individual subject".[5]

It is perhaps no coincidence that science writing that displays these moments of imaginative interlude appears to be a specific feature of late twentieth-century desert accounts; such texts appear at the same point as the ecocritical movement becomes established as an independent and politically alert discipline.[6] These texts share with that critical corpus a sense of the environmental concerns of the day and, in the moments in which they describe a "more even relationship" with nature, become part of a general agency for change. This study's contribution towards this agency for change is in identifying and analysing the moments when the Arabian desert is presented as a place of value in its own right and becomes part of what we might call a productive "greening of the desert".[7] As tidy as this sounds, however, the reality is obviously far more subtle, and the discussion concludes with a broader exploration, beyond science writing, of some of the ecocritical issues surrounding wilderness representation. The Arabian desert belongs to a constructed landscape that is no more "politically [or] historically innocent" than the literature and culture that describe it; the effects of this invested geography are felt even today, for example in issues of conservation and land management.[8] To understand the context of these modern ecocritical issues, it is important to review the prevailing historical discourses that inform wilderness writing in general, and Arabian desert writing in particular, and it is to this context that the discussion first turns.

Delighting in sand grouse

If for the Bedu of Gertrude Bell's description (cited at the opening of this chapter) the desert is peopled with a series of lived and remembered connections "thicker with human associations than any city", for Europeans, it remains resolutely connected, even in the main desert narratives of today, with emptiness, absence, and abandonment.[9] Locked in the

Wonderment and wilderness 145

"imaginative geography" of the West, the desert is generally presented as a place of implied mental and physical privation, symbolised by the solitary desert wanderings of biblical prophets.[10] As Roderick Nash notes, in his history of the concept of wilderness, such landscape has long been "instinctively understood to be something alien to man – an insecure and uncomfortable environment against which civilization had waged an unceasing struggle";[11] Western pilgrims, explorers, and scholars have been drawn to "this cruel land" – a land, which as Wilfred Thesiger famously suggested, "can cast a spell which no temperate clime can match" – and for centuries have weighed their accomplishment in terms of the challenge it represented.[12] As we have seen, much recent travel writing connected with the region weighs its own accomplishment in turn against the exploits of those earlier pioneers, particularly T. E. Lawrence and Wilfred Thesiger, whether literally in second or footstep journeys or metaphorically through intertextual reference. In analysing the effect of Joseph Conrad's work on the image of the Congo, Patrick Holland and Graham Huggan write that "every modern travel book that features the Congo as travel zone at some level reinscribes Conrad's classic novella *Heart of Darkness* (1898)". In the same way, almost every modern travel book on Arabia reinscribes Thesiger's *Arabian Sands*, turning the desert into an equivalent "abject zone of extreme yet undifferentiated 'otherness' within which every aspect of life – landscape, people, culture, politics – presents itself as always already wrapped in metaphor and myth".[13] As such, the Arabian desert, over the centuries of its literary delineation by Western travellers, has become a textual zone, at best "incidentally geographical".[14]

"Incidentally geographical", as a term used by Holland and Huggan for over inscribed places, may be a useful way of characterising the literary representation of the Arabian desert, but it should not obscure the fact that other modes of desert discourse have been "specifically geographical" in their objective and that, until relatively recently, both literary and geographical content could be found operating simultaneously in desert literature. If, as Melman suggests in reference to Doughty's work, desert narratives may be "superficially described as stories of the conquest of the void, or wilderness, as well as tales of risk which position the individual explorer in front of a hostile nature", then geography has provided one of the ways in which explorers have sought to make sense of the undifferentiated otherness – one of the ways, in other words, in which the human being has attempted to rationalise or tame wilderness.[15]

In an opening chapter of *Imperial Eyes*, Mary Louise Pratt identifies one of two seminal historical episodes that have impacted on travel and travel writing as the moment when, in the second half of the eighteenth century, Linnaeus introduced a comprehensive system of taxonomy in *Systema Naturae* published in 1735. Pratt shows how the systematic naming of things brought about a transformation in the manner in which

146 *Wonderment and wilderness*

people explored and, more to the point, wrote about their explorations. Instead of the compendiums of zoological and botanical data that formed the appendices of earlier travel tomes (as required under the general headings set by the Royal Society for reporting on natural history),[16] the "observing and cataloguing of nature itself became narratable. It could constitute a sequence of events, or even produce a plot. It could form the main storyline of an entire account".[17] This is significant when transposed to the context of desert explorations in Arabia because suddenly there is something to write about in an otherwise often prop-less landscape. The eye, lacking any immediate distraction, focuses in on the detail of the minimal life in view and becomes observant of the minutiae in a landscape of essentially unencumbered forms. It is of little surprise, then, that embedded in the exploits of each lonely traveller, copious descriptions of the natural world appear in all the major desert texts in a process that can be charted back to the eighteenth century. This is the point when travel writing in general becomes institutionalised in that it becomes sponsored by and presented to the Royal Society;[18] indeed, from the eighteenth century and for much of the Victorian age, as Paul Fussell notes, travel becomes "something like an obligation" upon those able and willing to contribute to the intellectual project of accumulating knowledge.[19] That activity is eventually streamlined into new disciplines. In this context, Holland and Huggan show that travel writing joined "anthropology, geography, and the human sciences generally as one strand of a new regime of knowledges" that helped to encode the region of scrutiny.[20] Journal writing in the early and mid-nineteenth century became key to the accuracy of observation where precise notes on time, number, and distance formed part of what Carl Thompson terms the "epistemological decorum" of the day,[21] and ensured that, as Fussell notes, travel writing was able to "share the space and borrow the authority" of human sciences.[22]

If, as these critics suggest, a literature of science and conservation grew from within travel literature, it could not be contained by it, and the observations of amateur gentlemen (and one or two lady) scientists over the late nineteenth and early twentieth centuries become less about making a record of the flora and fauna encountered at a given point in time and more about evidencing and legitimating the author's presence within a geographical location. Desert writers during this period were cognisant of their continuing duty to record the physical nature of the earth, but largely as a reflection of the human story within it. *Arabia Deserta*, the work of desert explorer Charles M. Doughty, is a classic of its kind:

> Of surpassing interest to those many minds, which seek after philosophical knowledge and instruction, is the Story of the Earth. Her manifold living creatures, the human generations and Her ancient rocks ... that vast mountainous labyrinthine solitude of rainless valleys.[23]

Besides the many detailed, scientific observations that Doughty makes on the desert lands in Arabia, attention is always drawn ultimately to man's (and the gender is specific here) interest in the landscape and the thoughts that it inspires about his place in the universe. This is reflected in the poetic literary tone in which the ponderous, multisyllabic words match the "mountainous labyrinthine solitude" of its subject and hyperbole helps to set the description within the specific aesthetic of the Romantic sublime. Described as "the Story of the Earth", this is in fact the story of Man, striding through a femininised landscape, looking for philosophical insights imposed on the construction of place. The landscape is made performative, in other words, for human instruction.

Similar devices are used in the celebrated passages of natural description in T. E. Lawrence's account of Wadi Rum (in *Seven Pillars of Wisdom*) and of *al-ramlah*, known as the "Empty Quarter" to Western travellers, in Bertram Thomas's *Arabia Felix*.[24] Thomas, learning from the Bedu with whom he is travelling, writes that

> the sands are a public diary, that even he who runs may read, for all living creatures go unshod. ... No bird may alight, no wild beast or insect pass but needs must leave its history in the sands, and the record lasts until a rising wind bears a fine sand along to obliterate it.[25]

Keen to make a more permanent record than a footprint in sand, Thomas details the fennec foxes, sand cats, the "twelve varieties of lizards, all alike endowed with pointed snouts for diving in the sands", the scorpions that were "of pale green colour", and three types of snake, "all of sand colour, boa, horned viper, and colubrid".[26] As an amateur scientist, Thomas is identifying, classifying, noting, and, indeed, celebrating nature for the education and enjoyment of learned society back home.[27] Given the Arab context, his work, and those of fellow explorers, also contributes to the academic tradition of Orientalism, "a specific kind of knowledge about specific places, peoples, and civilisations" that Said argues is a formidable part of the colonial project.[28] While science lends authority to the travel account, it also lends authority to the hegemonic perspective expressed therein.

The responsibility of travellers towards documenting wilderness areas loses traction after Bertram Thomas, as science forms into more individual disciplines. The human print in the desert (tangibly scratched as petroglyphs into the rocks of iconic Arabian landscapes) is reflected in desert texts that become increasingly more about the observer than the observed, and the almost obsessive recording of natural data that marked Victorian desert travel accounts runs its course in the first half of the twentieth century and more or less ends with Wilfred Thesiger's *Arabian Sands*. This narrative not only represents the last text in which scientific

148 *Wonderment and wilderness*

desert observations are confidently recorded by an amateur, but it also represents the apotheosis of self within the desert landscape; so strong is Thesiger's mark upon the desert in *Arabian Sands* that it is almost impossible for future travellers to cross the same landscape without recognising Thesiger's presence within it. After Thesiger, travel writing is no longer deemed the appropriate vehicle of scientific detail as the disciplines of zoology, ornithology, geography, anthropology, and ethnography claim this territory as their own, or as Thompson observes, "The growing specialisation of science ... generated an increasingly technical scientific vocabulary that could not easily be reconciled with the requirement for a plain prose style in the travel account".[29] Modern desert travel writers, such as Mark Evans, may take pleasure in referring to the wildlife they encounter, and in describing the features of erg and dune, but mainly as life-affirming events or challenges to overcome in the wilderness – as an ornament to their descriptions or as harbingers of meaning for the traveller – rather than as a deliberate contribution to the collection and expression of technical data. This minimalisation of scientific purpose in the modern desert journey is for some authors a subject of regret or apology; as Evans states, "In the past, expeditions like the first crossing of the Empty Quarter made significant contributions to scientific understanding. Our journey is not so much about that, but is more about communication, and connection".[30] While the stated intention of Evans's *Crossing the Empty Quarter* is less about the need to inform and more about the desire to create a sympathetic understanding of his subject – namely, Bertram Thomas whose route Evans follows, the communities who live along the desert rim and the natural world he encounters as he crosses the Empty Quarter – there is yet a wistful nod to the fellowship of the Royal Geographic Society to which the author belongs. This is evidenced by the traveller's excitement at finding rare new petroglyphs, an event that is described as a highlight of the entire journey.

If modern travel writers since Thesiger feel somewhat cut off from the tradition of "voyages and travels" of previous centuries, scientists have lost ground too. Modern scientists are clearly expected to use a register and vocabulary appropriate to their discipline, leading some desert commentators to renounce their professional authority in favour of a more literary approach that allows them to dip into the reserve of rich textual associations accruing to the subject. There is nothing new in this approach, as Holland and Huggan point out, "It is as common for travel writers to disguise their scientific authority as to invoke it – a strategy that supports their advantageous rhetorical position as inquiring amateurs".[31] Ralph A. Bagnold is one such self-styled inquiring amateur travelling in the 1930s who, despite being elected to the Royal Society for his work on desert physics, insisted on describing himself as "an amateur scientist of no academic standing".[32] His identification with amateurism suggests that he took pleasure in availing himself of the wider repertoire of narrative

Wonderment and wilderness 149

techniques more readily available to a travel writer than a modern scientist. The preface to *Libyan Sands* reads as part apology to science, part manifesto for future desert writing; its full title, *Libyan Sands: Travels in a Dead World*, captures the sense of lifelessness, of man centre stage in the landscape, and of fixed perspectives ("ideas preserved") projected onto the space:

> I have collected my travels [in] ... places where nothing exists, no sprouting grass blade nor worm of decay; where perhaps, in certain spots, nothing ever did exist; travels shared, companions changing but ideas preserved; and over all a sense of what travel is, and how it can be done with little pomp, little money, much love of it and very much preparation.

(p. 9)

The literary nature of this text allows Bagnold to describe the desert less in terms of its own inherent qualities and internal communities, and more of an "otherness" of his choosing and a familiar escape from urban society: "[A]ll the constrictions of civilisation, walls, fences, conventions and police", he writes, "surge up vigorously to the limit of the sown, there to shrivel to nothing before the freedom of the desert" (p. 60). In contrast, Bagnold's more scholarly *The Physics of Blown Sand and Sand Dunes* casts a more scientific eye on what might be called the "ergonomics of sand" for the explorer, finding reasons for the desert's enduring magnetism in mathematical terms through the "simplicity of form, an exactitude of repetition and a geometric order unknown in nature". Bagnold appears uncomfortable, however, with the straitjacket of science and frequently throws it off in literary asides. Psychological analysis of the power of landscape is uncommon in a physics textbook, but from the outset, Bagnold is inspired to write about the terrain in language that borrows from literature. Within the introduction, for example, he describes the dunes as an anthropomorphic structure "growing, retaining their shape, even breeding, in a manner which, by its grotesque imitation of life, is vaguely disturbing to an imaginative mind", giving insight into his values as a man, rather than as a physicist objectively observing the mechanics of form.[33]

The blended nature of Bagnold's text (part science, part travel writing) anticipates more recent desert narratives that similarly dissolve the boundaries between genres, either in a conscious acknowledgement of their travelling antecedents or more commonly as a visceral response to an alien environment. By blurring the distinctions between science and travel, their work moves in a reverse direction from the canon to which it belongs, returning to the early genre of "voyages and travels" in an attempt to replace some of the wonder lost in the expression of modern science. Wonderment, as noted by Stephen Greenblatt, is a recurring

150 *Wonderment and wilderness*

feature in colonial travel writing and a key trope of Oriental literature.[34] Bringing it back into descriptions of Arabian desert encounter, therefore, runs the risk of inviting comparisons with discredited and anachronistic modes of representation. Some critics, such as Aaron Sachs, recognise the value in trying to redeem science writing from the homogenising postcolonial critique of European explorers and their texts; in something of a homogenising statement of his own, he notes that this approach has "obscured any potentially useful, even radical ideas that might have been developed by European, literary, male, bourgeois scientists";[35] Sabine Wilke similarly suggests that an explorer may have been part of a project of domination, but he may also have had something useful to say.[36] This is where a *postcolonial* ecocritical approach is helpful, as it allows useful elements to emerge from a text that may be otherwise flawed by the values of its time: as Ursula Heise notes, most critical reading under the postcolonial ecocritical banner approaches literary texts by asking "how accurately they portray the realities of colonial exploitation and environmental devastation" while at the same time exploring "to what extent the works' authors can be credited with attempting to resist these processes or with imagining alternatives to them".[37] Set within this context, the science writers (as a distinct category of modern travellers in Arabia) who use spectacle and wonder as equally as anguish and alarm within their nature texts can similarly be seen to trouble Orientalist tropes, paralleling postcolonial attempts to foreground the object of Western gaze and give it agency. Identifying opportunities for agency in modern desert writing is important because, for as long as deserts are thought of only as *tabla rasa* upon which to project (in this case Western) human preoccupations, mapped and measured only for the next resource exploitation, they are likely to continue to be the chosen sites of atomic testing, oil extraction, indiscriminate land fill, and unsustainable sport.

In the work of four relatively obscure science writers, physicist Uwe George (1976), entomologists Donald Walker and Tony Pittaway (1987), and geographer Nigel Winser (1989), all of whom write about the deserts of the Middle East, some of the legacy of the old Orient lingers in the landscape they describe, but their work is about more than just these anachronisms. In literary asides and anecdotes, they abandon their scholarly objectives to express moments when they are surprised by joy in the desert and in so doing betray something of what Roslynne Haynes describes as the *mysterium*, *tremendum*, and *fascinans* that marked the origins of science writing as it grew from amateur roots. One reading of their work is to categorise it as part of what Haynes identifies as "the emerging neoromantic cult of the desert as a space for enlightenment and self-discovery", and indeed, all the writers insert or implicate the first person in their accounts.[38] A more productive reading, however, through ecocriticism, examines the moments in which emotion towards the subject overcomes the scruples of scientific analysis and allows the writer to communicate the wonder of nature in all its glorious adaptation and biodiversity; at such moments, the author retreats from the centre of the account to the periphery. Within this kind of reading, the desert has a presence not just as an inanimate zone for human study, endeavour, and exploitation but as a place in its own right with its own logic and pattern – a "bioregion", in socio-biologist Edward Wilson's phraseology.[39] The moments of agency may be small – a delight in the sand grouse, an encounter with a dust devil, a journey beyond the marked zone of scientific enquiry – but they unmistakably evidence a growing consciousness towards the environment and raise questions about the human place within it.

George and the neo-sublime

In an ambitious physics project, the German naturalist Uwe George sets out to account for the growing desertification of much of the world's surface. The result is a mostly technical book, translated into English as *In the Deserts of This Earth*, that at times requires specialist knowledge to read and is complemented by diagrams, illustrations, graphs, and scientific data.[40] It also includes, however, photographs of the scientist and his wife at work in the desert terrain, and resorts throughout to first person narrative to describe the emotional impact of working alone for extended periods in an Arabian desert environment.[41] In anecdotes and asides, George establishes the transgressive nature of his enterprise, moving beyond the scientific objective of his study to show how the desert environment impacts upon him as a traveller and dweller within the landscape. His work is chosen here to show how it connects to Haynes's "neo-romantic cult of the desert", demonstrating the prevalence of this concept in a broader Western European rather than parochial English context, but also shows how it breaks free from this anachronistic perspective by imagining a new and more equal alliance with other, non-human desert dwellers.

Setting out his opening premise under the anthropomorphic title "The Merciless Sun", George taps immediately into the psychology of wilderness encounter: "The sight of the black, sun-scorched landscapes of rubble", writes George, "produces a feeling of devastation and chaos" (p. 23). Words like "endless abandonment", "boundless region", belong to the vocabulary not of physics but of literature, and most especially to the aesthetic of the sublime. Fear, or at least the frisson of danger, a feeling of diminishment in a landscape of enormity together with an inability to verbalise superlatives of space and silence, are common sublime responses to the untamed fastness of the desert and as such have formed consistently recurring tropes throughout the history of European desert literature. These metaphors are informed by the vocabulary of the sublime, as most particularly defined by Edmund Burke in Britain and Immanuel Kant in Germany. Although by no means the first nor the most

152   Wonderment and wilderness

comprehensive study of the sublime in the eighteenth century, Burke's treatise, *A Philosophical Enquiry into the Origin of Our Ideas of the Sublime and Beautiful* (1756), was influential in providing a ready-made vocabulary for affecting visual experiences, and it is often in his terms that travel writers have traditionally couched their most hyperbolic desert passages.[42] The desert, with its heat and hardship, leant itself well to sublime treatment for, as East-bound traveller Clarke states, "Burke has instructed us to find [the sublime] in vastness and in terror".[43] Clarke's choice not to describe a scene because it is indescribable (part of the "words fail me" trope) seems to be informed equally by the Kantian notion of sublimity found in the indefinable, the indistinct, and the overwhelming as articulated, for example, in *Observations on the Feeling of the Beautiful and the Sublime* (1764).[44] Roslynn Haynes helpfully translates the sublime into a modern desert context in commenting on the traveller's "awe at its immensity, terror at its starkness and fascination at its wildness". She goes on to explain how these emotions trigger a psychological effect: "[T]his spatial-temporal combination", explains Haynes, is "intense, vision-producing, almost literally mind-blowing, since it transcends the rational", and indeed, desert literature abounds with set-piece reflections on man's relationship with the divine and with metaphysical contemplation in general.[45]

The desert in its vastness, then, has often provided the ideal platform upon which to present the lone figure in the landscape, where he (it is invariably he) enacts dramas of an existential nature. Uwe George appears to fit neatly within this trope when he writes,

> I was standing there wholly alone, my body the centre of a vast empty disk. The horizon around me formed one uninterrupted circle. The sky was a glaring, colorless brightness, with not a cloud to be seen. Aside from me and the ground on which I stood, there was nothing but the brilliantly white, shimmering disk of the sun.
>
> (p. 4)

There are immediately obvious similarities in this passage with a moment of extreme egoism in a nineteenth-century English travel text – namely, Alexander Kinglake's Eastern tale, *Eothen* (a popular Victorian travel account described by travel historian Peter Whitfield as "a best-seller, a popular classic, still immensely readable, but full of ambiguities").[46] Kinglake writes: "hour by hour I advanced, and saw no change – I was still the very centre of a round horizon … the same circle of sand still glaring with light, and fire".[47] Centre stage and spot-lit, this is the performative subject at the height of solipsistic contemplation, nature reduced to a set for the performing *id*. This is the supreme "monarch-of-all-I-survey" moment that Mary Louise Pratt notably writes of in *Imperial Eyes*, a seminal text that has provided a lexicon of postcolonial terms since

Wonderment and wilderness 153

1992.[48] But where Kinglake's egocentricity can be read as part of an exalted colonial dominion that stretches as far as the eye can see, George's centring in nature is troubled and impinged upon by fear:

> An indescribable sense of loneliness and forsakenness overpowered me. ... I felt as if I had lost all the inner standards that gave me an awareness of time and place. An infinite distance appeared to separate me from the nearest living being, and it would take me forever, it seemed, to cover that distance.
>
> (p. 4)

George is disoriented in this landscape, stripped of the calibrations (the "inner standards ... of time and place") that are both the tools of his profession as a scientist and the practical attributes that connect him to safety, community, home. Ironically, the distorting element of his experience helps to re-orientate George into a natural world that has a presence beyond his existence within it. Thus, at the same time as George identifies existential angst present in the utter silence (a silence peculiar to deep desert wilderness), he is also becoming reattached to a more planetary understanding of the human in relation to the natural. The sense of being overwhelmed by nature only retreats when the author catches sight of his own track that leads him back, metaphorically and topographically, to the safety of camp. Ecocritics read moments such as these as instructive; as SueEllen Campbell writes, "[T]he dry places we call deserts possess, and can teach us to see, their own kinds of beauty, richness, and wonder, and they offer lessons for us all of adaptation, flexibility, toughness, and resilience". George's lesson in relative scale in the vastness is one such moment of learning.

George may have shrunk in the landscape, but at least he is still present within it. The French anthropologist, Marc Augé, in his study of supermodernity writes of the way that the modern world has created "empirical non-places" in which the individual is "decentred in a sense from himself; he has instruments that place him in constant contact with the remotest parts of the outside world"; these portable telephones, computers, and cameras mean the individual can live in a detached space that is "wholly independent of his immediate physical surroundings".[49] George's moment in the centre of a round horizon is in one sense an extreme version of the decentring of self in a non-place (in a "land not sliced into places").[50] But this overlooks the fact that George goes naked into the wilderness (crucially he *walks*, travelling only with canteen of water and compass, leaving behind the tools of connection, such as a vehicle and two-way radio, with the outside world) and in this condition, becomes disorientated and frightened by his vulnerability. Charles Forsdick asserts in a recent essay entitled "Travel and the Body" that getting lost can be interpreted as an "extreme form of re-embodiment, the reassertion of the

154 *Wonderment and wilderness*

place of the corporeal – with its radical unpredictability – in the experience of travel".[51] Uwe is similarly forced by the experience of the location to be fully aware of his mortality in relation to his surroundings; in other words, he must be *in the place* – indeed his survival depends upon it. Reflecting on the experience from the safety of camp he states,

> [T]he experience of being dependent on ourselves alone as we tramp through the boundless expanses of the desert, of trusting only our own abilities, enables us to recapture our identity. We can shake off the dross that our production-oriented society has heaped up in our psyches.
>
> (p. 5)

This connection with the wilderness, rather than the apparent taming it first suggests, is a moment of transcendence, a moment of recognising, as Augé advocates, "that we inhabit a single planet, a fragile, threatened body, infinitely small in an infinitely large universe".[52] Augé suggests that this "planetary awareness is an ecological awareness" and as such George's project helps educate the reader, over the course of the book, in gaining an insight into the beauty and complexity of the desert as place and as planetary component.

If George's response to the desert shares some of the ways in which travel writers describe the desert as positioned in space (in other words, the desert as other than home and offering a site of what C. Kaplan calls "philosophical epiphany"), it differs in the way the desert is positioned in time.[53] The track that leads George back to the camp proves that he is "a being with a past and a future" (p. 5). This is interesting because it touches on a key feature of the Arabian desert experience (as cradle of civilisation) in which traditionally the past impinges on the present in an ontological kind of way. This connection with the past, a feature that Augé calls "anthropological place" and which, in Saidian terms, links the Arabian desert to its "imaginative geography", is not always present in descriptions of deserts in other parts of the world. In *The Tourist Gaze*, Urry and Larsen identify the desert landscape of America, for example, as having a specifically future emphasis, divorced from the past. Quoting Baudrillard, they note that deserts in the USA constitute a "metaphor of endless futurity, the obliteration of the past and the triumph of instantaneous time"; they go on to write that the empty desert landscapes "are experienced through driving huge distances, travel involving a 'line of flight' into the disappearing future".[54] For George, as for most British writers who describe desert travels in an Arabian context, the journey is less about blotting out and more about filling in – detailing the "natural history" of the region (in George's case, most notably his discoveries about the extraordinary survival techniques of the sand grouse) and engaging with the nomadic communities that help establish a continuity

Wonderment and wilderness 155

with, to use Augé terminology, "a collective history". This is very different from the way in which, as Urry and Larsen suggest, roads crossing American deserts have come to dominate, at the expense of the landscape and the communities through which they cut, developing their own homogenous characters (complete with fast food outlets and undifferentiated malls) that seal drivers off from the landscape beyond the tarmac strip.

While American accounts of desert often focus on the Anthropocene, the "human-dominated geological epoch" (with its proposed commencement of 1945, date of "the Trinity" experimental nuclear explosion in the New Mexican desert), modern anglophone Arabian desert accounts, as we have seen, consciously narrate a non-human space. Paul Shepherd suggests that the "key spatial metaphors" of boundlessness and emptiness make the desert experience the most sublime of all natural encounters.[55] To these spatial metaphors, one might add "uniformity", a term coined by H. and H. A. Frankfort to describe the way in which landscape continues without change or incident within an entire scope of view. "The interesting result of uniformity", as Frankfort suggests,

> is the way in which it accentuates any exceptional bit of relief that happens to break the monotonous regularity. Out in the desert one is conscious of every hillock, of every spoor of an animal, of every desert dust storm, of every bit of movement.[56]

These are the elements that are studied with intense scrutiny by George, who takes a holistic approach to the role all parts of the desert wilderness play in the evolution of the landscape and extrapolates from these scientific observations a prognosis for the future of planet Earth. Telescoping in and out of the macro- and micro-zones of planetary physics and earth sciences, the author focuses on details that are folded into a larger web of being that he makes tangible through his ornithological field study on the sand grouse. In a moment when he suppresses a scream on account of the bird's family sleeping nearby, he recognises that "now it was more than scientific interest that linked me to them". This is an expression that owes its origins to another aspect of eighteenth- and early nineteenth-century European Romanticism – namely, "pantheism". George describes a sense of overwhelming connectivity with the birds: "[W]e, the living, were linked in the face of what I felt to be the cruel coldness of the universe" (pp. 176–77). This identification of kinship as equal sufferers under the sun can be identified as a non-Anthropocentric perspective. Diletta de Cristofaro and Daniel Cordle suggest that such moments challenge us to "think beyond the human scale, to imagine – limited though such intellectual leaps must be – planetary forces, histories, and spaces in the face of which we shrink into insignificance".[57] In George's desert, the tiny adaptations of toads are brought under the same scrutiny as the

156   *Wonderment and wilderness*

geological events that have shaped the desert in which they live, helping to recreate that sense of scale; crucially, for the purpose of the present discussion, this is achieved not through the exposition of scientific data but by reference to the idiom of travel writing.

In George's desert, then, it is possible to read less of a reproduction of the Romantic sublime and more of a reconfiguration of that aesthetic attuned to today's ecological sensibilities. In the Burkean sublime, the moments of contemplation of the vastness and terror may similarly try to capture, in Melman's words, the "infinity of the universe and the human condition within it", but the undiminished focus of gaze remains on the subject: even at the moment that man is described as infinitely small within the landscape, he is still the protagonist of the scene he constructs.[58] In other words, the Romantic desert is all about the writer who describes it. George's sublime, in contrast, pushes the human element sidewise and allows the desert to become all about the sand grouse.

Walker and Pittaway in amateur pursuits

If Uwe George's work belongs to a European tradition (albeit one reconfigured for new purposes) of the Romantic sublime, the work of D. H. Walker and A. R. Pittaway references a more distinctly British aesthetic – namely, the picturesque. Whereas George is a professional scientist, the work of Walker and Pittaway emerges from an amateur tradition; even a casual user of field guides will instantly recognise the Linnaean nomenclature, the distribution maps, the illustrations belonging to each genus, the categorisation according to family in *Insects of Eastern Arabia* (1987).[59] At the time of its publication, this book represented a rare, if not the only, illustrated field guide on Arabian insect life, and in it, Walker and Pittaway cover the various species known by amateur entomologists as "bugs" in a field guide typical of the publishing house Macmillan. The acknowledgements give credit to subject specialists (renowned lepidopterists, apiasts, and general entomologists), as expected, but they also give the first hint that the field of study is larger than the world of expected entomological survey. The book, the reader learns, was "prompted by a love for the beauty and freedom of the desert", and the contents of the book are "records from a happy association with this environment" (viii); in the preface, there is a reference to William Wordsworth's "Solitary Reaper" and his "weary bands/Of travellers in some shady haunt,/Among Arabian sands" so that even before the book begins in earnest, it is clear that this is a hyperinscribed space that will permit the scientists to stray out of the normal territory of dry data description normally associated with practical field guides. The introduction gives further clues as to the taxonomy of the text – something that might be referred to in entomological terms as a "var", or "variation", on the described norms of the genre – as it opens with a lyrical description of the desert environment

Wonderment and wilderness 157

before embarking on general details common to a particular class of Arthropoda:

> [S]himmering in the heat, the view from the top of the sand dune was extensive … a delight of rolling sand and stone hillocks; … in the cool dark recesses beneath the rocks other life existed; the insects … belong to a large phylum or division of the animal kingdom.

> (p. viii)

The shift from lyrical to scientific language appears eccentric to the reader but natural to the writer, who swaps register with similar rapidity throughout.

By the end of the book, the lyrical takes over altogether. Liberated by the desert subject to step out of his scientific role, Donald Walker is responsible for a concluding section called "Reflections on Arabia".[60] Described as a "series of tales from experiences encountered in Arabia" (p. 155), the eight vignettes, still clinging to third-person anonymity and somewhat apologetically appearing in smaller font than the text in the rest of the book, are part travelogue, part memoir. The first of the eight tales, covering the author's arrival in the country of Saudi Arabia and his first encounter with the desert, marks a tentative foray into travel writing proper:

> Slowly this kaleidoscope of colour altered the scene, forming an unforgettable picture with the minaret of the mosque and a palm tree silhouetted against the deep red sky. He was deeply affected by the beauty of his new surroundings. The call to evening prayers drew him out of his reverie.

> (p. 155)

The third-person narrator, the expatriate of the tale's title, is not embraced by the landscape but standing at the respectful distance of a spectator. The scene is framed by a fixed viewpoint and organised into a familiar composition of silhouetted foregrounds and retreating sunset backgrounds. In the peaceful and neat arrangement of mosque, palm, and prayer, and in the reference to "scene" and "picture", it is easy to trace the Romantic legacy of Gilpin's Picturesque. William Gilpin, one of the leading proponents of this aesthetic in the eighteenth century, wrote that the Picturesque denotes "such objects as are proper subjects for painting", and he associated it closely with the "art of travel".[61] Writing about Gilpin's description of Tintern Abbey, Tim Youngs states that "travellers' accounts of the landscape do not provide a neutral version of it; they do not simply describe it; they *construct* it … not as it is but as it strikes and affects".[62] Holding up a Claude-glass to landscape in their travels East, travel writers similarly constructed the scenery in front of them: "both the reality and the fancy", writes Henry Holland, for example, of a view

158 *Wonderment and wilderness*

in the Near East in the early nineteenth century, "combine in giving to the scenery the character of a vast and beautiful picture spread out before the sight".[63] Part of this construction, of course, envisions the relationship between the East and the West. For the Romantics, the Orient consisted of a collection of illusory parts, observed from "true-life", but interpreted in Western terms, and reassembled to form a two-dimensional picture, voiceless, and vulnerable to further re-interpretations by the spectator. Without the linguistic ability, the time, or even the inclination, many travellers, not just in the 1800s but throughout Western travel East, are unable to graduate beyond the role of spectator, to glean anything more than a snapshot either of the land or its inhabitants. The splendid views of set-piece scenery, such as those of Keppel whose "numerous caravan tracing its way through the mazy winding of the road, added not a little to the living part of the picture"– and not a lot to literature, we might add, nor to a refreshed view of the East.[64]

Walker's painting of the Arabian desert in the colours of the Picturesque, whether conscious or not, could be cast in the same unflattering light, wearily recasting familiar tropes – that is, were it not for the bugs. Weaving between the discipline of science writing and travel writing, the field guide delights in its subject. Describing fleas, for example, as "small, wingless insects that live as parasites mainly on mammals", the register is predictably dry, but when the text describes the flea as "capable of *spectacular* leaps which sometimes exceed 100 times the length of its own body" (p. 111, emphasis added), it is possible to feel the excitement of the subject. This is travel writing as it extends from a heritage of desert exploration and amateur (without implying the modern pejorative now associated with the term) investigation. Edward Said, in an essay entitled "Professionals and Amateurs", remarks that specialisation means "losing sight of the raw effort of constructing either art or knowledge" in preference for "impersonal theories or methodologies". Specialisation, in other words, is one form of professionalism that "kills your sense of excitement and discovery" and reduces intellectual endeavour to an impoverished activity, carried out "for a living, between the hours of nine and five with one eye on the clock".[65] Said goes further to suggest that modern learning has become contained and restricted by the protocols of communication demanded by each specialist discipline, and this has impinged upon the intellectual opportunity to challenge. In contrast, amateurism, Said suggests, is an ethical practice motivated by virtues such as "care and affection rather than by profit". In contrast to "selfish, narrow" specialisation, it has the power to make "connections across lines and barriers" unhindered by what Said observes as the self-serving and self-imposed restrictions set up by the professions.

As an amateur in the Saidian definition of the term, Walker's eight stories and the excited frame tales of each insect family belong to a new species of wilderness travel writing that aims to bind and connect the human with, in this case, the minutely observed world of the desert insect.

Wonderment and wilderness 159

In one of the tales called "Time and Life", Walker describes a dying camel, imagining its role "when it had run for hours with long stride carrying its master effortlessly across the desert", now lying encircled by waiting ravens. The scientist does not attempt to intervene but returns to the scene over the course of three weeks and watches as death unfolds a whole drama of its own:

> Nature now assisted in its final departure. The work had been started by the ravens, then a Steppe Eagle had visited the carcase and then a Desert Fox. The remains were alive with activity as several different species of beetle and fly made it their temporary home, rapidly feeding and breeding, each carrying out its duty in the web of life.
>
> (p. 160)

In the way the tale moves the focus from human sentimentality for animal as owned by man, to animal as part of a "web of life", and in the way that it achieves this through combining the tools of travel writing with the lens of science, it resonates with the ethical scholarship advocated by Said, making "connections across lines and barriers". William Sherman writes that in the eighteenth century, "instead of presenting readers with a hodgepodge of marvels, travel accounts sponsored by and presented to the Royal Society began the systematic collection of nature knowledge in the name of reason and public utility".[66] Rather than seeing Walker as reductively returning to eighteenth-century aesthetics, his work can be seen as returning some of the wonder, "the hodgepodge of marvels", to the travel account in an age of hyperspecialisation. In so doing, he contributes knowledge for a new kind of "reason and public utility" put to the purpose of a modern concern for the environment. Sharing his fascination with the role of the beetle and fly in the desert's web of life brings a wider audience to the more scholarly parts of Walker's field guide and indeed supports the campaigns of Edward Wilson and others who advocate the importance of biodiversity.

While the field guide by Walker and Pittaway is by its very nature a celebration of biodiversity (in the entomology described therein), the discussion *about* biodiversity is only inferred through a reading of the book's vignettes. This chapter turns next, therefore, to a work wherein biodiversity is a significant theme in its own right. In a report that notes "some 16,500 invertebrates from 31 taxonomic groups" (p. 158), biodiversity is one of the resulting observations of Nigel Winser's work on a sand desert in Oman. While primarily an expedition report, Winser's work shares many of the neo-romantic elements of George and Walker with similar sublime and picturesque travel snapshots delineating the familiar representations of the desert. Where Winser's work makes an interesting contribution to the genre, however, is in a new note of anxiety about the scientific enterprise itself. George, Walker, and Pittaway appear confident

160   *Wonderment and wilderness*

in their activity, conducting science in the full expectation their work's value lies in some generic notion of its contribution to knowledge. Written contemporaneously, Winser's work in contrast betrays a thread of doubt. Winser the scientist has a confidence in the undertaking that is not wholly shared by Winser the travel writer. This is a productive dilemma that not only reveals a new postcolonial angst but affords agency to the environmental debate to which it contributes.

Winser in search of solutions

In *The Sea of Sands and Mists* (1989), Nigel Winser, a trained zoologist who identifies as a geographer, sets out to record a major Royal Geographical Society expedition in the late 1980s of which Winser was the main organiser.[67] The account is couched within the "ancien regime" of Royal Geographic Society exploration (p. xv) in which deserts "have long been a fascination for Britons" (p. xix), and the scientific pedigree of the text is carefully established. The reader learns, for example, that the study took a cross-disciplinary approach that involved the work of over 30 scientists and resulted in numerous scientific papers. The subtitle of Winser's expedition account, *Desertification: Seeking Solutions in the Wahiba Sands*, reveals the multidisciplinary nature of the project, capturing both a scientific and a political perspective, and it includes the major findings of the scientists from each of the represented disciplines (including earth science, biology, zoology, and geography), summarised by Winser for the layperson; the account concludes with an epilogue written by Dr. Roderic Dutton, the scientific coordinator of the expedition.

But the scientific pedigree is only part of the story: *The Sea of Sands and Mists* presents most consistently, in fact, as desert travel narrative. The account's credibility is anchored, for example, not as may have been expected by reference to fellow earth scientists, but by placing it within the tradition of desert literature:

> For all expeditioners Wilfred Thesiger is something of a hero. He is the last of the great desert explorers and for many he crowns the work of Burton, Doughty, Blunt, Lawrence, and Philby, familiar names for those who have taken an interest in the British presence in the Middle East.
>
> (p. 23)

The reference to the desert literary "greats" is not simply an acknowledgement in the opening pages, it informs the way in which Winser engages with the landscape, as he gains satisfaction, for example, in knowing that "across the wadi was the head of the same swale that Wilfred [Thesiger] and his companions had travelled through some thirty-eight years earlier" (p. 119).[68] Winser, illustrated seated on a camel, camel stick in hand, and

Wonderment and wilderness 161

in the company of the Bedu, is carving out his own space within the literary landscape, as equally as he is charting, mapping, and naming the features of a geographical location as befits the nature of the scientific expedition he leads. In amongst chapters with a distinctly scientific resonance ("Taylorbase – The Field University" and "Seeking Solutions"), there are chapters with more lyrical titles ("Sand of a Thousand Colours" and "The Sand Guardians") and even within the chapters, a change in register marks the shift between the two idioms of science writing and travel writing. In a chapter entitled "The Life Science Team", for example, the text is illuminating regarding the "nitrogen-fixing bacteria" in the roots of the *prosopis* tree and how these "bacteria combine gaseous nitrogen in the soil with other elements to produce nitrogen compounds that can be used as a fertilizer by the plant" (p. 63) while also exalting in the pantheistic joy of drinking rain in the desert "joining with the earth around ... with the trees and every living thing" (p. 85).

The bi-disciplined nature of the text, part science, part travel narrative, frames the central dilemma of Winser's enterprise: the scientist envisions the desert space as a problem to be solved or "come to terms with" (a phrase he repeats several times), while the traveller revels in the desert as it is and with all its imaginative possibilities.[69] The sense of the writer being pulled between these two positions continues throughout the text. Winser is proud that the work of the team (and indeed his own account of the expedition) "will inspire others to come and take a closer look" (p. 138), and he quotes Robin Hodgkin in *Playing and Exploring* (1985): "These [unknown] worlds will only come to life if someone acts on them, plays with and explores them and then shares the resulting surprises" (p. 138). Winser acknowledges, however, that a desire to communicate the value of the sands comes at a price. From a practical perspective, during the project he expressed concern that the work of the field centre could "turn into a circus if we were not careful", and he cites problems with controlling the hundreds of visitors received at Taylorbase (p. 31); he also concedes in interview that the expedition opened up the sands to tourism, and that gave rise to concerns about the conservation of the area. But there is also an imaginative price to pay for definitions and delineations too – as if naming somehow equates with taming the wilderness: "[I]t seemed a sacrilege to be condemning [the dunes] to such scrutiny, but knowledge of the geographical jigsaw requires intimacy; no corner could ever parry detailed inquiry" (p. 28). Throughout *The Sea of Sands and Mists*, Winser is presented as experiencing the conflicting interests of "man in the landscape". In the scientific work carried out, in the definition and identification of the desert inhabitants, in the mapping and naming of a hitherto uncharted region, in the very presence of 1,000 people in a space that formerly attracted none but the nomadic few, the sense of wilderness is eroded and with it the imaginative possibility it holds for freedom and escape.

162   *Wonderment and wilderness*

This tension between what can be summed up as science and art is of course familiar Romantic territory that is neither new nor uncontested. Indeed, Winser's use of the phrase the "condemning to scrutiny" immediately recalls to mind the famous lines in *Lamia*, written by the Romantic poet John Keats in response to Isaac Newton's theory of prismatic colour: "There was an awful rainbow once in heaven:/We know her woof, her texture; she is given/In the dull catalogue of common things"; the poet blames philosophy (for which we can read "science") for conquering "all mysteries by rule and line" – in other words, for "unweaving the rainbow".[70] The passage has often been held up to represent a supposed opposition between art and science, but, as evolutionary biologist Richard Dawkins points out, this is seeing a binary where it does not necessarily exist. In a book, taking its cue from *Lamia*, called *Unweaving the Rainbow*, Dawkins makes the case for science as a means of revealing rather than unravelling wonder. He gives as an example the wonder of being born at all, given the statistical odds against it: "The potential people who could have been here in my place but who will in fact never see the light of day outnumber the sand grains of Arabia", and Dawkins suggests that in unwrapping one mystery, another presents, and this in itself is beautiful.[71] "The feeling of awed wonder that science can give us", Dawkins writes with a presumed nod to the sublime, "is one of the highest experiences of which the human psyche is capable" (p. x). Given this perspective, Winser's work can be read as *releasing* the wonder of the desert through scientific study – a project affirming of the human place within nature and its controlling hand over it.

The trouble with this reading is that it requires a confidence in the scientific nature of the project that is not fully sustained in the text. Winser's narrative both unweaves the rainbow and nostalgically tries to put it back together again. Thus at the same time as Winser writes that he hopes the sands will become a "living laboratory for international desert research" (p. 45), at the same time as he writes that he looks forward to a time when the dunes are fully understood so that we will "be able to control them" (p. 140), and at the same time as he gives "confidence to all who believe that all deserts one day can be turned green" (p. 63), he is also wistfully straining after the "heartbeat of the sands" and feeling like "an intruder who had no right to be there" (p. 131).[72] This is the part that makes Winser's account relevant not just to an ecocritical reading of the text (where these moments can be interrogated for the doubt they cast on the human project of dominating the natural world) but even more specifically to a postcolonial ecocritical reading. Indeed, it is the very ambivalence towards the scientific nature of the enterprise, captured through the frequent lyrical asides, that troubles not just the sense of human dominance over the landscape but also Western dominion over (or at least interference with) Arab land.

To illustrate a postcolonial ecocritical reading of *The Sea of Sands and Mists*, it is necessary first to identify some of the Oriental tropes that

Wonderment and wilderness 163

appear in the text. An obvious foregrounding of the familiar Saidian project of othering, apart from the setting of the text within a British rather than local exploratory tradition, appears in the introduction. In a bid to demonstrate the pioneering potential of the project (a necessary authenticating device in both science and desert travel writing), we learn that very few had travelled through the sands or knew them intimately until the Wahiba project brought them to the attention of "over 1,000 individuals" (p. 9). As Pavel Cenkl points out, "[B]y implicating unexplored regions as largely unpopulated 'uninscribed and hence strategically emptied space[s]', cartographic and textual narratives [continue to] retail that emptiness as a hyperborean space of possibility".[73] Many ecocritics make a similar point: Campbell states that deserts are often projected as empty and therefore need to be "improved, redeemed, changed into something else. Hence our many dams and irrigation projects – and the familiarity of the phrase 'to make the desert bloom'", and some of this thought appears to influence Winser's mission to find a "solution to the desert" (Chapter 9).[74] Similarly, although the Bedu are mentioned throughout, they are not presented as part of a systematic understanding of the sands despite their having lived in the sands for centuries. This "native" knowledge of the desert may only exist in oral record rather than in scientific papers, but it conflicts with the Western assumption of "unknown", "unresearched" territory. Another Oriental trope presents in the form of the alien nature of the desert; described as mysterious, it is at times threatening and at other times alluring. Winser is drawn towards the desert, particularly the part marked out of bounds beyond their zone of scientific enquiry, like many earlier British travellers were drawn to Arabia itself: "[D]isappearing into the Sands", writes Winser as he enters the Sands as his own danger zone beyond the reach of the scientists' camp, "without much chance of being rescued with only small amounts of food went against all my expedition rules, but if we were to be desert travellers we had to do it properly" (p. 119) – and by "properly" he means challenging his Western identity in a zone of maximum otherness. These tropes are familiar to the Oriental discourse, part of the "distribution of geopolitical awareness into aesthetic, scholarly, economic … landscape and sociological description" that Said argues helps to "control, manipulate, even to incorporate, what is a manifestly different (or alternative and novel) world".[75] In this sense, and in the sense in which the whole desert project could be interpreted as mapping the region for Western interests, Winser, who read the eulogy at Thesiger's funeral, appears to be upholding the Western project of Orientalism.

This, however, is not a complete and therefore not a fair reading of Winser's work; indeed, there are three main objections. Firstly, this reading overlooks the counter-discourse that the text establishes through the moments of doubt in the enterprise and through expressed communion with nature. In "A Journey with Said Jabber Hilays", Winser accepts the invitation of his Bedu friend to undertake the journey beyond Taylorbase

164   *Wonderment and wilderness*

by camel, and this friend becomes not just a practical guide through the sands but also a spirit guide in interpreting the signs of nature – the wildcat tracks, the gazelle and fox prints, where a "small mammal had a squabble with a bird of prey" (p. 126) – that they encounter. At one point, Said Jabber Hilays sings a ballad, and Winser recognises that "here was desert data being communicated in verse" (p. 127), and Winser becomes wrapped, albeit for a short time, in the Bedouin experience. At length, they have to return to Taylorbase, and Winser suddenly has a moment of clarity about his project:

> Said was pushing the pace of the journey to suit us and this meant we had to disentangle ourselves from the warm hospitality being offered. The project as a whole suddenly seemed an intrusion in the life of these masters of the desert environment.
>
> (p. 131)

This is not Winser as a pioneering British desert explorer, forming his identity in opposition to the threatening space of the desert, nor as a scientist trying to impose a Western logic on an alien territory; even less is it an ethnographer metaphorically measuring Bedu heads (as desert traveller Bertram Thomas) for spurious notions of primitiveness.[76] Like Thesiger, Winser becomes a guest in a landscape he recognises is full of someone else's customs, ballads, resources, and rich with "innate knowledge" (p. 135). Indeed, he feels privileged to become "an integral part of desert life" (p. 132) and learns from the values he perceives through the Bedu's generosity. Unlike Thesiger, Winser's education with the Bedu is not an anachronistic experience of a "doomed race"; it embraces their modern notions of land use and land management.

The Omani scholar, Hilal Al-Hajri, writes, "The ultimate contribution of British travellers to Omani culture is that they described everyday life in Oman, which is almost neglected in the few Omani historical works".[77] He goes on to say that the observation and recording by these travellers, including on themes of "natural phenomena", help to "fill a gap in the cultural history of Oman". This brings us to a second objection of an Orientalist reading of Winser's work. Seen in the light of Al-Hajri's comment, the Wahiba project is more about partnership than domination – and indeed many of "the 1,000" included in the project were locally based Omani scholars, guides, drivers, fixers, and the project credits extend to the royal permission granted for the expedition, the sponsorship of the Diwan of Royal Court Affairs, and many Omani corporations that underwrote the project (p. 179). If only a few Omani scholars were involved, this is more of a reflection of the nascent education system in place at the time of the expedition (Oman's first university, Sultan Qaboos University, was only established in 1986), rather than as any exclusivity intended in the project design.

As a third objection to an Orientalist reading of Winser's work, there is the point that the desert acts upon Winser and the science team as equally as they imprint their work upon it; indeed, the desert becomes more of a home and a school rather than a zone of otherness. Winser writes that "four months in the Sands leaves an indelible mark; it had changed the lives of the team. Few could now speak of the area and its people without enthusiasm and we were all protective of our new-found friendships" (p. 144) – and by "friendship", Winser includes their relationship with the desert. As he wistfully admits in interview nearly 40 years later,

> There isn't a day I haven't thought about the Sands – we made friendship with the landscape and with all friends you respect them, and miss them, and want to go back to see them. The Sands are not a tamed space.[78]

These connections, these ties to place, are "no airy fantasy", to use Said's term; they translate into practical ends, but these ends, in Winser's case, are not sinister plots for postcolonial globalisation or resource exploitation. They result in positive environmental efforts that have involved supporting local conservation initiatives.[79] If "many scholars" in the fields of postcolonialism and ecocriticism

> see their academic, culture-focused work as part of a broader political effort to engage – critically, in many cases – with modernisation processes and their consequences, to imagine more equitable social structures, and to rethink the material bases on which such structures might be founded,

Winser's project (and indeed his life's work) fits into this category too.[80] In practical terms, for example, the legacy of the Wahiba project can be counted in the opportunities that it has created for local Bedu, not least in tourism – a result anticipated in the scientific overview of the project written by Roderic Dutton: "[T]he Centre, the tourist base and the guides will all create forms of local employment which use the unique knowledge of the Sands' people and allow them to combine local money-earning activities with their traditional way of life" (p. 167). If the Sands have been tamed, according to Winser's account, it is largely by the Bedu for the Bedu, building on some of the potential released through the Wahiba project.

In this light, it is possible to argue that despite suggested latent Orientalism, *The Sea of Sands and Mists* is an example of "healthy postcolonial environmentalism" that extends beyond the project's apparent imperial tendencies.[81] Although ecocriticism's focus on the wild (and of place as home, the locally observed but the universally connected) is

166 *Wonderment and wilderness*

markedly distinct from postcolonialism's probing of the civilised (and the hybrid, the displaced, and the disruption between local and global), the two share, in Graham Huggan's terminology, a "productive overlap". In Winser's text, the moments of integration with nature and the respect for the life of the Bedu point to the negotiations between the mapping and measuring of the scientist and the desire to convey a postcolonial disquiet through the text's travel writing counternarrative – part of the "fruitful alliance between the two critical/theoretical schools".[82] But problems remain, as inevitable in any act of representation, and a productive probing of these modes of representation is the subject of the final section of this chapter, the intention of which is not to come to any neat and tidy conclusions, but simply to engage with some of the complexities involved in the process of cross-cultural, cross-species delineation.

Staging the desert for Western audiences

The works of George, Walker, Pittaway, and Winser, as analysed hitherto, show how they perform differently from and within the traditional parameters of both science and travel writing, but, under the scrutiny of an ecocritical reading, all can be read as succeeding to some extent in transforming the imaginative geography of Arabia from barren legacy to fertile space for the productive discussion of the desert as a thing in itself. But all three writers operate in a zone that is "only incidentally geographical", built up instead "out of several different kinds of knowledge – historical, political, anthropological, cultural, mythical and experiential".[83] The accumulation of this investment invites the scientist to attempt a broader field than that narrowed by his or her discipline. In the preface to a later edition of his 1967 classic *Man in the Landscape*, Paul Shepherd notes the enduring appeal of an inter-disciplinary approach to engaging with landscape. Looking back on the "idiosyncratic mix of visionaries, young geographers and landscape architects" attracted to his work over the years, Shepherd writes,

> I now see that we were trying to reinvent "landscape", to see it as a middle ground if you will, where visual perception, nature esthetics, and ecological order might meet, to find an area of understanding released from the opposition between Art and Science, even from the tyranny of the disciplines.[84]

When analysed within this context, caught in a reshaping exercise to "reinvent" the Arabian desert, the work of the science writers such as those discussed herein performs as part of a newer tradition of wilderness philosophy and desert ecology. These desert writers each express a genuine affection for the wilderness they describe and try to encourage the

Wonderment and wilderness 167

reader towards a similar way of seeing that reveals the desert as habitat and home, rather than a land only of interest in its potential economic or imaginative use. In this, they attract a similarly new kind of ecocriticism that focuses less on the narrative of nature writing and more on the "textual tropes that establish the links between the natural world and the human observer, or between nature and culture".[85] Within that cultural context, however, "their Arabia" remains a construct that inevitably carries part of the imaginative legacy of the past. Furthermore, in writing to edify a primarily Western audience, and in their fashioning the space partially for Western discovery (and self-discovery), their work takes on a documentary quality that serves to fix the space in the familiar binaries of subject and object.

Alexander Wilson acknowledges of wilderness writing in America after 1945 that it establishes "a kinship with a natural world" that is seen to be somehow authentic but also treats nature like "a laboratory full of 'things' to be observed and increasingly managed in the name of social mobility and economic progress".[86] Karla Armbrusta sees the same contradiction at work in nature documentaries – on the one hand, nature is presented as a resource to be used (through the application of science), while on the other hand, it is presented as a lost Eden. Combined with technical staging devices that deliberately construct the landscape as "exotic", these features serve to distance the viewer, to strengthen rather than dissolve boundaries between subject and object, nature and culture.[87] This bind is exemplified in Michael McKinnon's text, *Arabia: Sand, Sea, Sky* (1990), which according to the preface was written to parallel a television series of the same name: even as McKinnon claims that their expedition was "not in the style of earlier travellers", he immediately contextualises their journey within that literary context.[88] That literary context imposes a particular way of seeing onto the desert that forbids fresh insight – the desert cannot be seen in any other way than a place of awe, quest, challenge, danger, extremes, purgation, absence because generations of travellers and scientists, almost despite their best intentions, have bestowed those dimensions upon it. Shepherd argues that this kind of stereotyping of the landscape not only closes the eyes of "subsequent travellers" but also releases them from the "trauma of confronting the unknown", and he makes the case that mapping has a similar effect, emphasising one particular element of the landscape at the expense of others.[89]

The dilemma confronting Western science writers, or indeed any wilderness writers, then, is how to overcome the overbearing inscriptions of the past. In common with fellow Arabist, Michael Asher, who espoused the term "deep ecology" to describe the integral connection between the natural world and an educative moral dimension to be intuited from wilderness encounter, McKinnon attempts to differentiate between *learning about* and *learning from* the desert.[90] This distinction helps unsettle the

168 *Wonderment and wilderness*

dominant discourse of imposing Western knowledge on Arabian land-forms and encourages instead a listening, passive approach that opens the desert up for a different kind of enquiry. McKinnon's specifically educational agenda uses the literary platform to communicate an ecological message – one that will be familiar to television audiences of the iconic wildlife programmes of the age. From the outset, he reflects ruefully on the changes brought about by the discovery of oil in the twentieth century and the infrastructure that has grown to support its extraction and recognises that as a result, "[t]oday, the preservation of rangeland and mountain habitats is the most important ecological issue confronting the people of the Arabian peninsula" (p. 13). He concludes his book on a somewhat mournful note: "The challenge today is to find a new equilibrium that will balance modern demands with the creation of a new ecological order that reverses the present trends and preserves a great inheritance for future generations" (p. 215). The problem remains, however, not only how to achieve that balance but also how to find a form of writing that is sufficiently released from the constructs of the genre (in this case desert literature) to allow for that equilibrium to be expressed. McKinnon, while identifying the problem, is unable to find a new form for this purpose, leaving it ambiguous as to *whose* inheritance he is talking about and *which* future generations.

Shepherd suggests that the exercise of determining merit in landscape is inseparable from the act of travel and that both are impacted upon by cultural determinants such as painting and drama, and he reminds us that the word "scenery" comes from the Greek word for "stage".[91] Just as farmland is of little interest as scenery to the farmer, the desert is similarly not an inanimate object to be gazed at by the desert inhabitant – even less is it a problem to be solved. Lynn Ross Bryant in her study of the psychology of national parks in the USA quotes William Cronon's essay "The Trouble with Wilderness" and argues that "the way we conceive of nature is exactly that: our conception, our construction". Nature is not something external but a way of seeing upon which we impose boundaries: "It is hard for us to see that nature and wilderness are not objects existing out there, but constructs that organise human perception of the environment".[92] Bryant reminds us that Native American cultures do not make a separation between nature, humans, and other animals; this distinction between human and nature is characteristic largely only of Judeo-Christian cultures. It also overlooks, as Graham Huggan and Helen Tiffin recognise in reference to the work of British eco-philosopher, Kate Soper, that human agency is evident in almost all aspects of the so-called natural world, leading to the concern as to which parts of that mediated space should be preserved or protected.[93]

Applying this perspective to McKinnon's conservationist project, it begs the question as to which type of Arabian desert McKinnon suggests we preserve – the desert as landscape of Bedu husbandry, the desert as

Wonderment and wilderness   169

watered by *aflaj* (traditional irrigation), the desert as place of oil extraction, or the desert as location of thriving cities. The Arabian desert is all these things to the people who live there, and there are obviously ethical and political concerns about a Western subject pontificating on the fate of land use when not invited by the owners to do so. McKinnon's comments can only be justified if the notional environment is somehow magically removed from the political and transported into the universal.

Exploring the barren triumphalism of human over nature, Huggan and Tiffin, in a postscript to *Postcolonial Ecocriticism*, trace the development of the concept of "post-natural", or the "death of nature", as articulated by eco-theorists and commentators such as ecofeminist critics Carolyn Merchant (1980) and Donna Harraway (1991), and Bill McKibben (2006).[94] The key concept that each of these critics explores is the extent to which humans have shifted away from a sense of holistic integration within an organic entity towards a sense of extrication from it; this then leads to a sense of entitlement over it. There are several problems ecocritics suggest with the notion of separating humans from nature: it diminishes the sense of responsibility towards the outcomes of human intervention; it encourages a museum mentality towards wild space that is discreetly defined in opposition to tamed space, locking it into a moment of time; it leads to difficulties about what to do with indigenous people for whom the landscape is an evolving environment; it leads to a sense of consternation that something intrinsically valuable has been lost if the landscape changes. These concerns translate both metaphysically and practically in the texts not just of economists, conservationists, and environmentalists whose work involves unravelling these dilemmas in a desert context but also, as we have seen, all those who invest an imaginative value in wilderness. As a consequence, many desert texts include a mournful tone that revolves around the kind of paradox that Enato Rosaldo refers to as "imperialist nostalgia":

> A person kills somebody, and then mourns the victim. In more attenuated form, someone deliberately alters a form of life, and then regrets that things have not remained as they were prior to the intervention. At one more remove, people destroy their environment, and then they worship nature. In any of its versions, imperialist nostalgia uses a pose of "innocent yearning" both to capture people's imaginations and to conceal its complicity.[95]

Holland and Huggan, in quoting Rosaldo, argue that many modern travel writers deploy this kind of nostalgia to "yearn for the 'simpler' ways of life – often rural, premodern, preindustrial, that they, and their metropolitan readers, persuade themselves they need".[96] It is this kind of nostalgia that proves highly attractive to succeeding generations of travellers, keen to visit "just in time" or "before it's too late", and this, in

170 *Wonderment and wilderness*

turn, leads to the promotion and exploitation of particular environments for their tourism potential, often at a cost to their sustainability. Sustainability, the carbon footprint, and ethical concerns in general are not just the subject of science writing and investigation; they are also the subject of travel writing and, indeed, as Tim Youngs points out, travel criticism too.[97] Much of today's broad ecological discussion on wilderness revolves around an ethical concern not just about the human relationship with the environment and if or how it should be preserved but also about whom should access it and who should constitute its guardianship. A century ago, these questions may have been of limited concern, but in an era of ever-increasing travel to ever-remoter destinations when some suggest that "by the simple act of travelling, you are contributing to the problem" of its piecemeal extinction, this has assumed importance on a number of philosophical and practical levels that are explored in the remainder of this book.[98]

As intimated earlier, there can be no neat conclusions to a chapter about the relationship of the human being within nature, even as traced within the narrow genre of desert travel writing, as the subject, as we have seen, is made complex by history. It is also further problematised by the unique sense of crisis with which the world currently grapples with rapid environmental change – a crisis brought about in part by the discovery of oil. Yes, the Arabian desert as the land of extremes has been crossed, mapped, exploited for resources, and described in various acts of human containment. Navigable on tarmacked roads, defined by satellite images, built upon by expanding cities, and cultivated for agriculture, today's deserts of Arabia appear to be conquered by science. This chapter, however, has tried to show how a careful reading of the work of some scientists contests that notion – that even in the act of conducting science, there is wonderment that causes the scientist to pause and reconsider his or her relationship with the natural world. Some of these moments, as captured in science writing, continue to contribute to the region's "imaginative geography" but, as has been shown, the layering of symbolism and nostalgic engagement can illuminate as well as obfuscate the human relationship with nature.[99] At its most productive, desert literature today presents the desert as a liminal space in which the old boundaries (containing unhelpful absolutes of science and exploration, nature and human, West and East) are made porous, and the perception of human mastery of nature is troubled. With the erosion of boundaries, inevitably some of the old authority of science is eroded too, particularly as tourism seeps across the divide in place of exploration. It is important to reflect on whether the democratising of the desert space, where the wilderness as a trophy site of a few hardy explorers has given way to its promotion as the destination of tourism and the reimagining of the space for local interest, is anything to regret. This tension between nostalgia for the wilderness by Western writers in the past and the new political realisation of the desert space today (and within which lies the educative possibility of intuiting human place within nature for a broader constituency of people) is brought to crisis in the following chapter.

Notes

1 Gertrude Bell, *The Desert and the Sown: Travels in Palestine and Syria* [Heinemann, 1907] (Mineola, New York: Dover Publications, 2008), p. 60. For a short biography of Bell, see Janet Wallach, *Desert Queen: The Extraordinary Life of Gertrude Bell* (London: Phoenix Giant, 1997).

2 Robert Kern, "Ecocriticism: What Is It Good For?" in *The ISLE Reader: Ecocriticism, 1993–2003*, ed. by Michael P. Branch and Scott Slovic (Athens: University of Georgia Press, 2003), pp. 258–81 (p. 260).

3 See Richard Nordqist, "Definition and Examples of Science Writing", *Glossary of Grammatical and Rhetorical Terms* [online], ThoughtCo (2019), available at: https://www.thoughtco.com/science-writing-1691928 [accessed 12 July 2019].

4 SueEllen Campbell et al., ed. *The Face of the Earth: Natural Landscapes, Science, and Culture* (Berkeley and Los Angeles: University of California Press, 2011), p. ix.

5 Lawrence Buell, *The Future of Environmental Criticism: Environmental Crisis and Literary Imagination* (Oxford: Blackwell, 2005), p. 48.

6 William Rueckert was apparently the first person to use the term "ecocriticism" in 1978, but the term took on its current usage as a subbranch of literary and cultural studies in the late 1980s and 1990s. See Ian Buchanan, *Oxford Dictionary of Critical Theory* [2010] (Oxford: Oxford University Press, 2018).

7 See Campbell, *Face of the Earth*, p. 183 where she usefully makes the point that "language itself can complicate our understanding of deserts"; Campbell mentions "green" is associated with ecological health, while the "brown" of deserts seems "ecologically injured or destitute, even when they may be vibrant with healthy biodiversity" (p. 183). Obviously, "desert" is itself a word that connotes absence.

8 Edward W. Said, *Orientalism* (Harmondsworth: Penguin-Peregrine, 1978), p. 27.

9 Bell, *Desert and the Sown*, p. 60.

10 Said, *Orientalism*, pp. 49–72.

11 Roderick Frazier Nash, *Wilderness and the American Mind* [1967] (New Haven, CT: Yale University Press, 2014), p. 8.

12 Wilfred Thesiger, *Arabian Sands* [1959] (Harmondsworth: Penguin Books, 1984), Prologue, p. 15.

13 Patrick Holland and Graham Huggan, *Tourists with Typewriters: Critical Reflections on Contemporary Travel Writing* [1998] (Ann Arbor: University of Michigan Press, 2000), p. 69.

14 Holland and Huggan, *Tourists with Typewriters*, p. 67.

15 Billie Melman, "The Middle East/Arabia: 'The Cradle of Islam'", in *The Cambridge Companion to Travel Writing*, ed. by Peter Hulme and Tim Youngs (Cambridge: Cambridge University Press, 2002), pp. 112–19 (p. 114).

16 See Daniel Carey, "Truth, Lies and Travel Writing", in *The Routledge Companion to Travel Writing*, ed. by Carl Thompson (London and New York: Routledge, 2020), pp. 3–14 (p. 7).

17 Mary Louise Pratt, *Imperial Eyes: Travel Writing and Transculturation* [1992] (London: Routledge, 2008), Chapter 2 and p. 26.

172 *Wonderment and wilderness*

18 Hulme and Youngs, *Cambridge Companion*, p. 29.
19 Paul Fussell, ed., *The Norton Book of Travel* (New York: W.W. Norton and Co., 1987), p. 130.
20 Holland and Huggan, *Tourists with Typewriters*, p. 92.
21 Carl Thompson, *Travel Writing* (Abingdon and New York: Routledge, 2011), p. 46.
22 Fussell ed., *The Norton Book of Travel*, p. 130.
23 Charles M. Doughty, *Travels in Arabia Deserta* [Cambridge: 1888] (London: Jonathan Cape and the Medici Society, 1926, 2 Vols), preface to second edition, p. ix.
24 See Chapter 62 of T. E. Lawrence's *Seven Pillars of Wisdom: A Triumph* [1935] (Harmondsworth: Penguin, 1986); see also Bertram Thomas's *Arabia Felix* (London: Jonathan Cape, 1932), where, for example, Chapter 14 is entitled "A Geographical Note on Rub Al-Khali".
25 Thomas, *Arabia Felix*, p. 178.
26 Thomas, *Arabia Felix*, p. 238.
27 See Thompson, *Travel Writing*, p. 60.
28 Said, *Orientalism*, pp. 55 and 203.
29 Thompson, *Travel Writing*, p. 82.
30 Mark Evans, *Crossing the Empty Quarter in the Footsteps of Bertram Thomas* (UK: Gilgamesh Publishing, 2016), p. 79.
31 Holland and Huggan, *Tourists with Typewriters*, p. 228 in endnote 11.
32 Ralph A. Bagnold, *Libyan Sands: Travels in a Dead World* [1935] (London: Eland Publishing, 2010), p. 227.
33 R. A. Bagnold, *The Physics of Blown Sand and Sand Dunes* [1941, 1954] (Mineola, Dover Publications, 2005), p. xix (Introduction).
34 See Stephen Greenblatt, *Marvelous Possessions: The Wonder of the New World* (Chicago, IL: University of Chicago Press, 1991).
35 Aaron Sachs, "The Ultimate "Other": Post-Colonialism and Alexander von Humboldt's Ecological Relationship with Nature", *History and Theory*, 42 (2003), pp. 111–35 (p. 116).
36 Sabine Wilke, "Performing Tropics: Alexander von Humboldt's *Ansichten der Natur* and the Colonial Roots of Nature Writing", in *Postcolonial Green: Environmental Politics and World Narratives*, ed. by Bonnie Roos and Alex Hunt (Charlottesville and London: University of Virginia Press, 2010), pp. 197–212 (p. 209).
37 Ursula K. Heise, "Postcolonial Ecocriticism and the Question of Literature", in *Postcolonial Green*, ed. by Roose and Hunt, pp. 251–58 (p. 255).
38 Roslynn D. Haynes, *Desert: Nature and Culture* (London: Reaktion Books, 2013), p. 143.
39 See Edward O. Wilson, *The Diversity of Life* [1992] (Harmondsworth: Penguin, 1994). For a useful summary of the concept of "bioregion" and its application to literature, see also Jonathan Bate, "Poetry and Biodiversity", in *Writing the Environment: Ecocriticism and Literature*, ed. by Richard Kerridge and Neil Sammells (London and New York: Zed Books, 1998), pp. 53–70.
40 Uwe George, *In the Deserts of this Earth* [1976], translated by R. and C. Winston (New York and London: First Harvest/HBJ, 1977).
41 George worked mostly in the Sahara but also covered parts of the northern Arabian desert.
42 Edmund Burke, *A Philosophical Enquiry into the Origin of our Ideas of the Sublime and Beautiful* [1759], ed. by James Boulton (Oxford: Basil Blackwell, 1987).

Wonderment and wilderness 173

43 Edward D Clarke, *Travels in Various Countries, 1810* (London: 1816–1820, 11 Vols), Vol. III, p. 108.

44 See Robert Doran, *The Theory of the Sublime from Longinus to Kant* (Cambridge: Cambridge University Press, 2015).

45 Haynes, *Desert*, p. 115.

46 Peter Whitfield, *Travel: A Literary History* (Oxford: Bodleian Library, 2012), p. 225.

47 Alexander William Kinglake, *Eothen: Traces of Travel Brought Home from the East* (London: John Ollivier: 1845), p. 276.

48 Mary Louise Pratt, *Imperial Eyes: Travel Writing and Transculturation* (London: Routledge, 1992), p. 201.

49 Marc Augé, *Non-Places: An Introduction to Supermodernity* [1992] (John Howe, trans., London: Verso, 2008), p. viii.

50 Zygmunt Bauman, "From Pilgrim to Tourist – Or a Short History of Identity", in *Questions of Cultural Identity*, ed. by S. Hall and P. du Gay (London: Sage, 1996), pp. 18–36, (p. 20).

51 Charles Forsdick, "Travel and the Body", in *The Routledge Companion to Travel Writing*, ed. by Carl Thompson (London and New York: Routledge, 2020), pp. 68–77 (p. 76).

52 Augé, *Non-Places*, p. x.

53 See C. Kaplan, *Questions of Travel: Postmodern Discourses of Displacement* (Durham, NC, and London: Duke University Press, 1996).

54 John Urry and Jonas Larsen, *The Tourist Gaze 3.0* [1990] (London: Sage Publications, 2011), p. 66.

55 Paul Shepherd, *Man in the Landscape: A Historic View of the Esthetics of Nature* [1967, 1991] (London: University of Georgia Press, 2002), p. 160.

56 H. and H. A. Frankfort, *The Intellectual Adventure of Ancient Man* (Chicago, IL: University of Chicago Press, 1946), p. 60.

57 D. De Cristofaro and Daniel Cordle, "Introduction: The Literature of the Anthropocene", *C21 Literature: Journal of 21st-century Writings*, 6, no.1:1 (2018), 1–6 (p. 4).

58 Melman, "Middle East/Arabia", p. 114.

59 D. H. Walker and A. R. Pittaway, *Insects of Eastern Arabia* (London: Macmillan, 1987). Pittaway supplied the technical entomological data on the specimens that both authors collected for study, but the narrative text was written by Walker.

60 This is known anecdotally: Don Walker was my late father, and I was privileged to assist him and my mother, Shirley Walker, in some field work in Saudi Arabia and to help in reading the early manuscripts, the illustrations for which were produced by my brother, Allan Walker.

61 William Gilpin, *Three Essays on Picturesque Beauty* (London: 1794), p. 36.

62 Tim Youngs, *The Cambridge Introduction to Travel Writing* (Cambridge: Cambridge University Press, 2013), p. 44.

63 Henry Holland, "Travels in the Ionian Islands", *Eclectic Review*, N.S.7 (1817), 353–72 (p. 358).

64 George Keppel, *A Personal Narrative*, II, p. 2.

65 Edward W. Said, "Professionals and Amateurs", in *Representations of the Intellectual* (New York: Vintage Books, 1996), pp. 73–83.

66 William H. Sherman, "Stirrings and Searchings (1500–1720)", in *Cambridge Companion*, ed. by Hulme and Youngs, pp. 17–36 (p. 29), in reference to eighteenth-century travel writing.

67 Winser, Nigel *The Sea of Sands and Mists – Desertification: Seeking Solutions in the Wahiba Sands* (London: RGS, 1989). The study focuses on Eastern

174 *Wonderment and wilderness*

Oman and one of the most compact sand deserts in the world, known today as the Sharqiya Sands. The sands were formerly known as the Wahiba Sands and are named as such in the expedition reports; the name changed as part of the unification project of the former Sultan of Oman, Sultan Qaboos bin Said; place names associated with tribes were largely replaced to transfer space from local tribal claims to serve a more national agenda.

68 Author's unpublished interview with Nigel Winser, 2 June 2016.

69 Desertification was considered in the 1980s as an issue that has since appeared less urgent. In Chapter 9 of *The Sea of Sands and Mists*, for example, Winser states, "By the end of the project we had come to terms with the Wahiba Sands" (p. 136). He uses the same phrase later in the chapter (p. 138).

70 John Keats, *Lamia* (1820) Part II, lines 229–38, *John Keats: The Complete Poems*, ed. by John Barnard (Harmondsworth: Penguin, 1973), p. 431.

71 Richard Dawkins, *Unweaving the Rainbow: Science, Delusion and the Appetite for Wonder* [1998] (New York: First Mariner, 2000), p. 1.

72 The full quotation is as follows: "Said was pushing the pace of the journey to suit us and this meant we had to disentangle ourselves from the warm hospitality being offered. The project as a whole suddenly seemed an intrusion in the life of these masters of the desert environment" (p. 131).

73 Pavel Cenkl, "Narrative Currency in a Changing Climate", in *Postcolonial Green*, ed. by Roos and Hunt, pp. 137–56 (p. 146).

74 Campbell, *Faces of the Earth*, p. 238.

75 Said, *Orientalism*, p. 12.

76 The reference is to Bertram Thomas who travelled with calipers to measure Bedu heads as part of an ethnography project. See Thomas, *Arabia Felix*, Chapter 3, on skull measuring and racial typing.

77 Hilal Al-Hajri, *British Travel-Writing on Oman: Orientalism Reappraised* (Bern: Peter Lang AG, 2006), pp. 24–25.

78 Author's unpublished interview with Nigel Winser, 2 June 2016.

79 Winser was invited to return to Oman as part of Earth Watch and continued to work thereafter with local environmentalists engaged in the protection of endangered species.

80 Heise, "Postcolonial Ecocriticism", p. 251.

81 Sachs, "Ultimate 'Other'", p. 111.

82 Graham Huggan, "'Greening' Postcolonialism: Ecocritical Perspectives", *Modern Fiction Studies*, 50, no. 3 (2004), 701–33 (p. 701).

83 Holland and Huggan, *Tourists with Typewriters*, p. 67.

84 Shepherd, *Man in the Landscape*, p. xxiii.

85 Heise, "Postcolonial Ecocriticism", p. 256.

86 Alexander Wilson, *The Culture of Nature: North American Landscape from Disney to the Exon Valdez* (New York: Basil Blackwell, 1991), p. 125.

87 Karla Armbrusta, "Creating the World We Must Save: The Paradox of Television Nature Documentaries", in *Writing the Environment*, ed. by Kerridge and Sammells, pp. 218–38.

88 Michael McKinnon, *Arabia: Sand, Sea, Sky* (London: BBC Books, 1990), p. 75.

89 Shepherd, *Man in the Landscape*, p. 234.

90 Michael Asher describes himself under the professional profile of his LinkedIn account as a member of the deep ecology movement.

91 Shepherd, *Man in the Landscape*, p. 119.

92 Lynn Ross-Bryant, *Pilgrimage to the National Parks: Religion and Nature in the United States* (New York: Routledge, 2013), p. 4.

93 Graham Huggan and Helen Tiffin, *Postcolonial Ecocriticism* [2010] (Abingdon: Routledge, 2015), p. 224.

Wonderment and wilderness   175

94 See Carolyn Merchant, *The Death of Nature: Women, Ecology and the Scientific Revolution* (London: HarperCollins, 1980); Donna Harraway, *Simians, Cyborgs, and Women: The Reinvention of Nature* (New York: Routledge, 1991); Bill McKibben, *The End of Nature* (New York: Random House, 2006).

95 Renato Rosaldo, *Culture and Truth: The Remaking of Social Analysis* [1989] (London: Routledge, 1993), pp. 69–70.

96 Holland and Huggan, *Tourists with Typewriters*, p. 29.

97 Youngs, *Cambridge Introduction*, p. 183.

98 Jeff Greenwald, quoted in Youngs, *The Cambridge Introduction to Travel Writing*, p. 183 (in reference to carbon emissions).

99 Said, *Orientalism*, pp. 49–72.

5 Desert as shared space

In *Wilderness Oman* (2002), a photographic memoir of travels in the Arabian desert, Malcolm MacGregor identifies the impact of tourism on the environment and singles out casual groups of visitors against whom he can distinguish his own photographic journey within the country, namely "wadi bashers [a local expatriate term for expeditions in four-wheel drive vehicles], mountain bikers and tour groups".[1] Yet in presenting lyrical passages of text and enticing photographs that invite the reader to follow MacGregor into "this unknown and remote country", it is contradictory, then, to complain of a diminishment in wilderness when others take up the challenge.[2] As shown in the previous chapter, the dilemma of wanting to bring the wonders of wilderness to a wider audience and a desire to keep it wild is a familiar bind of many desert writers, few of whom seem to see their own incursions into the area as part of the act of taming or indeed recognise their own implication in creating new paths for future tourists to follow. One of the distinguishing features, as we have seen, of many of the writers examined in the previous chapters is their desire to be recognised as accomplishing something worthwhile. For footstep travellers, this meant binding their journey to that of a predecessor; for others, intertextuality is used as a shorthand for "we, the travellers" as distinct from "you, the tourists". As Maria Leavenworth points out, "[T]here is a contemporary ambivalence towards travel when many want to travel but no one wants to be a tourist".[3] Even though the distinction between travel and tourism has been eroded by virtue of relatively risk-free desert encounter and facilitated access, desert expedition has continued throughout the past two decades, but within the resulting texts, it is possible to detect an increasing anxiety as to how to make the account appear meaningfully different from the casual desert outing. This chapter examines how this anxiety has resulted in desert literature of new or extenuating forms. Two of these forms – namely, the "accelerated sublime" and what might be termed the "secular pilgrimage" – are analysed here not just to show how they help twenty-first-century travellers distinguish their travels in an era when tourism has demystified the locus of

DOI: 10.4324/9781003197201-6

Desert as shared space   177

heroic adventure but also to show how they contribute to the broader critical debate on the value of travel as tourism.[4]

The need to make a distinction between travel and tourism has a long pedigree and as such has attracted much scholarly attention. Paul Fussell, for example, differentiates between the "self-directed" wanderings of the traveller as a higher-order activity than the "externally directed" itinerary of the tourist.[5] James Buzard documents the historical divergence of the two concepts, pointing out that the term "tourist", according to the *Oxford English Dictionary*, was originally used interchangeably with "traveller". Arising out of the individualistic sensibilities of the Romantic era, it only acquired its modern pejorative connotation with the development of mass, group-oriented tourism in the middle of the nineteenth century. Buzard suggests that it is at that point that travel came to be associated with "boldness and gritty endurance"; tourism in the meantime came to be seen as an imitative activity, the "cautious, pampered unit of a leisure industry", the roots of which can be traced back to Thomas Cook's first package holidays of the 1840s.[6] The use of guidebooks produced by Baedeker and Murray similarly contributed to both the democratisation and domestication of travel by creating a checklist of "must-see" sights and how to access and process the experience.

The definition of tourism and travel continues to evolve and, in an era when both concepts appear to be eliding, Carl Thompson pinpoints the current difference as the intervention of an agent in organising "most aspects of the journey for the traveller".[7] Tim Youngs meanwhile identifies that an enduring element of the distinction lies in the choice of, as much as in the planning required to reach, a destination – the "mass tourist" travels along the beaten track, the "cognoscenti" seeks to get off it.[8] The distinction between traveller and tourist, other critics argue, also lies in the quality of person attempting the track, opposing the "sensitive traveller" against the "vulgar tourist".[9] There is something contradictory, as Buzard notes, that tourists can be both "superficial surface-skimmers" – such as MacGregor's undiscerning wadi bashers, mountain bikers, and tour groups – and "the blundering agents of profound (and lamentable) social and cultural change", but nonetheless, there is little reward from a writer's perspective in belonging to the "wrong" camp. It could be argued that no tourist intends to have a negative impact on the wilderness, but the fact remains that en masse, that is often the perceived outcome. Buzard contends that "rhetorical attempts to exempt oneself" from the responsibility for the outcome (for example, in terms of landscape degradation) "are futile", but this does not stop recent desert travellers seeking a way in which to cast their journeys appropriately – othering themselves as sensitive travellers, not vulgar tourists.[10]

The traditional way of achieving merit for a desert journey was to cut new ground, but in an era where there is little new ground left, an alternative approach is to cover old ground in new ways. In the field of

178 *Desert as shared space*

Arabian desert literature, there are examples of both: almost all the modern travellers analysed in this book have sought to distinguish themselves from their tourist counterparts by claiming the competitive edge – the venturing into new territory, or into old territory in novel ways, in order to invest greater authenticity in the modern venture. Most admit that the endeavour is somewhat specious. Success, in terms of Arabian desert travel, is mostly measured in terms of having what the traveller regards as an authentic experience, and this is generally connected with the distance strayed from the beaten track; this sense of authenticity has been steadily eroding in direct proportion to the number of visitors following suit. This is no new sentiment, as the distinguished desert traveller, Freya Stark, lamented in the early twentieth century:

> Even now the crossing of the desert is an everyday affair, and although the Nairn Motor Transport do what they can, and cook your breakfast-sausage romantically for you in the open desert over a fire of camelthorn ... they do not quite succeed, one must admit, in giving the true nomadic feeling to any except most innocent travellers.[11]

Stark's sense of desert travel as tourist performance is the antithesis to Thesiger's purporting to reach Arabia "only just in time", before modern communications made enjoying an authentic experience more accessible to less extraordinary people.[12] For modern desert explorer, Levison Wood, little chance remains of a genuinely authentic experience: "Of course", he states in interview, "travelling in the desert is a form of escape – even Thesiger went home. You're always a foreigner in the desert and a foreigner travelling in the desert is always less authentic".[13] This realisation accompanies Wood as he walks or travels a punishing 5,000 miles through 13 Arabian countries alone (accompanied only by the cameramen) in just four months in order to prove that his travels amount to more than just a holiday in the sands.

As we have seen, modern self-styled professional explorers, such as Ranulph Fiennes and Adrian Hayes, make "a great show of the extent to which they journeyed 'off the beaten track', thereby avoiding tourists and the infrastructure that supports them", even at the expense of appearing foolish to the local people they encounter.[14] Mark Thomas, who circumnavigates the Israeli Barrier in *Extreme Rambling* (2011),[15] and Leon McCarron, who describes deliberately hiking along new recreational trails in the Middle East in *The Land Beyond* (2017), refashion the paths of their journeys as something more significant or exotic – "arteries that connect the disparate parts of a country built on nomadism and movement".[16] All are eager to prove they are not on holiday. Part of the way in which they persuade the reader of this fact is by appealing to the overtly political context of their journey. While the Arabian desert has become more readily accessible in practice, the perception of the region to which it belongs has appeared, post "9/11", to have remained intimidating, at least to non-Muslim, non-expatriate Western travellers. Until very recently when Saudi Arabia joined other Arabian Peninsula countries in opening its doors to tourism, the perception of Arabia as a hostile region of questionable politics was exacerbated by the relative complication (with the exception of certain Gulf cities) of gaining access due to the continuing need for visas to travel and work in some countries, and ongoing conflict in others. At the time of writing, furthermore, newly opened borders were being periodically closed due to the Covid pandemic, leaving little opportunity for two decades' worth of misinformation about Middle Eastern security and stability to be dispelled. Out of this context, a new, distinctly politicised type of desert text has emerged that capitalises on Arabia's resurrected danger-zone status; it is to a brief analysis of these hyper-modern accounts of extreme distinction between travel and tourism that the discussion now turns.

Post-tourism and the accelerated sublime

In his provocative study of today's travel writing, *Extreme Pursuits*, Graham Huggan analyses what he perceives as a growing cultural anxiety around the exponential growth of tourism and concludes that it has led, among other consequences, to a rise in travel texts that correspond to what has been termed the "accelerated sublime".[17] In reference to Claudia Bell and John Lyall from whom the term derives, Huggan defines this concept as a "hyperinscribed" natural space in which tourists engage in extreme activities as leisure pursuits in order to satisfy an "ever-intensified search for experiential authenticity".[18] This includes not just those activities that involve technology (such as daring adventure sports in wild places) but also "older, more endurance-based activities" that imply a "purer, less technologically mediated engagement with the site".[19] It also, crucially, involves risk. As has been demonstrated throughout this study, expeditions in the deserts of Arabia provide exactly this kind of "older, more endurance-based" activity, especially given the opportunity to travel by camel rather than motorised transport; it has also perennially involved at least the perception of danger as part of the traditional othering of the desert space. Indeed, ever since the Swiss explorer Jean Louis Burckhardt cut through the Siq at Petra in 1812 disguised as a *hajji*, anxious for his life in case he showed too much interest in the wonders he was rediscovering for Europe, Arabia, and the desert in particular, has provided just such a hyperinscribed space.[20] A survey of the superlatives of endurance in a desert context shows that the quest for the competitive edge, for the "more extreme, more dangerous, farther away, deeper, steeper, or faster", is evidenced in modern travel literature connected with the Arabian desert too, but taken to even more extraordinary extremes.[21] The excitement afforded by the prospect of danger in travelling within the region is still

180   *Desert as shared space*

underpinned by the vocabulary of the sublime as the so-called shock-and-awe military campaign of the 1990s showed. In modern critical theory, the term "accelerated sublime" has emerged to describe a peacetime equivalent, defining the connection between landscape and identity as realised through expedition, extreme sport, and what Kathleen Adams calls "Danger-Zone Tourism".[22]

Over the first two decades of the twenty-first century, self-aggrandising desert narratives, in which the (invariably male) author puts himself centre-stage in locations of real or perceived danger, form almost a subgenre of masculine-oriented desert travel literature associated with the region. Conforming to the characteristics of the general accelerated sublime, these male accounts are undercut with an ironic patina that is in itself a kind of self-distinction, reflected in titles such as *Misadventure in the Middle East* (2007), which features the author as "Tramp, Artist and Spy" in the subtitle of an otherwise fairly ordinary tale of a car journey through Iran, Iraq, and Arabia; *Bad Lands* (2007) and *Dark Lands* (2013), which deliberately place the author, according to the back cover blurb, in "some of the most repressive and dangerous regimes in the world"; and *A Tourist in the Arab Spring* (2013), which, despite the book's dedication to the "martyrs of the Arab Spring", is in fact less about the martyrs and more about the writer's supposed daring in venturing to countries in post-war chaos.[23] All these accounts are deliberately political and, to differing degrees, overtly aware of the Orientalism in which their work is contextualised, even if they find it impossible to provide an entirely new mode of representation. In the ironic, self-deprecatory tone familiar to the accelerated sublime, Henry Hemming, for example, mocks the pomposity of his project to "alter Western stereotypes about the region" (p. 5). Despite devoting two chapters to a discourse (verbalised as a dialogue) on how to manage the Oriental legacy, he nonetheless represents the stereotypes he seeks to unravel, casting the region as "on the one hand [as] the hotbed of modern-day suicidal terror, and on the other a more Orientalist, antique and sexually louche land of Ali Baba flying-carpet fantasy" (p. 5). All three of the authors are at their most interesting when grappling with the literary difficulties of representing the Other.

In the difficulty in finding anything new to say, in the use of parody, in the recycling of the past as nostalgia, and in the links with popular culture and mass media, it could be argued that accelerated sublime desert literature is illustrative of the last throes of postmodernism.[24] What makes it new is the political dimension to the work: these travels are conducted less in an imaginative geography and more along practical axes of the modern Middle East in an age of perceived terrorist threat. Tony Wheeler's contribution to the accelerated sublime in *Bad Lands* and *Dark Lands*, for example, describes visits to countries such as Saudi Arabia and Iraq that until very recently were determinedly off-limits by virtue of their internal politics and relationship with the world at large,

Desert as shared space 181

and he uses his travels in the region to express political opinions about what he perceives as the "failed state" status of the countries he visits. Writing for a largely Western readership, Wheeler's final assessment is in some measure re-assertive of old East-West relations: "For all the whining about how unfair the world is to Islam", Wheeler writes at the end of the Saudi Arabian chapter, "it's the country's inward-looking, tightly constrained, narrow-minded view of its religion and its position in the world that is the real cause of the Saudi problem" (p. 300). His prescription for "the Saudi problem" is increased tourism, and he notes, "[T]here's plenty to see, getting around is quite easy and the facilities are more than adequate" – a summary worthy perhaps of a guidebook. In mirroring the focus of Lonely Planet, the publishing house he co-founded, to promote travel that is off the beaten track, Wheeler writes, "My first thought, when George W. Bush announced his Axis of Evil, was 'I want to go there.' Well who wouldn't? He'd inadvertently created an adventurer's travel wish list".[25] If part of the prospect of encountering danger in zones that are off the beaten track is to heighten the sense of heroism involved in travelling there, it is also about trying to recapture an "imagined geography" and points to the broader sense in which the boundaries of the Middle East are frequently redrawn and reimagined according to the political and social interplay between West and East.[26] It is also, as Vincent Cheng argues, about travellers recapturing a lost sense of "their own cultural identity in an increasingly globalised world". The outcome, Cheng identifies, is the ability "to continue to be able to assert difference and superiority".[27] When Wheeler, as "Guidebook Guru", asserts that difference and superiority in relation to the Middle East, it carries with it the problematic potential to influence a wide readership, recalibrating the East-West relationship in the latter's favour.[28] At the beginning of the introduction to *Bad Lands*, Wheeler poses the question, "[W]hat makes a land bad?" He concludes that "it's got nothing to do with geography or topography".[29] The cover of *Bad Lands*, however, features palm trees and a camel together with skull and crossbones, an oil derrick, and army tanks, as if the anthropomorphised desert landscape is somehow complicit in, or at least symbolic of, human malady. However coincidental, the negative tropes of desert – dead, dying, barren, empty, baked, desiccated, sterile, encroaching on fertile land – help to re-establish this particular landscape as an objective correlative of failing statehood.[30]

Tom Chesshyre's romp through the Arab countries of North Africa and parts of Arabia a year after the Arab Spring of 2011, described in *A Tourist in the Arab Spring*, ostensibly shares some of the newly politicised stance of Wheeler's and Hemming's work but errs more on the side of "post-tourist", in the Maxine Feifer sense of the term. As Thompson points out, "[G]etting off the beaten track, and of being a 'traveller' rather than a 'tourist', are usually self-deluding fantasies and illusions".[31] In doing his best "to act like" a tourist (p. 118) while going to sleep

182 *Desert as shared space*

"counting gunshots above the rooftops" (p. 97), Chesshyre appears at best naïve. At worst, he appears to be courting the kind of "disaster tourism" that Graham Huggan describes in *Extreme Pursuits*: "Disaster tourism embraces a wide variety of sometimes incompatible activities: from safely insulated, unashamedly voyeuristic appreciations of other people's extreme misfortunes ... to deliberately risky visits to current war-torn zones and dangerously unstable political sites".[32] Disaster tourism and the texts that it produces can be seen as a sinister development because they create the new kinds of "global stereotypes" that Alan Keohane warns of in his work on the Bedu; these, he argues, promote the idea of Arabs as "villains ... and hooded faces" fuelling a new sense of cultural distinction.[33] It also fuels the apocalyptic rhetoric provoked by the events of 9/11: "[P]eople are more fascinated with apocalyptic prophecy than ever before", writes Jason Boyett; "this may be due to the dire events happening around the world on a daily basis, especially in the Middle East".[34] By mapping Arabia along the uninterrogated "axis of evil", the achievements made through postcolonial critique and more enlightened encounter, such as are observed in the modern desert writing hitherto highlighted throughout this study, are disappointingly reversed.

Part of the process of projecting Arabia back into the unmitigated hostile space traditionally associated with desert is to reverse the perceived domestication of the space through exploration and recreate a suitably challenging climate in which to define the modern quest. As Debbie Lisle writes in *The Global Politics of Contemporary Travel Writing*, "Travel writers can no longer have that treasured moment of being first anywhere, but they can certainly be the first to prove their masculinity by travelling in a dangerous, brave or impossible way".[35] In an age where former virtues of manly courage and strength are no longer taken for granted, it is perhaps notable that texts conforming to the accelerated sublime appear to be trying to regain the space for primarily male endeavour.[36] This has a commercial angle too; as Levison Wood puts it, "[I]f there's no risk, there's no expedition – without risk, it's a holiday!"[37] In other words, as Gary Krist writes, for it to be "real" travel writing, it has to depict the experience of hardship.[38]

If for some the modern desert experience offers a gendered space for proving male prowess, for others it represents an antidote to the banality that characterises much of the accelerated sublime. In the absence of extrinsic details, the desert has traditionally forced travellers inward, provoking introspection of either a solipsistic or of a productive kind. Those writers who embrace the desert experience as a "rite of passage" contribute to a more nuanced thread of recent desert literature. Indeed, if the accelerated sublime strand of texts is unencouragingly retrogressive, despite its attempt to be radically new, a more optimistic prognosis of the Arabian desert genre, as briefly explored in the following section, can be found in the modern secular pilgrimage.

The modern secular pilgrimage

Billie Melman, Michael Grimshaw, and Rosylnn Haynes are among many recent commentators to show how, over the centuries, travellers have endowed the desert with redemptive and purifying powers "which cleanse" the suffering soul.[39] The Arabian desert, as origin of the three great monotheistic religions forged from violent conflict and upheaval, has always represented a locus of inner journey and indeed of redemptive experience, and it is little wonder that modern writers draw on this tradition to give new meaning to their travels.[40] "There it was", writes William Atkins in *The Immeasurable World*, his 2018 hyper-referenced, instructive account of travel in seven deserts on five continents, "the hyper-arid zone in all its abundance: solitary, godless, lonesome, deathly, barren, waterless, trackless, impassable, infested, cursed, forsaken – and yes, at the same time, the site of revelation, of contemplation and sanctuary".[41] This work, allegedly arising out of a week's solitude and reading in monastic internship that provoked the idea of desert travel, shares with other recent Arabian desert texts a notion of the inner journey as quest with the power to transform. At the end of "The Desert Library", a chapter telling the story of his travels in the Omani portion of the Empty Quarter, Atkins describes the magnetism of the desert pulling him deeper into the sands while his destination lay along the road to Salalah. It is at this very point, however, that he recognises the value of the life left behind – the "palms and papaya of the coastal plain", the "glorious endowment" of community, husbandry, and fecundity. To remain within the purgatorial space, he suggests, is a betrayal of life that becomes more about flight than quest, grinding identity and humanity into oblivion until it acquires the "condition of sand" (p. 60). His, then, is the "search for individual identity conducted against a natural landscape" which, according to Tim Youngs, is an identifiable trope in travel literature as a whole with self-knowledge leading to "a rebirth ... which prepares one for a more fulfilling re-entry into society".[42] Throughout the remaining chapters of Atkins's book, the obvious love of the landscape is tempered by the notion of the desert being colourless – a "blank manuscript" that gives necessary contrast to the "illuminated page" of abundant life (p. 361).

Peter Hulme notes, "[A]s the earth's wildernesses get paved over, travel writing increasingly emphasises the inner journey, often merging imperceptibly into memoir",[43] and memoir is a good description for two other modern desert texts of a questing nature, Lawrence Osborne's *The Wet and the Dry: A Drinker's Journey* (2013) and James Budd's *Half Past Ten in the Afternoon: An Englishman's Journey from Aneiza to Makkah* (2014). The two travel accounts form an unlikely pair to consider in tandem, the one being close to the accelerated sublime texts considered earlier, while the other is a more earnest foray into the picturesque. The two are linked, however, in a quest that is little to do with the countries

184   *Desert as shared space*

described therein and much more to do with the inner quest, the defining of self in the search for the soul; as such, their pairing helps to remove the artificiality of divides between sacred and secular of which modern commentators are justifiably wary.[44]

Both texts, although perhaps not intentionally, build on antecedents such as Charles Doughty's *Arabia Deserta* (1888) and Geoffrey Moorhouse's *The Fearful Void* (1974).[45] The latter, narrating a journey within the Sahara, describes the extreme rambling – or nomadism – of the author (and an assortment of ill-judged companions) as he attempts, without any qualification or prior experience, to cross the Sahara from west to east on foot and riding camels.[46] The desert provides the conditions, nothing more, of a journey that is all about observation of self: "My primary aim in going to the desert", Moorhouse writes, "was not to establish a record, much as I might enjoy doing so, but to explore an extremity of human experience" (p. 29). So extreme is the undertaking that he suspects that even Wilfred Thesiger, with whom Moorhouse rehearses his plan, "thought my enterprise little more than a stunt" (p. 31). While Moorhouse fails to complete his proposed journey and has to return home "a defeated man" (p. 279), it could be argued that he nonetheless accomplishes his stated aim and *The Fearful Void*, with its description of the psychological effect of extreme physical endeavour – "Body was pain and it had no separate parts. I wanted release, nothing more. I wanted to sleep, nothing beyond" (p. 159) – has become a classic of the genre, often cited in literary, cultural, and theological criticism that probes representation of the modern travelling self.[47]

Lawrence Osborne's *The Wet and the Dry* identifies with the work of Moorhouse and the monotheistic pilgrimage inheritance, despite appearing at first glance to lie at the farthest extreme of the accelerated sublime.[48] The author tries to garner credit for his journey through the somewhat preposterous endeavour to drink his way around, among others, the countries of the Arabian Peninsula; deliberately provocative, prodding taboos, gloating in his ability to circumvent local custom by gaining access to alcohol in the Muslim countries through which he passes, his comments in the opening chapters are particularly glib as he hopes "in some dark way that I might eventually stumble across that most delightful phenomenon, a Muslim alcoholic" (p. 9). Two factors redeem his account, however: firstly, the way in which the choice of destination sets up a dialectic between "wet" and "dry", and secondly, how that desert context contributes to a moment of clarity within the parallel inner journey. Tapping into anxieties about globalisation and what Roger Scruton memorably described as the West's "addiction to freedom", Osborne's own personal addiction to freedom, in the form of alcoholic excess, makes it hard for him to avoid the faux Arabia of Western imagination that is recreated in the tourist resorts, malls, and bars across the Middle East and "present as a motif" of décor, iron lamps and Bedu tents

Desert as shared space   185

(p. 90).[49] In contrast to this homogenised zone of what he describes as "self-absorbed banalities", Osborne finds authenticity in stepping beyond the built environment. It is within this context that the desert becomes a site of pilgrimage and in which an identifiable moment of epiphany appears to occur:

> We lay together in the wildness, making words out of pebbles on the beach, walking through the dunes. We talked less and less, but this did not matter ... the days at the desert sea were crystal-clear, in terms of consciousness. It takes several days for all traces of alcohol to leave the bloodstream, and when that happens the clarification is surprising.
>
> (p. 94)

Austere and purgatorial, the landscape stripped of incidentals parallels the clarity enjoyed in sobriety, offering a transformational quality in which "you move differently, you think differently; you sense things differently" (p. 94). The landscape operates here not just as the site of personal redemption (however temporary) but also as a way of binding the individual back into the community from which he has become a pariah, making him more aware of his responsibilities and provoking greater respect for both the country in which he is travelling and for the companion he is sharing the journey with. The moment does not last long, but it is enough of an epiphany to make sense of the journey as pilgrimage and the opportunities that can be learned from the desert as "dry", as a holistic environment not just as an unproductive other to the "wet", and sets up opportunities for change on the author's return home.

In common with new nature writing, this is desert writing that contributes to the kind of transformative literature advocated by Robert Macfarlane – a kind of literature that is not "noisily game-changing" (as he identifies Mark Cocker as advocating) but which (as Rebecca Solnit proposes) sows its seeds quietly and awaits incidental fertilisation.[50] The connection between Osborne's narrative of a drinker's journey around the Middle East and James Budd's reverently sober memoir, *Half Past Ten in the Afternoon*, may appear tentative, but they both share a deep sense of attempted redemption through their desert encounter.[51] Budd's narrative, published in 2014 but focusing on the author's memories of his time as a teacher in Aneiza in Saudi Arabia between the years 1965 and 1970, may have remained as a pleasant, if unremarkable, account of an unremarkable town were it not for the parallel journey that charts the author's faith from its first stirrings in Aneiza to its apotheosis in Mecca many years later. The journey's spiritual heart is not in the journey to Mecca, nor is it as Budd suggests his journey from agnosticism to Islam; for the reader, the epiphany of the account is in the moment of expulsion from the Arab town Budd had made his home. Although Aneiza had changed

186   *Desert as shared space*

little since Doughty stayed in one of the mudbrick houses over half a century earlier, the town that Budd describes is rapidly modernising under the influence of globalisation. In the almost obsessive enumeration of fast-food outlets given in the narrative ("two McDonalds, two Dunkin Donuts, three Baskin Robbinses, a Pizza Hut, a Domino's Pizza, a Little Caesar, a Burger King, a KFC and a Starbucks" (p. 185)), Budd appears to be exiled not just from Aneiza but from an approximate garden of Eden that is forever locked in his memory. Indeed, in its painful evocation of displacement and exile, this is a text of "rupture", such as Caren Kaplan writes about in *Questions of Travel*. Throughout this book, similar moments of rupture have been interrogated for the insights they offer not just about representation of people and place but also about the human condition as hemmed in by modernity. In moments of exile, there is at least a productive sense of dislocation – of fortunate fall into nomadism or a wandering along the path "between", but never arriving "in". Exploration of the interstices of place and time, where the path is all, has a redemptive, postcolonial quality to it, and indeed, Deleuze and Guattari theorise that monotheism arises out of nomadic life, lived in the "smooth spaces" of desert, steppe, and ocean, precisely because a sense of the absolute is only possible to experience when freed from locale and conquest. In this sense, Budd's conversion to Islam, which translates into English as "surrender", can be read as the reward of expulsion.[52]

Accounts such as those of Osborne and Budd – superficially retrospective studies in the conquest of wilderness through adventure tourism and through globalisation – can be read, then, more productively as accounts in which modern man (or woman) goes "in search of a soul, in search of home".[53] In their new "spirituality and earnestness", these kinds of accounts cover similar territory, albeit through different modes, to the twentieth-century wilderness texts (encompassing mountain and desert) of Peter Matthiessen's *The Snow Leopard* (1978), Robyn Davidson's *Tracks* (1980) and Bruce Chatwin's *The Songlines* (1987).[54] The inner journey, framed by external wilderness, becomes a form of therapy, a retreat to a supposed simpler life that has not yet been, as Youngs puts it, "buried and distorted by the weight of the post-industrial, mechanised world".[55] In this, the twenty-first-century desert soul-seekers appear to herald another revival of Romantic primitivism, reached at through the extremities of experience – drinking to excess in the case of Osborne, for example, or undergoing religious conversion in the case of Budd.

As a result of modern infrastructure, it is not just the "extreme traveller", however, who is privileged to experience the redemptive quality of a desert experience; in today's Arabian desert, almost anyone with a guidebook (including those on limited means and of limited mobility) can find their way to a sand dune and commune with nature with potentially similar effect. Describing his own theological inner journeys, Clive Pearson asks, "Are we tourists, travellers or exiles as we negotiate our way through

Desert as shared space 187

the legacy of the Enlightenment and modernity?" And of the three, he appears to choose to cast himself as the former – an "intelligent tourist" with "a Lonely Planet at hand".[56] In the 1990s, Buzard posited that the distinction between traveller and tourist was "highly specious", and today, when all parts of life appear to be accelerating and travellers share with tourists the desire for the most pleasure in the least time,[57] Huggan is among other commentators who assume that the distinction is entirely dead.[58] There is an elegiac quality to Huggan's comment that mirrors a statement made by Fred Inglis who writes of the Romantic journey that it is always "on the point of vanishing", and the way of life the traveller encounters "is always on the edge of extinction".[59] He goes on to suggest, however, that travelling "after" does not necessarily mean travelling less meaningfully, and indeed, the reimagination of the desert as pilgrimage for a new generation of elided travellers and tourists, oppressed by the realities of their own digital era (not to mention the illusions of a "declining and decadent West"), are contributing further accretions to the Arabian desert legacy.[60]

Democratisation of the desert experience

"The 'otherness' of deserts", writes Haynes in the concluding sentence of her study of the cultural value of the desert, "has come to epitomise a new perspective; the unexpected beauty of minimalism, the acknowledgement of, and respect for, dissenting values and a questioning of economic rationalism and materialism as pre-eminent goals for our planet".[61] Stripped back to basics, but crucially full of potential for invigorated experience, the restorative and redemptive power of deserts is felt not only by those who engage with it academically or through literature but by the casual visitor also. While many, as we have seen, dismiss tourism as a shallow and consumer-oriented expression of modern society devoid of "deeper spiritual or cultural significance", others such as Lynn Ross-Bryant recognise in tourism "the pilgrimage of modern times".[62] Writing on the phenomenal success of the North American national park as a magnet for tourism, Bryant identifies that "pilgrimage and tourism are permeable experiences. Pilgrimage has always included 'seeing the sights' as well as worrying about finding the next bed and breakfast. And tourism frequently involves a search for personal transformation".[63] The Arabian desert similarly acts as "sacralised" space, to use MacCannell's phrase, in which visitors, with head bowed down beneath the sun, enter in awe.[64] Thompson argues that such spaces eventually become "fetishised and commodified" as they become embraced within the entire panoply of the tourism industry; in the Arabian deserts, this is evident in the growing number of tourist camps offering the obligatory camel ride to watch the sunrise, serving last suppers over dying embers, paying homage to the Bedu as caretakers of the Other, peddling trinkets such as camel bone as

188   *Desert as shared space*

talismans of the pilgrimage into the dunes – part of what Holland and Huggan call the "sanitised spectacles of mass tourism".[65] This commodification, however, does not necessarily mean that the redemptive or inspirational value of the experience is circumscribed; it could simply indicate that the space is functioning well as an authentic locus of wilderness engagement for a greater number of people, a kind of democractisation of the experience that has hitherto, as we have seen, been a somewhat elitist, male-oriented, able-bodied phenomenon. Tourism can be seen within this context as a force for good, rather than negatively as an erosion of wilderness and the values represented therein.

Paul Shepherd makes a surprising apologist for the tourist in *Man in the Landscape*: while he regards the tourist as a fool, "taken seriously only by those bent on fleecing him",[66] he also concedes that there is a reciprocal benefit flowing between tourism and wilderness and views tourism as a "bad performance of a true virtue" (p. xxvii). That virtue lies in the appreciation of the natural world and in seeing it as an instructive alternative to the mechanised and artificial environment that most tourists inhabit. In their enthusiasm for wilderness, Shepherd concludes, tourists could just "be the hope of mankind":

> The tourist moves in a sphere which has no immediate connection to the conduct of his daily business. … Out of his daily niche, his potential increases … for he is on a pilgrimage or he is wayfaring, the best thing for his soul. … In this plastic formative mood he is essentially a new and different person.[67]

The ability of the desert to become a transformative zone for those who enter that space, traveller or tourist alike, is most usually considered from the perspective of a Western as opposed to an indigenous gaze. Any manipulation of that space that does not conform to a sense of desert as other, tends to attract opprobrium in both travel and critical writing. Many desert cities, for example, are often weighed in the balance against the wilderness from which they appear to be in opposition. In *Arabia Through the Looking Glass*, Jonathan Raban attends the opening of the Dubai Petroleum Company's new headquarters and lampoons what he regards as the excess (a word that is often levelled at the modern desert city) on display: "A fountain played at my elbow as I lounged, marvelling, on a prettily cushioned stone bench; this was kitsch so magnificent and inventive that it totally transcended the category – it was a triumph of happy make-believe".[68] Urry and Larsen similarly single out the city of Dubai as an example of an "evil paradise", or a place of "monumental excess"; they chart Dubai's assumed rise and fall as an example of "twentieth-century hubris", prefiguring the end of the so-called tourist gaze, and predict that the city's glamour will gradually fade when oil revenues run out and sea levels rise.[69] Urry and Larsen wistfully wonder whether the city's demise

Desert as shared space   189

(as it turns out, incorrectly anticipated) might signal a "reversal beginning in an Arabian desert" of the kind of unregulated consumption represented by Dubai. Urry and Larsen are perhaps guilty of their own tourist gaze here, tending to airbrush away "undesired modern signs" which are contrasted against the supposed elemental wilderness. Why else mention "an Arabian desert"? As we have seen, this is not an innocent term, but a whole collection of values wrapped up in a Western appreciation of wilderness.

Urry and Larsen write of Dubai's transformation from a "sleepy village" into a shimmering Arabian Las Vegas as if the city has in some way been a victim, if not of its own success, then of Western capitalist forces upon it. While the growth of this and other desert cities in the region may have been accelerated through tourism (modern Dubai's commercial success has been built out of its capitalisation as a transport hub for long-haul travel), it is hard to argue that it is a victim. Like European countries after the First World War that deliberately courted tourism by fashioning their cultural activities to the "presumed or inferred interests of foreign visitors", similarly, the desert countries of the Middle East have collaborated with transport and travel agencies, with universities and foreign governments, to maximise tourism as part of their diversification strategies.[70] Part of this strategy has involved deliberately recreating a kind of mythical Arab Orient for Western consumption. Despite the regrettable collateral of homogenisation occasioned by this approach, the rise in tourism across the Arabian Peninsula is not necessarily to be lamented.[71] At the risk of stating the obvious, tourism is important to local economies. It benefits local people and can, with care, be conducted in a sustainable manner. While being cautious of lining up indigenous people as "natives" upon which globalising agencies "act", even Huggan and Tiffin recognise that local people have a role to play in deciding what is best for their communities.[72] This marks something of a departure from Huggan's scathing condemnation of tourism in his earlier work, *Extreme Pursuits*, which seemed to posit that tourism contributes to the kind of deliberate destruction and cultural appropriation of the lands it descends upon, rather as if tourism is like a plague of locusts stripping the local culture of its identity and worth. The problem with Huggan's earlier assessment of tourism is that it has overtones of what Michael Asher called the questionable spectre of "a rich man telling poor men that they are better off poor"; it could even be argued that such a perspective represents a second post-capitalist imperialism that appropriates to itself the self-determining capacity of a country to decide for itself if tourism is of value to its evolution within the global community. The desert countries of Arabia have invested substantially in tourism – it would be a pity for the people therein (who within living memory of many of their inhabitants were compelled to endure a life with insufficient education, health care, and infrastructure) if the whole institution of travel and tourism were now to be undermined by a neo-liberal crisis of faith in its power to benefit.

190 *Desert as shared space*

Within the ever-evolving debate about the potential benefits of travel and tourism balanced against the lament about globalisation, it is interesting to consider the impact that the increase in tourism has had on the sustainability of the imaginative wilderness. It raises the question as to whether the deserts of Arabia can remain as an effective other for Western preoccupations when, encouraged by the policies of local governments, more people are able to discover the landscape for themselves and potentially reach farther into the wilderness than ever before. Sustainability has become the new mantra for those involved in facilitating the journeys of these visitors in their interaction with the wild, and the modern guidebook has assumed an ever greater if contradictory role in purporting to transform the "vulgar tourist" into the "sensitive traveller", most recently through emphasising experiential, community engagement in place of mere sightseeing. Desert writing mirrors travel writing as a whole in this regard, and while some, such as Geoff Dyer, might contend that the travel narrative is a dying art form, it may just be that the baton is being taken up by a different form of traveller, writing a different, digitised form of text – that moments of travel can be experienced within the paraphernalia of tourism. This is certainly the conclusion of Carl Thompson who convincingly charts not just the resurgence of travel literature in the modern era but also its substantial change in form. In editing an influential new compendium of critical essays on the genre, *The Routledge Companion to Travel Writing*, published in 2016, he reflects on the "heightened self-reflexivity and greater concern with the ethical implications of travel and travel writing" but also concedes that the genre remains broad enough to embrace a reassertion of "old, colonial-era taxonomies of travel, traveller and place", albeit in "exaggerated, fetishized fashion".[73] As demonstrated in the preceding chapters, even within one small location (albeit writ large by imagination), modern travel writing now encompasses a divergent set of voices, expressive of widely varying agendas executed within a range of budgets and appealing to different audiences. These include the probing of postcolonial dilemma in deeply autobiographic works, as well as the retrospective "salvage ethnography" of some footstep travel; they range from an earnest return to wonderment in nature writing to the masculine heroic form of some of the dark tourism texts of the current decade. In common with today's travel literature as a whole, much desert writing is undercut by bathos as travellers grapple with the ethics of boarding an aeroplane or the perceived banality of writing a guidebook, and, particularly in the wake of a global pandemic where travel has recently been confined within borders, many wonder whether it is better to stay at home than risk becoming the tourist they suspect they identify with. But as the next major desert expedition (crossing the deserts of Saudi Arabia in 2022 with extensive regional backing and carried out by a multi-cultural, mixed-gender team with full technological support) takes shape, it is

Desert as shared space 191

clear that desert travel is not over yet, even if it looks very different today from the travels of St John Philby whose route it roughly follows. A book is likely to follow, together with a blog, vlogs, and a mosaic of contributing images and routes for others to follow in virtual space and in digital time. So while Dyer's "Round South America on a Pogo Stick" species of travel writing probably reached its desert apotheosis in Osborne's account of trying to find a bottle of champagne in Oman,[74] it would be rash to assume that a genre that has withstood the secularisation of pilgrims, the professionalisation of amateurs, and the commercialisation of explorers will not similarly survive the democratisation of travellers into tourists. In so doing, desert literature will continue to offer moments of insight if not about the region covered, then at least about the land left behind – wherever that may be in a world where home has packed a bag and gone travelling.

Notes

1 Malcom Macgregor, *Wilderness Oman* (Devizes: Ptarmigan Publishing, 2002), p. 22.
2 Macgregor *Wilderness Oman*, p. 6.
3 Maria Lindgren Leavenworth, *The Second Journey* [2009] (Umeå: Umeå Universitet, 2010), p. 24.
4 See Claudia Bell and John Lyall, *The Accelerated Sublime: Landscape, Tourism, and Identity* (Westport, CT: Praeger, 2002).
5 Paul Fussell, ed., *The Norton Book of Travel* (New York: Norton, 1987), p. 651.
6 James Buzard, *The Beaten Track: European Tourism, Literature, and the Ways to "Culture" 1800–1918* (Oxford: Clarendon Press, 1993), p. 2.
7 Carl Thompson, *Travel Writing* (Abingdon and New York: Routledge, 2011), p. 49.
8 Tim Youngs, *The Cambridge Introduction to Travel Writing* (Cambridge: Cambridge University Press, 2013), p. 58.
9 Buzard, *The Beaten Track*, p. 6.
10 Buzard, *The Beaten Track*, pp. 12–13.
11 Freya Stark, *Baghdad Sketches: Journeys through Iraq* [1937] (London: Tauris Parke Paperbacks, 2012), p. 1.
12 Wilfred Thesiger, *Arabian Sands* [1959] (Harmondsworth: Penguin, 1984), p. 11.
13 Author's unpublished interview with Levison Wood, 15 October 2017.
14 Thompson, *Travel Writing*, p. 124.
15 Mark Thomas, *Extreme Rambling* (London: Ebury Press, 2011).
16 Leon McCarron, *The Land Beyond: A Thousand Miles on Foot through the Heart of the Middle East* (London and New York: I.B. Tauris, 2017), p. 179.
17 Graham Huggan, *Extreme Pursuits: Travel/Writing in an Age of Globalization* (Ann Arbor: University of Michigan Press, 2009), p. 6.
18 Huggan, *Extreme Pursuits*, p. 99.
19 Bell and Lyall, *The Accelerated Sublime*, p. 193.
20 Jean Louis Burckhardt, *Travels in Syria and the Holy Land* (London: The Association for Promoting the Discovery of the Interior Parts of Africa, 1822).
21 Bell and Lyall, *The Accelerated Sublime*, p. 193.

192   *Desert as shared space*

22 Kathleen M. Adams, "Danger-Zone Tourism: Prospects and Problems for Tourism in Tumultuous Times", in *Interconnected Worlds: Tourism in Southeast Asia*, ed. by Peggy Teo, T.C. Chang, and K.C. Ho (Oxford: Pergamon, 2001), pp. 265–78.

23 See Henry Hemming, *Misadventure in the Middle East: Travels as Tramp, Artist and Spy* (London: Nicholas Brealey Publishing, 2007); Tony Wheeler, *Bad Lands* [2007] (Melbourne: Lonely Planet Publications, 2010); Tony Wheeler, *Dark Lands* (Melbourne: Lonely Planet Publications, 2013); Tom Chesshyre, *A Tourist in the Arab Spring* (Chalfont St. Peter: Bradt Travel Guides, 2013).

24 Tim Woods, *Beginning Postmodernism* [1999] (Manchester: Manchester University Press, 2009), pp. 68–71.

25 Wheeler, *Dark Lands*, p. 6.

26 Carl Thompson, "Introduction", in *The Routledge Companion to Travel Writing*, ed. by Carl Thompson, [2016] (Abingdon and New York: Routledge, 2020), p. xviii.

27 Vincent J. Cheng, *Inauthentic: The Anxiety over Culture and Identity* (New Brunswick: Rutgers University Press, 2004), pp. 2–3 and 6.

28 Tony Wheeler, "Philosophy of a Guidebook Guru", *UNESCO Courier* (July-August 1999), 54–55.

29 Wheeler, *Bad Lands*, p. 7.

30 Urry and Larsen, *The Tourist Gaze*, pp. 65–66 on the subject of desertification.

31 Thompson, *Travel Writing*, p. 126. See Maxine Feifer, *Going Places: Tourism in History from Imperial Rome to the Present* (New York: Stein and Day, 1986).

32 Huggan, *Extreme Pursuits*, p. 100.

33 Alan Keohane, *Bedouin Nomads of the Desert* [1994] (London: Kyle Books, 2011), Preface, p. 7.

34 For a satirical account of today's obsession with apocalyptic theories, see Jason Boyett, *Pocket Guide to the Apocalypse* (Orlando, FL: Relevant Books, 2005).

35 Debbie Lisle, *The Global Politics of Contemporary Travel Writing* (Cambridge: Cambridge University Press, 2006), p. 95.

36 See Huggan, *Extreme Pursuits*, pp. 100 and 103.

37 Author's unpublished interview with Levison Wood, 15 October 2017.

38 Gary Krist "Ironic Journeys: Travel Writing in the Age of Tourism", *The Hudson Review*, 45, no. 4 (1993), 593–601.

39 Billie Melman, "The Middle East/Arabia: 'The Cradle of Islam'", in *The Cambridge Companion to Travel Writing*, ed. by Peter Hulme and Tim Youngs (Cambridge: Cambridge University Press, 2002), pp. 112–19; Michael Grimshaw, *Bibles and Baedekers: Tourism, Travel, Exile and God* [2008] (Abingdon: Routledge, 2014), and Roslynn D. Haynes, *Desert: Nature and Culture* (London: Reaktion Books, 2013).

40 See Douglas Burton-Christie, *The Word in the Desert: Scripture and the Quest for Holiness in Early Christian Monasticism* (Oxford and New York: Oxford University Press, 1993) and Lane Belden, *The Solace of Fierce Landscapes: Exploring Desert and Mountain Spirituality* (Oxford and New York: Oxford University Press, 1998).

41 William Atkins, *The Immeasurable World: Journeys in Desert Places* (New York: Doubleday, 2018), p. 21.

42 Youngs, *The Cambridge Introduction*, p. 99.

43 Peter Hulme, "Travelling to Write (1940–2000)", in *The Cambridge Companion to Travel Writing*, ed. by Peter Hulme and Tim Youngs [2002] (Cambridge: Cambridge University Press, 2010), pp. 87–101 (p. 94).

Desert as shared space 193

44 See, for example, Ellen Badone and Sharon R. Roseman, eds., *Intersecting Journeys: The Anthropology of Pilgrimage and Tourism* (Urbana: University of Illinois |Press, 2004).
45 Charles M. Doughty, *Travels in Arabia Deserta* [Cambridge: 1888] (London: Jonathan Cape and the Medici Society, 1926, 2 Vols) and Geoffrey Moorhouse, *The Fearful Void* [1974] (London: Faber and Faber, 2008).
46 Peter Hulme, "Travelling to Write (1940–2000)", in *The Cambridge Companion to Travel Writing*, ed. by Peter Hulme and Tim Youngs [2002] (Cambridge: Cambridge University Press, 2010), pp. 87–101. Hulme makes the point that "Thesiger's themes may look old-fashioned (even for their time)" but notes nonetheless that "nomadic life is a constant theme throughout the last half century" (p. 88).
47 See, for example, Michael Grimshaw, *Bibles and Baedekers: Tourism, Travel, Exile and God* [2008] (Abingdon: Routledge, 2014), p. 1.
48 Lawrence Osborne, *The Wet and the Dry: A Drinker's Journey* (London: Harvill Secker, 2013).
49 Roger Scruton: *The West and the Rest: Globalization and the Terrorist Threat* (London: Continuum, 2002), p. 127.
50 Robert Macfarlane, "Why We Need Nature Writing: A New 'Culture of Nature' Is Changing the Way We Live – and Could Change our Politics, Too" [online], *New Statesman*, Nature (2015), available at: https://www.newstatesman.com/culture/nature/2015/09/robert-macfarlane-why-we-need-nature-writing [accessed 28 June 2019].
51 James Budd, *Half Past Ten in the Afternoon: An Englishman's Journey from Aneiza to Makkah* (London: Arabian Publishing, 2014). See the author's expanded discussion of Budd's narrative in *Studies in Travel Writing*, 20, no. 4 (2016), 425–27.
52 Cyril Glassé, *The Concise Encyclopaedia of Islam: Revised Edition* [1989] (London: Stacey International, 2001), p. 219.
53 Holland and Huggan, *Tourists with Typewriters*, p. 71.
54 Hulme, "Travelling to Write", p. 90.
55 Youngs, *The Cambridge Introduction*, p. 97.
56 Clive Pearson in Grimshaw, *Bibles and Baedekers*, p. vii.
57 Mark Evans talks about the frustration of not being able to sit around the camp fire on his crossing of the Empty Quarter because he was required to keep up with the demands of real-time media and had to complete the entire journey within a predetermined timeframe. Author's unpublished interview with Mark Evans, 19 March 2016.
58 Huggan, *Extreme Pursuits*, p. 5: "I am taking it as a given that there is no meaningful distinction between the tourist and the traveller".
59 Fred Inglis, *The Delicious History of the Holiday* (London: Routledge, 2000), p. 82.
60 Grimshaw, *Bibles and Baedekers*, p. 52.
61 Haynes, *Desert*, p. 208.
62 Lynn Ross-Bryant, *Pilgrimage to the National Parks: Religion and Nature in the United States* (New York: Routledge, 2013), p. 6.
63 Ross-Bryant, *Pilgrimage to the National Parks*, p. 6.
64 Dean MacCannell, *The Tourist: A New Theory of the Leisure Class* (Berkeley: University of California Press, 1999), pp. 42–48 and quoted in Thompson, *Travel Writing*, p. 162.
65 Holland and Huggan, *Tourists with Typewriters*, p. 2.
66 Paul Shepherd, *Man in the Landscape: A Historic View of the Esthetics of Nature* [1967, 1991] (London: University of Georgia Press, 2002), p. 150.
67 Shepherd, *Man in the Landscape*, p. 156.

68 Jonathan Raban, *Arabia Through the Looking Glass* [1979] (Glasgow: Fontana, 1980), p. 196.
69 Urry and Larsen, *The Tourist Gaze 3.0*, pp. 239–40.
70 Buzard, *The Beaten Track*, p. 332.
71 Before the current Covid pandemic, the World Bank trend analysis covering the period 1995 to 2017 showed a sharp increase in tourism in all Arabian Peninsula countries except Yemen; see "International Tourism, Number of Arrivals" [online], The World Bank (2019), available at: https://data.world bank.org/indicator/ST.INT.ARVL [accessed 10 July 2019].
72 Graham Huggan and Helen Tiffin, *Postcolonial Ecocriticism: Literature, Animals, Environment* [2010] (Abingdon: Routledge, 2015), p. 68.
73 Carl Thompson, "Travel Writing Now, 1950 to the Present Day", in *The Routledge Companion to Travel Writing*, ed. by Carl Thompson [2016] (London and New York: Routledge, 2020), pp. 196–213 (p. 197).
74 Dyer, "Is Travel Writing Dead?" As part of a series of "2 minute reads", this article in *Granta* could almost belong to the accelerated sublime that it appears to disdain. See Pico Iyer's rebuttal in the same journal in which he describes a different travelling demographic from the "somewhat colonial interaction" of former travel writing.

Conclusion
Barren legacy?

In an era when parts of the Arabian desert have been grassed over for golf courses (the example that the champion of wilderness, Jay Griffiths, uses as a symbol of "the absolute dominion of man over wild nature"), and their fringes turned into ludic playgrounds for tourists, it is reasonable to ask whether the Arabian desert trope has at length become a barren legacy – a space as empty as the imaginative geography often used to describe it.[1] New desert travellers earnestly simulate the act of exploration in supervised forays off-road, guided by satellite technology and comprehensive guidebooks – such as the ones I have authored or contributed to myself; others, with a deliberate dose of irony or self-mockery, don Arabian headdresses for a 30-minute camel-ride and inevitable "selfie" in which all hint of modernity (satellite dishes, mobile phone masts, shops, pickup trucks, and the other accoutrements of a typical modern desert life) is carefully edited out. Such self-casting in an ossified landscape of set-piece props (Bedu, camel, sand-dune) represents an act that John Urry and Jonas Larsen in *The Tourist Gaze* might identify as an effort to "tame the objects of the gaze", thereby reflecting and reinforcing stereotypes of the Western imagination, not just of the desert but of the Orient as a whole;[2] this contributes in turn to what Hayden White has termed the "fictions of factual representation" – texts that appear to perpetuate a dated literary legacy at the expense of reflecting today's Arab modernities.[3]

Even today's professional expeditioners, such as Ranulph Fiennes, Adrian Hayes, Mark Evans, and Levison Wood, recognise the slight absurdity of the modern desert endeavour, or at least register that the achievement of crossing the desert today is, in Ali Behdad's terminology, a "belated" activity, different in calibre to the accomplishment of former explorers.[4] In interview, for example, Evans is quick to point out that Bertram Thomas "had no map to follow and death was a distinct possibility"; now, in contrast, "the only thing that can't be controlled is the weather".[5] The anxiety about authentic endeavour is reflected in the resulting travel narratives that, as identified in the previous chapter, seek frequently to distinguish the experiences described therein from those found in a tourist blog. As observed by Levison Wood, an author who

DOI: 10.4324/9781003197201-7

196   *Conclusion*

recently walked around Arabia, as the distinction narrows between traveller and tourist, exploration has inevitably become "a profession, a job".[6] While this job obliges the traveller to generate stories to satisfy sponsors and fulfil publication and television contracts, the ability to write something distinctive has become increasingly challenging when anyone with a guidebook can do the same. Indeed, so apparently tame is the activity of exploration, given today's fully supported expeditions, that it has led Geoff Dyer to argue that it signals if not the death of travel literature, then at least the second journey form of it – or what Dyer calls the "literary equivalent of package tours in which destination and experience are so thoroughly predetermined that one is reluctant to make a booking".[7] In a region where travelling is heavily invested in the inscripted past, this suggests that the era of meaningful desert travel in Arabia may have run its course.[8] This in turn begs the question as to whether the Arabian desert genre has, in itself, become redundant – a weary trope over-invested with literary allusion.

The subtitle of this book – *A Barren Legacy?* – was chosen to reflect not just a recognition that travel in the region has changed dramatically since Wilfred Thesiger's travels, triggering a crisis of confidence in the modern desert journey, but also to reflect a weariness among today's critics and commentators with modes of representation that appear only to recycle insupportable tropes. The desert as empty and vacant, open to Western delineation and penetration; the desert as a place of unchanging landscape and free, primitive cultures – all these familiar tropes have over the centuries offered a gratifying other, or imaginative alternative to the claustrophobic, urban complexities of life back home. As shown throughout this study, they have also contributed to a presumed general engagement with the East conceptualised in Said's *Orientalism*. As Said famously showed, the impact of both manifest and latent Orientalism has resulted in material consequences, encouraging (if not facilitating) exploration and resource exploitation and resulting in tangible benefits for Western nations. From the perspective of postcolonial agency, then, desert literature that continues to resurrect latent Orientalism appears dispiritingly retrogressive and contributes to the notion of barren legacy.

But if the recycling of outmoded tropes continues in *some* of today's desert literature, it is not ubiquitous in *all* such travel texts, at least not all of the time. Indeed, as this book has endeavoured to show, desert writing is no more of a homogenous project than any other that contributes to the general legacy of Orientalist texts, nor is it a dying project, and the usefulness of this book may be considered not just in the way it has found desert literature to be continuing "in rude health" but also in finding prognoses within the genre for self-rejuvenation.[9] Even as travellers grapple with the modern dilemma of meaning in their journeys, and as the desert becomes ever more accessible to the casual tourist, elaborate expeditions continue to be planned and continue to be executed in the Arabian

Conclusion 197

desert, resulting in at least three key new desert texts, as we have seen, in the period between 2015 and 2020. Another major new journey, internationally sanctioned and involving a team led by Mark Evans, was launched by the British Princess Royal on 27 September 2022; following the very form that Dyer laments as sounding the death knoll of travel literature, it plans to walk in the footsteps of Arabist "Jack" Philby ("Sheikh Abdullah" on converting to Islam), and the journey is partially planned to celebrate the first European to cross the Rub Al Khali from East to West, as recorded in Philby's expedition narrative, *Heart of Arabia* (1922). What redeems this centennial journey – and the likely publication at the end of it – is that Evans is taking an old theme and forging something new with it. This is a project less about a white Western fascination with a white Western explorer and more about a locally blessed opportunity for cross-cultural interaction, carried out by a diverse team that includes a Saudi Arabian woman – namely, Philby's granddaughter Reem – in a country searching for ways to diversify away from oil through promotion of tourism.

What makes these new forms of desert expedition interesting is that in the place of once confident projects that describe self, other, and the land left behind, where nostalgia was once used largely as a tool for self-congratulation, doubt becomes a productive theme in itself – doubt about individual capability, about the ability to represent the Other, and about the hitherto unquestioned supposed superiority not just of a dominant culture but also in terms of human dominion over the natural world. If the habit of self-evaluation betrays a growing maturation in the individual, then it may also evidence an optimistic development within the genre of desert writing too, allowing for the experience of travel to be revived in its capacity to educate and to enhance intercultural understanding.

Encouraged by the work of postcolonial critics, an attempt has been made throughout this book to look beyond the stereotypes and, through the lens of postcolonialism, feminism, and ecocriticism, to investigate moments of what Fred Dallmayr calls "post-Orientalism" that "rupture or transgress the traditional Orientalist paradigm".[10] In Chapter 1's emphasis on presentations of self, for example, the discussion considered how, in evidencing an awareness of the complexities of representing "Arab" and "desert" in a postcolonial, postmodern, and increasingly globalised context, footstep travellers are able to arrive at more holistic and inclusive modes of representation. Similarly, Chapter 2's exploration of the Other through Eurocentric notions of nostalgia (particularly in reference to writing about the Bedu and in relation to the urban experience), concluded that a backward glance is not necessarily the same as a negative gaze: in recognising the educative potential invested in traditional ways of being while also showing how history is embraced by the modern lived experience in Arabian countries, desert writing can help to reveal rather than obfuscate today's Arab modernities. The way in which the

198 *Conclusion*

past impinges on the present and inversely the present mediates perspectives on the past has been shown by this study to be an inherent feature of desert literature in as much as it is expressed in the dominant discourse. For reasons examined herein, this discourse has tended to be white and male. By looking, in Chapter 3, at how the Arabian desert is not just written about by Western women but also how it is gendered by Western men, the study has shown that opportunities are being taken to represent the marginalised in a more representative manner. That discussion was developed, in Chapter 4's focus on natural wilderness, by showing how, in moments when scientists express wonderment in the desert landscape, a more equitable balance between subject and object is restored.

As shown throughout this book, the socio-historical context is continually referenced in Arabian desert writing and intertextuality as a recurring feature of the genre. If, as Heather Henderson writes, travel literature is "so highly intertextual that at times texts are actually substituted for experience itself", this is particularly the case with desert writing, and the result of this is an archive of work that reveals as much about the country left behind as the region of scrutiny.[11] It is this archive of material that continues to provoke visits to the Arabian desert, even as prospective authors suspect they are too late to experience anything "authentic". Primarily Western preoccupations have always been projected onto the Arabian desert – part of the metaphysical blank sheet that Mark Cocker recognises in the term "abroad" – that shifts as decisively over time as the region under scrutiny and the modes of travel available to explore it.[12] Far from a "barren legacy", therefore, the Arabian desert continues, as shown in Chapter 5, to be a zone of inspiration and quest for Western travellers and writers, albeit reconstructed to reflect today's cultural and environmental concerns. It acts, in other words, as a microcosmic projection of the broader discourses taking place "at home".

In summary, then, the imaginative geography of Arabia continues within desert literature to be charted along familiar axes but tends towards new and more promising destinations. But this is no cause for complacency. Looming over this entire discussion has been the spectre of globalisation and a general anxiety about what this signifies in the modern quest. Benita Parry alerts us to the fact that imperialism has "survived its formal ending" and continues to some extent under the new guise of globalisation.[13] Michael Hardt and Antonio Negri see globalisation as a new empire that sets up "its own relationships of power based on exploitation that are in many respects more brutal than those it destroyed".[14] While an era of postcolonialism has helped not just identify but also mitigate against irresponsible othering, there is, as Jenni Ramone reminds us, still more to be done,[15] and it is important to continue to provide, in the words of Graham Huggan, "more socially and ecologically responsible attitudes towards environment and place".[16] Some critics argue that

Conclusion 199

postcolonialism may be less potent as a critique of the global present because globalisation exploits the politics of difference (the key tool in challenging old binaries) albeit for a new agenda. This in fact is something that Said himself predicted in *Orientalism* when he wrote,

> One aspect of the electronic, postmodern world is that there has been a reinforcement of the stereotypes by which the Orient is viewed. Television, the films, and all the media's resources have forced information into more and more standardised moulds.[17]

In recognising and analysing some of that stereotyping tendency in the works of Arabian modern desert literature, while also revealing ways in which writers grapple with new tools to contest those tendencies, this book has endeavoured to add, albeit modestly, to the "planes of activities and praxis" that ensure that the gains made by postcolonial, feminist, and ecocritical critiques are maintained in an era of post-orientalism and in the age of the Anthropocene.[18]

Notes

1 Jay Griffiths, *Wild: An Elemental Journey* (London: Penguin, 2006), p. 6. The Dubai Desert Classic is played, for example, on one of the Peninsula's many green desert golf courses, the first of which was grassed in 1988; see "Golf Courses in the UAE" [online], Spikeson.com, available at: https://www.spike son.com/ countries/united-arab-emirates-golf-courses.php [accessed 11 July 2019].

2 John Urry and Jonas Larsen, *The Tourist Gaze 3.0* [1990] (London: Sage Publications, 2011), p. 167.

3 Cited in Patrick Holland and Graham Huggan, *Tourists with Typewriters: Critical Reflections on Contemporary Travel Writing* [1998] (Ann Arbor: University of Michigan Press, 2000), p. 10.

4 Ali Behdad, *Belated Travelers: Orientalism in the Age of Colonial Dissolution* (Durham, NC: Duke UP, 1994).

5 Author's unpublished interview with Mark Evans, 19 March 2016.

6 Author's unpublished interview with Levison Wood, 15 October 2017. See Levison Wood, *Arabia: A Journey Through the Heart of the Middle East* (London: Hodder and Stoughton, 2018).

7 Geoff Dyer, "Is Travel Writing Dead?" [online], *Granta*, 138 (2017), available at: https://granta.com/is-travel-writing-dead-dyer/ [accessed 13 July 2019].

8 See "Studying Arabia as a Country of the Mind" in the introduction to this study.

9 Anshuman A. Mondal reviewing Jenni Ramone, ed., *The Bloomsbury Introduction to Postcolonial Writing: New Contexts, New Narratives, New Debates* (London and New York: Bloomsbury Academic, 2018), back cover.

10 Fred Dallmayr, *Beyond Orientalism: Essays in Cross-Cultural Encounter* (New York: State University Press, 1996), p. 115.

11 Heather Henderson, "The Travel Writer and the Text: My Giant Goes with Me Wherever I Go", in *Temperamental Journeys: Essays on the Modern Literature of Travel*, ed. by Michael Kowalewski (Athens: University of Georgia Press, 1992), pp. 230–48 (p. 246).

200 *Conclusion*

12 Mark Cocker, *Loneliness and Time: The Story of British Travel Writing* (New York: Pantheon, 1993), p. 18.
13 Benita Parry, *Postcolonial Studies: A Materialist Critique* (London: Routledge, 2004), p. 18.
14 Michael Hardt and Antonio Negri, *Empire* (Cambridge, Massachusetts: Harvard University Press, 2000), p. 43.
15 Ramone, *The Bloomsbury Introduction*, p. 2.
16 Graham Huggan, *Interdisciplinary Measures: Literature and the Future of Postcolonial Studies* (Liverpool: Liverpool University Press, 2008), p. 15.
17 Said, *Orientalism*, p. 26.
18 Edward W. Said, "Orientalism Reconsidered", in *Literature, Politics and Theory: Papers from the Essex Conference, 1976-84* [1986], ed. by Francis Barker et al. (Abingdon and New York: Routledge, 2003), pp. 210–29 (p. 228).

Bibliography

Primary Sources

Al-Nahi, Donya, *Heroine of the Desert* (Bhopal: Manjul Books, 2006).

Anonymous, *The Way of a Pilgrim and the Pilgrim Continues His Way* [1930] translated by R.M. French (San Francisco: Harper and Row, 1952).

Asher, Michael, *The Last of the Bedu: In Search of the Myth* (Harmondsworth: Viking, 1996).

Atkins, William, *The Immeasurable World: Journeys in Desert Places* (New York: Doubleday, 2018).

Bagnold, Ralph A., *Libyan Sands: Travels in a Dead World* [1935] (London: Eland Publishing, 2010).

Bakewell, R. "Travels in Switzerland", *Eclectic Review*, N.S.21 (1824), 306–27 (pp. 306–07).

Beadell, Len, *Too Long in the Bush* (Adelaide: Rigby, 1965).

Bell, Gertrude, *The Desert and the Sown: Travels in Palestine and Syria* (New York: E.P. Dutton & Co., 1907).

Blackmore, Charles, *In the Footsteps of Lawrence of Arabia* (London: Harrap Limited, 1986).

Blunt, Lady Anne, *A Pilgrimage to Nejd: The Cradle of the Arab Race* (London: John Murray, 1881, 2 Vols.).

Brady, Adrienne, *Way South of Wahiba Sands: Travels with Wadiman* (London: Austin Macauley Publishers, 2013).

Bent, J. Theodore, *The Travel Chronicles of Mrs. J. Theodore Bent. Volume III: Southern Arabia and Persia* [1883–98], ed. by Gerald Brisch (Oxford: Archaeopress, 2010).

Brooks, Geraldine, *Nine Parts of Desire* (London: Penguin Books, 1995).

Budd, James, *Half Past Ten in the Afternoon: An Englishman's Journey from Aneiza to Makkah* (London: Arabian Publishing, 2014).

Burckhardt, Jean Louis, *Travels in Syria and the Holy Land* (London: John Murray, 1822).

Burckhardt, John Lewis, *Notes on the Bedouins and Wahabys, Collected During His Travels in the East* (London: Henry Colburn and Richard Bentley, 1831, 2 Vols.).

Burke, Edmund, *A Philosophical Enquiry into the Origin of our Ideas of the Sublime and Beautiful* [1759], ed. by James Boulton (Oxford: Basil Blackwell, 1987).

202   Bibliography

Burroughs, William S., *The Naked Lunch* [1959], ed. by James Grauerholz and Barry Miles (New York: Grove Press, 2001).

Burton, Lady Isabel, *Arabia, Egypt, India: A Narrative of Travel* (London and Belfast: W. Mullan and Son, 1879).

Burton, Richard, *Appendices to Pilgrimages to Al-Madinah and Meccah* [1855], ed. by Isabel Burton (London: Memorial Edition, 1893, 2 Vols.).

Byron, Lord, *Byron: Poetical Works* [1904], ed. by Frederick Page (Oxford: Oxford Univesity Press, 1970).

Chatwin, Bruce, *The Songlines* (London: Jonathan Cape, 1987).

Chesshyre, Tom, *A Tourist in the Arab Spring* (Chalfont St. Peter: Bradt Travel Guides, 2013).

Clapp, Nicholas, *The Road to Ubar: Finding the Atlantis of the Sands* [1998] (London: Souvenir Press, 1999).

Clarke, Edward D., *Travels in Various Countries of Europe, Asia and Africa* (London: T. Cadell and W. Davies, 1810–24, 11 Vols.).

Couchman, Helen, *Omani Women* (Muscat: Soloshow Publishing, 2015).

Cowan, James, *Desert Father: A Journey in the Wilderness with Saint Anthony* (Boston, MA: New Seeds Books, 2006).

Cust, Lionel and Sidney Colvin, eds., *History of the Society of Dilettanti* (London: MacMillan, 1898).

Davidson, Robyn, *Tracks* [1980] (London: Picador, 1998).

Dickson, Violet, *The Wild Flowers of Kuwait and Bahrain* (London: George Allen and Unwin, 1955).

Doughty, Charles M., *Travels in Arabia Deserta* [1888] (London: Jonathan Cape and the Medici Society, 1926, 2 Vols.).

Evans, Mark, *Crossing the Empty Quarter in the Footsteps of Bertram Thomas* (UK: Gilgamesh Publishing, 2016). http://www.gilgamesh.co.uk.

Fiennes, Ranulph, *Atlantis of the Sands: The Search for the Lost City of Ubar* [1992] (London: Signet, 1993).

Forbes, Rosita, *The Secret of the Sahara: Kufara* [1921] (Harmondsworth: Penguin Books, 1937).

Foster, Shirley and Sara Mills, eds., *An Anthology of Women's Travel Writing* (Manchester: Manchester University Press, 2002).

Fountaine, Margaret, *Love Among the Butterflies: Travels and Adventures of a Victorian Lady*, ed. by W.F. Cater (Boston, MA: Little, Brown and Company, 1980).

Galt, John, *Letters from the Levant* (London: T. Cadell and W. Davies, 1813).

Garnett, David, ed., *The Letters of T. E. Lawrence* (London: Jonathan Cape, 1938).

George, Uwe, *In the Deserts of This Earth* [1976], translated by R. Winston and C. Winston (New York and London: First Harvest/HBJ, 1977).

Gilpin, William, *Three Essays on Picturesque Beauty; on Picturesque Travel; and on Sketching Landscape* (London: R. Blamire, 1794).

Glen, Douglas, *In the Steps of Lawrence of Arabia* (London: Rich and Cowan, 1941).

Gordon, Lady Duff, *Letters from Egypt, 1863–65* [1865] (London: R. Brimley Johnson, 1902).

Griffiths, Jay, *Wild: An Elemental Journey* (London: Penguin, 2006).

Hayes, Adrian, *Footsteps of Thesiger* (Dubai: Motivate, 2012).

Bibliography 203

Hemming, Henry, *Misadventure in the Middle East: Travels as Tramp, Artist and Spy* (London: Nicholas Brealey Publishing, 2007).

Holland, Henry, *Travels in the Ionian Islands* [1813] (London: Longman, Hurst, Rees, Orme, and Brown, 1819).

Holland, Henry, "Travels in the Ionian Islands", *Eclectic Review*, N.S.7 (1817), 353–72 (p. 358).

Ingrams, Doreen, *A Time in Arabia: Life in Yemen's Hadhramaut in the 1930s* (London: Eland, 2013).

Johnson, Samuel, *A Dictionary of the English Language* (London: J.P. Knapton et al., 1755).

Keats, John, *John Keats: The Complete Poems*, ed. by John Barnard (Harmondsworth: Penguin, 1973).

Keohane, Alan, *Bedouin Nomads of the Desert* [1994] (London: Kyle Books, 2011).

Keppel, George, *A Personal Narrative of a Journey from India to England* (London: Henry Colburn, 1827, 2 Vols.)

Kinglake, Alexander William, *Eothen: Traces of Travel Brought Home from the East* (London: John Ollivier, 1845).

Kirkby, Bruce, *Sand Dance: By Camel Across Arabia's Great Southern Desert* (Toronto: McClelland and Stewart, 2000).

Lane, Edward William, *An Account of the Manners and Customs of the Modern Egyptians* (London: C. Knight, 1836).

Lane, Edward William, *The Thousand and One Nights* (London: Chatto and Windus, 1883).

Lawrence, A.W., ed., *T. E. Lawrence by His Friends* [1937] (New York: McGraw-Hill, 1963).

Lawrence, T. E., *Seven Pillars of Wisdom: A Triumph* [privately printed 1926, published 1935] (Harmondsworth: Penguin, 1986).

Macgregor, Malcom, *Wilderness Oman* (Devizes: Ptarmigan Publishing, 2002).

Mackintosh-Smith, Tim, *Travels with a Tangerine* [2001] (New York: Random House, 2004).

Mackintosh-Smith, Tim, *Yemen: Travels in Dictionary Land* [1997] (London: John Murray, 2007).

Mannin, Ethel, *A Lance for the Arabs: A Middle East Journey* (London: Hutchinson, 1963).

Maugham, Robin, *Nomad* (London: Chapman and Hall, 1947).

McCarron, Leon, *The Land Beyond: A Thousand Miles on Foot through the Heart of the Middle East* (London and New York: I.B. Tauris, 2017).

McClure, M. L. and C. L. Feltoe, eds., *The Pilgrimage of Etheria* (London: Society for Promoting Christian Knowledge; New York: Macmillan, 1919).

McKinnon, Michael, *Arabia: Sand, Sea, Sky* (London: BBC Books, 1990).

Mear, Roger and Robert Swan, *A Walk to the Pole: To the Heart of Antarctica in the Footsteps of Scott* (New York: Random House, 1987).

Montagu, Lady Mary Wortley, *The Letters of Lady M.W. Montagu during the Embassy to Constantinople, 1716–18* (London: John Sharpe, 1825, Vol. 1).

Moorhouse, Geoffrey, *The Fearful Void* [1974] (London: Faber and Faber, 2008).

Morris, James (now Jan), *Sultan in Oman* [1957] (London: Eland, 2008).

Morris, Mary, ed., *Maiden Voyages: Writings of Women Travellers* (New York: Vintage, 1993).

204   *Bibliography*

Morton, Christopher and Philip N. Grover, eds., *Wilfred Thesiger in Africa: A Unique Collection of Essays & Personal Photographs* (New York: HarperCollins, 2010).

Murray, John, *The Letters of John Murray to Lord Byron*, ed. by Andrew Nicholson (Liverpool: Liverpool University Press, 2007).

Nash, Geoffrey, ed., *Travellers to the Middle East from Burckhardt to Thesiger: An Anthology* (London and New York: Anthem Press, 2011).

Niebuhr, Carsten, *Travels through Arabia, and Other Countries in the East*, translated by Robert Heron (Perth, Edinburgh, and London: Morison et al., 1792, 2 Vols.).

Osborne, Lawrence, *The Wet and the Dry: A Drinker's Journey* (London: Harvill Secker, 2013).

Pryce, Lois, *Revolutionary Ride: On the Road in Search of the Real Iran* (London: Nicholas Brealey Publishing, 2017).

Raban, Jonathan, *Arabia Through the Looking Glass* [1979] (Glasgow: Fontana, 1980).

Robinson, Jane, *Unsuitable for Ladies: An Anthology of Women Travellers* [1994] (Oxford: Oxford University Press, 1995).

Ruete, E., *Memoirs of an Arabian Princess from Zanzibar* [1888] (Mineola, New York: Dover Publications, 2009).

Sasson, Jean, *Princess: More Tears to Cry* (London: Transworld, 2014).

Shelley, Percy Bysshe, *Ozymandias* [1817], *Shelley's Poetry and Prose*, ed. by Donald H. Reiman and Sharon B. Powers (New York and London: W. W. Norton, 1977).

Smith, John, *A System of Modern Geography* (London: Sherwood, Neely, and Jones, 1811, 2 Vols.)

Stanhope, Lady Hester, *Memoirs of the Lady Hester Stanhope: As Related by Herself in Conversations with Her Physician* (London: Henry Colburn, 1846, 3 Vols.).

Stark, Freya, *Baghdad Sketches: Journeys through Iraq* [1937] (London: Tauris Parke Paperbacks, 2012).

Tatchell, Jo, *A Diamond in the Desert: Behind the Scenes in the World's Richest City* [2009] (London: Hodder and Stoughton, 2010).

Thackeray, William Makepeace, *Contributions to 'Punch', Etc.* (New York and London: Harper and Brothers, 1903).

Thesiger, Wilfred, *Arabian Sands* [1959] (Harmondsworth: Penguin, 1984 with new preface).

Thesiger, Wilfred, *The Life of My Choice* [1987] (New York and London: W. W. Norton, 1988).

Thomas, Bertram, *Arabia Felix: Across the Empty Quarter of Arabia* (London: Jonathan Cape, 1932).

Thomas, Mark, *Extreme Rambling* (London: Ebury Press, 2011).

Toy, Barbara, *Travelling the Incense Route: From Arabia to the Levant in the Footsteps of the Magi* [1968] (London: Tauris Parke, 2009).

Van, Geldermalsen, Marguerite, *Married to a Bedouin* (London: Virago, 2006).

Walker, D. H. and A. R. Pittaway, *Insects of Eastern Arabia* (London: Macmillan, 1987).

Walker, Jenny and Paul Clammer, *Jordan* (Melbourne: Lonely Planet, 2015).

Walker, Jenny, *Jordan* (Melbourne: Lonely Planet, 2012).

Bibliography 205

Walker, Jenny and Mathew D. Firestone, *Jordan* (Melbourne: Lonely Planet, 2009).

Walker, Jenny et al., *Oman, UAE and the Arabian Peninsula* (Melbourne: Lonely Planet, 2013).

Wey, William, *The Itineraries of William Wey* [1857], translated by Francis Davey (Oxford: Bodleian Library, 2010).

Wheeler, Sara, *Terra Incognita: Travels in Antarctica* [1996] (New York: Modern Library, 1999).

Wheeler, Tony, "Philosophy of a Guidebook Guru", *UNESCO Courier* (July–August 1999), 54–55.

Wheeler, Tony, *Bad Lands* [2007] (Melbourne: Lonely Planet Publications, 2010).

Wheeler, Tony, *Dark Lands* (Melbourne: Lonely Planet Publications, 2013).

Winser, Nigel *The Sea of Sands and Mists – Desertification: Seeking Solutions in the Wahiba Sands* (London: RGS, 1989).

Wood, Levison, *Arabia: A Journey Through the Heart of the Middle East* (London: Hodder and Stoughton, 2018).

Secondary Sources

Abu-Lughod, Ibrahim, *Arab Rediscovery of Europe: A Study in Cultural Encounters* (Princeton, NJ: Princeton University Press, 1963).

Adams, Kathleen M., "Danger-Zone Tourism: Prospects and Problems for Tourism in Tumultuous Times", in *Interconnected Worlds: Tourism in Southeast Asia*, ed. by Peggy Teo, T. C. Chang, and K. C. Ho (Oxford: Pergamon, 2001), pp. 265–78.

Ahmad, Aijaz, *In Theory: Classes, Nations, Literatures* (London: Verso, 1992).

Ahmed, Leila, *Edward W. Lane: A Study of His Life and Works and of British Ideas of the Middle East in the Nineteenth Century* (London: Longman, 1978).

Ahmed, Leila, *Gender in Islam* (New Haven, CT: Yale University Press, 1992).

Aksikas, Jaafar, *Arab Modernities: Islamism, Nationalism, and Liberalism in the Post-Colonial Arab World* (New York: Peter Lang, 2009).

Aldington, Richard, *Lawrence of Arabia* [1955] (London: Penguin, 1971).

Al-Hajri, Hilal *British Travel-Writing on Oman: Orientalism Reappraised* (Bern: Peter Lang AG, 2006).

Allen, Graham, *Intertextuality* (London and New York: Routledge, 2000).

AlSayyad, Nezar, ed., *The End of Tradition?* (London and New York: Routledge, 2004).

Anderson, Benedict, *Imagined Communities: Reflections on the Origin and Spread of Nationalism* [1983] (London: Verso, 1991).

Anderson, Scott, *Lawrence in Arabia: War, Deceit, Imperial Folly and the Making of the Modern Middle East* [2013] (New York: Anchor Books, 2014).

Andrews, Malcolm, *The Search for the Picturesque: Landscape Aesthetics and Tourism in Britain, 1760–1800* (Stanford: Stanford University Press, 1989).

Anonymous, "To the Royal Geographical Society", *Punch*, 104 (10 June 1893), p. 269.

Anonymous, "Britons Relive Desert Legend of Lawrence", *The Times* (19 March 1985).

Anonymous, "Golf Courses in the UAE" [online], Spikeson.com, available at: https://www.spikeson.com/countries/united-arab-emirates-golf-courses.php [accessed 11 July 2019].

206 *Bibliography*

Anonymous, "International Tourism, Number of Arrivals" [online], The World Bank (2019), available at: https://data.worldbank.org/indicator/ST.INT.ARVL [accessed 10 July 2019].

Anonymous, "The Three Rio Conventions – On Biodiversity, Climate Change and Desertification – Derive Directly from the 1992 Earth Summit" [online], Convention on Biological Diversity, available at: https://www.cbd.int/rio/ [accessed 12 July 2019].

Appadurai, Arjun, *Modernity at Large: Cultural Dimensions of Globalisation* (Minneapolis: University of Minnesota Press, 1996).

Armbruster, Karla, "Creating the World We Must Save: The Paradox of Television Nature Documentaries", in *Writing the Environment: Ecocriticism and Literature*, ed. by Richard Kerridge and Neil Sammells (London and New York, Zed Books, 1998), pp. 218–38.

Ashcroft, Bill, Gareth Griffiths, and Helen Tiffin, *The Empire Writes Back: Theory and Practice in Post-colonial Literatures* (London: Routledge, 1989).

Asher, Michael, *Thesiger: A Biography* (Harmondsworth: Viking, 1994).

Augé, Marc, *Non-Places: An Introduction to Supermodernity* [1992] (John Howe, trans., London: Verso, 2008).

Awad, M., "Settlement of Nomads and Semi-Nomadic Groups in the Middle East", *Ekistics*, 7, no. 42 (1959), 338–43.

Bagnold, Ralph A., *The Physics of Blown Sand and Sand Dunes* [1941, 1954] (Mineola, Dover Publications, 2005).

Ball, Anna, *Palestinian Literature and Film in Postcolonial Feminist Perspective* [2012] (Abingdon: Routledge, 2017).

Barker, F., P. Hulme, and M. Iversen eds., *Colonial Discourse/Postcolonial Theory* (Manchester: Manchester University Press, 1994).

Barker, F., P. Hulme, M. Iverson, and D. Loxley, eds., *Literature, Politics and Theory* (London: Methuen, 1986).

Barr, James, *Setting the Desert on Fire: T. E. Lawrence and Britain's Secret War in Arabia, 1916–1918* (New York: W.W. Norton, 2008).

Barr, James, *A Line in the Sand: The Anglo-French Struggle for the Middle East, 1914–1948* (New York: W.W. Norton & Co, 2011).

Bassnett, Susan, "Travel Writing and Gender", in *The Cambridge Companion to Travel Writing*, ed. by Peter Hulme and Tim Youngs (Cambridge: Cambridge University Press, 2002), pp. 225–41.

Bate, Jonathan, "Poetry and Biodiversity", in *Writing the Environment: Ecocriticism and Literature*, ed. by Richard Kerridge and Neil Sammells (London and New York, Zed Books, 1998), pp. 53–70.

Baudrillard, Jean, *In the Shadow of the Silent Majorities* (New York: Semiotext, 1983).

Bauman, Zygmunt, "From Pilgrim to Tourist – or a Short History of Identity", in *Questions of Cultural Identity*, ed. by S. Hall and P. du Gay (London: Sage, 1996), pp. 18–36.

Behdad, Ali, *Belated Travelers: Orientalism in the Age of Colonial Dissolution* (Durham, NC: Duke University Press, 1994).

Belden, Lane, *The Solace of Fierce Landscapes: Exploring Desert and Mountain Spirituality* (Oxford and New York: Oxford University Press, 1998).

Bell, Claudia and John Lyall, *The Accelerated Sublime: Landscape, Tourism, and Identity* (Westport, CT: Praeger, 2002).

Bibliography 207

Bendle, Simon, "Lady Hester Stanhope: Kooky Desert Queen" [online], *Great British Nutters: A Celebration of the UK's pluckiest adventurers* (2008), available at: https://greatbritishnutters.blogspot.com/2008/07/lady-hester-stanhope-kooky-desert-queen.html [accessed 13 July 2019].

Bhabha, Homi K., *The Location of Culture* (Abingdon and New York: Routledge, 1994).

Bidwell, Robin, *Travellers in Arabia* (London: Hamlyn, 1976).

Bird, Dúnlaith, "Travel Writing and Gender", in *The Routledge Companion to Travel Writing*, ed. by Carl Thompson (London and New York: Routledge, 2020), pp. 35–45.

Birkett, Dea, ed., *Off the Beaten Track: Three Centuries of Women Travellers* [accompanying 2004 Exhibition] (London: National Portrait Gallery, 2006).

Blanch, Lesley, *The Wilder Shores of Love* [1954] (London: Phoenix, 1993).

Boyett, Jason, *Pocket Guide to the Apocalypse* (Orlando, FL: Relevant Books, 2005).

Branch, Michael P. and Scott Slovic, eds., *The ISLE Reader: Ecocriticism, 1993–2003* (Athens: University of Georgia Press, 2003).

Brathwaite, Edward Kamau, *History of the Voice* (London: New Beacon Books, 1984).

Brent, Peter, *Far Arabia: Explorers of the Myth* (London: Weidenfeld and Nicolson, 1977).

Bronfen, Elisabeth, *Over Her Dead Body: Death, Femininity, and the Aesthetic* (Manchester: Manchester University Press, 1992).

Buchanan, Ian, *Oxford Dictionary of Critical Theory* [2010] (Oxford: Oxford University Press, 2018).

Buell, Lawrence, *The Future of Environmental Criticism: Environmental Crisis and Literary Imagination* (Oxford: Blackwell, 2005).

Burton-Christie, Douglas, *The Word in the Desert: Scripture and the Quest for Holiness in Early Christian Monasticism* (Oxford and New York: Oxford University Press, 1993).

Butler, Judith, *Gender Trouble: Feminism and the Subversion of Identity* [1990] (New York and Abingdon: Routledge, 2006).

Buzard, James, *The Beaten Track: European Tourism, Literature, and the Ways to 'Culture' 1800–1918* (Oxford: Clarendon Press, 1993).

Buzard, James, "The Grand Tour and after (1660–1840)", in *The Cambridge Companion to Travel Writing*, ed. by Peter Hulme and Tim Youngs (Cambridge: Cambridge University Press, 2002), pp. 37–52.

Campbell, Mary B., *The Witness and the Other World: Exotic European Travel Writing, 400–1600* (Ithaca, New York: Cornell University Press, 1988).

Campbell, SueEllen, et al., eds. *The Face of the Earth: Natural Landscapes, Science, and Culture* (Berkeley and Los Angeles, University of California Press, 2011).

Canton, James, *From Cairo to Baghdad: British Travellers in Arabia* [2011] (London: IB Tauris, 2014).

Carby, Hazel V., "White Woman Listen! Black Feminism and the Boundaries of Sisterhood", in *The Empire Strikes Back: Race and Racism in 70s Britain*, Centre for Contemporary Cultural Studies (London: Hutchinson, 1982), pp. 212–35.

Carey, Daniel, "Truth, Lies and Travel Writing", in *The Routledge Companion to Travel Writing*, ed. by Carl Thompson (London and New York: Routledge, 2020), pp. 3–14.

208 Bibliography

Carr, Helen, "Modernism and Travel (1880–1940)", in *The Cambridge Companion to Travel Writing*, ed. by Peter Hulme and Tim Youngs [2002] (Cambridge: Cambridge University Press, 2010), pp. 70–86.

Carrigan, Anthony, *Postcolonial Tourism: Literature, Culture, and Environment* (New York and Abingdon: Routledge, 2011).

Cartier, C. and A. Lew, eds., *Seductions of Place* (London and New York: Routledge, 2005).

Caton, Steven C., '*Lawrence of Arabia*': *A Film's Anthropology*, (Berkeley, Los Angeles, and London: University of California Press, 1999).

Cenkl, Pavel, "Narrative Currency in a Changing Climate", in *Postcolonial Green: Environmental Politics and World Narratives*, ed. by Bonnie Roos and Alex Hunt (Charlottesville and London: University of Virginia Press, 2010), pp. 137–56.

Centre for Contemporary Cultural Studies, *The Empire Strikes Back: Race and Racism in 70s Britain* (London: Hutchinson, 1982).

Chatty, Dawn, *From Camel to Truck: The Bedouin in the Modern World* [1986] (Oxford: White Horse Press, 2013).

Cheng, Vincent J., *Inauthentic: The Anxiety over Culture and Identity* (New Brunswick, NJ: Rutgers University Press, 2004).

Choat, Colin, ed., *Seven Pillars of Wisdom* [online], Project Gutenberg Australia (2001), available at https://gutenberg.net.au/ebooks01/0100111.txt [accessed 12 July 2019].

Clark, Steve, ed., *Travel Writing and Empire: Postcolonial Theory in Transit* (London: Zed, 1999).

Clarsen, Georgine, *Eat My Dust: Early Women Motorists* (Baltimore, MD: John Hopkins University Press, 2008).

Clayton, Jay and Eric Rothstein, eds., *Influence and Intertextuality in Literary History* (Madison: The University of Wisconsin Press, 1991).

Clifford, James, *Routes: Travel and Translation in the Late Twentieth Century* (Cambridge, MA: Harvard UP, 1997).

Cocker, Mark, *Loneliness and Time: The Story of British Travel Writing* (New York: Pantheon, 1993).

Codell, Julie F. and Dianne Sachko Macleod, eds., *Orientalism Transposed: The Impact of the Colonies on British Culture* (Farnham: Ashgate, 1998).

Cole, Donald Powell, *Nomads of the Nomads: The Al-Murrah of the Empty Quarter* (Chicago, IL: Aldine, 1975).

Cole, Donald Powell and Soraya Altorki, *Bedouin, Settlers, and Holiday-Makers: Egypt's Changing Northwest Coast* (Cairo: American University in Cairo Press, 1998).

Conant, Martha Pike, *The Oriental Tale in England in the Eighteenth Century* (New York: Columbia University Press, 1908).

Coulbert, Esme A., *Perspectives on the Road: Narratives of Motoring in Britain* (unpublished doctoral thesis, Nottingham Trent University, 2013).

Curruthers, Douglas, "Captain Shakespear's Last Journey", *Geographical Journal*, 59, no. 5 (1922), 321–44.

Dallmyr, Fred, *Beyond Orientalism: Essays in Cross-Cultural Encounter* (Albany: State University of New York Press, 1996).

Das, K. C. and Nilambari Gokhale, "Omanization Policy and International Migration in Oman" [online], Middle East Institute (2010), available at: https://

Bibliography 209

www.mei.edu/publications/omanization-policy-and-international-migration-oman [accessed 13 July 2019].

Davey, Francis, ed., *Richard of Lincoln: A Medieval Doctor Travels to Jerusalem* (Exeter: Azure Publications, 2013).

Dawkins, Richard, *Unweaving the Rainbow: Science, Delusion and the Appetite for Wonder* [1998] (New York: First Mariner, 2000).

Dawson, Graham, *Soldier Heroes: British Adventure, Empire and the Imagining of Masculinities* (Abingdon: Routledge, 1994).

De Cristofaro, D. and Daniel Cordle, 'Introduction: The Literature of the Anthropocene', *C21 Literature: Journal of 21st-Century Writings*, 6, no. 1:1 (2018), 1–6.

Deleuze, Gilles and Félix Guattari, *A Thousand Plateaus: Capitalism and Schizophrenia* [1987] (London: Continuum, 2004), pp. 256–341.

Dillon, S., *The Palimpsest: Literature, Criticism, Theory* (London: Bloomsbury, 2014).

Doran, Robert, *The Theory of the Sublime from Longinus to Kant* (Cambridge: Cambridge University Press, 2015).

Duncan, James and Derek Gregory, *Writes of Passage: Reading Travel Writing* (London: Routledge, 1999).

Dyer, Geoff, "Is Travel Writing Dead?" [online], *Granta*, 138 (2017), available at: https://granta.com/is-travel-writing-dead-dyer/ [accessed 13 July 2019].

El-Aris, Tarek, *Trials of Arab Modernity: Literary Affects and the New Political* (New York: Fordham University Press, 2013).

Elsheshtawy, Yasser, ed. *The Evolving Arab City: Tradition, Modernity and Urban Development* [2008] (Abingdon: Routledge, 2011).

Euben, Roxanne L. *Journeys to the Other Shore: Muslim and Western Travelers in Search of Knowledge* (Princeton, NJ: Princeton University Press, 2006).

Fabian, Johannes, *Time and the Other: How Anthropology Makes Its Object* (New York: Columbia University Press, 1983).

Fairbain, Linda, "Maps and the Twentieth Century: Drawing the Line" (British Library Exhibition, November 2016 to March 2017).

Fedden, Robin, *English Travellers in the Near East* (London: Longmans, 1958).

Feifer, Maxine, *Going Places: Tourism in History from Imperial Rome to the Present* (New York: Stein and Day, 1986).

Forsdick, Charles, "Travel and the Body", in *The Routledge Companion to Travel Writing*, ed. by Carl Thompson (London and New York: Routledge, 2020), pp. 68–77.

Frankfort, H. and H.A. Frankfort, *The Intellectual Adventure of Ancient Man* (Chicago, IL: University of Chicago Press, 1946).

Freeth, Zara and Victor Winstone, *Explorers of Arabia: From the Renaissance to the Victorian Era* (London: George Allen and Unwin, 1978).

Freud, Sigmund, *Totem and Taboo: Resemblances between the Mental Lives of Savages and Neurotics* [1913] (London: W. W. Norton, 1989).

Fussell, Paul, *Abroad: British Literary Travelling between the Wars* (New York: Oxford University Press, 1980).

Fussell, Paul, ed., *The Norton Book of Travel* (New York: W.W. Norton and Co., 1987).

Gibb, Lorna, *Lady Hester: Queen of the East* (London: Faber and Faber, 2005).

Goudie, Andrew, *Great Desert Explorers* (London: Royal Geographical Society with IGB, 2016).

210   *Bibliography*

Greenblatt, Stephen, *Marvelous Possessions: The Wonder of the New World* (Chicago, IL: University of Chicago Press, 1991).

Grimshaw, Michael, *Bibles and Baedekers: Tourism, Travel, Exile and God* [2008] (Abingdon: Routledge, 2014).

Hall, Richard, *Empires of the Monsoon: A History of the Indian Ocean and Its Invaders* [1996] (London: Harper Collins, 1998).

Hall, S. and P. du Gay, eds., *Questions of Cultural Identity* (London: Sage, 1996).

Ham, Anthony, et al., *Middle East* (Melbourne: Lonely Planet, 2012).

Hannam, June, *Feminism* [2007] (Abingdon: Routledge, 2013).

Hardt, Michael and Antonio Negri, *Empire* (Cambridge, MA: Harvard University Press, 2000).

Harraway, Donna, *Simians, Cyborgs, and Women: The Reinvention of Nature* (New York: Routledge, 1991).

Harvey, David, "The Art of Rent: Globalization, Monopoly and the Commodification of Culture", *Socialist Register 2002: A World of Contradictions*, 38 (2002), 93–110.

Haynes, Roslynn D., *Desert: Nature and Culture* (London: Reaktion Books, 2013).

Heise, Ursula K., "Postcolonial Ecocriticism and the Question of Literature", in *Postcolonial Green: Environmental Politics and World Narratives*, ed. by Bonnie Roos and Alex Hunt (Charlottesville and London: University of Virginia Press, 2010). pp. 251–58.

Henderson, Edward, *Arabian Destiny: The Complete Autobiography* (Dubai: Motivate, 1999).

Henderson, Heather, "The Travel Writer and the Text: My Giant Goes with Me Wherever I Go", in *Temperamental Journeys: Essays on the Modern Literature of Travel*, ed. by Michael Kowalewski (Athens: University of Georgia Press, 1992), pp. 230–48.

Hissey, J.J., *Untravelled England* (London: Macmillan, 1906).

Hogarth, David George, *The Penetration of Arabia: A Record of the Development of Western Knowledge Concerning the Arabian Peninsula* (London: Lawrence and Bullen, 1904).

Holland, Patrick and Graham Huggan, *Tourists with Typewriters: Critical Reflections on Contemporary Travel Writing* [1998] (Ann Arbor: University of Michigan Press, 2000).

Holmes, Richard in Alexander Maitland, *Wilfred Thesiger: My Life and Travels, an Anthology* (New York: HarperCollins, 2003).

Huggan, Graham, "'Greening' Postcolonialism: Ecocritical Perspectives", *Modern Fiction Studies*, 50, no. 3 (2004), 701–33.

Huggan, Graham, *Interdisciplinary Measures: Literature and the Future of Postcolonial Studies* (Liverpool: Liverpool University Press, 2008).

Huggan, Graham, *Extreme Pursuits: Travel/Writing in an Age of Globalization* (Ann Arbor: University of Michigan Press, 2009).

Huggan, Graham and Helen Tiffin, *Postcolonial Ecocriticism: Literature, Animals, Environment* [2010] (Abingdon: Routledge, 2015).

Hulme, Peter, "In the Wake of Columbus: Frederick Ober's Ambulant Gloss", *Literature & History*, 3rd Series 6, no. 2 (1997), 18–36.

Hulme, Peter, "Travelling to Write (1940–2000)", in *The Cambridge Companion to Travel Writing*, ed. by Peter Hulme and Tim Youngs [2002] (Cambridge: Cambridge University Press, 2010), pp. 87–101.

Bibliography 211

Hulme, Peter and Tim Youngs, eds., *The Cambridge Companion to Travel Writing* (Cambridge: Cambridge University Press, 2002).

Hutcheon, Linda, *The Politics of Postmodernism* (London: Routledge, 1989).

Inglis, Fred, *The Delicious History of the Holiday* (London: Routledge, 2000).

Ingold, Tim, ed., *Companion Encyclopaedia of Anthropology: Humanity, Culture, and Social Life* (London: Routledge, 1994).

Irwin, Robert, *For Lust of Knowing: The Orientalists and Their Enemies* [2006] (London: Penguin, 2007).

Isendstadt, Sandy and Kishwar Rizvi, eds., *Modernism and the Middle East: Architecture and Politics in the Twentieth Century* (Seattle: University of Washington Press, 2008).

Jacobs, Jane M., "Tradition Is (Not) Modern: Deterritorializing Globalization", in *The End of Tradition?*, ed. by Nezar AlSayyad (London and New York: Routledge, 2004), pp. 29–44.

Jacobs, Jessica, *Sex, Tourism and the Postcolonial Encounter: Landscape of Longing in Egypt* (Farnham: Ashgate Publishing, 2010).

Jameson, Frederic, *Postmodernism, or the Cultural Logic of Late Capitalism* (London: Verso, 1991).

Janzen, Jörg, *Nomads in the Sultanate of Oman: Tradition and Development in Dhofar* (Boulder, CO: Westview Press, 1986).

Judd, Denis, *Empire: The British Imperial Experience from 1765 to the Present* (New York: HarperCollins, 1996).

Kabbani, Rana, *Imperial Fictions: Europe's Myths of Orient* (London: Pandora, 1994).

Kaplan, C., *Questions of Travel: Postmodern Discourses of Displacement* (Durham, NC and London: Duke University Press, 1996).

Kern, Robert, "Ecocriticism: What Is It Good For?", in *The ISLE Reader: Ecocriticism, 1993–2003* ed. by Michael P. Branch and Scott Slovic (Athens: University of Georgia Press, 2003), pp. 258–81.

Kerridge, Richard and Neil Sammells, eds., *Writing the Environment: Ecocriticism and Literature* (London and New York, Zed Books, 1998).

Kiernan, Reginald Hugh, *The Unveiling of Arabia: The Story of Arabian Travel and Discovery* (London: Harrap, 1937).

Knight, Wilson, *Neglected Powers* (London: Jonathan Cape, 1971).

Knightley, P. and C. Simpson, "The Secret Life of Lawrence of Arabia", *The Sunday Times* (9 June 1968).

Kowalewski, Michael, ed., *Temperamental Journeys: Essays on the Modern Literature of Travel* (Athens: University of Georgia Press, 1992).

Krist, Gary, "Ironic Journeys: Travel Writing in the Age of Tourism", *The Hudson Review*, 45, no. 4 (1993), 593–601.

Kristeva, Julia, *Desire in Language: A Semiotic Approach to Literature and Art* (New York: Columbia University, 1980).

Laderman, Scott, "Guidebooks", in *The Routledge Companion to Travel Writing*, ed. by Carl Thompson (London and New York: Routledge, 2020), pp. 258–68.

Laing, Jennifer and Warwick Frost, *Books and Travel: Inspiration, Quests and Transformation* (Bristol, Channel View Publications, 2012).

Leavenworth, Maria Lindgren, *The Second Journey: Travelling in Literary Footsteps* [2009] (Umeå: Umeå Universitet, 2010).

212 Bibliography

Lenzen, Cherie J., "The Desert and the Sown: An Introduction to the Archaeological and Historiographic Challenge", *Mediterranean Archaeology*, 16 (2003), 5–12.

Lewis, Bernard, *Islam and the West* (Oxford: Oxford University Press, 1993).

Lewis, Norman N., *Nomads and Settlers in Syria and Jordan, 1800–1980* (Cambridge: Cambridge University Press, 1987).

Lewis, Reina, *Gendering Orientalism: Race, Femininity and Representation* (Abingdon: Routledge, 1996).

Leys, Colin and Leo Panitch, eds., *Socialist Register 2002: A World of Contradictions* (Halifax: Fernwood Publishing, 2002).

Lindsay, Claire, "Travel Writing and Postcolonial Studies", in *The Routledge Companion to Travel Writing*, ed. by Carl Thompson (London and New York: Routledge, 2020), pp. 25–34.

Lisle, Debbie, *The Global Politics of Contemporary Travel Writing* (Cambridge: Cambridge University Press, 2006).

Lowe, Lisa, *Critical Terrains: French and British Orientalisms* (Ithaca, New York: Cornell University Press, 1991).

MacCannell, Dean, *The Tourist: A New Theory of the Leisure Class* (Berkeley: University of California Press, 1999).

Macfarlane, Robert, "Why We Need Nature Writing: A New 'Culture of Nature' Is Changing the Way We Live – and Could Change Our Politics, Too" [online], *New Statesman*, Nature (2015), available at: https://www.newstatesman.com/culture/nature/2015/09/robert-macfarlane-why-we-need-nature-writing [accessed 28 June 2019].

Macfie, A. L., ed., *Orientalism: A Reader* (Edinburgh: Edinburgh University Press, 2000).

MacInnes, John, *The End of Masculinity: The Confusion of Sexual Genesis and Sexual Difference in Modern Society* (Buckingham: Open University Press, 1998).

Mack, John E., *A Prince of our Disorder: The Life of T. E. Lawrence* (Boston, MA and Toronto: Little, Brown and Co., 1976).

MacKenzie, John, *Orientalism: History, Theory and the Arts* (Manchester: Manchester University Press, 1995).

Macleod, Dianne Sachko, "Cross-Cultural Cross-Dressing: Class, Gender and Modernist Sexual Identity", in *Orientalism Transposed: The Impact of the Colonies on British Culture*, ed. by J.F. Codell and D.S. Macleod (Farnham: Ashgate, 1998), pp. 1–10.

Maitland, Alexander, Wilfred Thesiger: Traveller from an Antique Land", *Blackwood's Magazine*, 328 (1980).

Maitland, Alexander, *Wilfred Thesiger: The Life of the Great Explorer [2006]* (New York: The Overlook Press, Peter Mayer Publishers, 2011).

Marchand, Leslie A., *Byron: A Portrait* (London: Knopf, 1970).

Marshall, David J., Lynn A. Staeheli, Dima Smaira, and Konstantin Kastrissianakis, "Narrating Palimpsestic Spaces", *Environment and Planning A: Economy and Space*, 49, no. 5 (2017), 1163–80.

Matar, Nabil, "Travel Writing and Visual Culture", in *The Routledge Companion to Travel Writing*, ed. by Carl Thompson (London and New York: Routledge, 2020), pp. 139–49.

Matos, Jacinta, "Old Journeys Revisited: Aspects of Postwar English Travel Writing", in *Temperamental Journeys: Essays on the Modern Literature of Travel*, ed. by Michael Kowalewski (Athens: University of Georgia Press, 1992), pp. 215–29.

Bibliography   213

McClintock, Anne, "The Angel of Progress: Pitfalls of the Term 'Post-Colonialism'", in *Colonial Discourse/Postcolonial Theory*, ed. by F. Barker, P. Hulme, and M. Iversen (Manchester: Manchester University Press, 1994). pp. 253–66.

McClintock, Anne, *Imperial Leather: Race, Gender and Sexuality in the Colonial Contest* (New York: Routledge, 1995).

McColl, R. W., ed., *Encyclopaedia of World Geography* (New York: Facts on File, 2005, 3 Vols.).

McKibben, Bill *The End of Nature* (New York: Random House, 2006).

McLeod, John, *Beginning Postcolonialism* [2000] (Manchester and New York: Manchester University Press, 2010).

Melman, Billie, *Women's Orients: English Women and the Middle East, 1718–1918: Sexuality, Religion and Work* [1992] (London: Macmillan, 1995).

Melman, Billie, "The Middle East/Arabia: 'The Cradle of Islam'", in *The Cambridge Companion to Travel Writing*, ed. by Peter Hulme and Tim Youngs (Cambridge: Cambridge University Press, 2002), pp. 112–19.

Mercer, Wendy, "Gender and Genre in Nineteenth-century Travel Writing: Leonie d'Aunet and Xavier Marmier", in *Travel Writing and Empire: Postcolonial Theory in Transit*, ed. by Steve Clark (London: Zed, 1999), pp. 147–63.

Merchant, Carolyn *The Death of Nature: Women, Ecology and the Scientific Revolution* (London: HarperCollins, 1980).

Mernissi, Fatima, *The Veil and the Male Elite: A Feminist Interpretation of Women's Rights in Islam* (Mary Jo Lakeland, trans., Reading, MA: Perseus Books, 1991).

Mills, Sara, *Discourses of Difference: An Analysis of Women's Travel Writing and Colonialism* (London and New York: Routledge, 1992).

Mills, Sara, *Discourse* (London and New York: Routledge, 1997).

Mohanty, Chandra Talpade, "Under Western Eyes: Feminist Scholarship and Colonial Discourses", in *Colonial Discourse and Post-Colonial Theory* ed. by Patrick Williams and Laura Chrisman (Hemel Hempstead: Harvester Wheatsheaf, 1993), pp. 196–220.

Mondal, Anshuman A., *Nationalism and Post-Colonial Identity: Culture and Ideology in India and Egypt* (London: Routledge Curzon, 2003).

Moore, Sharlissa, *Sustainable Energy Transformations, Power and Politics: Morocco and the Mediterranean* (Abingdon: Routledge, 2019).

Moore-Gilbert, Bart J., *Postcolonial Theory* (London: Verso, 1997).

Moore-Gilbert, Bart J., "'Gorgeous East' Versus 'Land of Regrets'", in *Orientalism: A Reader*, ed. by A.L. Macfie (Edinburgh, Edinburgh University Press, 2000), pp. 273–76.

Mousa, Suleiman, *T. E. Lawrence: An Arab View*, trans. by Albert Butros (London and New York: Oxford University Press, 1966).

Nash, Geoffrey, *From Empire to Orient: Travellers to the Middle East 1830–1926* (London: I.B. Tauris, 2005).

Nash, Roderick Frazier, *Wilderness and the American Mind* [1967] (New Haven, CT: Yale University Press, 2014).

Nordqist, Richard, "Definition and Examples of Science Writing", *Glossary of Grammatical and Rhetorical Terms* [online], ThoughtCo (2019), available at: https://www.thoughtco.com/science-writing-1691928 [accessed 12 July 2019].

214   Bibliography

Norton, Claire, "Lust, Greed, Torture and Identity: Narrations of Conversion and the Creation of the Early Modern 'Renegade'", *Comparative Studies of South Asia, Africa and the Middle East*, 29, no. 2 (2009), 259–68.

Nutting, Anthony, *Lawrence of Arabia: The Man and the Motive* (London: Clarkson N. Potter, 1961).

O'Brian, Rosemary, *The Desert and the Sown: The Syrian Adventures of the Female Lawrence of Arabia* (New York: Cooper Square Press, 2001).

Oakes, T., "Tourism and the Modern Subject: Placing the Encounter between Tourist and Other", in *Seductions of Place*, ed. by C. Cartier and A. Lew (London and New York: Routledge, 2005), pp. 36–55.

Orlans, Harold, *T. E. Lawrence: Biography of a Broken Hero* (London: McFarland, 2002).

Parry, Benita, *Postcolonial Studies: A Materialist Critique* (London: Routledge, 2004).

Patrick, F. A., *Cambridge History of English Literature* (New York: Cambridge University Press, 1927).

Perrault, Jeanne and Sylvia Vance, ed., *Writing the Circle: Native Women of Western Canada* (Norman: University of Oklahoma Press, 1993).

Petersen, Kirsten Holst and Anna Rutherford, *A Double Colonisation: Colonial and Post-Colonial Women's Writing* (Sydney: Dangaroo Press, 1986).

Pollock, G., "Territories of Desire: Reconsiderations of an African Childhood Dedicated to a Woman Whose Name Was Not Really 'Julia'", in *Travellers' Tales: Narratives of Home and Displacement*, ed. by G. Robertson et al (London and New York: Routledge, 1994), pp. 61–88.

Porter, Dennis, "Orientalism and Its Problems" [1983], in *Postcolonial Theory: A Reader*, ed. by Patrick Williams and Laura Chrisman (New York: Columbia University Press, 1994), pp. 150–61.

Pratt, Douglas, et al., eds., *The Character of Christian-Muslim Encounter: Essays in Honour of David Thomas* (Leiden: Brill, 2016).

Pratt, Mary Louise, *Imperial Eyes: Travel Writing and Transculturation* [1992] (London and New York: Routledge, 2008).

Raban, Jonathan, "The Journey and the Book" [1982], in *For Love and Money: Writing, Reading, Travelling, 1969–1987* (London: Collins Harvill, 1987), pp. 253–60.

Ramone, Jenni, ed., *The Bloomsbury Introduction to Postcolonial Writing: New Contexts, New Narratives, New Debates* (London and New York: Bloomsbury Academic, 2018).

Richardson, Neil and Marcia Dorr, *The Craft Heritage of Oman* (Dubai: Motivate Publishing, 2003, 2 Vols.).

Riffenburgh, Beau, *The Myth of the Explorer* [1993] (Oxford: Oxford UP, 1994).

Robertson, G., et al., eds., *Travellers' Tales: Narratives of Home and Displacement* (London and New York: Routledge, 1994).

Robertson, Roland, *Globalization: Social Theory and Global Culture* (London: Sage, 1992).

Robinette, Nicholas, *Realism, Form and the Postcolonial Novel* (New York: Palgrave and Macmillan, 2014).

Rodenbeck, "Dressing Native", in *Unfolding the Orient*, ed. by Paul and Janet Starkey (Reading, MA: Ithaca Press, 2001), pp. 65–100.

Rojek, Chris, *Ways of Escape: Modern Transformations in Leisure and Travel* (London: MacMillan, 1993).

Bibliography 215

Roos, Bonnie and Alex Hunt, eds., *Postcolonial Green: Environmental Politics and World Narratives* (Charlottesville and London: University of Virginia Press, 2010).

Rosaldo, Renato, *Culture and Truth: The Remaking of Social Analysis* [1989] (London: Routledge, 1993).

Ross-Bryant, Lynn, *Pilgrimage to the National Parks: Religion and Nature in the United States* (New York: Routledge, 2013).

Russell, Alison, *Crossing Boundaries: Postmodern Travel Literature* (New York: Palgrave, 2000).

Sabry, Tarik, *Cultural Encounters in the Arab World: on Media, the Modern and the Everyday* (London: I. B. Taurus, 2010).

Sabry, Tarik and Joe F. Khalil, *Culture, Time and Publics in the Arab World: Media, Public Space and Temporality* (London and New York: I. B. Tauris, 2019).

Sachs, Aaron, "The Ultimate 'Other': Post-Colonialism and Alexander von Humboldt's Ecological Relationship with Nature", *History and Theory*, 42 (2003), 111–35.

Said, Edward W., *Orientalism* [1978] (Harmondsworth: Penguin-Peregrine, 1985).

Said, Edward W., *Culture and Imperialism* [1993] (New York: First Vintage Books, 1994).

Said, Edward W., "Professionals and Amateurs", in *Representations of the Intellectual* (New York: Vintage Books, 1996), pp. 73–83.

Said, Edward W., "Orientalism Reconsidered", in *Literature, Politics and Theory: Papers from the Essex Conference, 1976–84* [1986], ed. by Francis Barker et al (Abingdon and New York: Routledge, 2003), pp. 210–29.

Sardar, Ziauddin, *Orientalism* (Buckingham: Open University Press, 1999).

Schechner, Richard, "Ritual and Performance", in *Companion Encyclopaedia of Anthropology: Humanity, Culture, and Social Life*, ed. by Tim Ingold (London: Routledge, 1994), pp. 613–647.

Scheele, J., *Smugglers and Saints of the Sahara* (Cambridge: Cambridge University Press, 2012).

Shepherd, Paul, *Man in the Landscape: A Historic View of the Esthetics of Nature* [1967, 1991] (London: University of Georgia Press, 2002).

Sherman, William H., "Stirrings and Searchings (1500–1720)", in *The Cambridge Companion to Travel Writing*, ed. by Peter Hulme and Tim Youngs (Cambridge: Cambridge University Press, 2002), pp. 17–36.

Skeggs, Beverley, *Formations of Class and Gender* (London: Sage, 1997).

Smith, Oliver, "In Search of Lawrence's Arabia", *Lonely Planet Magazine* (May 2010), 76–86.

Smith, Sidonie, *Moving Lives: Twentieth-Century Women's Travel Writing* (Minneapolis and London: University of Minnesota, 2001).

Spivak, Gayatri Chakravorty, "Can the Subaltern Speak?" [1988], in *Colonial Discourse and Post-Colonial Theory*, ed. by Patrick Williams and Laura Chrisman (Hemel Hempstead: Harvester Wheatsheaf, 1993), pp. 66–111.

Spivak, Gayatri Chakravorty, *Death of a Discipline* (New York: Columbia University Press, 2003).

Starkey, Paul and Janet, *Unfolding the Orient* (Reading, MA: Ithaca Press, 2001).

Steger, Manfred B., *Globalization: A Very Short Introduction* [2003] (Oxford: Oxford University Press, 2017).

216 Bibliography

Tarrant, Fiona, "Queen of the Desert" [online], *Oxford Mail* (1998), available at: https://web.archive.org/web/20140201102033/http://www.oxfordmail.co.uk/archive/1998/09/29/6638325.Queen_of_the_desert/?ref=arc [accessed 13 July 2019].

Taylor, Andrew, *Travelling the Sands: Sagas of Exploration in the Arabian Peninsula* (Dubai: Motivate Publishing, 1997).

Taylor, Andrew, *God's Fugitive: The Life of C.M. Doughty* (London: Harper Collins, 1999).

Teo, Peggy, T. C. Chang, and K. C. Ho, eds., *Interconnected Worlds: Tourism in Southeast Asia* (Oxford: Pergamon, 2001).

Thompson, C. W., *French Romantic Travel Writing: Chateaubriand to Nerval* (Oxford: Oxford University Press, 2012).

Thompson, Carl, *Travel Writing* (Abingdon and New York: Routledge, 2011).

Thompson, Carl, ed., *The Routledge Companion to Travel Writing* [2016] (Abingdon and New York: Routledge, 2020).

Thompson, Carl, "Travel Writing Now, 1950 to the Present Day", in *The Routledge Companion to Travel Writing*, ed. by Carl Thompson (London and New York: Routledge, 2020), pp. 196–213.

Thubron, Colin, "A Lifelong Search for Just Deserts: Thesiger – Michael Asher: Viking, Pounds 20" [online], *The Independent* (1994), available at: https://www.independent.co.uk/arts-entertainment/book-review-a-lifelong-search-for-just-deserts-thesiger-michael-asher-viking-pounds-20-1451083.html [accessed 13 July 2019].

Thubron, Colin, "Don't Forget Your Toothbrush" [online], *The Guardian* (2000), available at: https://www.theguardian.com/books/2000/sep/23/travel.travelbooks [accessed 15 July 2019].

Tidrick, Kathryn, *Heart Beguiling Araby: The English Romance with Arabia* [1990] (London: Tauris Parke, 2010).

Tindall, Gillian, *Countries of the Mind: The Meaning of Place to Writers* (Boston, MA: Northeastern, 1991).

Topping, Margaret, "Travel Writing and Visual Culture", in *The Routledge Companion to Travel Writing*, ed. by Carl Thompson (London and New York: Routledge, 2020), pp. 78–88.

Torgovnick, Marianna, *Gone Primitive: Savage Intellects, Modern Lives* [1990] (Chicago, IL and London: University of Chicago Press, 1991).

Trench, Richard, *Arabian Travellers* (London: Macmillan, 1986).

United Nations, "68% of the World Population Projected to Live in Urban Areas by 2050, Says UN" [online], United Nations Department of Economic and Social Affairs (2018), available at https://www.un.org/development/desa/en/news/population/2018-revision-of-world-urbanization-prospects.html [accessed 12 July 2019].

Urry, John and Jonas Larsen, *The Tourist Gaze 3.0* [1990] (London: Sage Publications, 2011).

Wa Thiong'o, Ngũgĩ, *Decolonising the Mind: The Politics of Language in African Literature* (Portsmouth, NH: Heinemann, 1986).

Walder, Dennis, "Writing, Representation, and Postcolonial Nostalgia", *Textual Practice*, 23, no. 6 (2009), 935–46.

Walker [Owen], Jenny, "Half Past Ten in the Afternoon: An Englishman's Journey from Aneiza to Makkah, by James Budd", *Studies in Travel Writing*, 20, no. 4 (2016), 425–7.

Bibliography 217

Wallach, Janet, *Desert Queen: The Extraordinary Life of Gertrude Bell* (London: Phoenix Gian, 1997).

Waring, Sophie, "Margaret Fountaine: A Lepidopterist Remembered", *Notes and Records: The Royal Society Journal of the History of Science*, 69, no. 1 (2015), 53–68.

White, Kevin, *The First Sexual Revolution: The Emergence of Male Heterosexuality in Modern America* (New York: New York University Press, 1992).

Whitfield, Peter, *Travel: A Literary History* (Oxford: Bodleian Library, 2012).

Whitlock, Gillian, "Tainted Testimony: The Khouri Affair", in *Australian Literary Studies*, 21, no. 4 (2004), pp. 165–77.

Wilke, Sabine, "Performing Tropics: Alexander von Humboldt's *Ansichten der Natur* and the Colonial Roots of Nature Writing", in *Postcolonial Green: Environmental Politics and World Narratives* ed. by Bonnie Roos and Alex Hunt (Charlottesville and London: University of Virginia Press, 2010), pp. 197–212.

Williams, Patrick and Laura Chrisman, eds., *Colonial Discourse and Post-Colonial Theory* (Hemel Hempstead: Harvester Wheatsheaf, 1993).

Williams, Patrick, and Laura Chrisman, eds., *Postcolonial Theory: A Reader* (New York: Columbia University Press, 1994).

Wilson, Alexander, *The Culture of Nature: North American Landscape from Disney to the Exon Valdez* (New York: Basil Blackwell, 1991).

Wilson, Edward O., *The Diversity of Life* [1992] (Harmondsworth: Penguin, 1994).

Wilson, Jeremy, *T. E. Lawrence Studies* [online], available at http://www.telstud ies.org/ [accessed 12 July 2019].

Woods, Tim, *Beginning Postmodernism* [1999] (Manchester: Manchester University Press, 2009).

Woodward, Richard, "Armchair Traveler: Travel Desk". In *The New York Times*, 30 December 2007.

Wordsworth, Jonathan, Michael C. Jaye, and Robert Woof, *William Wordsworth and the Age of English Romanticism* (New Brunswick, NJ and London: Rutgers University Press, 1987).

Wright, Gwendolyn, "Global Ambition and Local Knowledge", in *Modernism and the Middle East: Architecture and Politics in the Twentieth Century* ed. by Sandy Isendstadt and Kishwar Rizvi (Seattle, DC: University of Washington Press, 2008), pp. 221–54.

Young, Robert J. C., *Colonial Desire: Hybridity in Theory, Culture and Race* (Abingdon and New York: Routledge, 1995).

Youngs, Tim, *The Cambridge Introduction to Travel Writing* (Cambridge: Cambridge University Press, 2013).

Index

Page numbers followed by n indicate notes.

Abu Dhabi 47, 51, 70, 87–8, 91, 133
Ahmed, Aijaz 13
Aksikas, Jaafar 89
Al-Hajri, Hilal 4, 71, 73, 79, 82, 164
Al-Hani, Donya 123; *Heroine of the Desert* 123
Allen, Graham 18
Altorki, Soraya 69
Al-Wahibi, Amur 55
Al-Zadjali, Mohamed 4, 55, 75, 101n45
Anderson, Scott 43–4, 97
amateurism xiii, 54, 146–48, 150, 156–58; and professionalism 158, 191
anthropology 5, 7, 10, 19, 70–2, 120, 146, 148, 154, 166; quasi- 54, 93, 121
Anthropocene 155, 199
Arab: definition of 6, 54; heritage 55–6, 61, 68; identity 86, 88, 92; modernity 2, 5–6, 20, 68–9, 81, 85, 88, 195, 197; timekeeping 79, 102n58
Arabian desert *see* desert
Arabian Nights 12, 126
Arabian Peninsula 4–6, 10, 30, 48, 68, 75, 78, 108, 112, 168, 179, 183
archaeology 37, 109; inverse 91, 94
Asher, Michael 17, 20, 67–2, 75, 83, 167, 189; *The Last of the Bedu* 67, 72
Atkins, William 183; *The Immeasurable World* 183
Augé, Marc 23, 51, 153–55
authenticity: of the travelling experience xiv, 2, 11, 14, 18–9, 22–3, 30, 44–5, 47, 55, 85, 94, 124–25, 178–79, 185, 188, 195–96, 198
automobile 76, 80; *see also* car

Babaie, Sussan 127–29, 135
Bagnold, Ralph. A. 76–7, 148–49; *Libyan Sands* 76, 149; *The Physics of Blown Sand and Sand Dunes* 149
Ball, Anna 65n95, 132, 139n91
Bassnett, Susan 112, 115, 133
bathos 37, 104n99, 190; *see also* parody
Baudrillard, Jean 51, 154
beaten track 177–78; getting off the 23, 32, 49–50, 177, 181
Bedouin *see* Bedu
Bedu xiv, 6, 10, 14, 40, 47, 56, 68, 87, 120, 133; caravan 79, 81, 158; customs and manners 8, 12, 17, 53–4, 83, 164; guides 39–42, 48, 50–2, 56, 72, 164; hospitality 47–9, 57, 164; immutability of 17–8, 19; modernisation and 31, 48, 72, 74–5, 103n93; wearing of Bedu clothing 52, 64n64, 127, 195; as distinct from city-dwellers 69, 81; mobility 72, 75, 78, 90; adaptability 20, 72, 75, 83, 90–1; settlement 71–2, 90, 100n26; and the desert 142, 163; as villains 74, 182; way of life 1, 17, 19–20, 37, 40, 69, 71, 83, 90, 127, 165, 187; women 127–28
Behdad, Ali 19, 47, 77, 113, 115
belatedness 2, 18–9, 36–7, 45, 47–8, 51, 70, 76–7, 195
Bell, Claudia 23
Bell, Gertrude 9, 15, 21, 36, 68, 108, 111, 113, 116; *The Desert and the Sown* 142–43

Index 219

Bhabha, Homi 13, 20, 33, 72, 74, 82; *Location of Culture* 74
Bidwell, Robin 113; *Travellers in Arabia* 113
Bin Kalut, Sheikh Saleh 56–8
bioregion 6, 151, 172n39
Bird, Dúnlaith 118–9, 129
Birkett, Dea 109, 112; *Off the Beaten Track* 109, 112
Blackmore, Charles 3, 34, 69, 72, 106; *In the Footsteps of Lawrence of Arabia* 38–45, 47, 49, 51–3, 56
Blanch, Lesley 109; *The Wilder Shores of Love* 109, 114–5
Blunt, Lady Anne 42, 113
Blunt, Wilfred Scawen 9, 36, 42, 113, 160
borders 2, 21, 74; between countries 4–5, 31, 33, 55, 57, 96, 100n26, 132, 179, 190; zone 69, 82, 144
Bowden, Jamie 43–4
Brady, Adrienne 107; *Way south of Wahiba Sands* 118–9
Brent, Peter 71; *Far Arabia* 71
Brooks, Geraldine 3, 107; *Nine Parts of Desire* 123–26, 134
Budd, James 183–84; *Half Past Ten in the Afternoon* 184–86
Buell, Lawrence 144
Burckhardt, Jean Lewis 8, 108, 179
Burke, Edmund 151–52; *A Philosophical Enquiry into the Origin of Our Ideas of the Sublime and Beautiful* 152; *see also* sublime
Burton, Isabel 109, 113–4; *The Inner Life of Syria, Palestine and the Holy Land* 115
Burton, Richard xiv, 8, 15, 70, 108, 113–4, 120, 137n42, 160; Personal Narrative of a Pilgrimage to Al-Madinah and Meccah
Butler, Judith 116
Buzard, James 31, 39, 50, 73, 177, 187

camels: travel by 17, 22, 35, 39, 42, 47, 51, 55, 71–2, 121, 146, 160, 164, 184, 187, 195; unfitness of 49–50, 69; replaced by cars 75, 85, 88, 179
Campbell, Mary 22
Campbell, SueEllen 153, 163, 171n7
Canton, James 63n54, 88, 91, 93, 95, 111, 116

car travel xiii, 33, 37, 50, 60, 72, 75–8, 81–2, 91, 133, 180
Carby, Hazel 118, 125
Carr, Helen 8, 72
Cenkl, Pavel 163
Chatty, Dawn 71–2, 78, 81; *Camel to Truck* 75
Chatwin, Bruce 186; *The Songlines* 186
Chesshyre, Tom 23; *A Tourist in the Arab Spring* 181–82
Clapp, Nicholas 3, 106; *The Road to Ubar* 106, 129–30
Cole, Donald Powell 69
colonialism 21, 89, 115, 117, 119, 133, 147, 150, 153
Cocker, Mark 68, 185, 198
Cook, Thomas 8, 177
Conrad, Joseph 145; *Heart of Darkness* 145
Couchman, Helen 107, 127–29, 135; *Omani Women* 127
Coulbert, Esme 76, 78
Cowan, James 35; *Desert Father* 35
Cronan, William 168; "The Trouble with Wilderness" 168
culture: and representation xv, 2, 3, 70, 84, 97, 99, 181; cross-cultural representation 73, 78, 114, 119, 131, 166, 197; relativism 79, 125; intercultural relationship 57, 60, 197

danger zone 163; tourism 179–80
Dallmayr, Fred 98, 197
Davidson, Robyn 3, 108; *Tracks* 108, 130–31, 186
Dawkins, Richard 162; *Unweaving the Rainbow* 162
Deleuze, Gilles 132, 186
desert: as alien landscape xiii, 9, 83, 124, 145, 149, 163–64; complete study of xiii; definition of 5, 68; democratisation of 60, 81, 170–71, 177, 187–91; explorers of 1, 19, 35; emptiness of 6, 10, 22, 55, 75, 83, 86–7, 95, 98, 126, 133, 142, 145–46, 163, 181, 195–96; fascination for Western writers xv; as gendered space 12, 20, 22, 129–135, 140n106, 182, 198; history of 6–11; historicised 84, 91–9; immutability of 19, 67, 98; mechanised 49, 75–80; modern

220   *Index*

and urban impingement on 48–9,
70, 76; politicised 80–5, 133,
169–71, 178–89; and the sown 2,
16, 17, 20, 67–9, 73–4, 98;
traditional tropes 7, 12, 31, 68,
143–45, 151, 196; urbanised
84–91; value of 144
desert literature, Arabian xiv–v, 2–3,
5, 11–2, 18–9, 22–3, 41–2, 67–71,
95, 107–09, 195–98; as barren
legacy 2, 23, 166, 195–98; new
forms of 176–83; *see also* science
writing; women
desertification 11, 122, 151, 160,
174n69
disaster tourism 182
Doughty, Charles M. xiv, 1, 9, 35–7,
73, 78, 86–7, 120, 145, 160, 186;
Arabia Deserta 146–47, 184
Dubai 87, 188–89
Duncan, James 52
Dutton, Roderic 160, 165

ecocriticism 2, 5–6, 22, 143–44,
150–51, 153, 162–63, 165–67, 197,
199; postcolonial 150, 162, 169
ecology 45, 166–67, 170
Egeria 109, 136n14
El-Aris, Tarik 74
Elsheshtawy, Yasser 88; *The Evolving
Arab City* 88
Empty Quarter 4, 6, 10, 14, 36, 53–5,
57–8, 60, 90, 128–130, 132–33,
147–8, 183
Encyclopaedia Britannica 67, 98
entomology 36, 110–1, 136n22, 144,
156–59
environment: desert xv, 22, 143, 151,
159–60, 164, 168–69, 198
escapism 11, 39, 52, 73, 87, 122, 133,
149, 161, 178
ethnography 22, 48, 99, 112, 128–29,
148, 164, 190
Euben, Roxanne 94
Evans, Mark 4, 10, 34, 36, 38, 53–60,
75, 148, 195, 197; *Crossing the
Empty Quarter* 54–5, 148
existentialism 86, 95, 152; angst
51, 153
expedition: of Sharqiya Sands xiii–xiv,
159–62, 174n67; modern desert 4,
10, 46–7, 75–6, 176, 196; polar 40,
45, 53, 106

explorers and exploration: of Arabian
desert xiii, 18–9, 23, 32–7, 53, 106,
110, 112–13, 142, 146, 178

Feifer, Maxine 32, 181
feminism 5, 20, 86, 108, 197; feminist
theory 115, 116, 118, 123, 129,
132, 135
Fiennes, Ginnie 106
Fiennes, Ranulph 3, 14–5, 106, 178,
195; *Atlantis of the Sands* 106
footstep journeys 18–9, 30–66, 91–3,
143, 176
Forsdick, Charles 153–54
Foster, Shirley 113, 116, 119; *An
Anthology of Women's Travel
Writing* 113
Fountaine, Margaret 109–111,
136n22; *Love among the
Butterflies* 110
Frankfort, H. and H. A. 155
Freeth, Zara 5, 113
Freud, Sigmund 70; *Totem and
Taboo* 70
Frost, Warwick 45
Fussell, Paul 19, 72, 146, 177

Galt, John 41
Gauttari, Félix 186
Geldermalsen, Marguerite van 3, 21,
107–08; *Married to a Bedouin*
126–27, 134
gendered space 12, 20, 107–8, 134,
143, 182
geography: of Arabia 1, 5–10, 87,
111, 145–46, 148, 160–61;
imaginative 3, 5, 11–4, 23, 24n2,
68, 73, 86, 145, 154, 166, 170,
180–81, 195–96, 198; McColl's
*Encyclopaedia of World
Geography* 6
George, Uwe 11, 150; *In the Deserts
of This Earth* 151–56, 159, 166
Gilpin, William *see* picturesque
globalisation xiv–xv, 2, 19, 23, 31, 51,
53, 67, 73, 87–9, 96, 99, 165, 181,
184, 186, 190, 198–99
Goudie, Andrew 8, 10; *Great Desert
Explorers* 8
Greenblatt, Stephen 149–50
Griffiths, Jay 3, 58, 108, 195; *Wild:
An Elemental Journey* 58, 108,
131–32

guidebooks xiii–iv, 8, 35, 177, 181, 186, 190, 195–96
Gulf region, the 6, 10, 46–7, 57, 73, 88–90, 122, 179

hajj 3, 95, 179
Hannam, June 108
harem 7, 21, 117, 119
Hayes, Adrian 31, 34, 38, 45–7, 48–52, 54, 56, 59, 99n7, 106, 134, 178, 195; *Footsteps of Thesiger* 46, 49–50
Haynes, Roslynn 7, 107, 108–09, 150–52, 183, 187; *Desert: Nature and Culture* 7
Hemming, Henry 23, 80, 180; *Misadventure in the Middle East* 180–81
Henderson, Edward 84
Henderson, Heather 32, 198
heroic: endeavour 1, 14, 38, 40–1, 53, 77, 107, 114, 143, 177, 181, 190; figure 37–41, 43, 45, 56, 95, 134
Hijaz railway 39, 44
Hissey, J. J. 76
Hodgkin, Robin 161; *Playing and Exploring* 161
Holland, Henry 157
Holland, Patrick 13, 21, 145–46, 148, 169, 188
Holmes, Richard 37
Huggan, Graham 13, 21, 23, 121, 125, 145–46, 148, 166, 168–69, 187–88, 198; *Postcolonial Ecocriticism* 169; *Extreme Pursuits* 179, 189
Hulme, Peter 30, 183
Hutcheon, Linda 96
hybridity 9, 72, 112, 144, 166

Ibn Battuta 15, 17, 91–8, 104n113
imperialism 15, 46, 57, 60, 198; anti- 89; humanitarian 121, 189
inner journey or quest 23, 52–3, 77, 116, 183–86
indigenisation 34, 57, 59, 89
intertextuality 1, 18–9, 31, 34–8, 54, 59, 176, 198; tradition of 34–8
Iraq 6, 111, 116, 124, 180
Isendstadt, Sandy *Modernism and the Middle East* 88

Islam 4, 7, 9, 15, 89, 92, 181, 185; conversion to 111, 185–86, 197; and travel 94–5; and women 122, 124–27, 181

Jacobs, Jane 89
Jacobs, Jessica 73
Jeddah 8
Jordan 6, 39, 42, 86, 123, 126–7

Kabbani, Rana 12, 119; *Imperial Fictions* 12
Kant, Immanuel 152; *Observations on the Feeling of the Beautiful and the Sublime* 152
Kaplan, Caren 186; *Questions of Travel* 186
Keats, John 162; *Lamia* 162
Keohane, Alan 6, 74, 182
Kern, Robert 143
Khalil, Joe 5
Khouri, Norma 123; *Forbidden Love* 123, 125
Kinglake, Alexander: *Eothen* 152–53
Kirkby, Bruce 18, 34, 38, 45; *Sand Dance* 46–52, 59, 106, 121
Kristeva, Julia 34

Laderman, Scott xiv
Laing, Jennifer 45
Larsen, Jonas 77; *The Tourist Gaze* 154–55, 188–89, 195
Lawrence, T. E. xiv, 9, 14–7, 32, 34–6, 38, 56, 73, 87, 97, 115; *Revolt in the Desert* 14; *Seven Pillars of Wisdom* 15–7, 34, 39–44, 120, 130, 147
Lean, David 16; *Lawrence of Arabia* 16, 44
Leavenworth, Maria Lindgren 18, 31–3, 45, 51, 176
Lenzen, Cherie J. 68, 82
Lewis, Bernard 12
Lewis, Norman 33; *Sand and Sea in Arabia* 33
Lewis, Reina 21, 86, 115
liminality 20–1, 69, 82, 132, 170
Linnaeus, *Systema Naturae* 145
Lisle, Debbie 13, 112, 135; *The Global Politics of Contemporary Travel Writing* 182
Lyall, John 23, 179
Lowe, Lisa 13, 115

222 Index

MacCannell, Dean 49, 187
MacGregor, Malcolm 176; *Wilderness Oman* 176–77
Mackintosh-Smith, Tim 3, 10, 16–7, 20, 68, 74; *Travels with a Tangerine* 17, 84–5, 91–9; *Yemen* 97
male gaze 20, 86, 128
marginalisation 13; of Bedu 50, 82, 90–1, 143; of women 20, 107–8, 112, 115, 132, 134–35, 198
Marshall, David 59
masculinity 38, 106–08, 110–14, 120, 130, 133, 135, 142, 180, 182, 190
Matar, Nabil 4, 108
Matthiessen, Peter 186; *The Snow Leopard* 186
Matos, Jacinta 32
Maugham, Robin 42; *Nomad* 42
McCarron, Leon 178; *The Land Beyond* 178
McCleod, John 22, 108
McClintock, Anne 21, 71
McKinnon, Michael: *Arabia: Sand, Sea, Sky* 167–69
McWilliam, H. H. 33; *The Diabolical* 33
Mecca 7, 8, 15, 78–9, 108, 185
Mear, Roger 45
media: intrusion of 49; social 4, 37, 55–9, 180, 199
Melman, Billie 10, 90, 115, 145, 156, 183; *Women's Orients* 115
Middle East xiv, 2, 14, 31, 35, 68–9, 73, 85, 87–92, 109, 111–3, 130–3, 160, 179–185, 189
Mills, Sara 13, 21, 113, 115–6, 119; *An Anthology of Women's Travel Writing* 113
modernity: anti- 68 *see* Arab modernity
Mohanty, Chandra Talpade 123
Montagu, Lady Mary Wortley 109, 113, 120, 127
Moore-Gilbert, J. 46
Moorhouse, Geoffrey 3; *The Fearful Void* 184
Morris, Jan 3, 37, 59–60, 68, 112, 116; *Sultan in Oman* 37, 60, 80–3, 121–22
Morris, Mary 109–110, 116; *Maiden Voyages* 109, 112
Morrison, Jane 116

motorised transport xiii, 23, 74–8, 80, 179; Thesiger on 76
Muscat 56, 80, 82, 106, 127
Muslim 74, 89, 92, 184; women 108, 120, 123, 126–28, 135

Nash, Geoffrey 16, 115
Nash, Roderick 145
nature as desert environment 2, 11, 18, 21, 51, 59, 70, 74, 76–7, 130, 142–44, 146–47, 149, 150–53, 159, 195; as hostile and alien 109, 145, 163; representation of 162–71, 185–86
natural history 59, 146, 154
Niebuhr, Karsten 120
noble savage 16, 99, 105n118
nomadism 6, 49–50, 54, 57, 68–72, 75, 81, 87–8, 90–1, 95, 154–55, 128, 154, 161, 178; travellers and 184, 186
nostalgia 1, 16–7, 19, 32, 38, 53, 70, 77, 92–3, 97, 143, 180, 197; imperial 42, 169–70
Nutting, Anthony 15

oil: discovery of 5, 122, 133, 168–70, 188; benefits of 71, 74, 90; production of 10, 17, 23, 48, 82–4, 86–8, 90, 150, 197
Oman 4–6, 17, 46, 53–5, 57–8, 60, 80–1, 90, 94–5, 97, 118, 121, 128–29, 159, 164
oral tradition 50, 59
Oriental stereotypes 12, 21, 74, 79, 81, 85, 88, 99; of women 115, 120, 124, 127, 129, 180, 182, 195, 199
Orientalism xiv–xv, 5, 7, 79–80, 97–8, 117, 129, 147, 163, 180; latent 2, 11–4, 165, 196
Osborne, Lawrence 184, 186, 191; *The Wet and the Dry* 183–85
otherness 2, 6, 9, 20, 32, 47–8, 70, 72–3, 92–3, 96, 180; desert Otherness 84, 143, 145, 149, 163, 165, 187; othering xv, 13, 72, 80, 115, 163, 177, 179, 198

Palestine 25n22, 112, 132
Palgrave, Gifford 9, 96
palimpsest 53, 59, 65n95
pantheism 155, 161
parody 17, 53, 96–7, 180

Index 223

patriarchy 108, 119, 126
Patrick, F. A. 11
petroglyphs 147–48
Philby, St. John 10, 36, 42, 130, 160, 197; *Heart of Arabia* 197
picaresque travel writing 10, 47, 96, 115
picturesque, Gilpin's 156–58
pilgrim: Christian 35, 80–1, 109, 145; in nature 77; to Mecca 78–9
pilgrimage 23, 79–81, 91; Islamic 15; secular 176, 182–8, 191; *The Way of a Pilgrim* 91
Pittaway, Tony 150; *Insects of Eastern Arabia* 156–60, 166
Pitts, Joseph 7; *A True and Faithful Account of the Religion and Manners of the Mohammetans* 7
planet: -ary 153–55; -arity 99, 129
polyphonic and polyvocal description 59, 61, 87, 131
Porter, Dennis 12, 16
postcolonialism xv, 12–4, 20, 108, 165, 196–97, 199
postcolonial: anxiety 60, 160; theory 19, 21, 44, 82, 85, 123, 132, 153, 197; counternarrative 31, 34, 68, 150, 166; sensibility 73, 87, 133, 135, 142–44
postmodernism 17, 96, 104n113, 180, 197, 199
Pratt, Mary Louise 13, 115, 129; *Imperial Eyes* 145–6, 152–53
primitivism 10, 16, 70, 73, 164, 186, 196
Pryce, Lois 3, 30; *Revolutionary Ride* 80

Qaboos, Sultan 5, 55; University 164
Qatar 6, 54–5, 57, 90

Raban, Jonathan 10, 68, 73, 84–91, 126; *Arabia Through the Looking Glass* 84–6, 88, 91, 122, 188–89
Ramone, Jenni 198
renaissance in Arab states 5, 55, 73, 89
Riffenburgh, Beau 40–1
rihla 4, 94
Rizvi, Kishwar *Modernism and the Middle East* 88
Robinson, Jane 109; *Unsuitable for Ladies* 109, 112

Rojek, Chris 32
Rosaldo, Ernato 169
Ross-Bryant, Lynn 187
Royal Geographical Society 8, 42, 77, 110, 148, 160
Royal Society 146, 148, 159
Rub Al-Khali *see* Empty Quarter
ruins of empire 12, 41–2

Sabry, Tarik 5
Sachs, Aaron 150
Said, Edward xiv, 11–3, 87, 108; *Orientalism* 12–3, 16, 21, 67, 73, 82, 84, 88, 147, 196, 199; and women 115; *Culture and Imperialism* 86–7; "Professionals and Amateurs" 174
Sasson, Jean 107, 124; *Princess: More Tears to Cry* 123, 125
Saudi Arabia 6, 54–5, 57, 77, 122, 124–25, 157, 179–181, 185, 190, 197
science writing 21, 110–1, 142–170; definition of 143
Scott, Captain 40, 45, 131
second journeys *see* footstep journeys
sexual practices 73, 120, 139n80; harassment 116; sexuality 119–21, 126, 132, 180
Sharqiya Sands xiii, 51
Shepherd, Paul 155; *Man in the Landscape* 166, 168, 188
siren trope 22, 119–21, 129–130
Skeggs, Beverley 116
Smith, John 41
Smith, Oliver 44
Smith, Sidonie 131
social media *see media*
Spivak, Gayatri Chakravorty 13, 20, 33, 99, 122, 124; "Can the Subaltern Speak?" 122
Stanhope, Lady Hester 109, 112
Stark, Freya 10, 15, 21, 42, 108, 111, 113, 116, 178
subaltern 20, 122, 124, 134
sublime, the 12, 22, 151, 155–56; accelerated sublime 23, 134, 176, 179–84; Burkean 41, 147, 151–52, 156
Suez crisis 42–3, 63n54
Swan, Michael 45
Sykes-Picot agreement 4, 42

224 *Index*

Tatchell, Jo: *Diamond in the Desert* 108, 133
taxonomy 21, 144–45, 156, 159, 190
terra nullius 6, 22, 54, 87
Thesiger, Wilfred xiv, 1, 3, 10, 14–5, 17–8, 20, 31, 34, 37, 71, 73, 87, 96, 120, 145, 160, 184; *Arabian Sands* 52, 71, 145, 147–48; in the footsteps of 45–51; *My Life and Travels* 37; *The Life of My Choice* 37, 51; rejection of modern 70, 72
Thomas, Bertram 10, 34–6, 42, 53–8, 120, 130, 195; *Arabia Felix* 10, 14, 34–5, 59, 147–48
Thomas, Mark 178; *Extreme Rambling* 178
Thompson, Carl 2, 9, 70, 82, 96, 107, 109, 117, 146, 177; *The Routledge Companion to Travel Writing* 190
Thubron, Colin 98, 107
Tidrick, Kathryn 9, 54, 113–5, 130
Tiffin, Helen 168, 189; *Postcolonial Ecocriticism* 169
Torgovnick, Marianna 70
tourist: gaze 32, 188–9; post-tourist 33 *see* traveller
tourism xiv, 4–5, 10–1, 73, 161, 165, 170, 176–82, 187–90, 197; post- 32, 179–81
Toy, Barbara 3, 68, 77–80, 82–3, 112, 117–8; *Travelling the Incense Route* 77
travel literature: and truth 22, 44, 96–7; and lies 123
traveller: distinction with tourist 3, 23, 30, 49–50, 176–79
tribes, Arabian 31, 54, 57–8, 78, 80–1, 90, 132

Ubar 3, 15, 106, 129–30
United Arab Emirates 6, 47–8, 118
United Kingdom 57
urbanisation 2, 11, 48, 67, 69–70, 72, 74, 84–90
Urry, John 77; *The Tourist Gaze* 154–55, 188–89, 195
USA 154–55, 168

veiling, of women 88, 119, 122–30, 134
veiled best-seller 121–24, 134
voyages and travels 148–49

Wadi Rum 39, 42, 51, 61, 147
Walker, Donald 150; *Insects of Eastern Arabia* 156–60, 166
Wey, William 35
Wheeler, Sara 3, 40, 108; *Terra Incognita* 108, 131
Wheeler, Tony 23; *Bad Lands* 122–23, 180–81
Whitfield, Peter 35, 70, 87, 152
Whitlock, Gillian 121; *Forbidden Lies* 123
wilderness 95, 109, 133–34, 144, 151, 153, 158; diminishing 1, 3, 67, 77, 176; increasing 10–1; preservation 45; value of 46, 134, 144, 154, 166–7, 186–89; and wonderment 142–51, 162–63, 170, 176, 198; taming of 154, 161, 176
wildlife 133, 148; documentaries 166–68
Wilson, Alexander 167
Wilson, Edward 151, 159
Winser, Nigel xiii, 3, 150, 159; *The Sea of Sands and Mists* 160–66
Winston, Victor 5, 113
women: and desert literature 2, 20–1, 106–18, 121–29; and the domestic 107–08, 110, 115–6, 120, 125, 129, 134, 142; marginalised 20, 106–07, 115; Arab 86, 107, 117–121, 124–25, 128–29, 134; travellers 111–3; distinct voice 116–7
Wood, Levison 4, 15, 178, 182, 195–96
Woods, Tim 98
Wordsworth, Jonathan 41
Wordsworth, William 95, 156; *The Prelude* 95

Yemen 6, 77, 96, 111
Young, Robert 9, 13
Youngs, Tim 18, 20, 48, 75–6, 110, 117–18, 140n102, 157, 170, 177, 183, 186

Printed in the United States
by Baker & Taylor Publisher Services